# Tomorrow's

# Tomorrow's World
## Britain's Share in a Sustainable Future

*Written for Friends of the Earth by*

Duncan McLaren, Simon Bullock and Nusrat Yousuf

*With contributions from*

Abigail Goodchild, Heidi Morgan and Jacky Karas

Earthscan Publications Ltd, London

First published in the UK in 1998 by
Earthscan Publications Limited

A catalogue record for this book is available from the British Library

ISBN:  1 85383 511 0 (paperback)
       1 85383 510 2 (hardback)

Typesetting and page design by
PCS Mapping & DTP, Newcastle upon Tyne

Printed and bound by Biddles Ltd, Guildford and Kings Lynn

Cover design by Andrew Corbett


For a full list of publications please contact:

Earthscan Publications Limited
120 Pentonville Road
London N1 9JN
Tel: (0171) 278 0433
Fax: (0171) 278 1142
Email: earthinfo@earthscan.co.uk
http://www.earthscan.co.uk

Earthscan is an editorially independent subsidiary of Kogan Page Limited and
publishes in association with WWF-UK and the International Institute for
Environment and Development.

This book is printed on elemental chlorine free paper from sustainably managed forests

# Contents

# List of Figures

# List of Tables

# List of Boxes

# Acknowledgements and Dedication

*He who knows he has enough is rich*

Tao Te Ching

**To the memory of Andrew Lees (1949–1994)**

## WITHOUT WHOM...

The authors would like to extend their thanks to the following for their patience, support and assistance: Clare McLaren, Amanda Brace, Roger Levett, Nick Robins, David Lord, Alex MacGillivray, Jon Ralls, Jules Pretty, David Olivier, Professor Peter Smith, Anne Petherick, Paul Weaver, Chris Revie, Helen Snodin, Phillipe Spapens, Bertram Zagema, Andrew Dilworth, Ronnie Hall, Tim Jenkins, Anna Thomas, Tony Bosworth, Roger Higman, Matt Phillips, Frances MacGuire, Linda Fletcher, Tricia Allen, Rachel Western, Pete Hardstaff, Tony Juniper, Uta Bellion, Sue Riddlestone, Georgina Green, Joachim Spangenberg, Tim Jackson, Tim Rice, Vicki Hird, Charles Secrett, Mike Childs, Claudia Rawlinson and David Howarth.

This book forms part of Friends of the Earth's Sustainable Europe project – an unprecedented collaboration by over 30 groups across the whole of Europe. All of these groups are setting national sustainability targets for their countries, setting an agenda for government and business. This book is also a contribution from Friends of the Earth in the UK to the Sustainable Societies Programme of Friends of the Earth International which involves groups in every continent working for sustainability.

## DISCLAIMER

To illustrate the possibilities for resource-conserving practices, we cite the views and practices of specific companies at many points in this book. This should not be taken to imply any endorsement by Friends of the Earth of the companies named.

# Acronyms and Abbreviations

| | |
|---|---|
| ACRA | Aluminium Can Recycling Association |
| ATP | Aid and Trade Provision |
| BACMI | British Aggregate Material Construction Industries |
| BCSD | Business Council for Sustainable Development |
| BiE | Business in the Environment |
| BRE | Building Research Establishment |
| BWEA | British Wind Energy Association |
| CBA | cost-benefit analysis |
| CHP | combined heat and power |
| $CO_2$ | carbon dioxide |
| DOE | Department of the Environment |
| DSS | Department of Social Security |
| DTI | Department of Trade and Industry |
| ECF | elemental chlorine free |
| EIA | environmental impact assessment |
| EMAS | Eco-Management and Audit Scheme |
| EPAQS | Expert Panel on Air Quality Standards |
| ESCOs | energy service companies |
| EU | European Union |
| FAO | Food and Agricultural Organisation |
| FDI | foreign direct investment |
| FICGB | Forestry Industry Council of Great Britain |
| FSC | Forest Stewardship Council |
| GATT | General Agreement on Tariffs and Trade |
| GDP | gross domestic product |
| GMOs | genetically manipulated organisms |
| GNP | gross national product |
| GPI | Genuine Progress Index |
| Gt | gigatonnes |
| ICRP | International Commission on Radiological Protection |
| IEM | Institute of Environmental Management |
| IIASA | International Institute of Applied Systems Analysis |
| IIED | International Institute for Environment and Development |
| IMF | International Monetary Fund |
| IPCC | Intergovernmental Panel on Climate Change |
| ISEW | Index of Sustainable Economic Welfare |
| ISO | International Organisation for Standardisation |

| | |
|---|---|
| IUCN | World Conservation Union |
| LETS | local exchange trading systems |
| MDF | medium density fibreboard |
| Mt | megatonnes |
| mtoe | million tonnes of oil equivalent |
| NFFO | Non-Fossil Fuel Obligation |
| NIMBY | not in my back yard |
| NNP | net national product |
| NOx | oxides of nitrogen |
| NRA | National Rivers Authority |
| OECD | Organisation for Economic Cooperation and Development |
| PAHs | polycyclic aromatic hydrocarbons |
| PM10s | small particulate pollution from combustion processes |
| POST | Parliamentary Office of Science and Technology |
| ppmv | parts per million by volume |
| PVC | polyvinyl chloride |
| RCEP | Royal Commission on Environmental Pollution |
| SACs | Special Areas of Conservation |
| SAPs | structural adjustment programmes |
| $SO_2$ | sulphur dioxide |
| SSSI | Site of Special Scientific Interest |
| TCF | totally chlorine free |
| TRI | Toxics Release Inventory |
| TRIPs | Trade-related Intellectual Property Rights Agreement |
| UNCSD | UN Commission on Sustainable Development |
| UNDP | United Nations Development Programme |
| UN/ECE | United Nations Economic Commission for Europe |
| UNEP | United Nations Environment Programme |
| VOCs | volatile organic compounds |
| WCED | World Commission on Environment and Development |
| WEC | World Energy Council |
| WRME | wood raw material equivalent |
| WTA | willingness to accept |
| WTO | World Trade Organisation |
| WTP | willingness to pay |
| WWF | WorldWide Fund For Nature |

# Introduction

Gandhi reportedly rejected the Western model of development, saying: 'it took the exploitation of half the globe to make Britain what it is. How many globes would it take India to do the same?' Gro Harlem Brundtland, chair of the World Commission on Environment and Development (WCED) concluded that humanity would need ten Earths to allow the world's population to reach Western levels of consumption.[1]

It is now ten years since the WCED reported, and put the task of achieving sustainable development on every agenda. Since then the task they set has simply become more urgent, as it has become ever clearer that 'business as usual' with a few tweaks and a green gloss will not be enough. This year, the UN Environment Programme (UNEP) said that humanity's inefficient use of resources and patterns of wasteful consumption are 'driving us towards an environmental precipice'.[2] With continuing loss of the planet's diversity, the growing threat of global warming and the ever increasing demands for more metals, wood, and water to be taken from a finite planet, it is no exaggeration to say that we already have one foot over the edge.

This book sets out to do two things: to imagine what a sustainable society would look like, and to set concrete practical targets to help us get there. It starts from the explicit proposition that we must halt our rape of the Earth, and meet our needs within our environmental means.

Our vision of a sustainable society is not some woolly green utopia, nor a future of technological stagnation and a retreat to the stone age. Instead it is about a society in which everyone's needs are met – one in which people matter. It's not a left-wing vision, but one that explicitly rejects Margaret Thatcher's infamous claim 'there is no such thing as society' in favour of a recognition that not only is a good society the goal and foundation of a good economy, but that society, like civilisation, does not end at the Channel. The UK is not only part of Europe, but part of a global economy and a global society. Friends of the Earth wants to see a global society in which everyone can live fulfilling lives, free of insecurity, poverty of body and of spirit, and free of the fear that there may be no future for their children. In the words of Tony Blair:

> *All of us together must ... build the decent society ... a society in which every individual is valued, every person given a chance to develop their potential, a society to which we contribute and which contributes to us.*[3]

Five years ago, at the 'Earth Summit' held in Rio de Janeiro in 1992, ministers and prime ministers from virtually every country on Earth signed the Rio Declaration and agreed Agenda 21. Together these provide a mandate for radical changes in production and consumption, and the foundation of a collaborative process on all levels, from local to global. In 1997, progress on these agreements was reviewed by the UN's Commission on Sustainable Development (UNCSD). Inevitably, the conclusion was that progress has been slow and limited.

Most global environmental degradation is caused by a small minority of the world's population – the 20 per cent of mainly Western people who consume over 80 per cent of the world's resources. The planet cannot sustain current total levels of consumption, let alone five billion people, or almost ten billion within 60 years, consuming as Westerners do now. This leads to a dilemma for Western countries – either we continue to take far more than our fair share of the Earth's resources, and consign the majority of the world's population to get by with almost nothing, and still exceed the earth's capacity; or we must reduce the amount of resources we consume. We argue that to enable the global population to stay within limits the planet can sustain, and to allow Southern countries to develop, consumption in the West has to fall.

This book sets out what this imperative means for the UK, and what we need to achieve to reach this sustainable, equitable state of affairs. Major cuts in resource use are needed. However, the book also shows that the real goals for society – health, employment, quality of life, equality, a secure environment – are not determined by consumption of resources, and that reductions in consumption need not diminish our lives. Indeed, the current obsession of governments and businesses with economic growth, consumption and consumerism benefits only a small minority, and is the major obstacle to a sustainable and fair national and global society.

This book is about the future. It is necessary because humanity is on a development path that risks catastrophe. Despite widespread increases in human wellbeing in many countries, the current development model is failing us, our children and future generations.

The development model has three major shortcomings. First, its dependence on high throughput of energy and materials threatens ecological limits at a planetary scale. Humankind's use of environmental resources must be reduced to within sustainable levels. Second, the benefits of growth and development are distributed inequitably between and within nations. Global inequity has more than doubled since 1960, leaving around 1.3 billion people in poverty. Environmental space targets are set according to an equitable distribution of resources between countries by 2050. Third, many of the beneficiaries of increased material consumption have begun to discover that their quality of life is no longer enhanced by increased consumption. We therefore seek ways of meeting environmental space targets that meet needs directly, and avoid the overconsumption that is damaging quality of life. We call these 'sufficiency strategies'.

As Part 1 of this book shows, these three problems are not legacies of pre-industrial society which further growth will eradicate, or small and reparable faults in the model of economic development which can be solved by technological advances. They are not 'symptoms of the model's failure, but of its success ... the better the model performs, the worse these problems will get. They are endemic'.[4] Even so, we are optimistic that humankind can meet the challenge. This is not a blind optimism that technology and market forces will save the planet – the unproven thesis of the recent flurry of 'contrarian literature' – but informed optimism that strategies which will ensure that our planet remains habitable are possible, and compatible with continued increases in human wellbeing. As academic and environmentalist William Rees puts it: 'Global ecological change may well represent our last great opportunity to prove that there really is intelligent life on Earth'.[5] The current development model can be replaced by one which truly delivers sustainable development.

Friends of the Earth has previously set down the principles of sustainable development: equity within the current generation, and with future generations, and all decisions made with full and fair participation, and full regard for the environment.[6] In this book we express sustainable development in terms of fair shares in *environmental space* – an equitable distribution of environmental resources between the Earth's people now, and into the future. We advocate the use of the concept of environmental space to set practical targets for sustainable rates of use of environmental resources that reflect real ecological limits and the need for equitable access to those resources. The extent of change needed for any one country, such as the UK, can be illustrated by comparing the share of that sustainable production we consume with our share of the global population. With just 1 per cent of the world's people, Britain uses 5 per cent of the planet's capacity for carbon dioxide absorption, over 2 per cent of its sustainable timber yield, and almost 5 per cent of its sustainable steel and aluminium production. Specific environmental resources have been selected to cover the main inputs of our global economy and targets calculated for each in Part 2. In each case we have examined examples of good practice from the UK and elsewhere to quantify the ways in which we could meet the targets.

The environmental space approach suggests that sustainability for the UK will be a major challenge, but one that is practically achievable. Existing technology and good practice is at least adequate to meet interim targets and, for most resources, could make many of the savings required by 2050. The obstacles to sustainability are not technical, but economic, social and political. These can be overcome. Although the radical changes needed to achieve sustainable development challenge existing practices, they also offer opportunities to tackle problems in these fields.

The changes needed are outlined in Part 3 of this book. A sustainable economy is one which can provide employment and generate wealth for all. In other words, it is one in which all the stakeholders in companies and the economy – including employees and the wider community – are treated fairly. Inequality and exclusion undermine sustainability. If we fail to restore or create social justice in our communities then our efforts to make economic and environmental progress will be undermined by the costs of inequality. By focusing on needs, and developing and strengthening the social economy to help deliver them, we can reduce consumption without affecting wellbeing. The critical issues addressed here have somehow been banished to the margins of political debate, partly because they require an integrated long-term view of policy, and partly because they challenge too many influential vested interests. Democratic renewal is needed, with political and environmental rights and responsibilities for all.

So our vision is also optimistic. Even though the UK is one of the world's over-consuming nations, taking more than a fair share of the Earth's environmental resources, we have the opportunity to do something about it. Our destiny is in our own hands. If we choose to lead by example, we will enter the 21st century not only environmentally but economically healthier. The UK can be ready to compete in a global economy where the base of competitive advantage will be the environment, and our aim will be to provide for the needs of all, within the limits of environmental space.

Meeting the sustainability targets suggested by the environmental space analysis will not be easy, but it is possible, and the economic, social and political reforms needed will bring many benefits for us, for our children and for future generations. Those reforms are simply the first steps towards sustainable development. The longest journey, it is said, starts but with a single step. There is no longer and no more rewarding journey for humankind than that of truly sustainable and enduring human development – the journey into tomorrow's world.

# Part 1
# Sustainability and Environmental Space

# Introduction

The title of this part of the book might seem forbidding – so much that has been written on sustainability is either highly technical, exceedingly boring, or often both. No wonder people are confused as to what sustainability means. We hope to avoid being technical, or boring, but we have to be clear about our terms right from the beginning.

Sustainable development is now an accepted goal for policy in the UK, as in many other countries. The agenda has moved on to the questions of 'how do we achieve it', and 'how do we measure progress towards achieving it?' But underlying these questions is a continued and intense debate about what sustainability truly means. Definitions are generally vague, and permit widely differing interpretation. The term 'sustainable development' entered the language as a result of international political debate over the best development path for the so-called 'Third World countries'.[1] For many years, the question of economic development and increasing wealth in such countries has been closely intertwined with concern about environmental degradation as deforestation, soil erosion and desertification have worried development experts, but more recently global pollution concerns have taken centre stage.

The concept of sustainable development could be said to have been born at the Stockholm Intergovernmental Conference on the Human Environment in 1972, where both sets of concerns reached a global stage. A great deal was written in the next two decades about the integration of concerns over environment and development. But the term 'sustainable development' only became common parlance amongst environmentalists with the publication of the report of the World Commission on Environment and Development (WCED) – often known as the Brundtland report after the Chair of the Commission, the previous Prime Minister of Norway, Gro Harlem Brundtland. The report defined sustainable development, deceptively simply, as 'development which meets the needs of the present, without compromising the ability of future generations to meet their own needs'.[2]

The Brundtland report gave a new urgency to the whole question which culminated, in some respects, with the Earth Summit in Rio de Janeiro in 1992, attended by representatives of 176 countries, including more than 100 heads of state. This meeting agreed a global action plan for the 21st century – Agenda 21 – designed to deliver sustainable development. However, because of disagreement between rich and 'developed' Northern and the 'developing' Southern nations over who would pay –

and how much – Agenda 21 was never more than a voluntary declaration. Nonetheless, its language and many of its objectives have been adopted in sustainable development strategies at all levels from local authorities to the European Union. The term now appears four times in the cluster of treaties that govern the EU, and the Fifth Environmental Action Programme of the European Community, as it was then, issued in 1992, was entitled 'Towards Sustainability'. The UK Government has also published a strategy for sustainable development.[3]

Virtually all these plans and strategies ostensibly take as their basis the Brundtland definition, which can be expressed simply as meeting the twin needs of protecting the environment and alleviating poverty. In practice, sustainable development is often seen as an issue that concerns only Southern developing countries where environmental degradation is accelerating alongside continued widespread poverty. This is reflected in a complacent view that for rich countries such as the UK, sustainability can be achieved with a few small adjustments – a minor change of course, principally in terms of more integration of environmental concerns. Very few are taking seriously the approach to sustainable development defined by the world's major environmental agencies – the UN Environment Programme, the International Union for the Conservation of Nature (IUCN) and the WorldWide Fund for Nature (WWF) – 'improving the quality of life while living within the carrying capacity of supporting ecosystems'.[4]

As Figure I.1 shows, sustainability necessarily involves integrating the three conventionally separate domains of economic, environmental and social policy. As a result, as we shall see later, radical changes in the overarching political domain become necessary.

Implicitly, we can see very different interpretations emerging in practice. In the UK the official interpretation is weak, if indeed it can legitimately be described as 'sustainability' at all. For example, social issues such as poverty are largely ignored in the UK's strategy for sustainable development, which is based on the still unproven assumption that sustainability is achieved simply by further economic growth and a balancing of economic and environmental interests, according to a financial assessment of the relative costs and benefits. But, as we will see later, almost nothing could be less helpful.

Current trends predict a global population of perhaps 11 billion by 2050, 'with environmental problems at crisis level and poverty and social division rampant'. These are the words of the Independent Commission on Population and Quality of Life, established by seven governments including the UK, various intergovernmental institutions and several major foundations, which reported in 1996.[5] These are not just future problems for other countries far from England's temperate shores and green fields ... they are already here, and are set to get worse. Worse still, without global leadership from rich and influential nations such as the

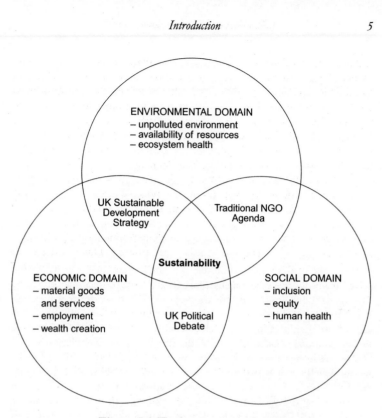

**Figure I.1** *The domains of sustainability*

UK, solutions will evade us all. If we are to achieve a sustainable future, rather than the bleak picture painted by the Independent Commission, then we need common targets and understanding of our goals.

In 1992 the US National Academy of Sciences and the British Royal Society issued a statement on population growth, resource consumption and a sustainable world. It concluded, in typically cautious scientific language:

> *The future of our planet is in the balance. Sustainable development can be achieved, but only if irreversible degradation of the environment can be halted in time. The next 30 years may be crucial.*

Before those 30 years are up, we believe we must be well on our way to achieving sustainability.

This first part of the book introduces the concept of environmental space, the reasons for its use, and ways of measuring it. It opens discussion on the needs and aspirations we seek to meet through consumption of environmental space. It is precisely because sustainability is such a difficult concept to pin down in practice, that we have to introduce this new term. We explain it in more detail below. However, the key point is that it will let us define sustainability in terms of real, practical and measurable targets.

# WHAT IS ENVIRONMENTAL SPACE?

Environmental space is an elegant new concept, if rather a clumsy term, brought into non-academic use by the Dutch. It describes the scope for human activities by defining environmental constraints. In everyday terms, we use it to set practical, realistic and measurable objectives. To understand the concept, it is perhaps best to begin with the realisation that struck so many when the first astronauts orbited the planet: we have only one Earth and we can't make it any bigger. Environmental space is the share of the planet and its resources that the human race can sustainably take. Or in other words, the share of the earth's resources that humanity can use without depriving future generations of the resources they will need. In a practical way, it is described in terms of the amount of different environmental resources, such as energy and timber, that we can use in a given time period without exceeding any environmental limits.

So environmental space can be conceived as the metaphorical space within which humankind can live and develop without fear of breaching any environmental limits or sustainability constraints. It can be described mathematically (for those who like that sort of thing) as the volume within defined limits on a set of axes. Figure I.2 shows the extent to which current global consumption exceeds sustainable levels, according to the figures we discuss in Part 2 of this book.

As an illustration, imagine a city enclosed in an enormous impenetrable transparent dome. It would not be long before the accumulation of wastes and the depletion of resources within it made life intolerable, or impossible. Every city and society needs a certain amount of resources to supply it and its people, and to absorb the wastes it produces. As societies grow and become more affluent, they generally need a larger and larger space from which to draw resources and absorb wastes. What is true for cities also holds for our planet; the entire planet is within such a 'glass bubble'. As our society has learnt more about the environment, it is becoming clear that the Earth does not have an infinite amount of resources, nor an infinite capacity to absorb pollution. There is a growing realisation that increasing population and increasing consumption are pushing at the limits of what the Earth can take.

Environmental space is a concept used to attempt to define these limits. There are, for example, limits to the amount of greenhouse gases, from power stations and traffic, we can put into the atmosphere without disrupting global climate. So environmental space defines global limits in terms of the rate of use of key environmental resources. As we will see

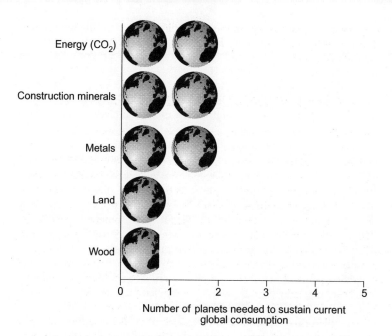

**Figure I.2** *Global overconsumption of environmental space*

later, such sustainable rates of use are determined by several factors, in particular, by the sustainable harvest of renewable resources and the ability of the environment to absorb our wastes and pollutants.[6]

We return to the definition of environmental space in Chapter 4. First we need to establish what these environmental limits or 'sustainability constraints' are.

## LIVING WITH LIMITS

The idea that there are limits to the expansion of human activities is not new. From religious prophets of doom to scientific modellers, the conclusion that humanity will suffer some catastrophic end has been a constant thread in human beliefs for millennia. So far they have been wrong. Humanity has survived! Indeed, it has developed to the extent that increasing numbers of people have the opportunity to live longer, safer, more comfortable and more fulfilling lives than ever before. In general, the current generation enjoys unprecedented material affluence, higher levels of education and the fruits of rapid technological progress in every field from transportation to healthcare.

Some argue that there is scope for technological development and economic growth to support many millions more at similar levels of wealth.[7] Writers like Herman Kahn[8] and more recently Julian Simon[9] have, depending on one's point of view, a touching optimism, or a blind faith in the power of the technical fix. They say that the Earth is far from the limits to its carrying capacity, or more importantly, that even if we are close, this doesn't matter because humans' ingenuity and intelligence can be used to push back those limits. Even more complacently, they claim that the working of free markets, virtually without guidance, will automatically deliver this transformation. These arguments are based on historical experience that apparent carrying capacities have been exceeded without disaster. The failings of such an analysis are a result of the overly narrow focus of academic disciplines. Such economists don't understand, or choose to ignore, the physical limits that underlie the economy, nor can they interpret ecological concepts effectively. By phrasing their arguments in terms of carrying capacity – a purely ecological concept – it is easy to demonstrate that it does not directly apply to humans.

Ecologists define carrying capacity as the maximum population of an animal species that can be supported in a given environment indefinitely. In the case of humans, however, carrying capacity is notoriously difficult to quantify in this way. Humans alter both the demand placed on the environment by each individual through consumption patterns, and the ability of the environment to meet these demands. Our activities can increase the latter by enhancing productivity through technological change, or reduce it through pollution and land degradation. Humans also transcend local limits through trade, as we shall see later. In a recent book, *How Many People Can the Earth Support?*, writer Joel Cohen presents a bewildering array of past estimates of global carrying capacity ranging from 1 billion to 100 billion; although over half of the estimates fall in the relatively limited range of 4 to 16 billion.[10] Despite the inherent uncertainties and varying assumptions, this implies that human interventions could influence effective carrying capacity by at least a factor of four.

This analysis seems to support the optimistic view. But there are three important reasons to doubt the optimists. First, the scale of environmental scarcity is increasing from the local to the global. We are now able to see environmental limits to human activity at a planetary scale. Second, the benefits of economic development are increasingly unevenly distributed between rich and poor and between North and South. And third, increasing material consumption levels in the richer groups and nations are no longer consistently reflected in increasing happiness and wellbeing.

We will examine these three problems with the optimistic view of the future in Part 1. They form the basis of our case that 'business as usual' will not deliver sustainable development. Part 2 explains environmental space in more detail and estimates the environmental resource basis available to humanity. Part 3 outlines how we can overcome the obstacles in the path to sustainable development, and how we can use environmental space targets to deliver it.

## Chapter 1
# Sustainability and Scarcity – Approaching the Limits

## INTRODUCTION

In this chapter we show how human consumption of environmental resources has grown in scale, and reach, and how our global economy, despite generally increasing the efficiency with which we extract resources from our environment, is now reaching global limits to such resource use. Climate change is one example of these limits, and as we put more stress on the planet in so many different ways, the risk of other, as yet unforeseen, ecological catastrophes is growing.

## FROM LOCAL TO GLOBAL

Historians and archaeologists suggest that previous local and regional human societies may have collapsed as a result of environmental scarcity, whether from the over-irrigation and salinisation of soils in ancient Sumeria, from the clearance of forests on Easter Island, or from irrigation and soil erosion in Mayan Central America. These can be seen as cases in which the activities of growing human numbers exceeded local carrying capacity. Similar consequences can occur today, as the case of Rwanda illustrates. The horror of genocide and civil war turned the world's attention to Rwanda in the mid-1990s. But before and beyond that conflict, hunger and poverty arose from severe land scarcity and degradation.[1] Rwanda's average rural population density of 574 inhabitants per square kilometre of arable land is the highest in Africa and most arable land is under cultivation. By 1991, half of the farmers reported declining productivity and half of the farmland was suffering from moderate to severe erosion. Per capita food production dropped by 25 per cent from 1984 to 1991.

In other cases, local resource scarcity has triggered not calamity, but economic transformation, as trade in resources or the search for alternative resources has had profound impacts on economies and societies. In the UK in the eighteenth century, the search for alternative energy sources to replace increasingly scarce wood and charcoal was a significant factor in the industrial revolution. But localised scarcity is not the norm today. Today most of human society is global. We do not rely only on local resources. In your house there will be magazines (most likely made from paper which originated in Scandinavian forests) and a TV (probably assembled in the Far East from materials mined and processed in China); the catalytic converter on your car contains platinum, perhaps mined in South Africa; the car itself may have been assembled in Spain from parts manufactured in the USA; in your fridge there may be butter from New Zealand, prawns from Thailand or green beans from Kenya, and the flowers on your mantelpiece could have been flown in from Colombia. In our modern economy, globalisation is everywhere. Virtually every commodity is traded internationally: from oil for energy, to financial services. As our demands grow, so the resources to meet them are drawn from all around the world.

The economy is not only global in its inputs, but also in its outputs: the effects of pollution are found everywhere from the Arctic to the Antarctic, from the Himalayas to the ocean deeps (see Figure 1.1). For example, DDT and other chlorinated hydrocarbons have been found in Antarctic organisms.[2] Heavy metals and other toxins have been found accumulating in the flesh of polar bears.[3] The ozone layer has been stretched thin by CFCs and other ozone-depleting substances – and hundreds of thousands of extra cancer cases are expected every year as a result.[4] Greenhouse gases are accumulating in the atmosphere with potentially devastating results, including mass extinctions, as habitats – especially coastal ecosystems such as coral reefs, and also forests – struggle to adjust rapidly to climate change.[5]

# GLOBAL LIMITS

It is difficult to measure global limits in a meaningful way. When we come to set targets we will not attempt to find a single global measure. However, global biodiversity is one good indicator of the stresses the planet is under. According to the *Global Biodiversity Assessment*, published by the UN Environment Programme in 1995,

> *humans are destroying the Earth's biodiversity at unprecedented rates, with between 5 and 20 per cent of some groups of animal and plant species possibly threatened with extinction in the foreseeable future unless present trends are reversed.*[6]

Over a hundred species are known to have become extinct since 1810, and at least 9400 are now threatened.[7] This does not include any of the 12 million or more species yet to be classified, many thousands of which

Ozone depletion: Current plans to phase-out ozone depleters mean that full recovery of the ozone layer will take until 2100

Transport: Road transport and air travel are the fastest growing sources of $CO_2$ emissions

Water shortages: 460 million people live in countries where there is serious scarcity of water

Climate change: Cuts of 60% in annual global $CO_2$ emissions would be needed simply to stabilise $CO_2$ concentrations in the atmosphere

Acidification: In parts of Scandinavia acid rain has leached up to 70% of the most important minerals from forest soils

Toxic chemical pollution: A grounded whale in the St Lawrence estuary had to be treated as hazardous waste because of the accumulation of toxic chemicals in its flesh

Deforestation: Each year some 15 million hectares of tropical rainforest is destroyed

Soil degradation: An area the size of China and India has suffered moderate to extreme soil degradation in the past 45 years

Species loss: The current rate of species extinction is 50–100 times the natural rate

Mining: In 1993 aluminium production created 980 million tonnes of wastes – over 20 times more than in 1945

Fisheries: 13 of the world's 15 major oceanic fisheries are in decline

**Figure 1.1** *Pressing against global limits*

might be already doomed by habitat loss.[8] The current rate of extinction is 50–100 times the average expected natural rate and in some areas may rise to 1000 to 10,000 times that rate due to habitat loss.[9] 'The adverse effects of human impacts on the Earth's biodiversity are increasing dramatically and are threatening the very foundation of sustainable development' according to Reuben Olembo, Deputy Executive Director of UNEP.[10]

Another useful indicator can be produced from a thermodynamic analysis: looking at the flows of energy through the Earth's systems. In such terms, all natural activity is constrained by the amount of incoming solar radiation. It is this energy that powers the planet. Not all of it can be exploited by plants and animals, but that which can be used in this way can be measured as 'primary productivity': the total solar energy captured by organisms through photosynthesis.[11] In practice, the measure of 'net primary productivity' is more useful. This subtracts the energy those organisms need to grow. Of 175,000 terawatts[12] of solar power the earth receives, less than 150 terawatts are transformed into NPP.[13] NPP is a helpful measure of the energy available to all other lifeforms including humans. In 1986, Peter Vitousek and other researchers based at Harvard and Berkeley calculated that around 40 per cent of terrestrial NPP was already being used by humankind,[14] directly or indirectly. In other words, agriculture and forestry to meet our requirements for food, fibre, timber and other natural resources take up four-tenths of the total energy available to the millions of species we share the planet with. Although it is inevitable that species at the top of the food chain will take a greater share of total productivity, the share taken by humankind, just one amongst about 14 million species,[15] is exceptional. And it is at a global scale, rather than just for a single ecosystem.

No one actually knows for sure how rapidly this share is increasing, but as more land is ploughed and more forests felled or brought into timber 'production',[16] we can be confident that it is growing. And although terrestrial NPP is easier to exploit, humans are also taking a significant share of marine productivity. Even if we include all marine productivity, Vitousek and his colleagues estimate that humans take fully one-quarter of global net primary productivity. Humans appropriate 8 per cent of net marine primary production but this rises to 25–35 per cent in the estuarine and continental shelf environments, the source of 96 per cent of the global fish catch.[17]

Despite our increasing use of it, the rapid increase in human population over the last few hundred years has not been based on our use of the energy in NPP, but on our exploitation of a historical stored surplus – the energy embodied in fossil fuels. As a result, as we will see, humankind is getting within touching distance of the determining factors for global carrying capacity. In the past, overconsumption led to local scarcity, local famine and local economic collapse. Today the whole planet is local.

The environmental space approach seeks to identify the global limits. However, this is not a repeat of the discredited 'limits to growth' debate of the 1970s, based on crude computer models and simulations (see Box 1.1). The world has not run out of non-renewable resources such as oil and metal ores, although there are those who argue that the limits of exhaustion are closer and more significant than is generally assumed (see

---

## BOX 1.1 *THE LIMITS TO GROWTH*

Physical restraints on growth were propelled into public debate by the 1972 report to the Club of Rome: *The Limits to Growth*. Using a large-scale computer model of the global economy, its authors concluded that unchanged growth trends in world population, industrialisation, pollution, food production and resource depletion, would deplete resources so severely that a sudden and uncontrollable decline in both population and industrial capacity would occur within 100 years. Even with their most optimistic assumptions about advances in technology, the model could not support present rates of economic and population growth for more than a few decades.

But the model was flawed both methodologically and factually. Feedback mechanisms of responses to scarcity were not included in the model. Some of the data it relied on regarding reserves and future trends in consumption have already been proven to be incorrect.

---

Chapter 9). On the other hand there is growing evidence that our rates of use of several renewable resources are exceeding sustainable rates, and that human pollution and wastes are affecting the global environment in an unsustainable manner.


## Overharvesting the Earth's Bounty

The European fisheries crisis of 1996 – with ministers unable to agree the cuts in catches that their scientific advisors had told them were necessary – was no isolated incident. It was part of a global trend. The annual world fish harvest has quintupled since 1950, and world fish stocks are severely threatened. In at least 13 out of the 15 main fishery areas, stocks are declining.[18] For example, before Independence in India, fishing was mainly a subsistence activity. But with the onset of economic planning deep-sea fisheries came to be regarded as a sector which could accelerate the growth of the rural economy. The key factor in this development was a UN-assisted Indo-Norwegian Project which introduced western style trawlers and freezer technologies for processing. For a decade until the mid-1970s the industry flourished. However after 1974 the overall levels of the fish and prawn harvest began to fall and by the end of the decade the marine fishery sector was heading towards an ecological and economic crisis caused by overfishing. Productivity and real per capita incomes halved between 1974 and 1982. Although monsoon trawl bans and deep sea fishing bans have been implemented over the past two decades, an increasing number of boats has put more pressure on the coastal fisheries. Higher catches in 1990 and 1991 (both over the estimated sustainable yield of 480,000 tonnes) resulted in a significantly smaller catch in 1992. The pattern is repeated time and time again. Between 1977 and 1987 the population of New England groundfish decreased by 65 per cent. Stocks reached record low levels in the early 1990s.[19] In some cases, not only are fish stocks being depleted, but the catches are not even consumed locally. Exploitation by European fishing fleets has been blamed for the decline in stocks in the coastal waters of Senegal.[20]

Renewable resources such as forests and fisheries can be swiftly pushed into decline, especially where pressures on them are growing as a result of increasing consumption or growing populations. As long as fuelwood gathering does not exceed the regrowth of the tree stock, then the activity, seen in isolation, is sustainable. But as soon as gathering does exceed regrowth, then the result, if unmanaged, is that the tree stock itself declines. Every year the gap between supply and demand grows bigger, and every year more of the 'capital' is used just to maintain basic needs. This too is a widespread problem, not an isolated concern. More than two-thirds of all people from developing countries rely on wood for cooking and heating. According to the FAO in 1980[21] nearly 1.2 billion people were meeting their fuelwood needs only by cutting wood faster than it was being replaced. Nearly 100 million people could not meet their minium needs even by over-cutting the woodlands around them. Projections for the year 2000 suggest that the number of people lacking wood or over-cutting will double, reaching nearly 2.4 billion.

In countries like Ethiopia, the human and ecological costs of wood scarcity are high. Boiling water becomes an unaffordable luxury where fuelwood is critically scarce. People often have no choice but to divert dried dung and crop residues from fields to cooking stoves and therefore reduce soil fertility. Not only have forests, potentially able to provide many resources besides fuel, been lost, but the rebound is affecting another fundamental resource – agricultural land. Fuelwood cutting is only one of the pressures on the globe's forest resources. In the 1980s rates of tropical deforestation remained high at around 15 million hectares – an area greater than the size of England – or 0.8 per cent of the remaining area, every year.[22] At the same time primary old-growth forests have been felled and replaced with plantation monocultures in many parts of the temperate and boreal zones of the world. These pressures are generated by industrial demands for wood, combined with (in tropical zones) clearance for agricultural use.

Similar problems of accelerating decline can result where agricultural land itself has been the scarce commodity. In the Philippines, agricultural reform, modernising and amalgamating farms, led to migration of now landless farmers. While land was still available in the lowlands, the environmental consequences were limited. But once that 'agricultural frontier' closed, and migration began into the forested uplands, defor- estation has been followed by massive soil erosion. The environmental toll has been enormous to the Philippines. Cultivated upland areas increased from 582,000 ha to 3.9 million ha from 1960 to 1987. Soil erosion was estimated at about 122–210 tonnes per hectare annually for newly established pasture, compared to only two tonnes under forest cover. These impacts resulted from a combination of social and economic processes and an environmental threshold.[23]

Fresh water, too, is becoming a critically scarce resource in many parts of the world due to competing demands for water for drinking and washing, for crop irrigation, and for industrial purposes. Around 1.3 billion people – over one-fifth of the Earth's population – do not have access to safe drinking water. There are an estimated 250 million cases of water-related disease annually, and between 5 and 10 million deaths.[24] In the Amazon region shortage of water has been exacerbated by deforestation which has affected the local climate, cutting rainfall by a quarter.[25] As we will see later, water resources have already become a source of political conflict in several regions. Global climate change threatens to make the situation even worse.

Overall, the outlook is bleak. The UN Environment Programme recently reported that use of a whole range of renewable resources such as land, forests, fresh waters and urban air is beyond their natural renewable capacity.[26]

## The Global Dustbin

As we saw in the fisheries sector, it's not just poverty and population pressure that can lead to such environmental collapses. The demands and pressures generated by Northern consumption levels are also a key factor. Even more worrying is the evidence that the outputs of our economies are unsustainable; that human pollution and wastes are affecting the global environment. Climate change, ozone depletion, and acidification have become the subjects of major international debate and negotiations. Their impacts are not just directly felt by human society, they are also depleting the productive base of the global ecosystem. For example ozone depletion reduces primary production by phytoplankton and studies suggest that in the Antarctic, the reduction may be in the order of 6–12 per cent.[27] In turn this could feed back into climate change, as lower phytoplankton populations will absorb less carbon dioxide.

Climate change can exacerbate or trigger desertification, the creation of deserts on previously productive land, and soil erosion. In Spain, Portugal, Greece and Italy, experts claim to be able to detect the beginnings of desertification with a trend towards long periods of drought, broken only by intense storms which erode weakened soils bare of vegetation as a result of drought.[28] In the UK, we don't risk desertification as such but as we shall see in Chapter 6 there is evidence of increasing susceptibility to erosion in an existing trend of declining organic matter levels in soil; a trend which is likely to be exacerbated by climate change.

Acid deposition has been blamed for widespread forest damage in many parts of the world, with perhaps the best known case this side of the Atlantic being the 'Waldsturben' or tree dieback experienced in many Central European forests. This reduces forest productivity and damages soils. In parts of Scandinavia up to 70 per cent of the most important minerals may have been leached from forest soils by acid rain.[29] Recent reports suggest that many newly industrialising countries, such as China and South Korea, are suffering from acid deposition over large areas.

The global limits we are approaching are not those of material resource depletion; we're not running out of coal or aluminium. They are the limits to the amount of abuse the Earth or our own health can take from the waste materials we are disposing into the environment, principally as pollution (see Box 1.2). We are overwhelming what are technically known as 'sink' capacities.

The Intergovernmental Panel on Climate Change (IPCC) is confident that unless action is taken to prevent climate change, then global temperature will increase by 1.0–3.5°C by 2100. The average rate of warming implied is greater than any seen over a similar period in the last 10,000 years. Even if action is taken, we are already committed to significant impacts as a result of the accumulated emissions of past decades.

---

## BOX 1.2 *HUMAN HEALTH AS AN ENVIRONMENTAL LIMIT*

For some wastes the sink capacity of nature is small, and the accumulation of toxic pollutants in natural systems is threatening human health. In the atmosphere, various pollutants, mainly produced by burning fossil fuels, are linked with respiratory diseases, cancers, cardiovascular diseases and the rapidly growing asthma mortality rates observed in many Northern countries. In Britain 10,000 premature deaths every year have been attributed to the effects of small particulates which can cause respiratory and cardiovascular problems.

In our food and water, the byproducts of agricultural and industrial processes include chemicals that disrupt hormones, and which are implicated in falling fertility rates and other reproductive problems. In addition, both heavy metals and organic chemicals have been linked with retarded mental development in children. Other species are also affected by such pollutants. Alligators in pesticide-contaminated lakes in Florida have become impotent due to the hormone disrupting effects of the pesticides.

These are just examples, but they illustrate the extent to which we have already passed safe thresholds in our abuse of the planet and her people.[31]

Source: Bullock, S (1995) *Prescription for Change: Health and the Environment* Friends of the Earth, London; Carley, M and Spapens, P (1997) *Fair Shares: Sustainable Living and Global Equity in the 21st Century* Earthscan, London

# BEYOND THE LIMITS?

Are we therefore 'beyond the limits'? Many experts believe so. In a large complex system where response times are slow, it is possible for us to have already exceeded some of the limits. The threat of climate change is perhaps the most important case in point. Past and current emissions of greenhouse gases have already committed us to a significant (albeit difficult to quantify) degree of global warming. This is expected to lead to sea level rise affecting low-lying coastal areas, climatic changes including more frequent extreme events such as hurricanes, desertification and more widespread agricultural damage as soils dry out and rainfall patterns change, drying wetlands, and – as a global consequence of the above – hundreds of thousands of deaths from a range of causes including the spread of malaria and other diseases, and severe and widespread famine.

The Maldives, an island state in the Indian Ocean which averages no more than 1.5 metres above sea level, is likely to be made uninhabitable within the next century. Low-lying productive land on major deltas around the world will be inundated: Bangladesh, with much of its population and productive land on the Ganges delta, will be severely affected, losing some 17.5 per cent of its total land area. Overall, the best estimate of sea level rise by 2100 – 50 cm – will double the number of people who will experience flooding in an average year.[30] The risks of desertification and soil erosion will rise in many other countries: tropical and temperate. Although these risks are being taken seriously in negotiations over the Climate Convention, there are several ways in which they are played down in the interests of slowing governmental responses and cutting costs. At the time of writing, the Northern media have picked up only on the possible, although unlikely, benefits of warming in countries like the UK, while economists seeking to estimate the costs of these impacts have used unjustifiable cost-benefit approaches (see Box 1.3). It is partly because cost-benefit analysis approaches cannot tackle such questions that a more objective quantified approach based on simple agreed principles is necessary. This is where environmental space measures can be invaluable. Targets can be derived objectively, rather than relying on disputed valuations of human life and environmental quality.

Returning to the likely effects of climate change, there are other possible consequences that we can't predict as specifically. The Gulf Stream is perhaps the largest single factor in the UK's equable climate. It keeps us several degrees warmer than most other places at the same latitude. Peter Wadhams' work at the Scott Polar Research Institute[31] has found evidence from Greenland that one of the natural pumps that drives the Gulf Stream has failed for three years running because the sea ice has failed to form. As yet, no one knows why, but climate change is the prime suspect.

# BOX 1.3 *COST-BENEFIT ANALYSIS OF CLIMATE CHANGE*

The application of cost-benefit analysis (CBA) to complicated issues such as climate change is beset with difficulties. Yet its use has produced estimates which imply a level of certainty which is quite unwarranted. For example, a draft paper by the third Working Group of the IPCC in 1995 estimated the cost of the global 'damage from increased mortality' at US$89.3 billion, with US$57 billion of this in Organisation for Economic Cooperation and Development (OECD) countries. However, these figures are based on mortality studies in the US which suggest that the direct effects of increased temperature would be 294 deaths per million population. This figure was then adjusted to 45 per million, to account for 'full acclimatisation, including biological adjustments as well as changes in the physical structures of cities', and further reduced to 27 per million, as temperature rises are expected to be higher in US cities than globally. This figure was then extrapolated to other regions of the world by population. The overall costs were derived using an estimated value for human life. The value used was US$1.5 million for developed countries, but just US$0.1–0.15 million for developing countries.

This approach can be legitimately criticised on several grounds. First, data for US cities are unlikely to be representative. Second, there are uncertainties in predicting the extent of ability to acclimatise and no grounds for ignoring the potential costs of so doing. Third, it fails to include indirect causes of mortality such as increased exposure to malaria, famine and flooding. Fourth, and worst of all, having different valuations of life depending on whether you are rich or not is plainly immoral. This difference in 'value' between developing and developed countries is not just for people. The draft paper valued the loss of a hectare of wetland in the South at only 13 per cent of the value given to a similar wetland in a developed country.

The implication of such biased valuation is that most of the damage from climate change will fall on developed countries, when this patently is not the case. But this is politically convenient – if the costs of developed countries' carbon dioxide emissions can be shown to fall mainly on developed countries, then there is a weaker case for developing countries to demand compensation for damages done to them.

Different assumptions change these figures radically. If we assume simply that deaths from climate change will be 294 per million (in the absence of balancing costs for acclimatisation) and that a human life is worth US$1.5 million wherever they lived, without changing any of the other assumptions, then the cost by 2050 increases to around US$4400 billion.

The reason that estimated values for life and property are lower in the South is because of a major failing in the CBA approach. CBA economists normally ask people how much they are willing to pay (WTP) to avert a given loss. The values obtained are limited by people's ability to pay. In theory, when seeking values from those who lose out, economists should ask how much compensation people are willing to accept (WTA), leaving the WTP approach for asking the winners what their gains are worth. But WTA, not surprisingly, often elicits infinite answers: would you accept any amount of money as compensation for your child's life, or even health? But the economists' mathematical models can't handle such answers, so as in this case, they normally choose WTP methods even for valuing losses. However, as John Adams, of University College London, says:

> *this is to throw away the theoretical foundation of CBA, the criterion of a Pareto improvement – any change that permits the winners to compensate the losers and still leaves something over is an indisputable improvement. It is a crucially important evasion; it sacrifices the principle, from which cost-benefit analysis derives both its theoretical and moral legitimacy, to expediency.*

So far, partly as a result of the outcry against this approach by NGOs and many Southern interests, the IPCC has avoided endorsing any particular set of financial estimates of the costs![a,b,c]

*a* Source: Adams, J (1996) Cost Benefit Analysis: The Problem, Not the Solution *The Ecologist* 26(1)
*b* The proportion of the world's population within the potential malaria transmission zone could grow from 45 per cent to 60 per cent by 2100.
*c* Meyer, A and Cooper, T (1995) *GCI critique of IPCC WG3 Social Costs of Climate Change: a Recalculation of the Social Costs of Climate Change* Cambridge: Global Commons Institute

As the extent of our ignorance about global climatic systems becomes clearer, the possibility that we have unknowingly disrupted other global environmental systems to a similar degree becomes more real.

## RISKING ECO-CATASTROPHE

We have already subtly altered the planet's rotation by the impoundment of ten trillion* tonnes of water in outsize dams. This has shifted water from the oceans to the continents, thereby reducing mass around the Earth's equator and increasing mass in the northern part of the planet. This has pushed the axis of rotation about 60 cm away from the North Pole towards western Canada.[32] No one knows what this will do, least of all the governments, funding agencies and engineers that have undertaken these projects.

Our ability to engineer new species and genetic changes has yet to be tested widely, but as single varieties of crops engineered to resist particular herbicides become more widespread, the potential impacts of catastrophic crop failure from some unforeseen side effect become

---

* Unless otherwise indicated in text, one trillion = 1,000,000,000,000; one billion = 1,000,000,000.

greater. In our efforts to eliminate particular disease vectors such as mosquitoes, we cannot be sure that we won't wipe out some essential organisms from our ecosystem. As hormone-mimicking chemicals, thought to be responsible for the expression of transexual characteristics in fish and shellfish, spread in the environment, we don't know that an accelerating decline in fertility – even in humans – will not result. After all, we drink the same water.

In the past, algal blooms, triggered by nutrient rich pollution, have depleted all life from lakes. In the wrong circumstances, why should the same not happen to entire seas, or even oceans? Smaller algal blooms have already been reported in seas such as the Adriatic. When the amounts of heavy metals and other toxic materials mobilised in our economies exceed the amounts moved by natural erosion processes, what will be the consequences for our health and the health of other species? When our environment becomes ever more acid? And when all of these threats combine? At present, to be sure, such disasters are in the realm of science fiction rather than science fact, but such catastrophe scenarios serve to illustrate the need for a more cautious approach in our dealings with the Earth. As any scientist knows, a theory can never be proven, but the more often we can repeat our experiments and obtain the same answer, the more confident we can be in a particular hypothesis. In this case the hypothesis is that humankind is capable of destroying the Earth's ecosphere, or, at least, damaging it to the extent that it cannot support human populations. This is an experiment we can run only once: we have just one Earth. If this hypothesis is true, then we will have no place to go.

Sometimes we get early warnings of problems in the making. But these are rarely clear and simple. We can suspect that the decline of amphibians, bleaching of coral reefs and oceanic phytoplankton blooms are a warning of some problem, but it isn't so easy to decide what the problem is and what is causing it. And worse, there are many instances where ecosystems absorb stresses over long periods without much outward sign of injury, but then reach 'critical' levels where the cumulative consequences finally reveal themselves in rapid change. Such environmental discontinuities can be seen in many ecosystems today. For example, as the world famous ecologist Eugene Odum has noted, forest ecosystems can undergo slow degradation through acid rain for decades before finally and suddenly displaying environmental injury in terms of tree dieback or death.[33] In such ways, theoretical limits show themselves in real environmental degradation.

## Catastrophe and Uncertainty

Scientists now recognise the study of catastrophe theory as an important advance in knowledge. Developing mathematical tools can help us understand how systems might change when pushed over a threshold, perhaps even into a different 'quantum state'. The application of such tools to environmental concerns has not progressed far enough to advise us how to solve such problems, but it has reinforced the case for a precautionary approach.[34]

Environmental discontinuities are perhaps particularly pertinent to climatic change. In the case of global warming, interactions in the climatic system are still not fully understood and we are often unable to predict the consequences of a particular change. However we do know that the earth's past climate has not reacted in a smooth, predictable manner. Commentators such as Sir John Houghton, co-chair of the IPCC's science working group, have suggested that dramatic changes or jumps in climate could be triggered by global warming.[35] Ozone depletion gives another good example of a system pushed beyond sustainability limits set by environmental capacity. It also highlights well the uncertainty associated with thresholds. We cannot predict whether non-linear or 'runaway' effects will emerge, such as the dramatic and unexpected appearance of the Antarctic ozone hole when levels of stratospheric chlorine reached about 2 parts per billion. Models of likely future Arctic and Northern hemisphere depletion do not take account of the possibility of further 'thresholds'. Nor do our calculations of what is or is not a 'safe' level of chlorine or bromine in the stratosphere take account of surprises, for example a prolonged cold winter or a large volcanic eruption such as that of Mount Pinatubo, spewing particles into the lower stratosphere which speed up ozone depleting reactions.[36]

We cannot afford to ignore such uncertainties in the political process. Nor can we simply continue with business as usual while we await better scientific evidence. We need to manage the uncertainty. Where there is good reason to believe that substantial or irreversible damage to the environment is resulting from a pollutant, or some practice, then we should take action to prevent or solve the problem, before scientific proof is available. For example, where there is good reason to believe that an atmospheric pollutant is a major contributory factor in thousands of premature deaths each year, we should control it first, rather than undertaking detailed epidemiological studies, which correlate exposure to the pollutant with rates of death and disease: using human populations as scientific guinea-pigs!

This concept of taking action before full scientific proof is available, where the risks of failing to take action are significant, is called the 'precautionary principle'. We will call on it often in this report. Fortunately, it isn't an invention of environmentalists, but a principle of policy action endorsed by virtually every government in the world, including the UK, and embodied in the Treaty of European Union. However, it is rarely applied as effectively as it should be. All too often the burden of proof remains with those seeking to defend the environment. We should not be surprised at this since it is difficult for governments to take potentially financially or politically costly decisions on the grounds of a principle. In the example above, the appropriate precautionary action would have been tighter emissions standards for many vehicles, and powers for local authorities to impose local traffic restrictions, or even bans, to improve air quality – both potentially costly, at least in the short term. Nonetheless, as we discuss targets in this book, we will apply a precautionary approach where necessary.

## FROM LIMITS TO POLICY TARGETS

If the preceding analysis is right, then humankind needs to restrain its combined impact on renewable and sink resources, or risk catastrophe. Friends of the Earth is developing the concept of 'environmental space' as a way to make the idea of global carrying capacity useful in policy terms. This is not as simple as it first sounds. There are a number of factors that we need to include in our framework at an appropriate stage.

First, despite the process of globalisation of our economies and societies, some resource constraints to our economic activities are still determined locally: the amount of timber that can be harvested from a forest, the amount of fish that can be harvested from a sea. Moreover, our cultures and lifestyles mean we impose very different burdens on the local environment. There are two broad options for implementation of local carrying capacity constraints in policy when the economy is an open global system. We could seek local or regional self-sufficiency, and forgo many of the benefits brought by trade and participation in a global economy, or we could set limits to our activities at a global scale and then cooperate internationally to best meet them. This report takes the latter approach, but seeks to make those targets measurable and achievable through national and local action.

Second, because of the uneven distribution of many environmental resources, reducing total impact to a certain level globally may not be adequate, as, for example, local or regional concentrations of pollution could poison a whole lake or sea – in turn reducing our sustainable supply of fish. This principle is illustrated by acidification of Scandinavian lakes by pollution. So our targets must be based on sustainable rates of resource use which in turn reflect the application of sustainable management techniques which minimise the likelihood of such local problems. Fortunately, this largely works with the grain of environmental awareness; local populations generally know more about and have the incentive, if not always the opportunity, to take better care of local environmental resources than they do of the wider global resources on which the environmental space approach focuses. This does not exonerate governments, national and local, from taking the action necessary to ensure minimum environmental standards, instead it mandates them to do so.

The environmental space approach interprets the global limits to human impact on the environment in terms of the rate at which humankind uses environmental resources, including 'sink' resources. At a global level we estimate the sustainable supply for each of a number of key resources representative of the global economy, and compare it with the current rate of consumption. We explain the methodology in more detail in Chapter 4.

# SCARCITY, TRADE AND THE FRONTIER

This chapter has focused on scarcity. Before moving on to discuss equity (in Chapter 2) we must briefly consider the key tool that humankind has previously used to overcome local scarcity, and see what its implications might be at the global level. It is entirely realistic to see human history as the result of a process of expanding the frontiers of our territory to overcome resource scarcity. The great emigrations to the New World offered access to vast amounts of new land and resources. The colonial era, as George Orwell points out in *The Road to Wigan Pier*, provided the UK with a wide range of resources and products that we could not have consumed otherwise. Today we can still see 'frontier capitalism' at work, especially in terms of the exploitation of tropical genetic diversity by Northern business, which is strongly supported by the World Trade Organisation's (WTO) new Trade-related Intellectual Property Rights (TRIPs) Agreement.[37] We can also see it at work in the oceans, not just in exploitation of undersea reserves, but in efforts to obtain other mineral resources from the seabed. And, more generally, new international negotiations to liberalise foreign investments are viewed by many as heralding a return to the colonial era.[38]

For centuries humankind has been able to overcome local scarcity by importing resources. But now the physical frontier is closing, we are approaching the global limits. In consequence we need to turn our attention more directly to another frontier – the frontier of knowledge. As we will see in Chapter 3, it is theoretically possible to obtain vastly more wellbeing from our present, or even much lower, level of resource consumption. This must be the driving objective for the extension of human knowledge in the twenty-first century!

We do not see this as implying an end to trade. But it does imply much fairer and more balanced trade, as we will see in Chapter 2. We are firmly of the opinion that properly managed and fair trade between equal partners can enrich both – culturally as well as financially – without damaging the environment unnecessarily. Although increased transport costs – essential if the price of transport is to reflect the environmental damage it does – will inevitably reduce total volumes of trade, they will also shift the balance of trade away from primary materials and towards finished products, which are of higher value, and for which transport costs represent a smaller share of total costs. One problem with trade, especially of finished products, is that of distance. People are more aware of, and have more control over, the impacts of production if it occurs locally. Where we consume locally produced goods and services we have more reason (at least psychologically) to care about the impacts of that production. If it's our jobs on the line if the fishery is over-exploited and exhausted, if it's our children with asthma exacerbated by pollution, if it's our local countryside scarred by opencast mining then we are more likely to do what we can to prevent such problems arising. Nowhere is the cliche 'out of sight, out of mind' more apt than for such environmental issues. So, with free trade, we risk displacing environmental degradation and social exclusion onto those least able to counter them. Allowing this trend to determine policy would be more than NIMBY,[39] it would run in contradiction to the equity principle (see Chapter 2). It is morally wrong to exploit other people's environments and affect their health for our own gain.

Fortunately, it is fundamentally a technical problem – one which demands improved political processes to manage trade – rather than an argument for no trade. As Caroline Lequesne, trade policy expert at Oxfam, summarises: 'Under certain conditions, trade liberalisation can have a positive impact on labour and environmental conditions ... [neither] of these impacts is automatic, however; they depend rather on certain kinds of intervention'.[40] This creates a major political challenge, to shift the emphasis of the World Trade Organisation, and the other multilateral institutions, from promoting 'free trade' at more or less any price, and from promoting investments and reforms in developing countries that are simply designed to open their economies to the world market. Instead the WTO must promote fair and efficiently regulated trade. On balance we believe this is more politically possible than reversing the process of trade, and that it would entail less economic disruption in the short term, thus making the transition to a sustainable global economy more feasible. However, this does not mean that environmental space targets could not be used to inform a more radical strategy of promoting local self-sufficiency with trade of surpluses only.

# CONCLUSION

There are pressing environmental limits to human activity. They have not yet shown themselves in ways which trigger major catastrophic loss of life. But the effects of unchecked climate change are likely to be substantial in these terms, and ozone depletion has already committed us to millions of extra cancer cases. The environmental space approach to limits is more sophisticated in its approach to scarcity than the 'limits to growth' debate of the 1970s. It considers sink resources and renewable resources as well as non-renewables in a framework which is sensitive to real-world economics. The assumptions underlying the estimation of available environmental space are explained in some detail in Chapter 4. The need to worry about the limits to our use of sink and renewable resources is not just the province of academics and pressure groups. The Independent Commission on Population and Quality of Life recognises that there are limits to carrying capacity.[41] They suggest that we should try to estimate those limits and try to remain within them. The environmental space approach does just this.

This chapter has outlined some of the most pressing environmental limits, and made the case for a framework for measuring them. Environmental space may not be the ideal approach, but it is practical, it is possible now, and it can be seen as a convenient first measure. Quantitative targets, that reflect global limits to total resource use, are an essential foundation for sustainability; however, they say nothing about the distribution of such resources within the current generation. It is to this thorny question that we turn in Chapter 2.

# Chapter 2
# Sustainability and Equity –
# Colonising Environmental Space

## INTRODUCTION

In Chapter 1 we saw in passing how inequitable access to resources can lead to scarcity for specific groups of people. Moreover, we saw how inequitable distribution of control over resources can be a driving force for local and wider environmental degradation, especially of renewable resources such as fish stocks. Inequity also creates a driving force for 'development', growth and increased consumption, thus fuelling the global environmental crisis. At the same time inequity, directly or indirectly, reduces the access of many developing countries to the resources they need for development, through economic competition. In other words current levels of inequity prevent the achievement of sustainability. We believe that it is a basic human right to have equal opportunity of access to the resources one needs to live a decent life. So when we talk of equity it is in terms of fairness, not of financial stakes; and in terms of equal opportunities, not a revolutionary vision in which the wealthy are hauled up against a wall.

In the introduction to Part 1 we asserted that business as usual had failed to reduce inequity, and indeed, that inequity was growing. In this chapter we look more closely at the issue of global inequity and some of the factors that help maintain and increase it, notably international debt and trade relations. We then discuss how we might take equity concerns into account in our sustainability targets. Finally we touch on equity issues within the UK.

## GLOBAL INEQUITY

The UN Human Development report of 1996 makes the extent of global inequity clear, concluding that 'widening disparities in economic performance are creating two worlds – ever more polarized'.[1] The UN Development Programme reports that growth has failed for more than a

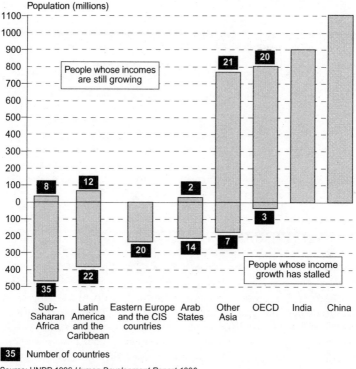

35  Number of countries

Source: UNDP 1996 *Human Development Report 1996*

**Figure 2.1** *Global inequity – the failure of economic growth*

quarter of the world's population who live in countries whose present per capita income was first reached in earlier decades (see Figure 2.1). To illustrate this even more sharply, the net worth of the world's 358 dollar billionaires is equal to the combined annual income of the poorest 45 per cent of the world's population – some 2.3 billion people.

Between 1960 and 1991 global inequality, measured by the ratio of income shares between the richest 20 per cent and the poorest 20 per cent, more than doubled, from 30 to 1, to 61 to 1![2] Furthermore, within countries, the marginalisation of the poorest bears little relation to national income. In the US, as in Nigeria, the poorest 20 per cent have per capita incomes around one-quarter of the average, while in both Bangladesh and Japan the income of the the poorest fifth is nearly half the average.[3] That said, absolute deprivation is much more severe in the South. The UN Development Programme reports[4] that over one-quarter of the world's population – 1.3 billion people – lives in poverty; 500 million are chronically malnourished; and in developing countries maternal mortality is nearly 12 times as high as in the rich Organisation for Economic

Cooperation and Development (OECD) countries. Moreover, more than 90 per cent of the world's 18 million HIV-infected people live in developing countries, and at the end of 1994 there were more than 11 million refugees in the developing world. To better assess the extent of poverty, the UN Development Programme has developed a measure of 'capability poverty' which considers the lack of three basic capabilites: to be well nourished and healthy, to be capable of healthy reproduction, and to be educated and knowledgeable. According to its estimates, some 1.6 billion people – one-third of the world's population – are 'capability poor'.[5]

Absolute poverty is also most concentrated in those developing countries most marginalised from the global economy: those which receive little foreign direct investment, and where aid is substantially outweighed by debt repayments. We will return to these issues later. First we turn to the factors maintaining global inequity.

# THE PERSISTENCE OF COLONIALISM

Recent British history is the history of a colonial power. For some time at the end of the nineteenth century and the beginning of the twentieth, the British ruled much of the known world. There is much to be proud of during that time, but also much to regret. Indigenous peoples suffered horrific indignities, land and resources were usurped, and British culture was imposed, often in the most inappropriate circumstances. Today, it would seem, these things are behind us. The British colonies, as with those of other nations, have mostly achieved self-determination, in some cases by amicable agreement. But in others, bitter and even bloody dispute was necessary before independence. Even so, many of those ex-colonies have remained as part of the British Commonwealth, often benefiting from their continued special relationship with the UK through trade preferences and other support. But it is not true to say that colonialism has come to an end. Although most countries have achieved political self-determination, few have achieved any real degree of economic self-determination. And as our economy becomes ever more global – the influence of economic factors controlled (loosely) by the rich OECD countries – this dominance by Northern countries has grown rather than declined. In virtually all economic relationships, developing countries are still the weaker partners. This is reflected in a cultural colonialism where the Western model of development and Western consumerist values are being promoted, and effectively imposed, globally.

Throughout this book we refer to the infamous North–South divide. But we use this as a helpful shorthand – a concept rather than a geographic rule. In particular, the newly industrialising countries of south-east Asia do not fit neatly into either category. In Korea, Malaysia, Indonesia and China, for example, governments are planning for rapid continued conventional economic development. Other things being equal, well before 2050 we can expect them to have reached or even outstripped OECD levels of economic activity and consumption. Many of the former communist 'countries in transition' are also difficult to categorise in this way. It is perhaps more useful to think of the 'North' as shorthand for the world's consumer class, most of whom are found in Northern industrialised countries, and the 'South' as shorthand for the world's low-wage or subsistence class, of whom the vast majority, landless or with very few resources, are to be found in Southern countries.[6] This division is reflected in the economic power and influence of different countries. This is the second reason for using the terms South and North – they reflect the current balance of power in world politics. The North controls the global institutions that set the framework for international relations, Northern companies control the vast majority of world trade, and Northern consumer lifestyles, reinforced by advertising and the ongoing liberalisation of the telecommunications sector, are determining an unfolding global culture. The influence of the North is not just indirect and unintentional. Governments and Northern-dominated inter-governmental organisations are using the leverage provided by international debt to make direct prescriptive interventions in Southern economies, in a process called structural adjustment.

## Debt and Structural Adjustment

From 1984 to 1993, total developing country debt to western banks and governments doubled.[7] Developing countries still owe over US$1300 billlion in 'external' debt to other countries, multilateral institutions such as the World Bank and foreign commercial banks.[8] Much of this debt built up in the 1970s with easy availability of petro-dollars, and has become a millstone since, as world interest rates have risen. Now debt servicing payments from South to North exceed aid flows from North to South, which total only US$60 billion each year. The UN Development Programme (UNDP) reports that 'debt repayments often absorb a quarter to a third of developing countries' limited government revenue, crowding out critical public investment in human development'.[9] The problem is worst for the 32 severely indebted low-income countries, many in sub-Saharan Africa. Between 1990 and 1993 debt servicing cost sub-Saharan Africa more than US$13 billion annually. UNICEF estimates that the total additional annual cost of meeting basic human needs for health, education, nutrition and reproductive health is only around US$9 billion.[10] At the latest count just US$7 billion of the debt of sub-Saharan Africa had been forgiven, leaving US$150 billion outstanding. Yet even if all existing debt relief measures were fully applied, 23 of these countries would still have what the UNDP describe as 'unsustainable' debt burdens – debts exceeding the value of exports by 200 per cent or more.

Many of the world's poorest countries are heavily indebted, but in order to borrow money from the International Monetary Fund (IMF) they are required to undertake innocuous sounding, but in fact immensely disruptive, 'structural adjustment programmes' (SAPs). These have largely dominated the economic policies of developing countries since 1980.[11] They involve tight monetary discipline, increased exports and reduced subsidies, even on basic necessities. The consequences are dramatic. At worst poverty and inequality have increased, with social unrest culminating in riots in, for example, Venezuela and Morocco.[12] More widely, land has been taken from local food production and pressed into cash cropping for export, because the need for hard currency overrides the need to ensure food security. Although those with jobs in cash cropping often have elevated incomes and a better life as a result, those who no longer have access to land to grow their own food suffer. The IMF designed SAPs to decrease domestic consumption and to generate more domestic savings, more investment – especially by foreign-owned corporations – and more exports. Specifically, these policies promote export-orientated growth, reductions in social public spending such as education and health, cutbacks in the state's role in the economy, removal of subsidies on basic foods and transportation, devaluation of the national currency and freezing the real wages of workers.[13]

The result of SAPs has been far from beneficial. For more than a decade, citizen organizations around the world have voiced their strong criticism of the impact and effectiveness of the IMF's SAPs. All reviews of SAPs have found, at best, mixed results in terms of their environmental and social impacts.[14] Where impacts have been found to be negligible or positive, more often than not it is not the result of the SAP, but of the corrective policies used to protect these interests against the SAP's negative impacts. More broadly, studies which have examined the practical economic results have more negative conclusions than those which assumed that SAPs would deliver the intended results. In reality, even the World Bank admits that their performance in delivering the intended economic results is patchy[15] and that they need supporting measures to protect the poor.[16]

Overall, adjustment policies have not resurrected developing countries' economies, but in practice have caused a severe deterioration of the living conditions of the poor, accelerated environmental degradation and increased the external dependency of developing countries.[17] So it would be difficult to justify their continuation even if they delivered on their economic objectives.

In Zambia (see Box 2.1), for example, SAPs have had significant negative impacts.

Social impacts have also been severe. Oxfam concluded that SAPs 'dramatically worsen the plight of the poor' in sub-Saharan Africa by adversely affecting food prices, health and education spending.[18] For

## BOX 2.1 *SAPs IN ZAMBIA*

In Zambia, implementation of a donor-funded structural adjustment programme began in 1983 and has continued intermittently to the present. SAPs have had a detrimental effect on Zambia's three main environmental problems: loss of wildlife, deforestation and urban water quality.The loss of big game species in Zambia has accelerated during the SAP period; for example, between 1960 and 1985, elephant numbers fell by 3 per cent per year from 270,000 to 75,000, but between 1985 and 1993 they fell by 9 per cent per year to just 22,000.The main cause of big game loss is poaching for trophies. Structural adjustment has increased urban unemployment and reduced farm incomes. These impacts have increased the incentives for poor people to collaborate with the organised poaching gangs. At the same time, public spending reductions have reduced the effectiveness of the National Parks administration.

About 45 per cent of Zambia's land area is covered by dry evergreen forest and miombo woodland, but during the 1980s this area was lost at a rate of 900,000 hectares, or 2.6 per cent, per year. The direct contribution of the SAP to this accelerated deforestation is difficult to distinguish. However, the proportion of the urban unemployed returning to the rural areas has increased as a result of the SAP, as has the area under maize cultivation. Both these factors have contributed to forest clearance. Pollution of water by mining and industrial wastes, and by sewage dumping has affected urban water quality. The SAP has contributed to this deterioration by cutting funding for the Ministry of Local Government, which is responsible for urban water supplies.

Source: Reed, D (ed) (1996) *Structural Adjustment, the Environment and Sustainable Development* London: Earthscan; Hogg, D (1993) *The SAP in the forest: The Environmental and Social Impacts of Structural Adjustment Programmes in the Philippines, Ghana and Guyana* London: Friends of the Earth

example, Uganda spends 12 times as much on debt repayment as on health, and in 1994 Zambia spent 30 times as much on debt repayment as on primary education.[19] The most severe costs fall on rural women who bear the brunt of meeting subsistence needs for their families. Kevin Watkins of Oxfam has reported that 'Zimbabweans have reinterpreted the acronym for their Enhanced Structural Adjustment Programmme, ESAP, as "Enhanced Suffering for African People".'[20]

Despite public commitments by the IMF and World Bank to favour the poor, Oxfam concludes that: 'in practice, the costs of adjustment are still being borne disproportionately by the most vulnerable sections of society'.[21]

Worse, as we noted above, SAPs have failed to achieve their own objectives as well as creating environmental and social chaos. SAPs encourage countries to focus on production and export of primary commodities such as coffee and cocoa to earn foreign exchange. But

prices for these are erratic and generally falling.[22] Deregulating agricultural markets has primarily benefited large-scale commercial producers,
while poorer farmers have been crippled by higher interest rates. In most
of Africa, at least, structural adjustment has not led to macroeconomic
stability or growth.[23] More widely, Oxfam concludes that 'there is little
evidence to substantiate the claim that adjustment policies are creating a
framework for more equitable growth and poverty reduction. In many
countries they appear to be doing precisely the opposite'.[24]

The Mexican Peso Crisis in early 1995 gives one good illustration of
the unreliability of SAPs in meeting their economic aims. High interest
rates on government securities, designed to attract foreign currency and
thereby prop up the exchange rate in the face of IMF policies focused on
reducing government expenditure and inflation, increased foreign
holdings of Mexican government securities from US$2 billion in 1990 to
almost US$30 billion in 1994.[25] When the government did not have
reserves to meet payments on bonds at the end of 1994 the peso
collapsed by 50 per cent of its value. The magnitude of capital flight out
of Mexico left the Mexican middle and lower classes with the bill of the
international capital bail out through yet more belt-tightening adjustment
policies. The IMF has been widely criticised for failing in its role of
surveillance, but the IMF's prescriptions also failed to stabilise Mexico's
balance of payments or regulate its monetary policies.[26]

As SAPs have clearly been unable to cure the financial problems of
its Latin American or African borrowing members, so it is unlikely that
the same economic reform recipe will be able to create sustainable
economic growth within the much more complex, further industrialised
economies of Eastern Europe, Russia and the newly independent states.
If these structural adjustment programmes remain in their current form,
the pattern of socially and environmentally destructive development will
continue, with the benefits being both short term and elitist. Nor will
debt be reduced. Years of SAPs have simply encouraged resource
exploitation and cuts in social welfare to maintain debt interest payments.
As the Religious Working Group on the World Bank and IMF concludes:

> *The human consequences of austerity measures to service the debt are
> felt disproportionately by the most vulnerable people in society ... who
> seldom have a voice in decision making processes around debt. The
> debt itself is unjust. Much of it was incurred by oppressive regimes
> which spent the borrowed funds on wasteful arms programs, projects
> benefiting the elites, or investments in the industrialised world by
> those elites. The majority of citizens did not receive any benefits from
> these borrowed funds, yet they pay the price for them.*[27]

This is not the place to set out an agenda for economic policy to replace
or reform SAPs. However two points must be made. First, targeted debt

relief – 'to deal rapidly and comprehensively with all outstanding debt'[28] in the most severely indebted countries – is still urgently needed, in combination with commitments to use part of the benefits of debt forgiveness for major investment in human development. Second, whatever mechanisms are advanced to help the sustainable development of Southern economies they must be developed in an inclusive manner with the full participation of both Southern governments and Southern people.

## Trade Relations and Trade Rules

The effects of SAPs are exacerbated by inequitable trade relations between the North and South. Originally, trade links were based on the export of natural resources from the colonies to industrialised countries for manufacturing purposes. This pattern, once in place, remained, but the severest economic repercussions were not really felt until world prices for non-oil primary commodities dropped dramatically between 1980 and 1993. Oxfam report that the estimated annual loss to developing countries over this period was around US$100 billion a year – more than twice the total value of aid flows in 1990.[29] Following the establishment of this 'colonial' trading pattern, trade liberalisation has always tended to favour the stonger trading partners. Thus, for example, Japan and the EU both impose a higher tariff on plywood than on raw logs, thereby encouraging the import of raw, unprocessed materials (a system known as tariff escalation). So the exporting country not only suffers economically through the loss of value-added processing, it must also produce more of the raw material, in this case logs, to earn the same amount of much needed foreign currency.[30] The late President Cheddi Jagan of Guyana starkly confirmed this picture, saying in 1994, in a letter to a US Congressman that: 'Our foreign debt, which we inherited from the previous government, is not only killing us, it is killing our forests as well'.[31]

Similarly, intergovernmental trade negotiations in GATT (the General Agreement on Tariffs and Trade) have always tended to favour the stronger partners. Thus, for example, agriculture, which is heavily subsidised in most Northern countries, has long been excluded from GATT negotiations. Even its recent inclusion, following the latest so-called 'Uruguay Round', has done little to change the situation. Continued subsidised overproduction in Northern countries depresses world food prices, with the result that farmers in developing countries receive a low price for their products and therefore often do not have the necessary resources to invest in sustainable production methods.[32] Overall, the World Bank and the OECD predict that the Uruguay Round will bring most benefits to the US and Japan, and least to the Southern countries, with Africa being a net loser.[33] Within Southern countries, certain groups amongst the poor will benefit less or even lose out, especially poorer agricultural producers. As the UN Development Programme points out, 'income inequality is clearly on the rise in many countries that have opened their economies' including Mexico, Sri Lanka and China.[34] Women, especially, are likely to see fewer of the benefits of trade liberalisation, as their activities generally take place outside of formal markets.[35]

The rules of the game themselves are often stacked against the weaker economies. Although the recently-formed World Trade Organisation (WTO) operates a one member, one vote system (in theory), the agenda of the Uruguay Round clearly demonstrated the North's influence. Issues of interest to the North, such as intellectual property rights and investments, dominated the Round, whilst issues of interest to the South, such as commodity prices, were absent. Furthermore, the rules on disputes, which permit what is known as 'cross retaliation' in other trade sectors, put weaker, less diverse economies at a major disadvantage, and thus under pressure to agree to the Northern agenda. Similarly, the poorer countries were virtually tricked into agreeing to implement the whole of the Uruguay Round as a 'single undertaking' if they wanted to join the WTO – and all feared the trade consequences of being excluded. This 'undertaking' included the so called 'Blair House' agreement on agriculture, struck between the EU and the US, which did little to help the South, as it enables the EU and US to retain permissible subsidies but forces developing countries to reduce restrictions on agricultural imports, which will exacerbate food security problems. Yet the poorest countries were not even consulted on the final text of the Blair House agreement![36]

Unsurprisingly, WTO rules continue to work against the interests of its weaker members. In theory, WTO rules require all countries to respond to liberalisation by their trade partners by offering equivalent measures. But where developing countries liberalise 'unilaterally', for example under SAPs, the industrialised countries are not required to reciprocate. For example, in the Philippines, tariffs were reduced by half and import restrictions removed from 2800 product categories between 1981 and 1995 without comparable reductions in industrialised countries.[37] Moreover, the WTO's aim to further free trade will principally benefit the companies that run world trade – the top 500 transnational corporations which control 70 per cent of world trade. These companies stand to benefit directly, for example, from the increased liberalisation of foreign direct investments and the tightening of intellectual property rights legislation agreed in the Uruguay Round. Many of these transnationals have consistently worked to influence the agenda of international trade negotiations, through lobbying at both the national and intergovernmental levels, and involve themselves directly wherever possible in international standards settings bodies, such as the International Organisation for Standardisation and the Codex Alimentarius Commission, for example. They are also set to gain from new negotiations on a free-standing 'Multilateral Agreement on

Investment' being negotiated in the OECD, which effectively seeks to remove all remaining national policy tools (in all sectors except security and defence) for regulating foreign investment and transnational corporation activities in any of its signatories.

While, as we saw in Chapter 1, environmental concerns need not imply protectionism and opposition to free trade, they do require a regulatory framework for trade which will protect environmental and social interests and promote fair trade practices. Otherwise, pressure for deregulated trade can lead to degradation of the environment and exploitation of workers; and if national regulations in these areas are lax or weakly enforced, this can lead to a downward spiral of standards while the rules governing trade can prevent or discourage governments from taking measures to safeguard labour and environmental standards. As Lequesne argues:

> *weak social and environmental regulations are not a source of legitimate comparative advantage, but an unacceptable form of exploitation. World trade rules should therefore be reformed to protect people's basic rights and to promote sustainable development.*[38]

## Aid Programmes

Aid programmes, also influenced by the interests of transnational corporations, have largely promoted similar outcomes to those of structural adjustment and trade. They have funded big dams, logging, new roads, new waterways and a host of other projects which have benefited specific interest groups, often in the lending countries themselves.[39] Although the worst excesses of the UK aid programme – those, such as the Pergau Dam, perpetrated under the Aid and Trade Provision (ATP), which only funds projects which in turn purchase UK goods – are a minor part of the overall programme, even mainstream lending through the World Bank and other multilateral lending institutions has largely failed to deliver the goods for their intended beneficiaries.[40] Poverty reduction is a stated aim of World Bank and bilateral aid programmes. In practice, however, not only have the poor missed out on the benefits, but they have, all too often, been the victims instead. For example, major aid-funded construction projects such as the Narmada Dam have damaged their livelihoods, or even led to forced relocation.[41]

In the World Bank, the 'big-project lending mentality' has persisted through years of struggle and opposition from community groups in the areas affected, and recently adopted procedures to take account of environmental and social factors have had little apparent impact.[42] Most recently it has been revealed – in a leaked document – that the limited project environmental impact assessment (EIA) procedures in the Bank are virtually useless. They are normally carried out too late to have any effect on the design or implementation of the project. No project has been cancelled as a result of a negative EIA report. Alternatives have rarely seen adequate consideration. Implementation on the ground has not adequately integrated recommendations for mitigation measures.[43] Even so, for the poorest countries, aid remains the main form of foreign exchange support and the largest source of financing for public expenditures such as health and education. But aid flows are falling in real terms. Private capital flows, on the other hand, are growing fast. But this means that an increasing amount of North–South financial flows is going direct to companies – often the same transnationals that have benefited from aid programmes – rather than to Southern governments and this through even less transparent and accountable institutions such as the International Finance Corporation, a part of the World Bank dedicated to supporting private sector investment in developing countries,[44] and the British Commonwealth Development Corporation.

## Private Capital Flows and Transnational Corporations

We have touched on the lobbying role of transnationals already. They can also influence developing country governments, perhaps even more easily than the multilateral agencies. Their objectives have been to liberalise trade, privatise resources and obtain government support for their investments in extractive, agricultural and processing industries. They have been amongst the principal beneficiaries of structural adjustment and trade liberalisation.

Between 1987 and 1994 private flows of capital, including foreign direct investment (FDI), private loans and equity investments, increased seven-fold. As a share of global GDP, FDI doubled between 1985 and 1994, while the fraction going to developing countries rose to more than one-third.[45] In allocation, private capital flows further reinforce inequities. Of total private flows in 1993, over two-thirds went to five 'emerging markets' – China, Singapore, Mexico, Argentina and Turkey. In 1994 FDI to developing countries totalled a record US$84 billion; 40 per cent of this went to China, and another 24 per cent to Hong Kong, Indonesia, Malaysia, Singapore and Thailand. Sub-Saharan Africa received only 3.6 per cent.[46] In 44 out of 93 developing countries the ratio of trade to GDP fell between 1985 and 1994.[47] The types of investment made mean that patterns of FDI reflect and accelerate the banks' lending programmes. The companies involved are generally active in the mining, timber, agriculture, power development and construction sectors. Such investments can have positive effects where transnationals introduce higher standards and more environmentally efficient processes. But in the arena of liberalised trade and liberalised investment regimes described above, this relies largely on voluntary action. As we will see in Chapter 10, the incentives for such action are especially weak where producers and consumers are so far apart.

# ECONOMIC DOMINANCE AND THE FAILURE OF THE DEVELOPMENT MODEL

The dominance of the global economy constrains developing countries' options. It also limits developed country options; but not so severely, as we will see in Chapter 10. It doesn't only mean that the richer North can afford to consume a greater share of the resources available globally, it also forces Southern countries to exploit resources to sell materials and commodities into a global market, to the point where the competition for sale depresses prices. But the normal market responses, which would be to produce less, are subdued by the pressures of international debt and structural adjustment.

Despite the efforts of international institutions and a host of charitable bodies, these processes have not delivered on the promises of the post-war agreements that established the World Bank and instigated the General Agreement on Tariffs and Trade (GATT) as measures to promote global economic development. Despite unprecedented economic growth in many countries, the absolute number of people in the world living in absolute poverty has grown, not declined, in the last 25 years.[48] In most continents this process has been accompanied by the growth of inequality within countries, as wealth has failed to trickle down from those who have gained from engaging in the global economy. Of course, we can't blame the current international institutions for all inequity; they have not forced Southern governments to squander vast sums on arms, or corrupt officials to salt away government funds in Swiss bank accounts. But the combination of their activities and the legacy of colonialism has created a great challenge for development. The conventional Western model has brought unacceptable environmental and social impacts. There is general agreement that widespread poverty is morally unacceptable, but disagreement on how best to eliminate it. There is also general agreement that 'development' in some form is desirable for poorer countries so that they can gain the benefits of participating in the global economy.

This consensus, rather than environmental concerns, has been the driving force behind the international processes which have spawned the idea of sustainable development. However, Southern countries have had little chance to set the agenda, so their participation in the global economy is not based on control of the resources they need for development. It is not on their own terms, but on those of the North, and those of the

Southern elites who have done well out of the current model. This is one reason why we must not entirely characterise a rich North:poor South split. Rich elites in the South are as much a part of the world consumer class, as the poor homeless in the North are part of a landless 'subsistence class'. And within the subsistence class it is women who bear the brunt of meeting subsistence needs such as childcare, housework, fuel gathering and water fetching.

All over the world, and in all sectors, it is the subsistence class who are losing ever more of their subsistence base to the 'Northern' elites. We noted above how fisheries in Senegal are being exploited for Northern markets at the cost of local subsistence. In Nicaragua, the rights to minerals resources, previously exploited by landless miners in small scale production, have been sold to transnational mining companies.[49] In the Philippines, commercial sugar production has appropriated the best land, leaving subsistence producers scratching an even poorer living.[50] In all these cases the story is of local control over resources which supported local livelihoods being lost as a result of the appropriation of those resources for 'Northern' use.

# 'ENVIRONMENTAL' COLONIALISM

Continued economic colonialism is therefore reflected in and arguably, based on, a new type of colonialism, over 'environmental space', or the resources needed for sustainable development. Above and beyond all the specific ways in which 'development' in the South reflects Northern interests, the impact of Northern consumption on Southern economies and societies is paramount. Not only are the rich developed countries of the North, with only a quarter of the world's population, consuming almost half of the total fossil fuels, around two-thirds of metals and three-quarters of 'industrial wood products', but as a result we are also consuming more than a fair share of the environment's capacity to absorb pollution. To take an extreme example, the richest (OECD) countries' current emissions of carbon dioxide already exceed the estimated global sustainable level of emissions for 2050, based on IPCC figures,[51] and those countries hold only 15 per cent of the world's population. Looked at another way, if the Chinese, currently emitting around 2.2 tonnes of $CO_2$ per capita, reach OECD average levels of emissions – almost 13 tonnes per capita – by 2050, then they alone will exceed those global sustainable levels by a factor of two.

Many politicians in Britain and other developed countries have taken such estimates as a cue to imply that there is no point in us taking action to reduce our emissions as it won't stop the Chinese or the Indians increasing theirs. This is not a helpful line of argument for at least three reasons. We do not naively believe that if the UK shows leadership on the international stage, that the rest of the world will meekly follow suit. However, first, we do believe that without more ambitious leadership from nations like the UK, we will never convince the developing world even to constrain the growth of its emissions. Our Southern partners in the Friends of the Earth International network have responded positively to our first efforts to promote equitable targets. They have told us that they need examples to follow that challenge the conventional development model and hold out the prospect of true sustainability. And they tell us that local control over critical resources such as land and water is critical to their future development.[52] Secondly, and equally importantly, unless we in the North develop analytical approaches and development policies that address such equity concerns directly, our posturing in international negotiations will not be taken seriously. Thirdly, such argument ignores the role, however modest in global terms that the UK actively plays in the management of the global economy, for example, as a member of the Group of Seven, or on the board of the World Bank, and through the investments and activities of UK government agencies and private companies.

In the longer term, consumption of natural resources by the rich industrialised countries needs to be diminished to such a degree that poor countries can strive for the same level of consumption without the ecological limits of the earth being violated. In some cases the limits are felt even more closely than where pollution is the most pressing problem. For renewable resources and land, every unit taken by the Northern countries is one that can't be used to meet indigenous needs in the South. In these cases an increasing share of total production is being taken to meet Northern demands. And although some in the South benefit, it is rarely the poorest. Those who work on cash crop farms producing bananas in Jamaica or in aquaculture to provide prawns for export from Ecuador often suffer poor working conditions and extremely low wages, while those who lose access to land or fish stocks for food production as a result are further marginalised, and deprived of food, especially protein.

More or less the only argument advanced to counter these concerns is that if the products were not exported for consumption in the North, there would be no effective demand, so they would not be produced at all. This may hold for many mineral resources, for example, at least in the short-term, but not where the product displaces subsistence production. And in the longer term this is just another way of saying that, if we do nothing to stop it, the rich will go on getting richer at the expense of the poor.

# FAIR SHARES IN ENVIRONMENTAL SPACE

The environmental space approach builds on the analysis of global limits to encompass a concept of global equity – of fair access to environmental resources for every nation. This is a moral approach based on a belief in equality of opportunity, rather than equality of outcomes. To illustrate this we start from the 'rule of thumb' assumption of equal rights: not that every individual must consume exactly the same, but that everyone has the same right to the resources our planet provides. So we calculate environmental shares by dividing environmental space equally, on a per capita basis, and then sum those shares to provide estimates of nations' fair shares in the global environmental space.

But this is for purposes of illustration of the scale of overconsumption in the North, not a prescription. We are not misguided tomato-like environmentalists – starting off green, but turning red overnight – who believe that central planning and reallocation can even begin to address the world's problems. We do not reject the role of the market in efficient allocation. But we do believe, as the Brundtland report proposed, that all human beings have the fundamental right to an environment adequate for their health and wellbeing, and more than this, that current rates of consumption and pollution deny this right to many of the world's poor and to many of our descendants. The British people may choose, through our democratic system, to allocate resources unevenly within our national society, but we do not have the right to appropriate the resources that another society needs for sustainable development. Sadly, it's not as simple as this suggests, for two reasons. First, practically, the ability to exploit environmental space is not always distributed equally – domestic electrical appliances are not going to see much use in a country without an electricity grid, for example. Even mining natural resources may be impossible without the capital to invest in mining equipment and processing technology. However, this is an issue of the timing of the transition rather than a fundamental problem.

Second, and more significantly, an equal distribution in this way may well not be enough – not enough politically and not enough morally. It is not without reason that Afro-Americans in the ghettos of Chicago demand the right to consume for a hundred years[53] – our culture already has! If we add together all the historical emissions of greenhouse gases, for example, we find that the developed countries are responsible for an even greater share of the threat of climate change than it appears at first sight. According to work by the Stockholm Environment Institute, the UK ranks third in the world in terms of cumulative carbon emissions over the period 1860–1986 (see Figure 2.2).[54] If a fair share were calculated to take this into account, the UK would have no quota left!

In a very real sense we have built up a massive 'environmental debt' to the rest of the world, one that makes the financial debts of developing countries seem puny by comparison. Friends of the Earth is not proposing to take this 'environmental debt' into account in the sustainability targets suggested here. But we explain it to illuminate the moral bankruptcy of arguments that permits to pollute, or emissions targets for pollutants, or 'rights' to consume should be 'grand-fathered', or in other

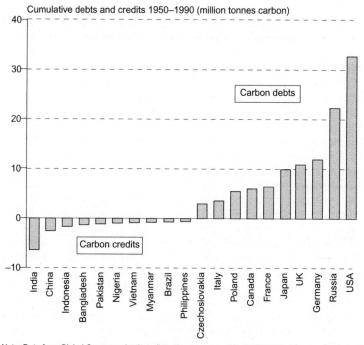

Figure 2.2 *Global inequity – 'environmental debts' in greenhouse gas emissions*

words, that those who have consumed and polluted more in the past will be allowed to consume and pollute more in the future. There may be strong technical, practical and even political arguments for such an approach, but there is no moral basis to it at all. It is therefore not adopted by Friends of the Earth, although we do recognise that there must be a transition to a fairer distribution, rather than some instant shift. This also allows those of us in Northern countries to gradually unlock ourselves from our resource intensive lifestyles such as patterns of urban development that demand high car use. We have made the investments in infrastructure and development that could permit such a shift through a historic process in which we have converted our natural resources into physical and human capital – our towns, cities, railways, factories, technology, skills and knowledge. This gives us opportunities to reduce our impacts that are not open to poorer countries.

Environmental space allows us to set targets and development paths which allow the 'headroom' for developing countries' consumption to grow without tipping the global balance. In a world where resource use is limited, then development can be achieved only through redistribution – not in the form of handouts, but through access to the resources needed for true self-determination. If the developed countries do not plan for such redistribution then the people of the South will either be increasingly marginalised, or will look to take control of resources for themselves, either directly as, for example, Sem Terra, the Brazilian land rights movement has begun to do in its occupation of agricultural land, or through increased rates of migration: as so called 'environmental refugees'. Involvement of the disenfranchised and marginalised communities of the South in the development process is essential to avoid such outcomes.

Wars over scarce resources are nothing new; any conflict over territory is such. But land is not the only reason for such conflicts now. In many parts of the world there is a threat of water wars, over scarce water for irrigation, or over the quality of water. These are set to arise where nations share the same river, and an upstream nation can abstract more water, or even dam the flow; or pollute the water. The Middle East seems a likely flash-point for wars of the first type, whilst further east, wet season flooding triggered by deforestation which increases sediment loads, and reduced dry season flows blamed on water management practices at the Indian Farakka Barrage on the Ganges, are stressing international relations between Bangladesh and India.[55] These types of conflict are relatively small scale now, but as environmental scarcity grows, few areas will be able to escape such impacts. Fish wars are another example. We're getting used to Navy ships getting involved in fishing disputes even here in Europe where pressures on fisheries have led to political conflicts between countries. But in other cases violent conflict has already arisen. For example, it has been reported that Russians have shot and killed Chinese fishermen in the Okhotsk sea.[56]

These add a strong practical reason why the rich of the world should worry about inequity just as much as the poor. Not only is it morally indefensible to argue that the benefits of ever more growth outweigh the deaths from preventable hunger and disease of 34,000 children every day,[57] for example, but in the longer term the social and economic costs will return to haunt even the wealthiest amongst us (see Box 2.2).

# INEQUITY IN THE UK

We cannot conclude this chapter without touching on equity concerns within the UK. In our view one of the strongest challenges to reducing Northern consumption comes from the concern that such changes would impact most severely on the poorest and most disadvantaged groups in Northern societies. However, this does not invalidate our arguments but merely extends them. We should not just seek to redistribute access to resources between North and South, but also within the North. We will

## BOX 2.2 *GLOBAL INEQUITY*

To illustrate the degree of global inequity, here we present some comparative figures for the USA and India as a benchmark.

- Per head the US consumes 36 times as much aluminium, 15.7 times as much steel as India, 42.7 times as much oil, and 400 times more wood pulp.
- Per head each American owns almost 150 times as many cars, consumes 10.5 times as much beef and veal, and three times as much water.
- In purchasing power terms, the average Indian income is just over one-twentieth of that of the average American.

The differences between the UK and India are smaller but just as stark. The average UK income is 14 times that of the average Indian, while our consumption of energy and aluminium is 35 times greater.

Source: World Resources Institute (1994) *World Resources 1994–95 – A Guide to the Global Environment* Oxford: Oxford University Press

return to this issue at greater length in Chapter 11, but here simply review some of the issues.

In recent years the UK has become one of the most unequal societies in the World.[58] Official figures suggest that by 1994 the poorest tenth of the population were 13 per cent worse off than in 1979, whilst the richest tenth had become 65 per cent better off.[59] That this inequality is widely perceived is illustrated by the extent of political uproar over the salary increases of MPs and 'fat-cat' directors, especially in the recently privatised utilities, whose profits come from selling basic necessities such as energy and water to the public. Although there is no official measure of poverty used in the UK, the Child Poverty Action Group has applied two commonly used yardsticks: the number on or below the level of income support benefit, and the number below half average wages. By the early 1990s both had grown sharply to approximately 25 per cent from 14 per cent and 9 per cent, respectively, in 1979.[60] That inequality is growing is borne out from a very different angle by a recent report in *The Economist* magazine, not normally known for its radical views, which noted that 'official economic indicators present a confusing picture at the moment'.[61] The magazine then suggested some 'unofficial indicators' including sales of 'flash cars', up by 640 per cent since the previous year; exotic holidays, bookings for the Dominican Republic up by 58 per cent on the year; and 'bigger bosoms', demand for cosmetic surgery up by 20 per cent on the year. The conclusion? 'Those at the top end of the income scale are seeing rather more of the recovery than those lower down'. In other words, income inequality is growing.

# Unemployment, Insecurity and Poverty

Will Hutton caused something of a political furore when his book *The State We're In*[62] argued that the UK had become a deeply divided society, with broadly 30 per cent disadvantaged, another 30 per cent insecure, and 40 per cent privileged. Some 28 per cent of the adult working population are either unemployed or economically inactive; to this can be added another 1 per cent who are occupied on government schemes to alleviate unemployment, and the proportion of the population living at the edge is close to 30 per cent. These, with their children poorly fed, their families under stress and without access to amenities like gardens, are the severely disadvantaged. The next 30 per cent are the marginalised and the insecure. People in this category work at jobs that are insecure, poorly protected and carry few benefits. These are often part-time jobs. There are now more than five million people working part-time, of whom over 80 per cent are women. The remaining 40 per cent or so are the privileged – those whose market power has increased since 1979. These are largely full-time employees and the self-employed who have held their jobs for over two years. Statistics on families bear out this analysis. Between 1979 and 1991 the proportion of families with no full time earner rose from 29 to 37 per cent and the average length of time it took a member of a household without work to find a job increased from 18 months in 1979 to four and a half years in 1993. On the other hand the proportion of two-adult households where both work, rose.[63]

The level of debate over such suggestions led the Department of Social Security (DSS) to commission research which revealed that such categorisation conceals substantial mobility between groups.[64] Peter Lilley, Secretary of State for Social Security at the time, claimed that the results proved that there is no such thing as poverty in the UK. However the DSS figures are only for male heads of households, so exclude some of the poorest groups, such as women, children, the elderly and homeless people. Peter Townsend, Emeritus Professor of Sociology at Bristol University, dismisses the DSS research as worthless.[65] Even if the DSS figures are correct in suggesting that many households moved in and out of poverty over the study period, this simply reinforces the arguments that insecurity for a wider group is on the increase.

In fact, in the UK there is real poverty – malnutrition and homelessness are at significant levels, and growing, yet safety nets have been cut back to finance tax cuts for the comfortable and reduced government borrowing. Malnutrition is now evident in the UK on a scale not seen since the 1930s. A survey of 179 local authorities and 36 health authorities found evidence of poor nutrition and poor growth rates in children from low income families in all but one area. Longer-term studies have found IQ deficiencies in such children.[66] Since 1979, official figures show that the number of children in households with an income only half that of the poorest 10 per cent has risen from 860,000 to 1,180,000.[67] The government's Low Income Project Team has warned that rising poverty is denying whole communities a healthy diet, putting them at risk of cancer, heart disease and debilitating anaemia.[68] Overall, such government welfare spending cuts are self-defeating, as the costs of health care rise in the longer term.

# IS INEQUALITY NECESSARY?

Proponents of the conventional development model argue that inequality is necessary and indeed desirable to drive economic participation. They claim that by providing rewards for success and penalties for failure, inequality promotes growth, which in turn generates greater wealth for all. But this view is not borne out by the evidence. The UK economy did not grow faster as inequality increased in the 1980s – and our successful competitors generally have more equal income distribution. In fact, as we will see in Chapter 11, poverty depresses economic efficiency, by increasing unproductive social costs and reducing the ability of the poor to afford education and training, thus reducing the skills base in the economy. Instead the justification for increasing inequity is political; poverty for some allows the 'comfortable majority' to be made materially better off – through tax cuts for example – maintaining their political support. Similarly, at a global level, the same motor that provides increasing material standards of living for a global minority generates environmental degradation and increases inequity.

However, the consensus view that drives the global economy, and in turn drives open economies such as the UK's, is that the less regulated and restrained the free market, the more wealth it will deliver. At the same time, however, it delivers more inequality. If this was truly only a relative phenomenon, perhaps we need not worry. But absolute material poverty still persists, and indeed, grows. Worse still, poverty is not just a material issue, poverty of mind and spirit is almost more important. This derives in part from the obvious inequalities that so devalue the more vulnerable groups in our society. For example, in August 1996 the DSS replaced a benefit helpline with a hotline for reporting suspected benefit cheats. This view is supported by research measuring happiness and wellbeing which suggests that inequality within societies directly reduces wellbeing. We return to this issue in the next chapter.

# POVERTY AND ENVIRONMENTAL LIMITS

The implications of global limits to resource use are serious. Conventional economic policy suggests that we can provide best for the

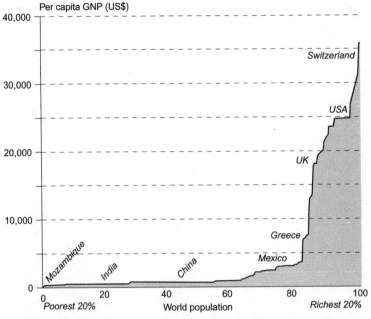

Source: UNDP 1997 *Human Development Report 1997*, with illustrative country examples

**Figure 2.3** *Global distribution of national income*

poorest groups in society by increasing the total size of the economy and, according to different political perspectives, allowing wealth to 'trickle down' to the poorest, or actively redistributing it by taxation and public provision. At a global level a similar approach is advocated, especially by the proponents of trade liberalisation at any cost, who argue that liberalisation drives economic growth, which will then trickle down to the poorest. But at both scales, the system is failing. As we saw earlier, wealth is increasingly concentrated in the pockets of the richest (see Figure 2.3). The richest 20 per cent now take 85 per cent of world income.[69] Worse, such high degrees of inequity are a direct consequence of current models of growth.

To provide even a minimum level of welfare for the poorest on the planet based on current production and consumption patterns, in other words without reducing inequity, would imply vast increases in total consumption. As we will see in Part 2, average rates of consumption of environmental resources per person in the UK are already amongst the highest in the world. Yet even at these average rates a significant proportion of British people are left without a roof over their heads or unable to afford a healthy and varied diet. In other words, with current distributional patterns, poverty is a driving force for growth in consumption and consequent growth in environmental degradation. There are also strong practical reasons for seeking to reduce inequity and poverty. As we will see later, cooperative efforts will be needed to deliver solutions to the environmental problems we face. Inequality, however, dissolves the social glue that is vital to such collective action, both within and between nations. As we approach global limits, we cannot go on consuming more materials to bake an ever bigger cake in the hope that there will be enough crumbs for the poorest. Instead we must become more efficient in how we meet needs through production and consumption.

## CONCLUSION

This chapter has outlined how inequity is growing, both regionally and globally. It has also sketched out how the causes of growing inequity are linked to the neo-classical consensus view of free market economics forged after the Second World War. The view that economic growth, regardless of its nature, could deliver benefits for all has been shown to be, at best, misplaced. The institutions and systems put in place to facilitate development through growth have instead facilitated continued 'environmental colonialism' by the wealthier industrial countries in a way which has maintained and even exacerbated inequity. And developing countries have been largely unable to influence the agendas of these institutions and processes.

We touched on the UK experience of colonialism above, and suggested that there was much to be proud of in the Commonwealth. But there is a need for a new 'Common Wealth' that includes all countries. A Common Wealth in which all have fair access to environmental resources and in which all have the opportunity for sustainable development. We all share this planet, we all rely upon it, but we could so easily further damage or destroy its ability to support us if we do not cooperate in the conservation, development and use of resources.

We believe that the extent of poverty and inequity described in this chapter demands a response if sustainable development is to be achieved. Equity concerns must, and can, be addressed within a framework of sustainability targets. So in this book we will outline an 'equity scenario' in which equitable access to resources is the basis of the environmental space targets for each country.

## Chapter 3
# Sustainability and Wellbeing – Delivering Quality of Life

## INTRODUCTION

For those of us in the UK with a secure job and income, and a home and all the other benefits these bring, past economic development has been, in most respects, 'a good thing'. But as we saw in the last chapter, not all have shared in the benefits. There are now 1.3 billion people on earth who live in absolute poverty – more than ever before. Over 12 million children die before the age of five each year, 95 per cent of them from poverty related illnesses.[1] And in the UK, 200,000 people have no home to go to. Many more live increasingly insecure lives, relying on part-time work, short contracts, the informal and even the criminal economy to earn a living. More still live with the threat of redundancy and unemployment.

In this chapter we address the third basic concern we have with the conventional growth model, that despite increasing money incomes, it is no longer actually increasing human wellbeing or the totality of human welfare. Wellbeing is a helpful concept here, as it includes both material affluence or 'standard of living' and 'quality of life' yet is distinct from both of them. This third failure partly results from the increasing extent of insecurity which stems from growth in inequality. But it is also partly a result of the breakdown, for very good reasons, of the assumption that we will necessarily be better off in the future. In the conventional model, from generation to generation, wealth increases. We have been able to ignore the future, because we could rely on an apparently natural economic process in which future generations are always wealthier than the current one. The best way to provide for our descendants was simply to generate wealth, or in other words, to strive for maximum economic growth. This simplistic argument is still voiced by some contrarian economists who have not grasped the difference between their abstract theories and the real, material and imperfect world.[2] The phenomenon of 'jobless' growth demonstrates the reality and is worrying policy makers the world over.[3] Yet politicians still woo our votes with promises of future growth in our standard of living. But a growing share of the public no longer believe them: for the first time since the war many parents believe they will not bequeath a better life to their children.[4] The day has arrived when we should listen to what our grandparents are saying, 'that things were better when they were young'. It seems likely that many of the current generation will share this view within their lifetimes, unless we respond to the challenge now.

At the heart of the problem is the fact that the byproducts of conventional economic growth cannot be assumed away. Growing environmental degradation and increasing inequality combine to undermine the benefits of growth by directly reducing wellbeing. And they also combine to undermine the ability of the economic system to sustain growth, especially in the longer term. So this chapter explores the relationships between economic growth, material consumption and wellbeing. Through doing so we are able to suggest key strategies for reducing the former without adversely affecting the latter. As a result we can find ways of meeting the environmental space targets suggested earlier, that will be welcome to the relatively well-off global consuming class, as well as to the global subsistence class.

# ECONOMIC GROWTH AND ENVIRONMENTAL RESOURCES

We cannot rely on growth to make us truly better off in the future for several reasons. First, it will not continue to deliver when our use (or abuse) of resources such as fossil fuels, old growth forests and rich fertile soils is effectively a spending spree of the accumulated natural capital of millennia. While economic growth built up the total capital base of the economy, then we could (at least in theory) safely leave the future to our descendants. However, if our activities deplete that capital base without making effective provision for the future then we are acting unsustainably. Natural capital is part of that capital base. Gretchen Daily of Stanford University outlines some of the aspects of that capital base:

> *one in three mouthfuls of our food derives from plants pollinated by natural pollinators living in natural ecosystems. About 44 billion metric tons of waste is processed annually by natural ecosystems. About half our increases in agricultural productivity each year derive from infusions of genetic material from other organisms that are sustained by natural ecosystems.*[5]

The annual value to humanity flowing from the natural capital of productive land, the atmosphere and oceans has been estimated at US\$20–30 trillion, at least as great as global gross national product![6] But human activities are blindly running down that capital. Both resource depletion

# BOX 3.1 *NATURAL CAPITAL IN THE CAPITAL ACCOUNTS*

Net National Product (NNP) subtracts a value for depreciation from Gross National Product (GNP). But it only accounts for depreciation of human-made capital. A 'green' NNP would also make deductions for depreciation of natural capital. Green NNP is equal to consumption plus the value of saving, minus the sum of depreciation on the overall capital stock – natural and human-made alike.

David Pearce and Giles Atkinson have suggested an indicator called 'net savings', adjusting the measure of gross financial savings in the country by values for depreciation, depletion of natural resources and pollution costs (in practice they suggest using depletion of oil and gas, and air pollution to represent these categories). Expressed as a proportion of GDP this gives a measure of the extent to which the country is 'investing in the future'. Pearce's estimates suggest that even with this crude measure the UK's 'genuine savings were negative for most of the 1980s'.[a] The World Bank has been pursuing a similar approach to estimate the 'wealth of nations' in terms of human resources, produced assets and natural capital. Their initial estimates suggest that human resources are the most significant component, and that, on average, the contribution of natural capital exceeds that of produced capital by a quarter.[b]

But these methods are of limited use. This conceptual framework cannot easily be translated into monetary values in the ways the neo-classical economists suggest. The 'net price method' Pearce suggests using for resource depletion treats the value of the depletion as the difference between the marginal cost of extraction and the market price. Unfortunately, in practice this is overwhelmed by other influences on the market price, and constitutes a poor indicator of real scarcity. The methods suggested for arriving at a measure of the monetary value of environmental degradation, based on the largely unknown costs of abatement or restoration or the widely criticised 'contingent valuation' techniques such as 'willingness-to-pay' surveys, are even more removed from reality. An alternative approach in the economics profession suggests that the only realistic way to measure the value of the environment for such purposes is by estimating the costs of maintaining the environment intact through the imposition of standards and protective policies in practice.[c] More fundamentally, the neo-classical approach would fail to deliver sustainability becauses it pays little regard to differences in types of capital (as Pearce admittedly recognises). It assumes that natural capital is directly equivalent to human-made capital and that different types of natural capital are effectively interchangeable.

This logic has been partly followed in the preparation of Satellite Environmental Accounts; although based on the concept of measuring natural capital depreciation, these often reject monetary valuation and simply report physical amounts. In the UK however, in a first attempt to produce satellite accounts, Pearce's valuation approach has been attempted for deple-tion of oil reserves and air pollution. Sadly this relies on the limited assumption that the value of depletion of oil and gas reserves is exactly equivalent to the profits made by the industry in excess of a normal rate of return. Even so it concludes that the costs of depletion are equivalent to £2.2 billion a year – about 25 per cent of the contribution of this sector to GDP.[d]

Different approaches can be taken to the question of monetary valuation in the preparation or modification of indicators – some are simpler, more transparent and therefore more robust than others. We return to this discussion later in this chapter.

Sources: *a* Atkinson, G and Pearce, D (1996) Indicators to change policy *New Economy* 3(1) pp10–14;

*b* Serageldin, I (1996) *Sustainability and the Wealth of Nations* World Bank Monograph;

*c* Rennings, K and Wiggering, H (1995) Weak and Strong Sustainability: How to combine economic and ecological indicator concepts? *Proceedings of International Sustainable Development Research Conference* March 27–28 Manchester pp76–79;

*d* Vase, P and Balchin, S (1996) *The Pilot UK Environmental Accounts* London: Office for National Statistics

and environmental degradation represent capital depreciation which is uncounted by conventional economic measures. In theory, it should be possible to adjust conventional measures of economic growth to take account of such depreciation. But such an undertaking is fraught with practical and theoretical difficulties (see Box 3.1).

The second reason growth cannot be relied upon to make us better off is that we are 'trading off' our natural capital: resources and clean air and water, for economic capital: factories and roads. This process is not without direct impacts on the future. We are leaving not just productive capital, but also a poisoned legacy, including climate change, genetic damage to our children, and the legacy of waste itself, for the few thousand years before landfill sites stabilise, and the tens of thousands of years before nuclear wastes become safe. Most fundamentally, the run-down of natural capital is undermining the global environmental systems that human life still depends on, such as the future stability of the climate and the ozone layer. These things can be described as 'critical natural capital', because we cannot afford to destroy them, however much profit we can make in the process! We can set out a similar argument with respect to human capital. Investments in human capital are only partly measured in economic indicators, and the depreciation of human capital by social inequity, and ill health, for example, is not accounted for at all.

All of this does not deny that economic growth can contribute to increased wellbeing. Much wellbeing is derived from material consumption. However, this is not an immutable relationship. Later we will turn to the question of how continued conventional economic growth has actually undermined the growth of wellbeing. But first, we have a major question to answer: 'how can we provide the economic basis for wellbeing for today's poor, and for future generations without running down our capital – economic, human or natural?' This is where our focus on inputs becomes especially relevant because there are ways of getting more wellbeing from less material consumption if we make the effort.

## EFFICIENCY AND WELLBEING

In practice, limiting inputs need not mean limiting the wellbeing derived from our economies. The history of economic development has been the history of increased efficiency of use of the resource in shortest supply, whether that is labour, capital, land or materials. For example the three and four-field rotations developed in the eighteenth century revolutionised use of agricultural land in the UK with rapid increases in productivity. The development of modern banking and investment activities revolutionised the efficiency of use of capital. Henry Ford's production line model for manufacturing vastly increased labour productivity. Countries and businesses have obtained competitive advantage from such revolutions. But because environmental inputs have for long been effectively free – whether as inputs to production or as sinks for pollution – there has been relatively little pressure to increase efficiency in their use and the abuse of the environment has grown to planetary levels.

But there is a silver lining in this cloud – there is vast unexploited potential to adopt efficiency measures to improve environmental 'productivity', much of which is financially cost-effective, even at current levels of environmental costs. As the CBI put it in the title of their recent report, currently, *The Environment Costs*.[7] In other words, the failure to address environmental productivity issues is already reducing companies' efficiency and profitability. As the costs of environmental inputs rise to reflect their increasing scarcity (whether as a result of simple market mechanisms, environmental taxes or more stringent regulation), then the costs to business will rise too. And it will inevitably be those companies and countries with the foresight to stimulate broad environmental efficiency that will come to dominate future markets. Because environmental scarcity is increasing at a global level, this 'efficiency revolution' generally cannot operate by substitution of one resource for another, but must take effect across the board.

It is more than theoretically possible to increase efficiency in the use of environmental resources, so that a smaller resource flow can maintain the same or higher level of consumption of goods and services. Experience with energy use has begun to demonstrate this principle in practice, with the efficiency of the Japanese economy being the best known case.[8] But measures such as product design and durability, and reuse and recycling are also critical in increasing overall efficiency. We call this change in the consumption of resources by industry 'delinking': reducing the environmental impact associated with each unit of goods and services produced. We return to these issues in Chapter 10.

Development is intended to add to human wellbeing, directly (for example, provision of schools and hospitals) or indirectly (by providing for or supporting economic activity which provides goods and services for consumption, and employment). Historically, development, like economic growth, has been directly linked to the consumption of environmental resources. The idea behind delinking is that this need not be so. Future human wellbeing can be obtained for less environmental cost. Delinking can operate at several points. Taking the example of energy use, if we use renewable energy sources rather than fossil fuels then the level of greenhouse gas emissions per unit of power generated is several orders of magnitude lower. But even within our use of fossil fuels, there are effective measures that can be taken. For example, if we burn the fossil fuel in combined heat and power plants the efficiency of power generation is higher – we get both electricity and useful heat – so we need use less fossil fuels for the same amount of useful energy.

But such delinking alone does not necessarily solve our problems. Each unit of output may be produced with less environmental inputs, but because of growth in the total outputs, overall environmental damage can still increase. For example, catalytic converters relatively delink toxic emissions from growth in road transport. But growth in the number of cars can be expected to overwhelm the gains so that, as a whole, pollution levels in the environment are not permanently reduced. At present emission of nitrogen oxides ($NO_x$) from cars is 1.4 million tonnes and expected to fall. But with traffic levels predicted to more or less double by 2020, emissions are predicted to rise again after reaching a low of 0.5 million tonnes in 2010. And in this case it appears that the predictions are overoptimistic with actual nitrogen dioxide levels rising, rather than beginning to fall in 1994.[9]

If environmental damage is to remain stable or decline, however much development or growth occurs, then more stringent and effective measures are needed. Such 'absolute' delinking is a bigger challenge. Achieving such a transition will require widespread substitution of ways of meeting needs which are intensive in their use of environmental resources with alternatives which are resource-efficient, such as replacing car journeys with walking, cycling and use of public transport. Although absolute delinking could theoretically continue to increase human wellbeing with no further increase in the rate of consumption of environmental resources, the figures outlined above suggest that this would not necessarily guarantee sustainability. To return to the example of $NO_x$, the temporary cut in traffic emissions should be seen in a context in which road traffic contributes almost half of total $NO_x$ emissions (and more in urban areas), and a return of total emissions to 1987 levels by 1994 was seen by the UN Economic Commission protocol as simply a prelude to cuts in total emissions to protect human and ecosystem health.[10] In Switzerland on the basis of critical loads analyses a cut of two-thirds in $NO_x$ emissions has been suggested.[11] In Northern countries we currently consume too much of the planet's environmental capacity and therefore need to achieve actual reductions in our use of those resources.

Environmental space begins by measuring the resources extracted from the environment. These resources are converted into inputs to our economy by the economic activities of mining, logging and so forth. These inputs are processed for use in manufacturing industry where they are converted into material goods. Many of these goods are used within the economic process, in the extractive, processing, manufacturing and service industries to produce consumer goods and services. Laying aside non-material sources of wellbeing for the moment, we in turn consume these goods and services to meet our needs, thus increasing wellbeing. It is clear that there are several transformations in this system, each of which can be challenged to increase efficiency and reduce wastage. For example if we can meet the same needs with 10 per cent less consumer goods and services, produced with 10 per cent less material goods, in turn produced with 10 per cent less inputs, extracted 10 per cent more efficiently, then we get the same needs for an overall reduction in environmental space consumed of one-third. If we achieve a 20 per cent improvement at each step, then the overall impact is cut back to just 40 per cent of the previous level. And such efficiency improvements can be rooted in a host of different advances in techniques and technologies including reductions in wastage or increasing recycling and reuse.

There is growing consensus – notably amongst leading business interests – that within the first half of the twenty-first century we need to have achieved 'delinking' by a factor of ten. In other words, reducing our consumption of environmental resources to one-tenth of its current level.[12] Other things being equal this would require a 40–50 per cent improvement in each economic transformation outlined above. The same business leaders are confident that with the right regulatory framework and effective market mechanisms, they can deliver such improvements!

# CONSUMPTION AND WELLBEING

The preceding section concentrated on the 'technical fix' approach to sustainability: measures to increase efficiency. But this is only part of the equation. Both increasing efficiency and reducing consumption can reduce the environmental impact of a given population. Here we return to the thorny issue of consumption.

First let us consider why we consume in the first place. To meet needs – that much is clear – but which needs? We consume far more than we need to meet basic needs for food, shelter, clothing and warmth. We consume to meet needs for status, self-image, entertainment, education, a whole range of things that are best summarised as wellbeing. In other words we consume because by doing so we make our lives better – we improve our quality of life. And we don't only consume material goods, we find it more pleasant to breathe clean fresh air, we enjoy the experience of fine art or pleasant landscapes, we watch and play sports. Not only are many of the things that make our lives better not material goods (or services that rely on material goods such as travel),but many of them have no monetary price. We don't have to pay for air or our experience of nature. The pleasure of seeing our children grow up is priceless. For many, simply knowing that our children will be able to enjoy their lives is the most important thing in the world.

The existence and importance of such 'non-monetary factors' in the quality of our lives means that it is, at least in theory, possible to reduce material consumption to increase total wellbeing, even at the individual level. To put this in a more commonplace way: in the UK millions of people are 'on a diet' at any given time: the vast majority of them are healthier, and feel better and happier for it. They are (in general) voluntarily reducing their consumption in a way that improves their wellbeing. Over-consumption is not limited to food, although it is one of the few cases where overconsumption is directly reflected in ill health.

Many religions have advocated restraint in material consumption. We are not advocating that everyone should live the life of a religious ascetic, nor are we promising salvation in the hereafter. But we are seeking a way of life in which we recognise when we have enough, and avoid overconsuming in a way that damages our own best interests. Interestingly, the British public is beginning to recognise this: eight in ten of us believe society is too materialistic.[13] It might appear irrational to systematically consume more than is good for us. Certainly most economists would argue that we consume only until our demands have been fulfilled, and no more. But this ignores the fact that the development of modern mass-consumerism involved a social and cultural transformation in which companies and government policies actively encouraged and promoted additional consumption in efforts to increase economic growth. Born in the USA in the 1920s, the new 'economic gospel of consumption' was preached by manufacturers such as General Motors which introduced annual changes to its models, and used advertising to make consumers dissatisfied with the car they already owned. As the economist John Kenneth Galbraith summed it up: the mission of business became to 'create the wants it seeks to satisfy'.[14]

Victor Lebow, a US retail analyst, put it bluntly in 1950:

> *Our enormously productive economy demands that we make consumption our way of life ... that we convert the buying and use of goods into rituals ... that we seek our spiritual satisfaction, our ego satisfaction, in consumption. We need things consumed, burned up, worn out, replaced and discarded at an ever-increasing rate.*[15]

Many of Lebow's convictions have been shown to be true, and in doing so have created a culture in which we seek to meet far too many of our needs by further material consumption, even where they could be met more fully and with less environmental impact, in other ways, as we will see below.

## MEETING NEEDS

Philosophers and researchers have put a lot of time and effort into thinking about human needs. Unlike neo-classical economists, who assume that needs are simply reflected in economic demand and, therefore, that meeting those demands will meet needs, they have developed sophisticated ways of looking at needs. Maslow developed the theory of a hierarchy of human needs (see Box 3.2) over 25 years ago, with the argument that some needs were more basic than others and, other things being equal, that people would seek to meet these first, but once these needs were satisfied, would not continue consuming things designed to meet those needs but would seek to satisfy their 'higher-order' needs. To put this in more practical terms, basic physiological needs for food and shelter come first, while needs for security and affection, for example, would emerge only once basic needs were satisfied.

Many have interpreted this hierarchy to suggest that demands for environmental protection will only emerge once the basic needs are satisfied. And there is some truth in this view. However, Maslow's hierarchy implies a far more rigid structure to human needs than really exists, and does not directly address the way in which environmental resources

---

### BOX 3.2 *MASLOW'S HIERARCHY OF NEEDS*

Most basic – Physiological needs such as food and shelter
Security and safety needs such as law and order
Social needs such as affection and 'belonging' needs
Esteem needs such as independence or status
Highest - Self-actualisation or individual self-fulfilment

Source: Maslow, A (1970) *Motivation and Personality*
New York: Harper and Row

underpin the meeting of all these needs, not just those higher up the pyramid. Still, it is not unusual for environmentalists to be damned for ignoring the basic needs of the many poor in favour of the 'higher order' needs of the fewer rich. Loggers and miners in the United States accuse environmentalists of 'taking the food out of babies' mouths' when they oppose clear felling of old-growth forests or new open-pit mines. Even though the arguments of the loggers and miners may be misguided, their concerns are no less real than those of the environmentalists. We cannot ignore them. But we can seek to reconcile them.

There is more than one way to view needs. In a collaborative project on 'human-scale development' based in Sweden, Manfred Max-Neef[16] suggested nine fundamental human needs. Two 'material' needs: for subsistence and protection, and seven non-material needs: for affection, understanding, participation, identity, idleness, creativity and freedom. From this it can be suggested that much of our material consumption is actually an attempt to fulfil non-material needs. This is not to say that such an attempt is fruitless. For example, our need to be creative is as much met by building our own furniture as by writing poetry, but the former requires far more materials than the latter. The nine needs are envisaged as occurring in four categories: being, having, doing and inter-acting. The emerging matrix of 36 categories of needs is in stark contrast to the single measure of utility which underlies classical economics. There are clear parallels between the work of Maslow and Max-Neef. Max-Neef's concept of subsistence needs corresponds to the basic physiological needs in Maslow's model. Max-Neef goes beyond Maslow by drawing the distinction between needs and satisfiers. Food and shelter are not needs in themselves, but satisfiers of the needs for subsistence and protection. Needs categorised in this way can be seen as universal, whereas satisfiers are cultural.

Max-Neef[17] characterises satisfiers as:

- Destroyers or violators, which occupy the paradoxical position of failing to satisfy the need towards which they are directed, and damaging the potential for fulfilling other needs. The classic example is the 'arms race', supposedly meeting the need for protec-tion, but not only did it increase that need rather than meet it, but it restricted our freedoms too.
- Pseudo-satisfiers generate a false sense of satisfaction of the need. Max-Neef includes prostitution (as a satisfier for affection) and fashion (as a satisfier for identity) in this group.
- Inhibiting satisfiers satisfy one need to which they are directed but tend to inhibit the satisfaction of other needs. Our TV culture is an excellent example, good at meeting leisure needs, but often stifling our creative capacities.
- Singular satisfiers manage to satisfy a single category of need

without affecting satisfaction elsewhere. Curative medicine and insurance fall into this group.

- Synergistic satisfiers manage simultaneously to satisfy several different kinds of needs. Examples include self-build housing, simultaneously meeting needs for shelter, creativity and participation; and breast-feeding babies, meeting a subsistence need, but also meeting needs for affection and identity.

Tim Jackson and Nic Marks at the University of Surrey[18] have begun to look at the relationship between economic goods and Max-Neef's view of needs and satisfiers. It is relatively easy to see how economic goods meet material needs, but beyond these simple material considerations things get more complex. There is no clear one-to-one relationship between economic goods and the underlying fundamental needs. Food may also be consumed in an attempt to satisfy other non-material needs. For example, eating chocolate may be a false satisfier for affection. On the other hand, the preparation and consumption of food contributes to the satisfaction of non-material needs such as affection, creativity, participation and identity.

Nor are economic goods the same thing as satisfiers. Economic goods are related to the physical manifestation of needs satisfaction. But satisfiers include forms of organisation, political structures, social practices, subjective conditions, values and norms, spaces, contexts, modes, types of behaviour and attitude.[19] By looking at needs and satisfiers in the way Max-Neef does, we can separate them from the conventional way in which they are met in modern economies. We buy food to relieve our hunger, we buy cars to both provide access to ways of meeting other needs, such as participation, and to enhance our self image or identity.

## Making Things Worse – An Example

As Max-Neef recognises, some 'satisifiers' are destructive or inhibiting. The case of transport shows exactly how bad the problem can get. We want access to facilities and experiences – or in other words we want to be able to meet our friends, get to the shops, to work, and to the park, and travel for the sake of the new experiences it can bring. Most of us don't want to sit in our car because it is powerful, comfortable, fast or any of the other reasons advertisers give us to choose it; those features may make it a more pleasant experience, but in practice we normally get in our cars because we want to get somewhere else and we want to get there conveniently and quickly. But because so many of us want the same thing, the roads are congested and dangerous. For many journeys, the car is no longer even meeting our needs. And, of course, it's contributing to a whole range of both obvious and insidious environmental problems.

As road transport has become the main mode of travel, governments have built more roads, public transport services have declined through lack of use, and people have adopted lifestyles which are highly dependent on the car. The benefits those trends have brought to the individuals concerned are clear, but no one has been counting the costs, the costs to the environment, the costs to health from air pollution, the costs to those who live on heavily trafficked commuter routes and rat-runs, or who are forced to escort their children to school for fear of traffic. Once these are taken into account, it's easy to see that we would be better off if our need for access to the same facilities and experiences could be met with less car travel.

With measures in transport planning to reduce road traffic, as a whole, we would be better off, with cleaner air, safer streets, better health, lower stress ... and so on. Our needs would be met without any of the damaging or inhibiting characteristics of current transport satisfiers.

## SUFFICIENCY – MEETING NEEDS WITH RESTRAINT

At heart, the case of car travel is an example of the idea we call 'sufficiency' – knowing *how much is enough*. We don't have to reduce car use to this level by voluntary sacrifice, or by central planning and imposition. We can use market mechanisms, both to reduce car use, and to increase public transport provision. The issue is not whether we regulate, or whether we leave it to the market, but how we regulate the market. The general principle is to accept that we can regulate in ways which leave the market only able to affect supply, or in ways which allow and even encourage 'demand management'. The latter is desirable where it is clear that current levels of consumption are too high for our collective good. So it is important that companies can profit from reducing demand through selling more efficient products and services rather than only by selling *more*. We will return to this question in the final section of this book.

This example illustrates another key point. Not only can individuals be better off by forgoing consumption, but often that opportunity is withheld from them because it is only by collective action – to provide good public transport and restrain traffic – that the benefits for every individual can be reaped. Such collective benefits based on social action may require public expenditure based on taxes, but then, as President Roosevelt is reported to have said, 'taxes are the price we pay for living in a civilised society'. We return to these political challenges in the final section of this book.

This analysis of collective or community interest also implies the possibility that constraining some individuals' wellbeing can increase the overall level of wellbeing in society as a whole. We accept this in the context of crime: preventing theft makes most of us better off, but not those who steal or deal in stolen goods. Such a social contract is clearly necessary to maximise social wellbeing.

## WELLBEING AND QUALITY OF LIFE

Material consumption measured conventionally in national income accounts is not directly equivalent to wellbeing. It only reflects quality issues insofar as they are valued or priced by markets. If we can better measure quality of life we can better assess different strategies for future development. A range of researchers, coming from many different backgrounds, have attempted to address the question of how to measure quality of life. Much of the best work has been done under the rather drab heading of research into 'indicators'. In essence, indicators are used because it is difficult to measure something directly, so surrogate or representative measures are found which help us understand what is going on.

One example is the Index of Social Health, published each year by Fordham University in New York. This indicates that despite GDP growth, quality of life – as measured by 16 indicators of wellbeing including infant mortality, drug use, the high school drop-out rate, access to affordable housing and income inequality – has been declining in the USA. By 1993, the most recent year for which data are available, the Index had declined to 40.6 out of a possible 100. A score of 100 would mean that all the indicators were at the highest level achieved since 1970. In 1993, in reality, six of the measures – including child abuse and income inequality – reached their worst recorded level.[20] In Norway, Friends of the Earth undertook research to quantify trends in suicide, crime, and the divorce rate, amongst other things, because these would appear to be good indicators for how happy people were.[21] Economists have created the so-called 'misery index' which adds together how fast prices are rising (the rate of inflation) and how many are out of work (the rate of unemployment) as a shorthand way of assessing the same thing. But even such social and economic indicators miss out on a lot of important factors.

More complicated attempts to measure wellbeing have been led by the work of John Cobb, an American theologian, and Herman Daly, previously a senior economist at the World Bank.[22] Cobb and Daly realised that conventional measures of economic progress were of little real value. So they set out to reform the central one, Gross Domestic Product (GDP), so that it would take account of a wide range of important social and environmental factors, as well as economic ones. It is easy to criticise the measure they created: the so-called Index of Sustainable Economic Welfare (ISEW) (see Box 3.3 and Figure 3.1), but the scoffers would do well to remember that GDP is no less a creation of its time.

## BOX 3.3 *THE INDEX OF SUSTAINABLE ECONOMIC WELFARE (ISEW)*

The ISEW adjusts the standard measure of consumer expenditure as follows.

*   Defensive expenditures or 'expenditures necessary to defend ourselves from the unwanted side-effects of production' are subtracted from the index, eg health, education, environmental externalities and commuting. However some government expenditures are included in the index.
*   The index includes measures relating to the formation and depreciation of human-made capital.
*   Account is taken of environmental degradation and the loss of natural capital, in other words, a value for depreciation of environmental capital based on the accumulated damage to the stock.
*   The contribution of domestic labour is taken into account.
*   Changes in the distribution of income and labour in the economy are considered on the basis that an extra pound for a poor person is clearly a greater contribution to wellbeing than the same pound for a millionaire.

Source: Jackson, T and Masks, N (1994) *Measuring Sustainable Economic Welfare – a Pilot Index: 1950–1990* Stockholm: Stockholm Environment Institute; Jackson, T *et al.* (1997) *An Index of Sustainable Economic Welfare for the UK, 1950–1996* Guildford: Centre for Environmental Strategy, University of Surrey

GDP was devised by Simon Kuznets in the 1930s and developed in the work of John Maynard Keynes and his collaborators during the 1940s. Most of Keynes' other economic work, although highly influential for many years, is no longer regarded as 'gospel truth'. GDP measures the rate at which money circulates in the economy, by measuring transactions, or purchases of goods and services. It is based on private consumption, or expenditure by individuals, with various adjustments.

ISEW begins from the same place, accepting that personal consumption is a real contribution to wellbeing, but not that it is the only significant factor. It attempts to value and include unpaid labour, so childcare, for example, is treated as an economic gain. GDP, on the other hand, ignores childcare unless you pay someone else to do it. ISEW also subtracts the costs of so-called defensive expenditures, such as the healthcare costs of road traffic accidents, or the costs of cleaning up oil spills which don't actually make us better off – but just get us back to where we were before the accident. GDP, however, goes up more if we have more accidents.

John Cobb has continued this work, alongside his son Clifford, to create the Genuine Progress Index (GPI). This incorporates a wider range of social factors into the index to begin to take account of things

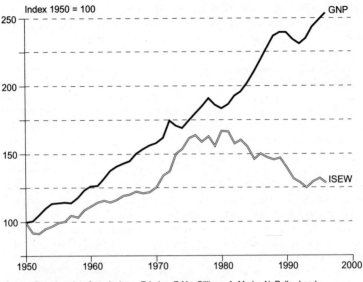

Source: Based on data from Jackson, T, Laing, F, MacGillivray, A, Marks, N, Ralls, J and Stymne, S 1997 (forthcoming) *An Index of Sustainable Economic Welfare for the UK 1950–96* Guildford: Centre for Environmental Strategy, University of Surrey

**Figure 3.1** *UK GNP growth compared with changes in the Index of Sustainable Economic Welfare*

like the costs of divorce and crime and the loss of leisure time. The GPI for the USA shows an even more worrying trend than the ISEW. The latest estimates suggest that the average American is almost one-third less well off today (in these real terms) than in 1950.[23]

In Daly and Cobb's work, environmental degradation is a major factor. In the UK ISEW it accounts for a significant part of the decline in the index since 1970. This is partly because their methodology treats long-term environmental damage in an ecologically realistic way, as cumulative. So the more forests are cleared, wetlands drained, stratospheric ozone depleted, and greenhouse gases emitted, the larger the negative adjustment in the index. This has drawn criticism from mainstream neo-classical environmental economists such as Giles Atkinson, who says that 'changes in stocks should be reflected in income flows, not the stock itself',[24] or in other words that only the reduction in the current year's income should be subtracted. But we don't know how to measure that reduction accurately. Daly and Cobb's approach may not be ideal, but it's better than assuming that there are no additional costs associated with fragmenting our remaining natural habitats still further – a practice long associated with accelerated species extinction – or in increasing greenhouse gas levels in the atmosphere even further above the critical levels expected to cause climate change. To do so is parading our ignorance about the risks of environmental damage in a way that makes the widespread use of asbestos in buildings until the 1970s look positively cautious.

The biggest weakness of the ISEW is actually one that the mainstream environmental economists support. It assumes that we can put monetary values on the various factors we want to include. However, it offers a more realistic measure of wellbeing than the current economic indicators that so infatuate too many of our policy-makers. Clearly we need to continue with constructive debate to establish a usable and practical measure of wellbeing. Research in Norway, based on long-term historical trends, also found economic growth to be a poor indicator of wellbeing. Dag Hareide found that as economic growth continued, increases in life expectancy tailed off, indicators of social pathology (suicide, loneliness and violence) first declined, and then in recent decades increased again, and also in recent decades, inequality grew and employment declined. Hareide believes that these trends are typical of the so-called 'developed' nations.[25]

It is, of course, possible to ask people how happy they are feeling and although there are great dangers (in research terms) in relying on such information, and in particular in trying to use it to make comparisons across time or space, some interesting results have been derived. The Dutch social scientist Ruut Veenhoven took this approach in his analysis of data from over 20 different countries.[26] He compared how happy people said they were with average levels of income, and demonstrated, as one would expect from Maslow's theory of needs, that there was a broadly curvilinear relationship with little long-term correlation between income growth and happiness above a certain level of income. In Veenhoven's study this level seemed to occur somewhere around the income level of Mexico, rather giving the lie to claims that environmental concerns and other 'higher-order needs' are only relevant to the wealthiest people in countries like the UK. Similarly, the evidence in the UK suggests that additional income increases sense of wellbeing, but only for the poorest fifth of the population, with very little correlation above that level.[27] And even this may well be more to do with unemployment than income itself. Joblessness is strongly correlated with mental stress and suicide attempts.[28]

Veenhoven's conclusion bears out the theoretical argument that as countries become richer it becomes more, not less, likely that the costs of further economic growth will outweigh the benefits.[29] Jacobs has argued that the growing impact of these costs in modern Britain is responsible for our growing sense of unease. He suggests that politicians should not be surprised to find in such circumstances that the 'feel-good factor' which normally accompanies economic upturns has proved remarkably elusive in recent years.[30]

More evidence that standard of living (measured in terms of income) and quality of life cannot be correlated comes from a range of studies done to assess people's preferences in places to live. These find that key factors determining quality of life – crime, health and environmental quality – are ranked higher by people than conventional measures of standard of living or economic success, and areas which rate higher on the latter factors do not necessarily feature in overall preferences.[31] Even at the individual level, there is evidence to support this assessment. The recent media buzz about 'downshifting' and the 'voluntary simplicity' movement in the USA are similarly based on a clear trade-off of more material consumption in favour of a better quality of life.[32] Michael Argyle, a psychologist who has spent more than a decade researching what makes people happy, concurs. Leisure, friends and family are critical, and fufilling jobs can make people happy, but extra spending money is way down the list.[33] In Max-Neef's terms, extra money is a pseudo-satisfier!

The United Nations have recognised the problem too, and use a Human Development Index in which economic growth is only one of three factors, the others being the infant mortality rate, and the adult literacy rate, to compare progress of developing countries. But the most intriguing research in this field suggests that not only are non-material factors of great significance in determining quality of life, but that the distribution of wealth within a country is particularly important. The most unequal societies seem to show the highest level of dissatisfaction – and not just amongst the poorest groups.[34] Physical and mental health within a society are also strongly influenced by inequality – the most unequal societies being most unhealthy too (see Chapter 11).[35]

## GROWTH, CONSUMPTION AND WELLBEING

The evidence to challenge the oft-assumed direct link between consumption and wellbeing is growing as more researchers recognise the importance of the question. It remains difficult to prove anything, because it's so difficult to separate out all the different factors involved when comparing countries or examining trends over time, and even more difficult to attribute causality. However there is enough evidence to challenge the political assumption that the single-minded pursuit of increasing standard of living in monetary terms will make the voters happy. And this goes beyond conventional political arguments over the extent and quality of public goods. Of course, access to and the standards of health care, education, social services, the arts and heritage all contribute to quality of life both for individuals and in their expectations for their children. But the impacts of inequality and environmental degradation are both more fundamental and more insidious than these.

# More is Worse

There are good reasons to believe that there is a causal relationship between conventional economic growth and those factors which detract from our wellbeing. This case is persuasively and clearly argued by Michael Jacobs in his book for Friends of the Earth and other UK NGOs in the Real World Coalition: *The Politics of the Real World*.[36] Both inequality and environmental degradation detract from our quality of life, directly and indirectly. For example, persistent inequality is at the root of the rising trend of crime. Social cohesion depends on contact between social groups, and on a political contract between social groups. As this contract has been eroded, so social exclusion has grown, reinforced by physical segregation as areas have become virtual ghettos of high unemployment and poverty. Crime and the fear of crime are a powerful brake on wellbeing, not just financially – although insurance premiums and the costs of security have soared – but as all victims of crime know, the greatest costs are physical and psychological. Recorded crime has risen ten-fold since the 1950s and, according to regular British Crime Surveys, only about a quarter of all crimes are recorded.[37] The latest Surveys reveal that the proportion recorded has been falling. Between 1993 and 1995, while recorded figures fell 8 per cent, the survey revealed a 2 per cent increase in crime. Even more alarming is the suggestion that violent crime has been growing much more rapidly than crime as a whole, up by 17 per cent in the last two years.[38]

Unemployment and, perhaps more importantly, the decline in job security is another key cost in the personal balance sheet of wellbeing. And the increase in insecurity is directly related to the increasingly global scale of competition and resultant labour market policies designed to increase flexibility. More mobility up the income scale has been paralleled by more mobility down it. It's no wonder that not even those in full-time employment are as happy as the conventional model suggests they should be. On top of lower job security, many are increasingly required to work overtime, or shifts. Similarly, environmental degradation has lowered wellbeing, most dramatically through fear for the future, but also more directly through air pollution, traffic congestion and noise, uncertain food quality and related impacts on health. The loss of countryside and natural habitats impinges not just on locals and visitors to the countryside, but also on a wider public whose sense of nature and culture feels increasingly violated. And public concerns for nature elsewhere are equally real; most people will never see a whale but they recognise the immorality of driving a species to extinction, and more widely, people do value the incredible diversity of life on this planet.

# CONCLUSION

This chapter has argued that conventional approaches to economic growth and increasing material consumption are no longer delivering increases in real wellbeing, for those who have, in the past, benefited most from economic growth. Environmental and social degradation resulting from unbalanced growth have harmed the wellbeing of the materially well off, as well as increasing inequity and bringing us up against global environmental limits. However, this chapter has also suggested that we need not retreat to the stone age to reduce our material consumption to sustainable levels. But it has shown the need for fundamental reform in our economic and social systems if we are to maintain or increase levels of human wellbeing while reducing material consumption. In fact, the evidence suggests that business-as-usual will not continue to increase wellbeing, and may even reduce it. So such fundamental reforms are the only option for the twenty-first century on this count, too. Those reforms offer a structure for practical sustainable development strategies designed to meet needs and increase wellbeing while decreasing material consumption.

# Conclusions

In the Introduction to this part of the book, we gave three reasons to doubt the optimistic 'business as usual' view of the future. Until recently, we used to be able to be phlegmatic about the risks of pursuing business as usual: the limits seemed to be far off, we had an apparently effective welfare state, global poverty could be eliminated in time, and overall wellbeing appeared to be growing. Now things look very different: the balance of risk has changed.

We have seen that the scale of environmental damage has been increasing: so that environmental limits are now being exceeded at a global level. And we have seen how inequality in the UK and globally has persisted and even grown. It has become clear that these are not legacies of pre-industrial society which further growth will eradicate, or small and reparable faults in the model which can be solved by technological advances. As Jacobs argues, they are not 'symptoms of the model's failure, but of its success ... the better the model performs, the worse these problems will get. They are endemic, not incidental'.[1] Equally importantly, since each is related to the others, they cannot be dealt with separately and incrementally. Even if, as politicians argue, we can tinker with the model to allow us to redistribute wealth nationally or even globally, as long as we have more of it to begin with, in a world of limits this approach is no longer practical. Moreover, we have seen, too, that benefits of global economic growth are not always reflected in real wellbeing; material consumption and growing income have not met people's needs, partly because at the same time as they provide material benefits, they damage other aspects of wellbeing. In other words, increased income does not necessarily equate to increased quality of life.

Michael Carley and Phillipe Spapens, who have been exploring environmental space from a wider global perspective, express these conclusions in a very similar way. They say that environmental space can be seen as based on three simple principles: that sustainability depends on reducing the throughput of natural resources in our economies to within global environmentally determined limits, and also, depends upon equity in access to the world's resources; and that production and consumption should serve to enhance quality of life rather than degrade it.[2] So we must seek a much more fundamental reform of global and national economic systems. There are two pillars to this reform: recognising ecological limits, and meeting needs. These underlie the concept of sustainable development. As the UN Environment Programme put it recently, inefficient use of resources and patterns of wasteful consumption are 'driving us towards an environmental precipice'. To reverse our course, it concluded, requires 'a worldwide transition towards resource equity and resource efficiency'.[3]

Below, in Part 2 of this book, we explore how we can use the concept of environmental space to set practical targets for our economies and societies that directly reflect real ecological limits and account for equity. In Part 3 we will turn more explicitly to the question of how we can meet needs within those limits and directly pursue quality of life.

# Part 2
# Sustainability Targets for Key Resources

# Chapter 4
# Measuring the UK's Sustainability

## INTRODUCTION

Environmental space targets are designed to make it possible for us to put sustainability into practice.[1] For many, sustainability is summed up by the famous cliché, 'we do not inherit the world from our parents: we borrow it from our children'. If we borrow from the future and fail to repay, then we are acting unsustainably. Sustainability also has a geographical dimension – we can 'borrow' environmental resources from the future, but we can and do, equally unsustainably, also 'borrow' them from other countries.

Our national impact on global environmental space can be expressed in terms of another key concept: our 'environmental footprint' – the impact of the UK's consumption on all different aspects of the environment, derived by adding together all the different impacts resulting from all the goods and services consumed in the UK. The UK is a significant net importer. In 1994 the visible (accounting only for material goods traded, in purely financial terms) balance of payments deficit was £10.6 billion.[2] We import resources such as fossil fuels, minerals, timber and agricultural commodities from all over the world. For example, all aluminium used in the UK comes from foreign mines, and 73 per cent of our paper and pulp is imported.[3] This net import can be seen as a measure of the UK's environmental footprint. The footprint analogy is especially helpful because so many of the environmental impacts of our Western lifestyles are felt in remote corners of the world – we cannot simply measure sustainability in terms of the environment in the UK.

## SUSTAINABILITY TARGETS

We have not tried to identify a single measure of sustainability, even though a single measure or metric would make it much easier to quantify sustainability, at least in theory.[4] It would be easier for policy makers and even the public to grasp and respond to. Comparison of different countries and changes over time would be much simpler. Alternative policies and strategies could be assessed easily in terms of their impacts.

In other words, all the advantages that modern economics has obtained by reducing everything to a single monetary measure of value. But although it would allow us to challenge the use of monetary value as the single comparative measure, it would be subject to similar weaknesses.

Comparing environmental impacts is like comparing chalk and cheese, not apples and pears. Different resources have different impacts on the environment, and can meet very different human needs. But even if these problems can be overcome, then we reach an even more significant problem. This is the same problem that defeats attempts to put meaningful monetary values on the environment – that some environmental resources cannot be traded away however much money or any other resource we get for them. We can't get by with either the ozone layer or the tropical forests; we need both. And we need clean air and clean water. And a stable climate. And so on.[5] Sustainability is about meeting multiple goals in complex systems – complex natural and human systems. Ecosystems don't reduce to one measure, nor does quality of life. So we have chosen a small number of resources to represent the basic material and physical inputs into the global economy: energy, land, water, timber and non-renewable materials (steel, aluminium, cement and chlorine).

*Energy* is fundamental. The availability of useful energy allows human society to extract metals, refine chemicals, travel and trade widely – it is essential to our modern economies and way of life. But energy use also underlies many of our most pressing environmental concerns, such as climate change and acidification of forests and lakes.

*Land* is similarly basic: it provides us with living space, and supports agricultural and natural ecosystems. The vast majority of our food comes from agriculture.[6] Natural and seminatural habitats are the fundamental base of biological diversity on the Earth. A major study sponsored by the UN Environment Programme suggests that 3 per cent of global soils are severely degraded and a further 8 per cent moderately degraded, mainly by overgrazing and poor agricultural practices.[7]

Forests provide *wood* for paper production, construction and energy generation, but they are also crucial for the protection of wild species, the regulation of the water cycle, as carbon sinks in the carbon cycle and valued for their contribution to landscapes and for recreation. As an economic resource, timber is representative of a number of renewable resources.[8] Deforestation, especially in the tropics, is probably the largest cause of species extinction and accounts for almost one-fifth of global carbon dioxide emissions.[9]

*Water* is another vital resource; without water there would be no life on Earth. It is essential not only for drinking and for growing crops, but it also forms the single largest input into the UK economy, accounting for about 90 per cent of all inputs by mass.[10]

*Steel* was the basic material of the industrial age and still accounts for around 90 per cent of all metals input into the UK economy.[11]

*Aluminium* is more typical of modern economies. Its use is growing in many sectors from construction to car-making.

*Cement* is a major construction material across Europe, especially where timber is in short supply. Its manufacture is a major source of $CO_2$.[12] Because it is less representative of construction in the UK, we also look at crushed rock aggregates which account for around 45 per cent of material inputs into the UK economy (excluding water and fuels).[13]

*Chlorine* is the largest chemical input to the UK economy, but is included principally because of its role in ozone depletion and a variety of other environmental and health problems. This, unfortunately, makes it rather less representative of the transformations needed in the chemical sector as a whole. However, it provides a good example of a high risk substance – environmentally dangerous in many forms and uses, such as CFCs, organochlorine pesticides and dioxins.

The UK's resource economy is summarised in Table 4.1. This highlights the relative significance of the materials included in the environmental space methodology.

# The Global Limits and Sustainable Rates of Use

The environmental space approach defines global limits in terms of the rate of use of key environmental resources. These sustainable rates of use are determined by a number of factors. Technically, the limits to environmental space are a function of:

- the carrying capacity of ecosystems (the sustainable supply of renewable resources including food and timber);
- the recuperative ability of the natural environment (its ability to absorb our wastes and pollutants); and
- the availability of non-renewable raw materials (fossil fuels and minerals).

In practice it appears that, of these factors, the first and second are being hit first, and that our rates of non-renewable material use are limited by the impacts of extraction and disposal on the second factor, rather than by their intrinsic scarcity.

**Table 4.1** *The UK Economy: Material Inputs*

| Material | Annual Input (million tonnes) |
| --- | --- |
| Energy (fossil fuels) | 222 |
| Aggregates | 120 |
| Food | 35 |
| Paper and fibre | 11.5 |
| Plastics | 3.5 |
| Glass | 2 |
| Timber | 18 |
| Steel | 15 |
| Non-ferrous metals | 2 |
| Total solid | 491 |
| Water | 4600 |

Note: the figures given here will not necessarily be directly comparable to detailed figures given in later chapters, but these have been compiled on a comparative (by weight) basis, excluding any wastes generated by their extraction or production.

Source: Jones, P (1995) *The UK Environmental Economy – Do We Value it or Weight it?* Working Paper. High Wycombe: Biffa Waste Services

To establish a common framework for our concerns about different resources the environmental space approach treats all of them as a function of the rate of resource use.[14] Firstly, this allows us to address both renewable and non-renewable resources within the same framework. In each case the sustainable rate of use of the resource is that which can be continued without significantly damaging any other resource. Therefore, rates of food production or timber extraction which led to rapid soil erosion would be unsustainable, as would rates of fossil fuel burning which lead to accumulation of greenhouse gases in the atmosphere. Secondly, it takes account of the fact that the limits to use of non-renewable resources are rarely defined by absolute scarcity (at least in the short and medium terms), but more often by the impacts of their use on sink resources, particularly in terms of the pollution generated.

For each resource, the fundamental question is, what rate of use is sustainable? For the various renewable and non-renewable resources it is reasonably easy to define, at least in theory, the sustainable rate. For instance, up to a certain amount of wood can be harvested from the whole forest estate each year without reducing the total productive base. In the most basic terms, if it takes 50 years for a tree to grow, then one-fiftieth of the trees in our forests can be felled each year. In practice it's not quite so simple, but it is still possible to come to a reasonable estimate of a sustainable supply. We can also arrive at an estimate of sustainability for non-renewable resources, even though as we use them up their total reserves get smaller. It is sometimes argued that as minerals become more scarce, their price rises, and thus more effort will be put into finding and developing new reserves of the mineral, into using it more efficiently or into finding other material substitutes. This has generally been the case in the past. In fact, mining firms tend to stop searching for new ore bodies when their existing reserves exceed 20 to 25 years' supply.[15] But as minerals become more scarce, as well as prices rising, the environmental impacts of finding, extracting and processing the same amount of mineral will grow. Long before the resource reaches economic exhaustion, when it is no longer worth extracting it because the financial costs are so great, its continued use will become unsustainable because of the related impacts.

To assess sustainability, instead of looking at a resource, say of a particular mineral, in isolation, we can look instead at the needs we meet by using it and at different ways of meeting them. Taking a simple example, we burn fossil fuels to get light, heat and motive power. We can also meet these needs from renewable energy sources such as wind power. The more we invest in wind power the less fossil fuels we will burn to meet the same needs. So in theory, the sustainable use of non-renewable resources is limited by the rate of investment in renewable alternatives for meeting the same need.[16] Even though the resource is declining, as long as the need for it is being reduced at the same rate, then the process can be seen as sustainable.[17] For fossil fuels and other mineral resources, in practice, the impacts of extraction or use are a more pressing constraint than absolute reserves of the resource. For example, the UK has large reserves of hard rock which could be quarried to provide construction aggregates. But people value our upland landscapes and habitats highly, and quarrying them would destroy this value.[18] Similarly, the rate of use of fossil fuels is limited by the resulting carbon dioxide emissions, which in turn cause climate change.

For most resources, the constraint to resource use is relative (in other words a certain rate is sustainable, but any greater rate is not). The environmental space approach is most valuable in such cases. However, some sustainability constraints are effectively absolute. In other words, no use of the particular resource is acceptable, because of the irreversible or long-term nature of the impacts of such use. For example, the legacy of nuclear power – wastes that remain dangerous to human and other life for many thousands of years – is unacceptable, and therefore nuclear power should be rapidly phased out. To ensure consistency, all the different types of constraints are integrated into the calculations to estimate figures for annual sustainable use of the resource as inputs into the economy. In other words, we use our knowledge of the constraints to calculate the sustainable supply of the resource.

## Sustainable Supply or Environmental Space

In theory, the sustainable supply could be estimated at any one of a number of scales – national, European or global. This is important because the scale we choose makes a big difference once we take the question of distribution into account. For example, in the case of timber, if we treat the resource as national, then we can estimate the amount available simply from national sustainable production. If instead we treat the resource as continental, since Europe is actually a relatively well forested part of the world, the total and per capita amount available increases. If we treat the resource as global, although the total available goes up still further, the population that it must be shared between goes up by more, and the per capita amount available falls. Where commodities or resources are widely traded, then it is most realistic to treat them as global, even if the volumes traded are relatively low. So we treat energy, steel, aluminium, cement and chlorine as global resources. For land and timber, we also choose to use the global scale – food and timber products are globally traded and increasingly so. Only water will be treated as a national resource. This is because water trading beyond water catchments is unusual and potentially ecologically devastating. Once we have decided on the appropriate scale, then to estimate the amount available for the UK economy we simply multiply the per capita environmental space by our expected population in 2050 (59.6 million).

We recognise that the limits as we conceive them are not entirely fixed. It may be possible to increase sustainable supply.[19] However, unlike some technological optimists, we do not think that there is substantial scope to extend the limits materially rather than virtually. Strategies such as fertilising the oceans to stimulate higher productivity, and thus greater absorption of carbon dioxide, are fraught with further environmental risks. The scope to change the relationship between resource use and environmental damage in such ways, thus changing the acceptable level of use, is limited, and generally brings us closer to another limit. Constraints for renewable resources can also vary. For example, forest areas can be increased. But such effects are not large enough to invalidate the broad overall estimates of the limits, and could be incorporated transparently into our approach.

# THE EQUITY PRINCIPLE – FAIR SHARES IN ENVIRONMENTAL SPACE

To apply the equity principle, outlined in Chapter 2, we need to look at supply in relation to population. This is potentially the most controversial aspect of the environmental space method. Our fundamental assumption is that everyone should have access to a fair share of the resources and opportunities they need to live a pleasant and fulfilling life. In other words, we notionally share out the sustainable supply equally amongst countries according to their relative population. This does not imply a prescriptive allocation method in practice. We recognise that there are variations between countries in terms of culture, climate or the legacy of past development, all of which can affect the different needs we use resources to meet. This does not undermine the principle of fair shares, although it may well mean that those shares are used to meet needs in very different ways.

We believe that the equity principle is the most logical starting point for our targets. We reject the idea, used for instance by many Northern nations in international negotiations over greenhouse gas emissions, that they need a larger share of the environmental capacity of the planet to deal with these emissions, because their economies and societies are based on high levels of energy use. This 'grandfathering' approach is extremely short-termist. In looking to the middle of the next century we do not need to be bound by current requirements for resources. Over that time scale Northern nations have the ability to adjust far more than Southern nations. The Northern industrialised nations have taken far more than a fair share for over a hundred years. We have built up, in the eyes of Southern nations, a vast 'environmental debt' to the South, which we should repay. Northern nations must therefore gradually cut their use of environmental resources, working towards fair shares.

So for the UK, we can compare our estimated total environmental footprint for each resource with our estimates of the fair share of environmental space available, to establish a quantitative measure of how far from sustainability we are at present. As a result the sustainability scenario set out in this book could also be described as an 'equity scenario'. The equity principle can be interpreted as stopping 'importing' sustainability, because to do so takes the resources others need to live sustainably, too. The UK's overall dependence on 'imported' environmental space resources may well be even more extreme than simple figures for net imports suggest. As UK manufacturing industry has declined, and our economy has become ever more dominated by services, so our apparent contribution to global pollution and resource use has declined. But a real measure of that contribution can only be made when we take full account of imports and exports, so as to judge the full extent of the environmental impacts resulting from our consumption.[20] In theory, if all commodities, goods and services were traded at prices that fully reflected environmental costs then it might be possible to make such an assessment of our impact simply from our spending. But this is not possible at present.[21]

In setting our environmental space targets we will use data for 'apparent consumption' as our base. We will not attempt to adjust the figures for embodied resources. This is for three reasons: first, in most cases it would be of little significance at the level of precision we can achieve at present.

Second, in practice it would be a mammoth task, as will be seen in Chapter
6 where it has been necessary to begin a similar process to assess our use
of land overseas. Third, it would mean that the targets derived for the UK
were no longer comparable to those produced for other countries in the
Sustainable Europe project. A further area where we have not been able
to quantify the effective import of resources is where British people
consume resources while abroad on holiday. We take almost twice as many
more visits abroad than foreign visitors take to the UK,[22] so generating a
higher net resource use. Overall we do not believe this effect would
substantially change our targets at present, but the amount of foreign
travel undertaken is growing fast, up by about 35 per cent between 1991
and 1995 according to International Passenger Survey data. Even at
present the impacts of tourism can be especially important for certain
resources in particularly popular holiday destinations.[23]

## The Population Base

Within the equity scenario, population remains a thorny question. There
are a range of United Nations forecasts for future population growth,
from 7.9 billion to 11.9 billion.[24] These not only imply very different
figures for per capita environmental space, but because population growth
rates are widely variable between countries, also imply a very different
distribution of environmental space between countries. Assuming, as is
expected, that UK population will remain around 60 million, then in the
low forecast the UK's share of global environmental space will be 60 per
cent greater than in the high case. It has been argued by some researchers
working on environmental space that we should base our targets on a
smaller global population figure based on a more rapid stabilisation. This
seems dangerously optimistic. Population growth is most rapid in those
countries which have the least resources to deal with the factors which
result in high rates of growth. To suggest that developing countries which
fail to stabilise populations by, say 2010, will get smaller per capita shares
of environmental space as a result, cannot be justified when the likelihood
of population stabilisation depends as much on the economic, aid and
development policies of the developed countries as on the developing
countries themselves. On the other hand there must be a deadline after
which additional population growth will not increase a country's share of
environmental space, otherwise practical targets cannot be set.

   Our central estimates are based on a stable world population of 9.8
billion, achieved by 2050. But we also present figures based on larger
(11.9 billion) and smaller (7.9 billion) final populations. We choose the
year 2050 because it will take time for Northern countries to escape high
energy and resource use patterns, and similarly, it will take time for
Southern countries to stabilise population growth.

# THE SUSTAINABILITY EQUATION

The share the UK currently takes of global environmental space depends on three factors: the number of consumers (in other words, our population), the amount of goods and services each of us consumes (our average rate of consumption), and the efficiency of our economy in converting environmental space into goods and services (the technological factor). These factors can be related in the form of an equation: the total impact we can impose on the environment (I) is a function of the total population (P), the per capita level of consumption or affluence (A), and the technological efficiency (T) with which we use the environment to generate wealth. This gives us the 'Ehrlich' equation: $I = P * A * T$.[25]

Such an analysis can be applied at any scale or to any group or country. The equation allows us first to separate out the different factors influencing total impact. Doing so shows that increases in consumption are more significant in terms of the expected increase in impact, than are increases in population. Population increases are expected mainly in those parts of the world where per capita consumption rates are very low. Consumption however is forecast to grow rapidly, from an already high level, in the Northern industrialised countries like the UK. To illustrate this point crudely, if population and consumption increase according to established trends then overall impact will increase around five-fold by 2050.[26] If population alone increased, then our impact would only double. Second, the Ehrlich equation allows us to estimate the necessary improvements in technological efficiency needed to achieve any given goal for the total level of impact. The environmental economists Michael Jacobs and Paul Ekins estimate that by 2050, simply preventing any increase in total impact implies a five-fold improvement in technological efficiency.[27] If economic growth in developing countries reaches the annual rate of 5.5 per cent – the level regarded by the Brundtland Commission as necessary to eliminate the most extreme forms of poverty – then the average global improvement in technological efficiency needs to be twice as high – ten-fold.[28]

Technology is the focus of the current environmental debate, with increasing demands for 'eco-efficiency' improvements of a factor of ten reflecting these type of calculations. Many of our suggestions later in this book are for technological improvements. However, the estimates presented so far assume that current rates of environmental degradation are sustainable, which is patently untrue. We shall see later that we need to reduce the total impact – especially in the critical area of energy consumption – by at least 50 per cent. This doubles the improvements needed. Moreover, technology is not the only variable.

# Population

It is self-evident that in a world of finite resources, population must be part of a long-term strategy for sustainability. Although there is still debate about this critical question, current understanding of the links between poverty, environmental degradation and population suggests that the best way of reducing population growth is to create the social and economic conditions that provide people with the security they require before having smaller families. If we are to achieve the low growth forecasts then we must deliver access to birth control for the 350 million couples who want no more children, but have no access to birth control.[29] And we must focus aid resources on education for women and girls to provide primary health care, promote literacy, elevate their status, and empower their equal and active participation in the economy through access to income generating employment. Upholding women's rights in these ways has been demonstrated, time and time again, to be the best tool for reducing birth rates by reducing the desire for large families. But to set targets for world population stabilisation as early as some have, for example for 2010, is unrealistic.[30] In practice it is almost inevitable that developing countries will not be able to stabilise population at that level. Our own targets for 2010 are merely interim targets to assist policy making, broadly based on a rule of thumb that at least 25 per cent of the total reduction required should be achieved by 2010.

# Consumption and Economic Growth

While the lower estimates of necessary technological improvements cited above are feasible, at least according to those businesses that have taken these concerns seriously,[31] the higher estimates seem somewhat less plausible, at least in the next 60 years. Even optimistic population growth assumptions don't bring the figures entirely into the realms of realism. There are technical limits to improvements in efficiency, based on funda-mental thermodynamic laws. This is especially important where the limiting factor to use of a resource is the resulting pollution. We can reduce per unit pollution, but this will require some additional input of energy or other materials. This means that even in such cases, measuring sustainability in terms of inputs is not misleading. Indeed, it ensures that attention is not focused disproportionately on 'end-of-pipe' measures to cut pollution which tend to incur higher additional costs in these terms.[32] In most areas we are still far from thermodynamic limits, but as we approach them, the rate at which we can improve efficiency slows.

But even with focused effort and the right incentives for businesses and governments to utilise the scope for such technological improve-ments, they do not simply lead to reductions in impact. Efficiency gains can be consumed in several ways: we cannot assume that, in practical terms, for example, if cars become more fuel efficient and therefore cheaper to drive, people will not choose to drive further as a result. In other words, in our consumer culture, efficiency improvements are likely to trigger increases in consumption that undermine the gains resulting from each unit of consumption being made less environmentally damaging. If technology alone will not achieve sustainable levels of impact then we may need to reduce levels of consumption. Fortunately, reducing consumption does not necessarily mean being worse off.

## Applying the Sustainability Equation to the UK

The approach we take is fundamentally different to that of economic forecasters, indeed, it has been dubbed 'back-casting'. It starts from the future target level, and works back to the present, rather than starting from present trends.[33] Our environmental space targets can be seen effectively as determining the acceptable level of 'impact'. So we can then examine the opportunities for influencing the other terms in the equation to achieve the desired level of impact. Our central targets are expressed in terms of percentage reductions in total resource use over a 1990 base.[34] Wherever data are available we also set out current projections for increases in consumption, although in many cases such forecasts are generated on the simplistic assumption that the relationship between economic growth and the use of that resource will remain unchanged. Where possible, we also try to separate out factors which will lead to higher consumption as a result of a material change – such as increasing numbers of households – from those which are merely economists' speculation. However reliable such projections have proved in the past, and in practice their record has been poor,[35] we can be confident that if policies are in place to try to break and even reverse past trends in resource consumption, then the future will not look much like the past in this respect. This is one reason why, where we see pressing need and scope for more rapid change than implied by a mechanistic approach to interim targets, we do not hesitate to urge the adoption of more stringent targets for 2010.

We will examine not only the potential for efficiency strategies which reduce the value of the 'technology' term in the equation, but also seek sufficiency strategies which directly reduce the 'consumption' term without reducing wellbeing. We do not assume that all sectors of the economy must achieve the same percentage cuts in resource use. This would patently be economically inefficient. However, neither do we exempt any sectors, or take an approach based entirely on 'cost-effectiveness' as such analyses tend to suggest only limited potential, because they assume that current low prices for resources – which do not reflect real environmental costs – will persist.

---

## BOX 4.1: *ENVIRONMENTAL SPACE TARGETS FOR THE UK*

For each resource:

- Determine the 'environmental space' or 'sustainable global use' for that resource – in terms of an annual rate – by identifying the limiting constraint on its use, and estimating the rate of use which avoids breaching that constraint.
- Calculate a per capita fair share in environmental space, based on forecast world population of 10 billion in 2050.
- Calculate a UK target on the basis of 59.6 million population in 2050.
- Estimate current UK consumption, taking account of trade in the resource.
- Calculate the reduction needed in UK consumption in percentage terms by 2050, and an interim target for 2010.
- Examine the major uses of the resource to identify potential savings by efficiency and sufficiency strategies.
- Review the likely impacts of those strategies on levels of consumption of other resources.

---

## CONCLUSION

The environmental space methodology and our application of it is summarised in Box 4.1.

The target figures derived are not seen as absolute limits, or expected to be exactly accurate. As Opschoor and Weterings stress, they do reflect some ethical judgements.[36] However, we are confident that not only do they reasonably accurately represent the speed and direction of change needed, but that they also indicate at least the order of magnitude of the changes in production and consumption levels which are needed to deliver sustainability. Most importantly they form a foundation for scientific and public debate about appropriate and effective strategies for sustainability.

The next five chapters turn to the specific resources, outlining the targets and the key reasoning behind them resource by resource. We will also note relevant policy and targets at the UK scale, and compare them with the environmental space targets. Details of the calculations and explanation are relegated to endnotes. Each chapter suggests practical measures that can contribute towards meeting the targets, and outlines the conflicts or synergies between measures to reduce use of different resources. In each case we will examine a few specific measures for reducing our use of each resource, with estimates of the potential based on case studies. These are not intended to be prescriptive, but illustrative of the possibilities. Indeed, in practice the best ways of meeting the targets may well be ones we have not considered. However, the case studies illustrate how far we could get simply with wider adoption of current best practice or realistic expectations of technological advance.

# Chapter 5
# Energy

## INTRODUCTION

For the last 200 years exploitation of fossil fuel reserves has been a powerful liberating force for our economies and societies. However, humankind's unsustainable use of energy lies at the heart of the global environmental crisis. Burning fossil fuels – coal, oil and gas – is the main cause of global climate change, acid rain and a host of more localised pollution problems. Without this massive energy subsidy, the rates of material extraction and use that underlie so many environmental concerns, from waste generation to traffic congestion, would not be possible. The time has come when the transition to a fossil-free, sustainable energy future must be planned.

## THE IMPACTS OF UNSUSTAINABLE ENERGY

### Climate Change

Early in 1996, probably the most prestigious group of scientists ever assembled to work on a single project reported that 'the balance of evidence suggests a discernible human influence on the global climate'.[1] This Intergovernmental Panel on Climate Change (IPCC) is confident that unless action is taken to prevent climate change, global temperature will increase by 1–3.5°C by 2100. The average rate of warming implied is greater than any seen over a similar period in the last 10,000 years. Burning of fossil fuels for energy is the main source of human-generated greenhouse gases, especially carbon dioxide. Combustion of fossil fuels accounts for about 85 per cent of global $CO_2$ emissions. Carbon dioxide was responsible for about half of the total 'climate forcing' in the 1980s, and a larger share historically.[2]

As the world warms, the climate in the UK will change. According to the Department of the Environment, if there are no major global policies to reduce greenhouse gas emissions, then in the 'most likely' scenario for the 2020s, climatic zones in the UK will shift 200 km northward.[3] The scenario shows a northward shift of natural habitats, wildlife species and farming zones by about 50–80 km per decade. By 2020 annual precipitation will have increased by 5 per cent and the UK will be on average 1°C warmer. Drought in the drier southeast and flooding in the wetter northwest might both become more common. By 2050, under the same scenario, annual precipitation will increase by 8 per cent, and temperatures by 1.6°C. The frequency of extremely dry summers such as 1995 could increase from 1 in 90 to 1 in 3 by 2050, sea levels rise by up to 37 cm and general gale frequencies by 30 per cent. The frequency of extreme coastal flood events would also increase. By 2050 what is now a 1 in 100 year flood would be likely to happen every year in Holyhead and Southampton, and every four years in Great Yarmouth. After 2030 the effectiveness of the Thames Barrier may be compromised.

These effects are expected to benefit forestry, some agriculture, tourism and recreation. But adverse effects are likely on soils, wildlife, especially species on the edge of their range, water resources, arable agriculture in the southern half of the UK, the insurance sector and on human health.[4] Health risks include increasing incidence of infectious diseases as well as heat-induced deaths and indirect effects from increased urban smogs. Insurance costs, which have quadrupled in some areas over the past 30 years because of weather related damage, could easily double again.[5] This 'most likely' prediction is not certain, however. The UK is currently blessed with the warmth of the Gulf Stream. Changes to the Gulf Stream as the world warms could, perversely, leave the UK with a climate more akin to Newfoundland than the Mediterranean. Again this would have significant adverse impacts on the UK's ecological and human systems. The precarious position of the UK's climate and the difficulty of prediction makes the UK particularly vulnerable to the rapid shocks and changes of global climate change. And the global impacts of climate change seem likely to be even more severe.

## Pollution, Ecosystems and Human Health

Carbon dioxide is not the only byproduct of our profligate use of fossil fuels. Other pollutants are also released in combustion processes, whether in vast quantities such as oxides of nitrogen ($NO_x$) and sulphur dioxide ($SO_2$), or in trace amounts such as polycyclic aromatic hydrocarbons (PAHs) and other volatile organic compounds (VOCs). $NO_x$ and $SO_2$ are major factors in the problem of acid deposition which has been blamed for forest dieback and the acidification of lakes, as well as for damage to buildings. Despite the lack of media interest since the 1980s, the problem has not been solved. Although the UK has agreed to reduce emissions, the process has been slow, and critical levels are still widely exceeded.

Acid deposition is also causing widespread damage to the upland landscapes that well-meaning but often misguided anti-wind farm protestors aim to protect. A detailed survey of the impacts of acid rain by the WorldWide Fund for Nature in 1995 found that, with only the agreed reductions prior to the 1994 sulphur protocol, 83 per cent of the most valuable protected areas surveyed in the UK would continue to exceed critical loads for acid emissions.[6] Even under scenarios with more stringent cuts than those agreed in 1994, 43 per cent of these sites would lie in areas where critical loads were exceeded. This would not necessarily damage the biodiversity interest of all these sites, but many of the upland sites concerned – notably bogs, heaths and mosses – can be highly sensitive to acid depositions.[7]

Energy-related pollutants also lead to ill health for humans. Recent research suggests that breathing urban air, polluted with combustion byproducts from industry and transport, costs each city dweller, on average, a year from their lives.[8] A report from consultants ECOTEC for the Department of the Environment estimated that the benefits of the current UK programme of reductions in sulphur dioxide (the main contributor to acid rain) were worth £18 billion – this being mostly human health effects.[9] It has been estimated that 10,000 deaths a year in the UK are attributable to small particulate (PM10) pollution. These particulates come from combustion processes – half of them from road transport. Economists have estimated that PM10s cost the UK £14 billion a year in damage to health and the environment[10] although these estimates are based on value-laden cost-benefit valuation procedures. The DOE has set up the Expert Panel on Air Quality Standards (EPAQS) to recommend air quality standards designed to minimise the risk to public health. But such standards are regularly exceeded. For example it has been estimated that, in 1991, some 19 million British people lived in areas where air breached European quality standards for $NO_x$. And in some of the worst cases in 1994, the 50 $\mu gm^{-3}$ standard for PM10s was exceeded in Cardiff on more than 50 days, the 50 ppb standard for ozone was exceeded on more than 50 days in Lullington Heath and the sulphur dioxide standard was exceeded on more than 30 days in Belfast.[11]

## Resource Depletion

We should also not ignore entirely the question of resource depletion. It has been estimated that every year as much oil is consumed as it takes nature 1 million years to create.[12] We need to be alert for signs that new reserves are becoming more difficult to find or exploit. This would signal that we were 'over the hump' into accelerating depletion, having used more than half of all the reserves. Some resource economists believe that this point is being reached for oil.[13]

# The Environmental Costs of Fossil Fuel Extraction

Increasing exploration and extraction costs are not just financial. As new reserves become more difficult to find, the energy costs incurred also increase – an unpleasant positive feedback mechanism. Environmental costs also increase as we establish production in remote and fragile wilderness areas, in the Alaskan Arctic for example. The impacts of oil extraction and distribution, for example, are already significant. Major oil spills such as the *Exxon Valdez*, and more recently the *Sea Empress*, are just the tip of an iceberg – oil spills account for only 5–12 per cent of oil entering the sea. Pollution from land, ballasting and washing of tankers, and deliberate illicit dumping account for the remainder of the estimated 2.5 million tonnes of oil released into the oceans every year.[14] Despite the efforts of industry apologists to argue otherwise, the impacts of oil spills on marine ecology are long lasting and can be severe.[15] Pollution resulting from the oil industry is not limited to oil itself. The debate over sea-disposal of the Brent Spar platform focused on the amounts of toxic wastes left on the platform. The linked environmental and social impacts of oil development have been seen in many places, for example in Ogoniland, Nigeria. The activities of Shell and others have led to widespread environmental devastation. Protests from native Ogoni people have been violently put down by the Nigerian government. Since 1993 the Nigerian Internal Security forces have killed over 1000 Ogonis, and executed many of their leaders, including Ken Saro-Wiwa.[16]

Global demand for energy – especially electricity – is growing fast. All of its environmental impacts are likely to worsen. According to the World Energy Council,

> *In the absence of widespread, determined and effective steps to curtail demand growth – by dramatic efficiency improvements, technological developments and because of environmental concerns – primary energy demand is likely to expand 2 to 2.5 fold by 2050.*[17]

With a business-as-usual approach to meeting energy demand this would double $CO_2$ emissions. Current rates of use of fossil fuels are unsustainable. All the evidence gathered by the IPCC suggests that the threat of climate change is the most pressing constraint to our use of energy.

## A NUCLEAR ALTERNATIVE?

Some still hold out the hope of a nuclear-powered future, despite the technical and economic failures of the last few decades. Like the techno-optimists of the fifties, with their promises of 'power too cheap to meter', they now promote nuclear development as the solution to global climate change. The UK nuclear power programme was established on the basis that it would provide cheap power to the UK economy, but this was never achieved. Nuclear power has always been heavily subsidised, and it is in fact one of the most expensive options for reducing greenhouse gas emissions. Indeed, the Government's nuclear review in 1995 concluded: 'additional capacity provided by new nuclear build is currently too expensive to be justified for $CO_2$ policy purposes alone'.[18] Overall, vast sums have been invested in nuclear power, even without considering the, as yet, little known costs of the long-term management of nuclear wastes, and still these technologies require state subsidies to generate power competitively.

While it is true that the emissions of $CO_2$ associated with nuclear power are low, there are other reasons why nuclear power has no place in a sustainable society.[19] Accidents at nuclear power stations have been widely publicised, but even under normal working conditions there is the danger of radiation exposure at every stage of the nuclear fuel chain. Moreover, the risk of accidental exposure to radiation from accidents, although small, carries major impacts. The Chernobyl disaster has resulted in increased cancer incidence in children, massive psycho-social damage and disruption, and a cost to Belarus alone of US$235 billion to 2015.[20] Many of the old reactors in operation in Eastern Europe, which use obsolete technology and are inadequately maintained, are disasters waiting to happen, according to many scientists. Even in France the Inspector for General Nuclear Safety has indicated that there is as much as a one in twenty chance of a serious reactor accident before 2010.[21] Similarly, PWR reactors, similar to the Sizewell B reactor in Suffolk, run the risk of a Chernobyl type accident.[22] Other reactors in the UK built in the 1950s and 60s have operated well past their intended lives.

The impacts of mining uranium for nuclear power are serious too, putting the health of workers at risk. A Working Group convened by the Uranium Institute's Committee on Nuclear Energy and the Public in 1993 found that 35 per cent of workers receive an annual dose greater than 20 mSv.[23] This is the dose limit recommended for worker safety by the International Commission on Radiological Protection (ICRP). Also, people have been displaced from their land by uranium mining companies, including Australian aboriginal people. Aside from the relationship of nuclear power and nuclear weapons and the risk of terrorist activity at nuclear installations, the legacy of nuclear waste is too substantial and too long-lived for us to contemplate. Radioactive wastes can remain hazardous for hundreds of thousands of years and need careful management to ensure that radioactivity does not escape into the environment. The British Government Panel on Sustainable Development reported to the Prime Minister in January 1996 that how to dispose of radioactive waste safely in perpetuity is one of the most intractable problems currently facing industrial countries. There are major scientific and technical difficulties with permanent disposal underground.[24]

As more is understood about the difficulties of safe long term management of nuclear waste from the fuelling, operation and decommissioning of nuclear reactors, the huge potential long-term costs are only just beginning to be realised. The risks of nuclear power are typically inter-generational, with the principal costs and risks falling not on those using the electricity generated from nuclear power now but on future genera-tions. Future generations will bear the costs up to 2100 – estimated by the OECD at a total of £45 billion for the UK – but enjoy no benefits.[25] This runs counter to the principles of sustainable development. It cannot be allowed to happen again.

# ENVIRONMENTAL SPACE TARGETS FOR ENERGY USE

The environmental constraint for fossil fuel use in terms of $CO_2$ emissions is based on the understanding that climate change greater than 0.1°C per decade is unacceptable and that $CO_2$ stabilisation at 350–400 parts per million by volume is needed to meet this condition. There are many different routes to stabilisation, but all imply deep cuts in carbon dioxide emissions in the long term. Precise targets and their timing vary, however, according to a whole spectrum of factors including: emissions of other greenhouse gases, deforestation and land use changes. In this report, global targets are estimated from IPCC emission profiles and scenarios for stabilisation selected to give a smooth transition from 1990 emissions to stabilisation.[26] On the basis of the most likely IPCC scenar-ios for the amount of the carbon budget to 2100 that will have been used up by 2050, we can estimate that globally, current emissions of 22.2 gigatonnes of $CO_2$ should be cut by around half by 2050. Other reliable studies based on the same data appear to support still greater cuts. For example, work by Krause suggests that a more rapid reduction in emissions is needed and cuts of up to 75 per cent may be required by 2050. We work from the basis that global cuts in the range 50–75 per cent will be needed.[27]

Our central scenario assumes a 50 per cent global cut, and a UN medium population projection. This produces global targets for 2050 of $CO_2$ emissions of 11.1 gigatonnes, equivalent to just 1.13 t-$CO_2$ per person.[28] Even this cannot be seen as a long-term stable level of emissions. The IPCC consider that by 2100, global emissions of $CO_2$ should be less than 2.0 gigatonnes! Table 5.1 shows the various options we have considered for our scenarios to 2050.

According to government figures, UK carbon dioxide emissions in 1994 were 552 million tonnes, or 2.5 per cent of global emissions. This

**Table 5.1** *Per Capita Environmental Space for Energy (t-$CO_2$)*

| CO$_2$ cuts required | World population 2050 | | |
|---|---|---|---|
| | *7.9 billion* | *9.8 billion* | *11.9 billion* |
| 50% | 1.4 | 1.1 | 0.9 |
| 75% | 0.7 | 0.6 | 0.5 |

translates to 9.5 tonnes of $CO_2$ per person. Present UK emissions take about 5 per cent of the global capacity for $CO_2$ emissions, even though the UK has only 1 per cent of the world's population. To reach the environmental space target of 67.3 Mt or 1.13 t-$CO_2$ per capita, a reduction of 88 per cent is required over the 1990 base figure.

The year 2050 seems a long way off, so we also set an interim target for 2010 which achieves a quarter of the total reduction required by 2050. For the UK such an interim target is 449 Mt of $CO_2$. This implies a reduction from 1990 emissions of 22 per cent for the UK. Our figures are broadly in line with a stabilisation scenario developed by the World Energy Council (WEC) and International Institute of Applied Systems Analysis (IIASA). This suggests that OECD countries should be aiming to reduce energy-related carbon dioxide emissions by about 32 per cent by 2020 and by around 75 per cent by 2050.[29] However, there are reasons to suggest that a more stringent medium term target would be appropriate. The long-term targets for 2100, implied by IPCC figures, are even lower than those for 2050, and the more rapidly they are achieved, the less the risk of catastrophic disruption.

Moreover, in the short to medium term developing countries' emissions are likely to increase rapidly, especially as most of them – the so-called non-Annex 1 countries – are not currently bound by the Climate Convention. Conversely, the developed countries could cut emissions more rapidly. This would help maintain a smooth approach to global targets. Research into 'safe emissions corridors' based on the assumption that non-Annex 1 countries' emissions continue to increase according to current trends, reaching 5.5–7.0 Gt C per year by 2010, suggests that as a result, Annex 1 countries, including the UK, will need to make much more substantial cuts in that period.[30] Total emissions for the Annex 1 countries will need to be cut by 33–60 per cent by 2010, just to keep within the safe corridor.[31] This implies, in turn, cuts of 20 per cent or more by 2005.

These estimates do not affect the environmental space targets for 2050 as, by then, all countries should have converged to the same per capita emissions rate. However, they do imply that for carbon dioxide, the environmental space methodology underestimates the cuts required by 2010 in the UK. This is because in practice, convergence will not be

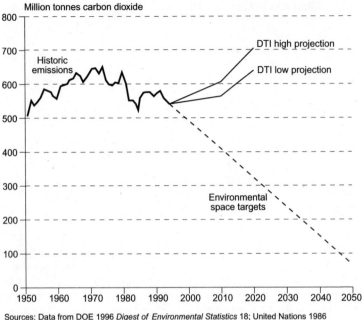

**Figure 5.1** *UK CO$_2$ emissions – projections and targets*

Sources: Data from DOE 1996 *Digest of Environmental Statistics* 18; United Nations 1986 *World Energy Database*; Department of Trade and Industry 1995 *Energy Paper* 65

linear and gradual from now. Instead there will be a period where developing country emissions grow faster than gradual convergence would suggest, so in the short term the UK and other developed countries will need to cut emissions faster. We would therefore endorse the CO$_2$ reduction targets for 2010 suggested by the European Environment Agency of at least 30 per cent.[32] Figure 5.1 compares the targets for the UK with projections for environmental space use with business as usual.

As a result of economic recession and the 'dash for gas' in energy generation, alongside some limited CO$_2$ reduction policies, the UK has already made some progress towards the target levels.[33] To achieve the rest of the reductions without relying on recession will be more challenging, but still feasible.

## MEETING THE TARGETS – TACKLING THE CLIMATE CONSTRAINT

There are various sources of useful energy that produce less CO$_2$ than conventional oil and coal burning power plants. Even within fossil sources, some produce more useful energy for each tonne of CO$_2$

emitted than others. This is why the recent 'dash for gas' – the development of 8847 MW of gas power stations, or 93 per cent of new capacity developed since energy privatisation – in the UK has helped us stabilise the growth of $CO_2$ emissions over the last few years. In the short term, through to 2010 and perhaps beyond, further increased use of gas for power generation is going to be a help in meeting emissions reduction targets.[34] Fuel-switching to gas will also help reduce emissions in the domestic sector. But even if there were enough gas to meet our energy needs, such fuel-switching to a less carbon intensive fuel is not a long-term solution. In the longer term we need fuel-switching to carbon-free renewable energy technologies.

Renewable energy technologies (see Box 5.1) have received only a fraction of the investment given to fossil fuels and nuclear power. Even after the privatisation of most of the power sector, only 6 per cent of the so-called Non-Fossil Fuel Obligation (NFFO) funds renewables.[35] Even with this limited support, many renewable technologies are rapidly approaching economic viability. Renewable energy costs have been falling rapidly since the early 1980s, despite a 40 per cent decline in research funding in OECD countries between 1982 and 1993.[36] And this trend is bucking the market – which largely ignores the external environmental and social costs of conventional fossil fuels.

The external environment costs represent a massive effective subsidy for fossil fuels, which in many countries is further reinforced with direct subsidies for fossil fuel exploration, extraction or use.[37] For example, the DTI spends twice as much money on 'publicity and promotion' for the oil industry than on all photovoltaics.[38] In the USA, on the other hand, ten different producers are active, and government initiatives aim to expand the photovoltaics market tenfold before the millennium.[39] Globally, the costs of photovoltaics are on a rapid downward curve, the efficiency of the technology is improving and sales are rising. World shipments of photovoltaic cells rose by 17 per cent in 1995, the largest percentage increase in ten years. The price of cells is now US$4 per watt, down from US$80 in 1975.[40]

Although the potential of renewable energy is vast – the solar radiation received by the Earth is about 10,000 times more than current human energy use – we cannot see it as unlimited. Much of it is very 'low-grade', in other words, of limited value for doing 'useful work' because too much energy would be needed to convert it to 'high grade' useful energy. Thus, although billions of megawatts of solar power are received by the Earth, we can only use a small fraction of it.[41] Nonetheless, this tiny fraction – several hundred terawatts – is an order of magnitude greater than the total amount of energy humans currently use, and two orders of magnitude greater than the tiny amount of renewable energy we currently exploit.[42] However, perhaps the most significant under-exploited energy technology is in fact what the Association for the Conservation of Energy describes

## BOX 5.1 *RENEWABLE ENERGY TECHNOLOGIES*

| Technology | Status |
| --- | --- |
| Large scale hydro | Limited further capacity for development |
| Micro-hydro | Potential largely unexploited |
| Passive and active solar heating | Proven and mainly economic, but not widely deployed |
| Photovoltaics (pv) | Technology developing rapidly, costs falling and potential enormous |
| PV-fuel cells | To produce hydrogen as fuel. Components proven, but economics speculative |
| Wind (onshore) | Proven, often competitive and expanding |
| Wind (offshore) | Components proven, not yet competitive |
| Biomass – gasification | Pilot technology, economics speculative |
| Biomass – direct combustion | Widely used, variable economics |
| Geothermal – aquifers | Proven, potential largely exploited |
| Tidal – estuarine dams | Technology proven, can be economic, but large schemes environmentally disruptive |
| Wave – shore-based | Test stations, uncertain economics |
| Wave – offshore | Various prototypes, economics speculative |

Source: Jackson, T (1997) *Power In Balance* London: Friends of the Earth

as 'the fifth fuel'. Energy efficiency improvements could dramatically reduce our dependence on primary energy while retaining our home comforts: warmth, light and other services and entertainment. To put energy saving into practice, there are a variety of technical and cultural reforms that must be considered in assessing how we might meet the need to vastly and rapidly cut our $CO_2$ emissions. We return to these after introducing the key sectors for $CO_2$ savings.

## Reducing $CO_2$ Emissions – the Key Sectors

Although energy efficiency in industry has improved substantially since 1970, energy consumption per household has barely changed, despite promotion of energy efficiency measures and increasing use of natural gas use. In the transport sector, limited improvements in the fuel efficiency of vehicles have been completely overwhelmed by the increase in car and lorry numbers and use.[43] Energy consumption in passenger transport almost doubled in the last 25 years, and use per passenger mile increased slightly, principally due to the increasing use of cars. Freight transport energy use increased by over 50 per cent with no change in use

**Table 5.2** *Carbon Dioxide Emissions, 1994, and Projected Energy Use Increases to 2020*

| Category | Carbon dioxide production (Mt) | DTI projected increase in energy use to 2020 (%) |
|----------|-------------------------------|--------------------------------------------------|
| Domestic | 153 | 12–16 |
| Commercial | 34 | 28–45 |
| Industrial | 161 | 0–41 |
| Roads | 127 | 49–79 |
| Others | 78 | n/a |
| Total | 553 | 27–30 |

Note: the projected energy use for industry varies widely. The increase in the iron and steel industry is predicted to be 0–23 per cent, in all others 12–41 per cent. This table attributes $CO_2$ to end-users, omitting the energy generation industry.

Sources: AEA Technology (1995) UK emissions of $CO_2$ *Fax to Friends of the Earth* 18 December; Department of the Environment (1995) *Digest of Environmental Statistics* London: HMSO; Department of Trade and Industry (1995) *Energy Paper 65. Energy Projections for the UK* London: HMSO

per freight mile. Commercial energy consumption per unit of output has fallen by over 35 per cent in the last 25 years, and industrial energy consumption per unit of output by over 50 per cent, partly as a result of changing patterns of trade. Table 5.2 shows the current breakdown of $CO_2$ emissions by sector, attributed to end-users of energy, alongside projections of the future increase in total energy use by those sectors.

# REFORMING THE POLICY FRAMEWORK

## Energy Prices and Energy Use

Environmental economists tell us that energy is overused because it is under-priced, or more precisely that its price does not reflect the true costs, including the environmental costs, of its use. They argue that upward pressure on prices is needed to change consumers' behaviour in the market. Higher prices should encourage the uptake of efficiency measures by increasing the financial incentive, and making more efficiency measures cost-effective. Higher prices for energy will also make more renewable energy production profitable, and stimulate further research and development. And if prices are not increased uniformly, with clean renewable technologies exempted from the measures used to increase prices, then as long as consumers can choose the source of their energy, this would give an even more substantial boost to the development of the renewable energy industry.

The last UK government argued consistently that environmental policy tools which use the market in this way are preferable.[44] But there has been little action because of the possible impact of increased energy prices on international economic competitiveness – despite the mass of evidence suggesting that higher energy costs lead to greater overall efficiency and better economic performance[45] – and because of the equity implications of higher domestic energy prices, leading to legitimate and vocal opposition to energy price rises from groups with social concerns. This political impasse was reinforced by the débâcle over the introduction of value added tax (VAT) on domestic energy. Ostensibly to bring the UK into line with the rest of Europe, and to encourage energy saving, the Government proposed to apply VAT to domestic energy in two stages: an 8 per cent tax in April 1994, rising to the standard 17.5 per cent in April 1995. Practically, this helped them balance the budget and many have suggested that this was the main reason the tax was introduced, rather than sustainability concerns. Certainly, it took massive political outcry and debate to establish adequate compensation for those in 'fuel poverty'. The outcry also meant that the second phase of the tax increase was cancelled, leaving energy VAT at 8 per cent, while the costs of insulation materials, for example, are already rated at 17.5 per cent. The Labour Government has now cut the rate to 5 per cent.

The Government suggests that a 20 per cent saving in energy would be cost effective.[46] But there are several barriers to uptake. People currently waste energy, because, in their particular circumstances, it is actually the sensible thing to do. In terms of cash flow, it may be easier to pay electricity and gas bills than to find and finance the capital investment required to improve the energy efficiency of their homes or premises, appliances or processes. For low income householders and small businesses, these problems are even more profound as they have poor access to credit, and little or no chance of making the required capital investment. For tenants and landlord alike, there is little direct incentive to invest in improving the energy efficiency of the building fabric because neither gains the full benefits of so doing. Because of the poor availability and labelling of suitable higher efficiency technologies and techniques, it may be too frustrating to bother trying to find them. Moreover, with electricity and gas companies currently controlled by regulations which encourage sales expansion, the overall balance of propaganda materials in the energy market is dominated by advertising which drives consumption rather than conservation, and which encourages poor fuel choices in environmental terms, such as the use of electricity for heating.[47]

# Government Policy and the Energy Market

Government policies have often sent the 'wrong' signals through their intervention in the existing energy market. Higher relative prices for carbon and nuclear based energy in comparison with renewable generation are a key policy measure – but only if proper attention is given to equity implications. Government policy already sets standards for the energy efficiency of new buildings, which are too low. It establishes the regulatory framework which controls the behaviour of electricity and gas companies. It decides that VAT will be charged on energy efficient building improvements. And it grants planning consent for new nuclear and fossil fuel power stations. Yet it also pays for public information campaigns to promote energy efficiency. Such policies could easily be altered to be consistent, and to shape the market differently. Then householders, businesses and public sector bodies would start to redirect some of the £50 billion they spend each year on energy supply into financing investments in energy saving options. It is not so much a question of finding new money, but of ensuring that this investment is redirected.

# Liberalisation – Setting the Framework

The policy framework for the energy market has been driven by political demands for privatisation and increased competition, in other words, an agenda of liberalisation. This can deliver efficiency improvements in the system as a whole, but there is no guarantee that environmental efficiency ends will be served. The critical issue is the policies that set the framework for the liberalised market. If we get them right we will gain the benefits of effective market competition *and* meet our environmental objectives most cost effectively. If we get them wrong, liberalisation could further impair progress towards sustainable energy systems by rewarding short-termism and environmental irresponsibility. The regulatory framework determines how different companies compete and profit: if they can only profit by selling more energy, then they have little incentive to promote efficiency. If, on the other hand, the framework reflects the principles of 'least cost planning' or 'integrated resource planning' which provides a fair comparison between the costs of increasing supply and the costs of managing demand, then, as has been found in parts of the USA, companies can profit by selling 'nega-watts', in other words, selling reductions in energy use by focusing not on energy itself but on the energy services we require. In California in 1991 Pacific Gas and Electric announced that it would 'stop building large central power stations and would obtain all future expansions in energy needs through customer efficiency (with financing and information from the company) and such alternative sources as wind and solar'.[48] The regulatory framework has helped. 'At least three states have decoupled utilities' regulated profits from energy delivered, allowing them to profit from efficiency improvements, and more than 20 others are considering doing so'.[49] At present, in the UK, energy service companies (ESCOs) are trying to develop a market niche in which they provide householders with energy efficiency measures paid for, over time, out of the savings in energy bills they give. But so far they have not been able to establish themselves in domestic 'small users' markets, supplying mainly the commercial and industrial users in the over–100 kW market.[50] The framework of the liberalised market must allow consumers to actively choose 'green energy' for such a price differential to be effective. With a little imagination, a framework which allows renewable suppliers to compete directly in the domestic market could be developed as the market is liberalised in 1998.

There are also opportunities for major improvements in building energy efficiency in new and refurbished buildings but these require integrated assessment of all the costs and benefits. For example if enough energy savings can be made to require not just less fuel, but a smaller boiler in a commercial or industrial building, the financial savings jump. Similarly if solar gain is managed to the extent that no air conditioning is required, then again the financial savings leap upwards. But too often all these decisions are made separately in the design process. It's partly an issue of training and knowledge, but also of reform of building development and planning regulations. In addition, certain specific policies are critical, especially if higher prices are to work as a policy mechanism. Support for research and development into renewables innovation will be needed, while direct investment in energy efficiency will help compensate those on lowest incomes, especially those in very energy-inefficient homes.

# ENERGY GENERATION

The first main area for $CO_2$ emission cuts lies in power generation. In the medium term, major $CO_2$ savings could be delivered by developing our wind energy resource, and exploiting the proven technology of solar water heating, rather than further development of fossil fuel power generation. In the longer term we anticipate that, alongside wind, photovoltaics will provide a substantial and growing share of energy needs and there is also possible scope for biomass, depending on availability of land. But despite interest and investment, the scale of shift needed will not happen on its own.[51]

## Renewable Energy

The UK is well endowed with renewable energy resources both on and offshore. So far, these are generally poorly developed. In particular, the

UK has by far the largest wind resource in Europe with 40 per cent of the total. Some 20 per cent of the UK land area has the annual mean wind speeds considered necessary for the economic generation of electricity even with existing technology. But the share of electricity generated by non-hydro renewables such as wind is just 0.71 per cent at present, despite an ostensibly impressive increase of 200 per cent in the last four years.[52] The Conservative Government of 1992–97 set targets for increasing renewable energy generation. Although these are small (equivalent to only 3 per cent of current consumption), they are indicative of the changing direction of policy. Renewable energy is particularly important because it replaces fossil-fuelled electricity generation capacity which is especially inefficient in terms of its $CO_2$ emissions for each unit of energy delivered to the final user. The UK used 286 TWh of electricity in 1994. This is 25 million tonnes of oil equivalent (mtoe). However it took 70.3 mtoe to make this electricity, a gap of around 45 mtoe.[53] This difference accounts for a large part of the inefficiency in the energy supply system. As an indication of that inefficiency, we use 219 mtoe of primary fuels and, including electricity, consume 154 mtoe of final energy (a gap of around 65 mtoe).

Media reports might suggest that the renewables industry is heavily subsidised. But the subsidies given to renewables are insignificant in comparison to the billions the nuclear industry has received and the direct and indirect subsidies for fossil fuels, ranging from tax breaks on oil exploration and development, to the vast implicit subsidy granted by the fact that the environmental and health costs of fossil fuel burning are not met by the industry. So it should be no surprise that there is effectively under-investment in renewable power generation in the UK, as in so many other parts of the world. But there are further obstacles. One of the biggest is the fact that there is substantial overcapacity in the UK electricity generation market. In 1994–95 maximum demand reached 82 per cent of capacity and average demand was just 54 per cent.[54] This overcapacity is principally due to the introduction of competition, and the subsequent dash for gas undertaken by the power generators in an effort to make maximum profits from the current relative cheapness of gas.

Even so, the costs of wind-generated electricity have dropped from 11 pence to around 4 pence per kilowatt hour in just six years, and it now looks set to be highly competitive in a liberalised market (see Table 5.3).[55] In the longer term, as generation plant is naturally replaced, the opportunities for renewables seem particularly good. But in the short term, the industry still needs some help from the government and the market if it is to be ready for the massive expansion implied by the environmental space targets. Critically, this means an ambitious target for expansion, and practical measures to support it, especially in terms of the regulatory framework for the liberated market.

**Table 5.3** *Current Electricity Generation Costs*

|           | Generation costs (pence/kWh) |
|-----------|:----------------------------:|
| Wind      | 3.8–4.8                      |
| Coal      | 4.3–5.0                      |
| Nuclear   | 4.0–6.6                      |
| Gas       | 2.3–2.9                      |

Source: British Wind Energy Association (1996) *The Economics of Wind Energy* London: BWEA

Friends of the Earth has previously urged the adoption of a UK target of 3500 MW of renewables development by the year 2000. The House of Commons Energy Committee has already endorsed this, in 1992 calling on the Government to adopt a target of 3000–4000 MW.[56] Achieving such a target would set us on a path to deliver perhaps 10 per cent of total primary energy supply from renewables by the year 2010. In the face of climate change, and the current failure to act decisively in this direction, this is no longer enough. If renewables are to meet their potential and supply what energy expert Mike Flood sees as practical – one-third of our primary energy requirements by the year 2025[57] – a more vigorous programme is needed to promote renewables, and to pull the financial plug on coal, oil and nuclear development.

# Wind Power

The UK wind resource is 28 times larger than that of Denmark although the country is only six times bigger in area.[58] Yet Denmark, as of April 1996, produced 3.7 per cent (600 MW) of its electricity supply from windpower,[59] and has set a target for wind of meeting 10 per cent of electricity demand (1500 MW) by 2005 as part of a total renewable target of 12 per cent.[60] Although presently the UK only produces 0.25 per cent of its electricity from wind[61] as we will see, a target almost twice as high as Denmark's could be achieved. In practice there are a number of constraints which make it difficult to utilise all the potential resource. The accessible wind energy in the UK is estimated at anything from 300 TWh/year to 1000 TWh/year.[62] The current best estimate for the maximum practicable resource for onshore wind power (by 2005), taking account of physical and environmental constraints, is 55 TWh/year.[63] More optimistic assessments, such as that by the Department of Energy in 1990, suggest a practicable resource of more than twice this (122 TWh/year). Here we will take the more conservative estimate as the basis for our analysis.[64]

The UK presently has over 500 turbines, providing over 200 megawatts of generating capacity in over 30 wind farms.[65] This is enough to provide electricity for approximately 200,000 homes at current rates of energy use. If, as the Building Research Establishment suggests, energy demand from households can be cut by 40 per cent (see below), then the same capacity would serve over 330,000 homes. The energy output from a single turbine or wind farm can be significant in terms of local electricity consumption,[66] while collectively wind turbines can make a significant contribution to meeting the UK's needs. To provide 55 TWh/year with wind turbines would require around 22,000 1MW turbines.[67] This level of renewable capacity displaces 41–55 million tonnes of $CO_2$,[68] which is roughly equivalent to 24.1 million tonnes of coal a year or about half of current UK total production.[69] Despite the reduction in demand for coal, much of which is imported, such a transition in energy generation would actually create more jobs than it destroyed. If wind energy replaced coal-fired capacity, up to 18,000 additional jobs could be created by the installation of 22,000 MW of capacity.[70] As wind technology develops there is also scope in the UK for offshore wind development which exploits more reliable winds, and uses negligible areas of land. The usable offshore wind resource was estimated to be 134 TWh/year by the Central Electricity Generating Board[71] and more recently, given improving technology, at 340 TWh/year by the British Wind Energy Association.[72]

Public concerns over the development of wind power have focused on visual intrusion and noise. Noise can be adequately controlled through the use of more modern gearing technology and three-bladed turbines. Opinion survey work has suggested that much concern over noise is misplaced, and that, more generally, the vast majority of people in the localities where wind farms have been developed, like them. A summary of nine surveys by the DTI, the BBC, the Countryside Council for Wales and Liverpool University students found between 61 per cent and 96 per cent in favour.[73] Visual intrusion, although – or perhaps because – it is more subjective, is still a significant concern in some cases. Higher (and thus more economical) wind speeds are found largely in and around areas designated for their landscape beauty. In supporting wind development the Government set a threshold wind speed which largely restricts developers to such areas. Friends of the Earth has produced Good Practice Guidelines for wind development, which suggest ways of reducing both noise and visual concerns. Friends of the Earth does not support building wind farms on Sites of Special Scientific Interest or big developments in Areas of Outstanding Natural Beauty and National Parks. Even outside such sensitive areas, wind development should be subject to environmental impact assessment on a case by case basis, considering, however, not only the local negative impacts, but the wider beneficial impacts of wind development such as reduction of the acid rain and global warming caused by non-renewable energy sources.[74]

# Other Renewable Energy Sources

Wind is not the only renewable resource we could harness in the medium term. Even in UK latitudes and with our notorious climate, there is a significant solar energy resource. Active solar heating systems are extensively used in many similar countries, usually for water and space heating applications. So far, solar development in the UK has focused on the supply of low temperature heat using solar panels. It is estimated that there are currently over 42,000 solar water heating systems in the UK. Almost all have been designed to provide hot water for domestic consumption. Users of the latest systems estimate that at least half of their annual hot water needs are met by their collectors, with most of their needs met in the summer and about half of their needs in winter. On average the most recent systems save householders approximately £200 per annum on their fuel bills. The reduction in carbon dioxide emissions is estimated as 350–1300 kg per year for a typical domestic water heating system. If 50 per cent of the households in the UK were to fit solar domestic hot water systems the annual $CO_2$ saving would be in the range of 4 to 15 Mt-$CO_2$.[75] The range is wide because the efficiency of existing hot water systems is equally diverse at present.

In the longer term, towards 2050, there is wider scope for other renewables to contribute to meeting the environmental space targets. Of these, photovoltaics and wave power are the most exciting, and biomass could offer substantial economic potential if the land area for biomass crops proves to be available (see Chapter 6). Photovoltaics are fast approaching economic competitiveness, even with the continued effective subsidies given to fossil energy. Amoco and Enron are currently promoting plans for a 50 MW photovoltaic power plant on Crete, which will be the first of its kind in the developed world.[76] In principle, the Department of Energy has estimated that large-scale photovoltaic power plants covering 6000 km², or 2.5 per cent of the UK's land area, could supply all of the UK's current electricity requirements, if not more. Even without additional land use, by incorporating photovoltaics into existing and new buildings, Mike Flood estimates that thousands of megawatts of power could be generated.[77] An experiment in Berlin using roof-mounted photovoltaics, as part of a refurbishment scheme for high density inner city housing, suggested that 30 per cent of the city's current electricity needs could be met from this source.[78]

The Oxford Solar House (OSH), completed in March 1995, was built to evaluate the potential of photovoltaics to contribute cost-effectively to UK domestic energy supply. The house was designed to function as an ordinary single-family standard house but to use as little energy as possible. Heating demand was reduced by maximising passive solar gain, by providing thermal mass to minimise temperature variations, and by good insulation. Energy demand was cut by installing a solar hot water system.

And electricity demand was reduced by installing energy efficient appliances, and by mounting a photovoltaic array on the roof. Over its first year in use the house has been a net exporter of electricity to the grid. The house was built for £800 per square metre, a typical price for an architect designed detached house in the UK, and it has extremely low running costs. Prices today would be lower because the costs of photovoltaics are still falling at around 20 per cent a year.[79]

The potential for using photovoltaic technology on new and existing buildings is growing fast. 'Solar shingles' have been developed by Energy Conversion Devices (ECD) of Michigan. These are designed for use on roofs, and are around 100 times thinner than traditional solar panels. They are easy to install, and with the economies of scale of mass production should be half the cost of conventional photovoltaic cells. The Japanese are investing heavily:

> *From next year, thousands of Japanese residents will be eligible for a government subsidy that pays for half the cost of installing the photovoltaic system of their choice ... Japan plans to eliminate the subsidy gradually as economies of scale help solar energy to compete with fossil fuels. ECD already has a foot in the door of the Japanese market through a partnership with Canon.*[80]

For 2050 we assume conservatively that 30–50 per cent, or 80–130 TWh of current electricity demand could be generated by photovoltaics, with no net land use implications.

Wave power is the other potentially major renewable resource for the UK; we have a lot of coastline, and the seasonal distribution of wave energy matches our energy needs, being greater in winter. Studies have suggested that wave energy could meet between one-sixth and one-third of current UK electricity use.[81] But investment in research and development is desperately needed to begin to realise this potential, and take the opportunity to become a world leader in this cleaner technology.

# Market Liberalisation – Threat or Opportunity for Renewables?

Without political intervention it seems unlikely that the rates of investment in renewable energy and demand side management will reach the levels needed to meet environmental space targets. There is an outstanding opportunity to set the right framework as full energy market liberalisation occurs in the UK in 1998. Market liberalisation will allow consumers to choose their energy supplier. In theory, consumer demand for renewable energy and more efficiency could be exercised to stimulate the renewable energy industry by redirecting major private investment.

That consumers will welcome such an opportunity is demonstrated by the response to Dutch electricity company PNEM's initiative to offer 'green electricity' from renewable sources at a higher tariff. Having exceeded their first monthly target for households signing up, they extended the scheme to a regional level, and a target of 10,000 households by the end of 1996.[82] In the UK, a recent opinion poll by MORI found that 86 per cent of the public would prefer to buy electricity generated from a renewable source and 24 per cent of these would pay a premium for the privilege.[83]

However, at present in the electricity sector 'must-take' contracts operate for certain stations. In Scotland they cover the nuclear and gas powered stations. This means that the generators must take the electricity that is supplied from these stations. Thus if the demand from consumers falls, the power stations that are turned off first are the coal-fired and hydro powered stations. In the rest of the UK, nuclear capacity is 'last off the grid'. Liberalisation is not anticipated to affect these arrangements significantly. However, under liberalisation, although the regional electricity companies will be bound by these various agreements, consumers could in theory enter into contracts directly with the energy suppliers of their choice, as long as the mechanics of billing for transmission costs can be resolved. In this way the potential benefits of liberalisation, to use the market effectively for environmental objectives too, could be realised.

## Conclusions on Renewable Energy Generation

The existing official target for increasing renewables capacity, at 1500 MW (in place or under construction by the end of 1998), is equivalent to just 2 per cent of generating capacity, or 3 per cent of current electricity use.[84] The European Union has agreed that 15 per cent of all energy demand should be met by renewable sources by 2010.[85] In the UK, official figures show that a target of 100 TWh per year (34 per cent of current electricity use) is achievable by 2015.[86] By 2050, much higher figures are possible. Our optimistic estimate is equivalent to almost 120 per cent of current electricity demand. Yet the Labour Party has set only a modest target of 10 per cent by 2010 and a longer term target of 20 per cent by 2025.[87]

We estimate that by 2010, renewables could be providing at least 55 TWh, therefore saving 55 $Mt-CO_2$, and by 2050, this saving could be increased to at least 180 $Mt-CO_2$ by vigorous promotion and investment (see Table 5.4).

**Table 5.4** *Estimates for Renewable Energy Generation for the UK for 2050*

|  | Conservative (TWh) | % of current electricity demand | Optimistic (TWh) | % of current electricity demand |
|---|---|---|---|---|
| Wind (incl offshore) | 55 | 18 | 190 | 60 |
| PVs | 80 | 25 | 130 | 41 |
| Wave | 45 | 14 | 90 | 29 |
| Total | 180 | 57 | 370 | 118 |

# ENERGY EFFICIENCY IN HOMES AND OTHER BUILDINGS

Although we are suggesting long-term targets for $CO_2$ saving, this does not mean that there is no call for short-term action. We categorise efficiency measures into short and long term as such an approach can aid planning for their introduction. Some measures can be introduced into any home, others will be appropriate only in new or refurbished dwellings. Thirty per cent of UK energy is used in houses – 525 TWh/year – producing 150–165 Mt-$CO_2$.[88] The Association for Environment Conscious Building has calculated the shares of energy consumption taken by different uses of energy in our homes (see Figure 5.2). However, this breakdown is based on energy use, not carbon dioxide. In emissions terms, electrical appliances are more significant than this figure might suggest, as on average electricity generated in the UK creates over three and a half times as much carbon dioxide as using natural gas for heating.

The Buildings Research Establishment (BRE) suggests that cost effective energy efficiency measures in housing could save 63Mt-$CO_2$ per year.[89] This is approximately 40 per cent of the total $CO_2$ emissions from households. These energy savings would also save households over £2 billion a year.[90] In the longer term, according to European Commission estimates, as the stock is gradually replaced, super-efficient housing could reduce energy consumption in the home to as little as 10 per cent of current levels.[91] The BRE estimate is based on an analysis of the cost-effectiveness of a range of energy efficiency measures.[92] The assumptions used mean that the savings calculated are conservative estimates at 1995 energy prices. The measures considered include low energy lighting, fitting loft/wall and other insulation, double glazing and draught-proofing together with using efficient electrical appliances (see Table 5.5). Space heating for buildings can be made even more efficient by using waste heat from power generation in the form of combined heat and power (CHP) schemes. These can boost the effective efficiency of generating capacity. Traditional coal fired

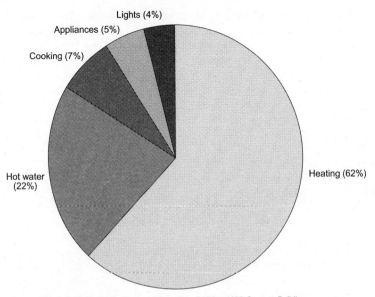

Source: The Association for Environment Conscious Building 1995 *Greener Building*
Coaley: Green Building Press

**Figure 5.2** *UK Domestic energy use*

electricity generation is about 35 per cent efficient in converting primary
energy to usable energy;[93] gas fired generation is around 55 per cent
efficient. CHP schemes can be as much as 90 per cent efficient.[94]

Electricity use in homes accounts for around 66–70 Mt $CO_2$,[95] or
40–45 per cent of the total attributable to the domestic sector. A recent
study by the Lothian and Edinburgh Environmental Partnership
estimated that savings from replacing inefficient lighting and appliances,
such as fridges (in low income households), could alone reduce domestic
electricity consumption by as much as 30 per cent.[96] The potential for
savings from more efficient appliances is so great because domestic appliances on the market vary so widely in efficiency. A survey published in
*Ethical Consumer* in 1995 reported ovens which ran on half the energy of
typical models.[97] For cookers, the most striking difference is in the choice
between electric or gas; swapping from an electric to a gas cooker would
save around 360 kg of $CO_2$ a year. For fridges, a Consumer Association
survey suggested that energy efficient refrigeration uses up to 70 per cent
less energy than average models.[98] Similar differences can be found for
washing machines. The market-leader machines are mainly German,
reflecting high energy efficiency standards in the German domestic
market. The UK, on the other hand, does not set high standards, and we
are missing out on the chance to sell premium products in European
markets because of this failure.

**Table 5.5** *Domestic Energy Savings*

| Measure | Potential saving (Mt-$CO_2$/yr) |
|---|---|
| Loft Insulation increased to 150 mm | 1.87 |
| Cavity wall insulation | 8.58 |
| Solid wall insulation | 9.75 |
| Full double glazing | 3.34 |
| Extra double glazing | 1.32 |
| Full draught-proofing | 1.10 |
| Extra draught-proofing | 0.40 |
| Cylinder insulation | 0.66 |
| Extra cylinder insulation | 0.84 |
| Condensing boilers | 6.64 |
| Low energy lights | 6.78 |
| Efficient dishwashers | 0.26 |
| Efficient refrigerators | 2.53 |
| Efficient fridge/freezers | 5.32 |
| Efficient freezers | 4.77 |
| Efficient televisions | 1.69 |
| Efficient electric cookers | 5.57 |
| Efficient gas cookers | 1.06 |
| Total potential savings | 62.48 |

Source: Building Research Establishment (1995) *Information Paper IP 15/95 Potential carbon emission savings from energy efficiency in housing* Garston: BRE

Guidance from the DOE for householders advocates a range of measures suitable for typical UK houses, such as installing six inches of loft insulation and efficient condensing boilers.[99] The package of measures would cost between £1079 and £2090, and could save each household £325–580 per year and around 60 per cent of annual average emissions. However, only a tiny proportion of homes have adopted these measures. Even though they are presently cost effective, as we saw earlier, the obstacles are big. In the longer term, even larger savings are possible, especially in new and refurbished buildings where design principles can also be applied to improve solar gain and reduce heat loss. The design principles to maximise passive solar gain have been known for many years, but are still rarely incorporated into UK designs. This is not because UK housing is built at densities which are too high to incorporate these principles, but because of a lack of pressure from central and local government to encourage the house builders to adopt them. Mike Flood suggests that with little effort, but the right regulatory framework, at least 3 million passive solar buildings (new and refurbished) could be in place by 2020.[100] Our expectations for urban redevelopment, discussed in Chapter 6, suggest that this may be a conservative estimate.

# Improving Old Homes

The DOE's Energy Efficiency Office (EEO) case studies show how a range of different measures can be implemented to achieve large cost-effective savings in energy use. These range from draught proofing and cavity wall insulation to double glazing and lagging hot water tanks. These do not rely on new or unproven technology, and given the economic as well as social and environmental benefits it is triply important that these measures are more widely used in all types of properties.[101] Current Government spending plans commit around £150 million in funding to various energy efficiency schemes including the Home Energy Efficiency Scheme, which provides around £70 million each year in grants for basic insulation and draught-stripping for low income, disabled or elderly householders; and the Energy Savings Trust (EST), established as part of the Government's Climate Change Programme, which promotes energy efficiency to domestic and small business sectors. It was expected that Government and energy efficiency industry funding of £50 million a year for the EST would be more than matched by funding from the energy utilities.[102] However, only a fraction of the envisaged support has been provided – just £10–£15 million per year. Although these schemes achieve a great deal with limited funds, the Government needs to invest more in energy efficiency. Compared with the subsidies to the nuclear industry or the oil exploration and development industry, £150 million is peanuts. The desire to see increased investment in energy efficiency inspired groups including Friends of the Earth to promote the Home Energy Conservation Act which was passed in 1995, albeit in a much weaker form than first envisaged. Nonetheless, it does provide duties for local authorities to undertake energy efficiency surveys and prepare reports setting out measures to achieve a 'significant' improvement in residential energy efficiency.

# Investment to Tackle Fuel Poverty

Investment in energy efficiency is needed not only for environmental reasons. It is critical for equity reasons too. It has been estimated that as many as 8 million households suffer from fuel poverty (the inability to heat the home without having to make tradeoffs in other areas of vital expenditure, such as food).[103] For relatively modest investments in energy efficiency to improve heating systems and insulate dwellings, fuel poverty can be eliminated while reducing total fuel use in such households.[104] Friends of the Earth is promoting the idea of a national £1 billion per year investment programme in domestic energy conservation over 15 years to eliminate fuel poverty. This could create in the region of 45,000 additional jobs throughout that period installing insulation and efficient appliances,[105] while substantially reducing the 30,000 'extra winter deaths' from respiratory and cardiovascular diseases that occur annually in the UK, many of which result from the combination of fuel poverty and poor energy efficiency.[106] Also, total energy consumption in those households would fall by up to 5 per cent from a relatively low base.[107]

## Energy Efficient New Housing

Building regulations for new buildings in the UK do include energy efficiency standards. However, the minimum standards required are still well below those mandated in Scandinavia, where a house built to the current regulations will consume only 31 per cent of the energy of a house built to UK standards[108] despite the more severe climate. The UK standards fall even further short of what is technically achievable. More is left to the voluntary Home Energy Rating scheme, which, at least in theory, allows house buyers to take energy efficiency into account by giving a clear standard measure of efficiency. But the minimum standards are not always met[109] while the Home Energy Rating scheme is making only slow progress in improving standards. The best designs, such as the Energy Showcase Project, and the 'Lower Watts' house, are already coming close to the 90 per cent reductions in energy use that the European Commission sees as possible in the longer term.[110] The Lower Watts house, a 'super insulated' house in traditional masonry construction, has demonstrated Scandinavian insulation and airtightness levels, but in conventional UK building methods.[111] Its initial construction cost – about £550 per m² floor area – was similar to non-energy efficient houses completed in the same locality in Oxfordshire at the same time and in similar materials. Including the benefits of fitting efficient lighting and appliances, total energy use is reduced to just 22 per cent of normal, and energy costs to 35 per cent of normal (see Table 5.6).[112]

Such houses are not just for the rich. Demonstration projects have achieved similar savings – of 66–75 per cent over Building Regulations standards – in provision of affordable housing both in inner Manchester and in suburbs in Milton Keynes and Swansea.[113] In all three projects the savings on fuel bills exceeded the additional rent or rent and mortgage costs incurred by at least 50 per cent. But these are isolated examples at present.

## Energy Efficiency Outside the Home

Using growth forecasts and historical data on the trend of energy consumption per unit of gross domestic product, we can make a rough prediction of energy consumption trends in industry. By 2010, energy

**Table 5.6** *Comparison of 'Lower Watts' House with Conventional Houses*

|  | Lower Watts house | | Normal house | |
|---|---|---|---|---|
|  | Gigajoules used (pa) | Cost (£) (pa) | Gigajoules used (pa) | Cost (£) (pa) |
| Space heating | 30 | 133 | 217 | 946 |
| Water heating | 11 | 49 | 18 | 79 |
| Cooker | 7 | 32 | 7 | 32 |
| Lighting and electrical appliances | 10 | 215 | 24 | 552 |
| Total | 58 | 580 | 266 | 1680 |

Source: Energy Advisory Associates (1994) *A superinsulated house in 'traditional' masonry construction* Leominster: Energy Advisory Associates

consumption by industry can be expected to fall a further 45 per cent, equivalent to 71 Mt-$CO_2$.[114] However, the historic trends also suggest that the rate of improvement in the ratio of energy use to GDP is slowing, so after 2010 we estimate that the scope for further reductions is limited.[115] Nonetheless there is still scope for further improvements, and not simply by further exports of the energy-intensive sectors of industry – one of the factors that has driven this trend in the past. Indeed, some energy experts argue that there are substantial further savings to be achieved even beyond those which are cost-effective according to conventional estimates. Amory Lovins of the Rocky Mountain Institute, pioneer of the so-called 'soft-energy paths', points out that conventional assessments compare just the costs of the specific energy-saving improvement with the costs of the energy saved by it. But low-energy buildings technology combining several technical improvements can cross thresholds which provide much greater savings.[116]

Twenty per cent of the UK's total energy use is in non-residential buildings. Figure 5.3 shows how this breaks down.

Air conditioning in offices uses large amounts of energy. Data from the Building Research Energy Conservation Support Unit show that best-practice naturally ventilated offices use less than one third of the energy per square metre of typical modern air-conditioned offices.[117] However, there is 'a tendency to equate "air conditioned" with luxury, instead of simply "poorly designed"'.[118] In Jarrow, the 15,000 sq foot Groundwork Eco Centre has just been built, which claims to be the greenest office building in the UK. It uses a combination of wind turbines, solar panels and the most up to date design techniques to create a building which produces half the carbon dioxide of a typical office building. The building's efficient use of daylight, natural ventilation and heat retention

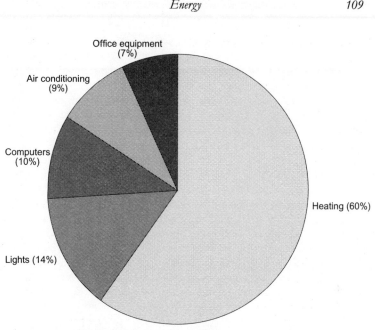

Source: The Association for Environment Conscious Building 1995 *Greener Building*
Coaley: Green Building Press

**Figure 5.3** *UK commercial energy use in buildings*

obviates the need for air-conditioning systems. The Eco Centre uses a quarter of the energy of a similar sized air-conditioned office.[119]

For the domestic sector alone, by 2010, other things being equal, we would expect to be able to deliver all the savings in homes suggested by the BRE: 63 Mt-$CO_2$. Taking into account growth in the number of households to around 30 million by 2050, the combination of these measures and a refurbishment and redevelopment programme could produce a saving of around 77 mt-$CO_2$.[120]

## TRANSPORT AND ENERGY USE

Road traffic emits around 125 million tonnes of $CO_2$ every year.[121] Even if there were no $CO_2$ emissions from houses or industry, if we fail to reduce emissions from car use, they alone will exceed the 2050 environmental space target for carbon dioxide! This is not to belittle the other problems associated with unsustainable transport but merely to stress the importance of tackling $CO_2$ emissions.[122] Transport, principally road transport, is the fastest growing source of $CO_2$ in the UK.[123] Indeed, road transport is the only major sector whose $CO_2$ emissions are currently increasing. Road transport accounts for 23 per cent of all $CO_2$

emitted in the UK. Emissions in 1994 were 125 Mt $CO_2$, up from 66 Mt in 1970, 92 Mt in 1980, and 121 Mt in 1990.[124] This increase is due to growing volumes of road traffic. Journeys have become longer and transferred to the car from other modes.[125] The key measures for reducing emissions from road traffic are improving fuel efficiency; shifting journeys back to more energy-efficient modes (such as public transport, walking and cycling); and reducing the need to travel.

## Fuel Efficiency

Prototype cars that can travel 100 miles on a gallon of petrol exist, such as the Renault Vesta which was 'borrowed' and exhibited at several motor shows by Greenpeace during 1994. Indeed, the Society of Motor Manufacturers and Traders (SMMT) is clear that the technology is not the problem, they blame lack of customer demand for 'low performance cars'.[126] The current average for new cars in the UK is 36.7 mpg.[127] Major technical improvements to reduce weight and increase drive efficiency are possible. But car manufacturers are remarkably conservative, in this case, pursuing development and sales of cars on the proven road of increasing power, speed and status.[128] The low interest of manufacturers in achieving further efficiency improvements by developing smaller, lighter cars reflects the relatively low cost of fuel. Relevant legislative pressure has focused on safety and emissions, rather than efficiency, so manufacturers have treated these issues as a greater priority.

The last Government encouraged improvements in fuel efficiency on a voluntary basis. But the voluntary target set by the SMMT of a 10 per cent improvement in efficiency by 2005 is little short of derisory. The Royal Commission on Environmental Pollution (RCEP) has urged the adoption of a target of a 40 per cent improvement in new car fuel efficiency by 2005 (over 1990 levels).[129] While past trends would suggest a 14 per cent increase in efficiency by 2010, raising average fuel consumption in the UK car fleet to around 34 mpg, from the arguments above we can expect manufacturers to achieve more than this. Extrapolating from the RCEP target, we suggest a 50 per cent improvement for new cars by 2010 is feasible. We believe that a 55 mpg new car average efficiency is feasible for the UK car fleet on this timescale, given that the first 100 mpg models should be in production as early as 2000 and the average fuel efficiency of the fleet would have increased by 25 per cent. By 2050 such models should be the average in the fleet.

Fuel efficiency improvements alone are not adequate. Much of the efficiency gains driven by previous oil price shocks have been traded off by drivers, either choosing to buy more powerful or bigger and safer (but heavier) cars, or simply by driving more as cars become more fuel efficient and thus car travel relatively cheaper. Claire Holman notes that:

> *research and development instigated after the second oil price shock*
> *came to fruition at a time of far lower real fuel prices and dwindling*
> *customer concern. As a result, technological developments, such as*
> *multiple valve engines, have been used to produce ever more powerful*
> *cars, rather than smaller and more efficient engines of comparable*
> *power.*[130]

So other measures are needed, too. We need to make less journeys by car, and reduce the need to travel as often or as far as we do now.

## Modal Shift

'Modal shift' is the jargon term for the switching of journeys from one way of travelling (or mode) such as the car, to another, such as the train. Although in $CO_2$ terms, efficiency measures are more significant, in a broad analysis of the sustainability of transport, modal shift away from the car is likely to be more important than such technological measures. There are few immediately effective policies for cutting $CO_2$ emissions from transport in this way, but in the medium term there is scope for a range of measures. Transferring air journeys to high speed rail is one. Shifting car journeys back to public transport and thus reducing emissions is another. In the 1980s and early 1990s ideological political pressure led to widespread privatisation and deregulation of public transport systems. Bus passenger journeys have fallen by 21 per cent between 1985/86 and 1992/93, while in the same time bus kilometres have increased by 21 per cent.[131]

But, as the example of Freiburg, Germany shows, such decline can be reversed. Freiburg (population 280,000) has a proactive travel policy involving reduction of car traffic, parking restrictions, promotion of 'clean' modes of travel and public awareness campaigns. At the beginning of the 1980s there was a persistent decline in public transport, mainly attributed to the relatively high cost of public transport use. The city council introduced a cheap 'environmental travel card' to encourage more people to use public transport. As a result, over the whole year, there were 4000 fewer cars on the road in the city centre every day, saving around 4000 tonnes of $CO_2$ emissions a year.[132] One way in which this scheme helps reduce car use is by levelling the playing field. When all the costs of a journey by public transport are paid at the time it is taken, and most of the costs of a car journey are paid in advance, there is a strong incentive to use the car once those costs have been paid. But once a monthly pass has been paid for, the extra cost of each journey by public transport is zero.

### Reliable, Convenient Public Transport

Cost is not the only obstacle to use of public transport. It does not offer the 'door-to-door' convenience of the private car. In the worst cases, a simple trip by car might require several changes on public transport, including changes of mode, for example from bus to train. As a result journey times are generally increased, especially where service frequencies are low. One example of the benefits of improving intermodal connections is Karlsruhe, Germany.[133] Karlsruhe generates considerable suburban travel. The outlying location of the two train stations previously required a large number of commuters arriving by train to transfer to the tramway. Now trams use the railway lines, linking the city centre directly with suburban communities. The average trip time was reduced by 15 minutes, to 30 minutes, and the share of public transport journeys over the route rose from 5–7 per cent to 35–45 per cent. The wider lesson is that improved intermodal links can increase public transport use significantly.

Reliable public transport is also essential if drivers are to be lured from their cars. Although in most UK cities buses are the most appropriate form of public transport in terms of cost and infrastructure investment, they are unreliable, especially where car traffic volumes are high. While separated routes and bus lanes can help solve this problem, they still suffer from poor perceptions – both of their reliability and their general image – as dirty and dingy public transport. The importance of reliable performance and a good image is shown by successful examples of new public transport schemes such as the Manchester Metrolink 2000.[134] Opened on 17 July 1992, the Metrolink provides a reliable, swift and high profile service. It now carries 13.4 million journeys (up 6.6 per cent on 1995's 12.7m): of these almost 20 per cent were previously made by car. Thus, despite the fact that it replaced an already well used suburban railway, a staggering 2.5 million car journeys have been taken off the roads every year. If we make the conservative assumption that the car journeys diverted to Metrolink average 2 kilometres in length then the total $CO_2$ saving is $1Mt\text{-}CO_2$.[135]

## Package Funding

There is a clear opportunity to increase funding for public transport, walking and cycling without any net increase in government spending, by exploiting the 'package funding' approach, which was initiated in 1993. This approach means that local authorities are encouraged to develop coordinated strategies with clear objectives and targets, looking at all modes of transport rather than developing individual schemes based on a single mode. However recent analysis of local transport practice has found that only 10 per cent of local transport expenditure was going on package funding. Of the £1 billion of public money going to local transport, 74 per cent is still going on schemes which will primarily benefit cars and lorries, and only 4 per cent is going on projects for cyclists and pedestrians.[136] In some regions there are more positive signs. In West Yorkshire, analysis by local Friends of the Earth researchers showed that authorities adopting the package approach were successful in a higher proportion of their bids than those that pursued a more conventional approach.[137] The new Government has an opportunity to match green rhetoric on transport with consistent decisions on transport funding that promote the package approach in all regions and shift emphasis within it to public transport. Integrated schemes elsewhere have shown great potential. In Lüneburg, Germany, combined traffic restraint and public transport measures have cut car use by 15 per cent, increased cycling by 59 per cent and walking by 48 per cent. Accidents resulting in injuries were cut by 13.5 per cent.[138]

## Cycling Targets

Cycling targets are another important element of an integrated transport policy. The last Government's target of doubling the proportion of journeys by cycle by 2002 from its present level of just under 2 per cent and quadrupling it ten years later is a move in the right direction but still leaves us far behind continental Europe. In Switzerland cycling accounts for 15 per cent of trips, in Denmark 18 per cent and in Holland 27 per cent of trips are made by cycling.[139] If we were to raise our proportion of journeys made by bicycle to the Danish level we would save over 10 million tonnes of $CO_2$. A realistic target could be to achieve 10 per cent by 2010 and 20 per cent by 2050.[140] Cycling also brings tangible health benefits. The British Medical Association has noted that 'even in the current hostile traffic environment, the benefits gained from regular cycling are likely to outweigh the loss of life through cycle accidents for the current population of regular cyclists'.[141]

## Reducing the Need to Travel

Between 1952 and 1992 virtually the same tonnage of people and freight has been carried for every unit of GDP, but the movement of vehicles to carry it around has actually increased by 25 per cent per unit of GDP.[142] The CBI now says that reducing transport intensity is 'the key challenge' for the future of the UK economy.[143] In particular, we need to cut commuting to work. In the UK as a whole, 8.3 miles is the average journey distance for car commuters. Relatively few longer distance commuters account for a relatively high proportion of total mileage. Only some 6 per cent of all car commuters have journey lengths of 35 miles or more but these 6 per cent account for half of the total car commuting miles. Conversely, 30 per cent of all UK car commuters have journey distances of five miles or less, but the accumulated commuting travel of this 'short journeys' group makes up only about 5 per cent of total car commuting miles.[144]

## Information Technology and Telecommunications

Information technology can help reduce both freight and business passenger mileage. Better communications and computer-aided planning can ensure that freight vehicles travel empty less often. One large brewing firm has reported a reduction of 5 per cent in its total annual kilometres through introducing a computerised vehicle routing system.[145] Video-conferencing can substitute for many business journeys, including many that would have been undertaken by air. BT estimates that the meetings it holds internally by video conference are equivalent to over 4 million passenger miles, or 1300 tonnes of $CO_2$ annually if they were all under-taken by car.[146] Some of these meetings, however, will have been made possible by the technology rather than representing a decrease in travel.

Increasingly services such as home banking are provided over the phone and computer networks which can avoid journeys by both the customer and the operator. Financial services are a business with great scope for homeworking.[147] Homeworking has a large potential to reduce travel, and hence to save time, and reduce costs, pollution and energy use. Digital UK, for example, has adopted an 'aggressive' approach to teleworking. In their Newmarket offices, for example, the ratio of staff to desks is eight to one. Overall, Digital has over 1200 'flexible workers' who, it estimates, save the firm £4.2 million net each year and are also 20–30 per cent more productive.[148]

Studies have shown that productivity gains from homeworking are in the region of 10–20 per cent.[149] It has been estimated that with produc-tivity gains of 5 per cent, employers' financial gains more than offset setting up costs.[150] Moreover, according to the Industrial Society, employ-ers who accommodate working from home, and other flexible employment practices, enjoy lower than average absence rates.[151] Homeworking also offers the potential to help a return to more mixed functions in cities, with work places being near to homes. In their compre-hensive review of homeworking, consultants EA Technology say:

> *A combination of homeworking and more living in cities would reduce the tidal flow of commuters each day, and prevent cities being deserted by night and suburbs deserted by day. This could lead to a reduction in crime in both areas.*[152]

They found that homeworking requires less than a sixth of the energy used in a 'good practice' office, and less than one-eighth of that used in a typical office, when all factors, including travel costs, energy costs in the home and in the office were included.[153]

As an estimate of carbon dioxide savings, on the basis of these findings, 2.5 million people (a quarter of the estimated office working population) switching to homeworking for four days a week would save 4.3 million tonnes of $CO_2$. And this is not an unrealistic proposition: in the US the number of telecommuters had reached almost 8 million in the early 1990s (or 6 per cent of the workforce), and was growing by up to

20 per cent per year. Some forecasts suggest that 20 per cent of the entire workforce will be homeworking for at least part of the week by the year 2000.[154] In Europe it is estimated that there are some 1.25 million teleworkers, and the European Commission wants to see the number exceed 10 million by the year 2000.[155] A study by Management Technology Associates for the Department of Transport found that among one group of UK teleworkers there was an average net saving of 113 car miles per week,[156] or 1.5 tonnes of $CO_2$ a year, about half of an average car's emissions. Grossed up to the total number of current UK teleworkers, this suggests that in 1993 home based teleworkers were already contributing a net saving equivalent to about 1 per cent of UK car miles, or some 5 per cent of total UK travel to work mileage.

Since half of all car commuting miles are generated by just 6 per cent of car commuters,[157] in theory we would only have to persuade those commuters to work at home in order to cut car commuting miles in half, a reduction of almost 22 million miles[158] (or around 6.5 million tonnes of $CO_2$). Although those jobs are not necessarily the most appropriate for conversion to teleworking, the above estimate is probably pessimistic, as uptake of teleworking will be most enthusiastic amongst those with the longest journeys. An overall annual saving in the order of 5 Mt-$CO_2$ is certainly feasible.

## Car Pooling and Other Measures

Even in the context of business travel, teleworking is only part of a package of measures including limiting car parking provision, supporting car sharing or car pooling schemes for commuting and similar measures (see Box 5.2).

All these measures to reduce work-related travel, and more, come together in the idea of Green Commuter plans, where organisations and companies manage the transport needs of their staff.[159] Employers improve the environmental impact of their operations by developing a package of measures, in conjunction with staff and unions.

Nottingham's new Green Commuter plan aims to cut car commuting journeys by 30 per cent in the first three years. Experience in the Netherlands and California shows that this can be achieved. In the De Maas office complex in Rotterdam, part of a national experimental project in the Netherlands, the share of commuting by car was cut from 49 per cent in 1989 to 32 per cent in 1993: a 35 per cent cut.[160] In California, there are 37 towns and cities with 'trip-reduction' bylaws that require employers collectively to appoint a transport coordinator and to implement a programme that reduces commuting to a required target, through reducing peak-hour trips by increasing car sharing and promoting homeworking and telecommuting.[161] The City of Torrance, for example, has used a wide range of different schemes, in particular car sharing, to increase the 'average vehicle ridership' from 1.1 people per car

---

## BOX 5.2 *EXAMPLES OF WORK TRAVEL SCHEMES*

*Southampton University Hospitals* have calculated that an average of £300 a year is spent on maintaining each parking space. They offer a 60 per cent discount to car sharers for parking. Approximately 25 people are now car sharing for travelling to and from work which has taken about 13 cars off the road. They also offer a bonus of £50 to employees opting into their new cycle allowance scheme in place of payment of car allowances.

The *Boots Company* in Nottingham operates Works Service Buses for its staff from Nottingham City Centre. The bus carries about 1300 people a day, 300 of whom own a car but choose to use the public transport instead. The company has also recently set up a car sharing scheme which has gained 500 members in four months.

*Nottinghamshire County Council* plans to set up a computer database for its car sharers. A guaranteed ride home by taxi in event of emergency will be made available. Showers and changing facilities are already provided to encourage more people to cycle together. Where there is a need for employees to have access to a car for work related journeys a fleet of vehicles can be made available for use by employees. *Nottinghamshire Health Authority* have successfully introduced the use of work pool cars to cover the needs of their 250 staff, 75 per cent of whom may need to use a car for work related journeys. Just three cars are used in the car pool scheme.

Sources: Nottingham County Council (1995) *Green Commuter Plans, A Resource Pack for Nottingham's Employers* Nottingham: NCC; Miller, B (1996) Collision Course *Health Service Journal* 1 August

---

in 1989 to 1.51 in 1995, through the Torrance Transportation Network (TTN), a scheme where 30 local business representatives work jointly with the City to share information on how to encourage employees to use alternative means of transportation.[162] Recent successes in Californian cities have been based on setting targets using local regulations, and this has been a marked improvement over previous voluntary systems. In the UK, voluntary schemes, for example in Edinburgh, have also proved ineffectual.[163]

If such measures are not to be undermined by non-participants' employees responding to less congested roads by shifting into their cars, the national policy framework must be right. This is the most critical part of the package, with the ability to convert what can seem like marginal tinkering right into the mainstream. The UK Government has grasped this nettle – if not yet firmly – by imposing a fuel-tax accelerator to increase the price of petrol by 6 per cent over inflation every year. This needs to be a yet higher rate of around 8 per cent to overcome the inertia in travel patterns and overwhelm the historical trends that have reduced real fuel prices by about 40 per cent since 1980[164] and the current competitive price-cutting efforts of the petrol companies that have limited forecourt price rises so far. The Royal Commission on Environmental Pollution has argued that the real price of petrol should double by 2005.[165] As with any tax, its effectiveness in encouraging less car use will depend on how easy it is for those faced with it to avoid paying: in this case, for car drivers to avoid, shorten or shift their journeys at another mode. Investment in, and other support for, alternatives to car use is therefore vital.

*Planning to Reduce the Need to Travel*

In the longer term, reducing traffic volumes and emissions depends crucially on breaching the trend of 'counter-urbanisation',[166] or as the august Royal Town Planning Institute described it, the 'californication' of the UK countryside. The pros and cons of more compact cities are discussed in more detail in Chapter 6. However, the potential to reinvigorate our towns and cities with a mix of land uses and functions, putting employment and a range of services within walking distance of quality homes, is exhilarating. Not only can $CO_2$ emissions be cut, but the social impacts of commuting can be replaced by the social benefits of community life. As psychiatry professor Hugh Freeman comments:

> *There can be little doubt that the time and energy wasted by many millions of people every day in travelling – whether in overcrowded mass transit or in crawling private cars – together with the stress that comes from this frustrating activity, must be factors harmful to all aspects of health.*[167]

Mixed, high-density urban developments, even where not totally car-free, do permit lifestyles free of car-dependency, the great addiction of the modern age. The withdrawal symptoms may not be pleasant, but the end result will be more than worth the effort.

The network of so-called 'car-free cities' established in Amsterdam in March 1994 has promoted the idea of areas where the freedom from providing for cars can massively improve quality of life. At the forefront of car-free initiatives is the city of Bremen in northern Germany. Here, as in other member cities, car-free does not mean absolutely car-less, since the need for residents to use cars on occasion is recognised. Research by the German and Swiss Governments suggests that members of car sharing schemes reduce their car mileage by 50 per cent while increasing their use of public transport. It is reported that in Bremen each shared car replaced five private cars.[168]

In Edinburgh, housing association Canmore has obtained planning permission for a 120 dwelling car-free development on industrial land in the inner city, close to rail and bus links. Residents' tenancy agreements and deeds will include clauses committing them not to own a vehicle. And demand for such high-quality environments is high: the proposed Berlin car-free neighbourhood was oversubscribed with thousands of applications – 20 per cent of which were from car owners prepared to give up their cars to live in such a development.[169] These projects are not 'anti-car'. There is access for cars, and pooled cars can be available for the community. The advantages: less noise, pollution, energy use and danger, and more green space, money (the average car costs £3117 a year to run),[170] local trade and freedom for children, are what attract people.

A perhaps more widely applicable approach in the next few years is to use the planning system to reduce journey lengths and reduce the need to travel. A report for the DOE and DOT revealed significant potential:

> *One of the simulations undertaken in this study indicated that planning policies in combination with public transport measures could reduce projected transport emissions by 16 per cent over a 20 year period. These findings are similar to those of other work which indicates that 10–15 per cent savings in fuel usage for passenger transport might be achieved through land use changes at the city region scale over a 25 year period.*[171]

And such approaches can save money too. A study into travel costs in San Francisco found that households in a car-dependent suburb spent US$13,000 a year more on travel than those living in a high density pedestrian-friendly neighbourhood with good public transport.[172]

## The Road Traffic Reduction Act

All the measures considered under 'modal shift' and 'reducing the need to travel' come together in the concept of road traffic reduction. The Road Traffic Reduction Act 1997, promoted by Friends of the Earth, the Green Party and Plaid Cymru with support from over 200 members of parliament and 100 local authorities, became law in March 1997. The Act requires local authorities to develop local traffic reduction plans. The Road Traffic Reduction (National Targets) Bill, introduced by Cynog Dafis MP in 1997, will if passed require the Secretary of State for Transport to draw up a national traffic reduction plan to achieve a 10 per cent reduction in road traffic mileage by 2010 (over 1990 levels). This target is practically achievable through the measures outlined in this section. Also, modelling conducted for Friends of the Earth suggests that depending on the pace of improvement in car technology and the uptake of car sharing and leasing, between 87,000 and 122,000 additional jobs would be created by 2010 by such a strategy.[173]

Other things being equal, implementation of the Road Traffic

Reduction Bill could be expected to lead to a 10 per cent cut in $CO_2$ emissions from road transport.[174] This conclusion tallies broadly with ECOTEC's conclusions on the scope for planning and land use measures of 10–15 per cent cuts in $CO_2$ emissions from transport over 20–25 years. We also need to add-in the effects of efficiency improvements. On the basis of current scrapping and purchase rates, the targets suggested earlier would raise average fuel efficiency by 25 per cent by 2010.[175] So the net effect of traffic reduction and fuel efficiency improvements would be to cut emissions by 41 Mt-$CO_2$.[176] Continued 10 per cent per decade reductions in traffic would be feasible for some time. This would suggest a target for 2050 of about a 40 per cent cut over 1990 levels. A conservative estimate of continued enhanced fuel efficiency trends, achieving the equivalent of the 100 mpg car as the average in the fleet, would cut emissions by 70 per cent. Combined, these factors could cut emissions by 102 Mt-$CO_2$.

# IMPLICATIONS FOR OTHER RESOURCES

The measures proposed in this chapter would have limited implications for our use of other limited environmental resources. The land required for energy generation would, at worst, increase slightly in comparison with that needed for fossil and nuclear (including mining). Twenty-two thousand 1MW wind turbines would directly occupy some 5000 ha in a total area, mainly remaining in agricultural use, of 500,000 hectares.[177] Wind energy would require a more dispersed land area, but the area directly occupied would be less than that used in coal mining for fossil power. An equivalent cut in coal use, of 24 million tonnes of coal a year, would free up roughly 8500 ha, or 85 km$^2$.[178] In our renewables estimates we have not included increased use of biomass, or use of photovoltaics (other than on buildings) both of which rely on using extra land area. The redesign of residential buildings to increase energy efficiency should, on balance, decrease land use. With effective planning, the land used for transport functions could be reduced by traffic reduction policies. In practice, we can assume that the overall effect of these factors will be negligible.

Use of water would be slightly reduced by increasing the renewable share of power generation, as less water for cooling and other uses would be required. However, only evaporative losses from cooling are included in our calculations in Chapter 8, so the effect on net consumption would be small; even eliminating water use in electricity supply would save only 4 per cent of total water use. Increasing the efficiency of domestic appliances may also help reduce water use as, in practice, more energy efficient showers and washing machines are also more water efficient. Increased uptake of such appliances is taken into account in Chapter 8. There should be no net effect on the use of wood, as neither biomass nor waste incineration are included in the estimates of the potential for renewable energy. If additional land were available for biomass production, then this would not affect the calculations in Chapter 7, as these are based on existing forest area.

The only area where we judge that the effect of the energy strategies set out above may be significant is for non-renewable materials. Although reduced road transport should reduce material demands in this sector, the combination of increased investment in renewable generation capacity, and in building refurbishment and improvement could increase use significantly in the short to medium term. One pessimistic review of the global effects of a transition to renewables estimated that demand for steel, concrete and glass could be tripled if a total of 20 terawatts were to be provided from renewable sources.[179] However, current global energy use is only 10 terawatts at present, and we do not anticipate such an increase in total demand. There will also be offsetting effects. Measures to reduce energy demand will provide longer term savings in materials as generation capacity is replaced by efficiency measures. This, along with improving material efficiency of renewables, should counterbalance much, if not all, of the increased material demand.

# CONCLUSION: MEETING THE ENVIRONMENTAL SPACE TARGETS FOR ENERGY

Table 5.7 shows the targets for energy environmental space, in terms of carbon dioxide emission. The UK is projected to have reduced its $CO_2$ emissions to 4–8 per cent below 1990 levels by 2000.[180] Despite this, in the UK, existing targets are not ambitious. The new Government has adopted stricter targets for carbon dioxide emissions, but these still fall short of the goals suggested by the environmental space analysis. The interim target proposed in this book for 2010 is for a reduction of at least 30 per cent. This exceeds the new Government's target of a 20 per cent reduction by 2010.[181]

If nuclear capacity is to be phased out, this needs to be factored in to our estimates. At present it seems unlikely that any new nuclear plant will be built in the UK. Both economically, and politically, the industry is dead in the water.[182] To advance the closure dates for all nuclear capacity to no later than 2010 would be practically feasible, given the generating overcapacity in the system, and our estimates of the potential rate of expansion of renewable capacity. For simplicity's sake we will just add an equivalent amount of $CO_2$ back into our figures for 2010 and beyond. In 1994 nuclear stations in the UK produced around 80 TWh of electricity.[183] This would produce 60–80 million tonnes of $CO_2$ if generated with fossil fuels.

**Table 5.7** *Carbon Dioxide Emissions and Environmental Space Targets*

| Year | Carbon dioxide (Mt) | Percentage cut from 1990 | Per capita (t-$CO_2$) |
|---|---|---|---|
| 1990 – actual | 576 | n/a | 10.0 |
| 1994 – actual | 552 | 4% | 9.5 |
| 2010 – target | 406 | 30% | 6.8 |
| 2050 – target | 67 | 88% | 1.1 |

The case studies and analysis set out above suggest that feasible – and with increasing energy prices, generally cost-effective – measures could reduce our $CO_2$ emissions by 147 million tonnes by 2010, or 25 per cent. This is another reason to set a more stringent target for 2010; as suggested above, these targets should be aspirational. By 2050, a reduction of at least 455 million tonnes, or 79 per cent, can be envisaged (see Table 5.8 and Figure 5.4).

**Table 5.8** *Carbon Dioxide Savings*

| Sector | Carbon dioxide savings – 2010 (Mt) | Carbon dioxide savings – 2050 (Mt) |
|---|---|---|
| Domestic energy efficiency | 50 | 77 |
| Transport | 41 | 102 |
| Power generation / renewables | 55 | 275 |
| Industrial energy efficiency | 71 | 71 |
| Nuclear phase-out | −70 | −70 |
| Total | 147 | 455 |

The potential savings figures for 2050 suggest that if these are the only areas where we make progress, then we will fall short of the necessary reductions. But they are not exhaustive, they merely illustrate the scope for the UK to begin the process of reducing its consumption of environmental space for energy to within a fair share, without imposing excessive costs or hardship on the British people. We must, however, repeat our caveat that this analysis does not assume that ever-increasing demands for material consumption will increase basic energy demands in the future (although it does allow for the increasing number of households). These savings are only what we see as practical from our current viewpoint and easily predictable advances in technology. Closing the gap, and achieving the full environmental space target should be possible, as long as we set it as an objective for policy and society. In this respect we share an encour-

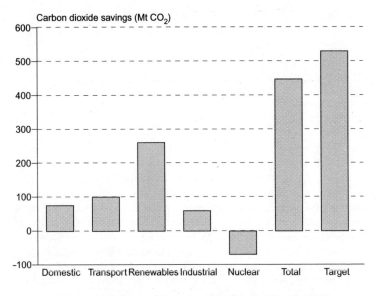

**Figure 5.4** *Potential for cutting UK $CO_2$ emissions by 2050*

aging conclusion with many of the energy response scenarios that have been developed, including those by the IPCC[184] and the World Energy Council.[185] These all suggest that achieving cuts in emissions of this order of magnitude is possible. Studies by the OECD and others also suggest that the economic effects over that period could be almost negligible if the process is well managed.[186] All that is lacking is the will to do it.

*Chapter 6*
# Land

## INTRODUCTION

Land is a fundamental resource. The core issue in this chapter is fair share of productive land. Our focus will be on the vital issue of production of food, meeting one of our basic needs. But before we can even look at food production, we must look at other competing uses for land which also meet basic needs: how much land needs to be protected exclusively or principally for the conservation of biodiversity? How much land do we need for urban use? And in each case, what does this mean in the UK in respect of future land availability for agricultural production?[1]

## BIODIVERSITY AND HABITAT PROTECTION

According to the UN Environment Programme, the destruction of natural and seminatural habitats to service human demands means that 'tens of thousands of species now existing are headed for certain extinction' and many more are under threat of extinction.[2] But maintaining biodiversity requires more than simply leaving something for other species, but also providing for and, where necessary, managing ecosystems to maintain diversity, a rather delicate diversity that is dependent upon change and disruption yet also threatened by it.[3] That threat grows as remaining ecosystems are fragmented by agricultural, forestry and urban development and as climate change becomes reality.[4] Niles Eldredge, curator at the American Museum of Natural History, argues that the widespread and rapid alteration of habitats, principally as a result of climatic fluctuations, is the common feature of previous episodes of mass extinctions observed in the fossil record. Humankind, however, is the first species on Earth capable of reproducing those effects.[5]

So why conserve biodiversity? If the planet has survived previous episodes of mass extinction, why should we worry? It may be simply a question of survival. But even if humankind can survive when the dinosaurs could not, there would be other losses. Not just the pleasure of experiencing the richness and beauty of life, but yet more genetic resources, possible food plants, medicines and useful materials would also be lost. In other words the social and economic sustainability of human society could well depend on the retention of biodiversity. Although natural diverse ecosystems are not necessarily more stable than modified simple ones, they are more sustainable, as their very diversity offers more potential for evolution. And even though there is no consensus on their wider applicability, a number of practical experiments both using plots in the open, and in a sealed, controlled environment, have shown that diversity in comparable grassland ecosystems increases productivity and resilience in the face of drought.[6]

In establishing sustainability targets for land use, for a range of practical and moral reasons, the protection of habitats and associated biodiversity is assumed to be the first priority for the use of land. The environmental space methodology takes a relatively crude two-fold approach to the need for land space for biodiversity. First, it assumes that one criterion of the sustainability of productive management techniques for forests and farmlands is that they will be sympathetic to species diversity, and thus our estimates of the areas needed and available for agriculture and forestry reflect this criterion. But second, it also takes a precautionary approach in calling for a minimum of 10 per cent of land area to be protected or actively managed for biodiversity conservation. This figure reflects expert estimates of the minimum area needed.[7]

Although around 8 per cent of the UK is designated as Sites of Special Scientific Interest (SSSIs or ASSIs) the protection granted by this designation is not adequate.[8] Although many SSSIs are used for agriculture or forestry without damaging their special interest, 200–300 sites are damaged every year and many more are at risk: at least 838 of the 6103 SSSIs are currently under some form of threat of damage.[9] For example, Thorne and Hatfield moors have been repeatedly damaged by planning permissions pre-dating SSSI designation and are now under threat from excessive water abstraction; at Twyford Down conservation designations were overridden by the Department of Transport; at Cardiff Bay the Urban Development Corporation persuaded the last Government to use a Parliamentary Private Bill to allow the construction of a barrage to destroy the site. But beyond these celebrated cases (and a host of others) where habitat destruction is legalised, are many cases where damage is in contravention of the law, but even if brought to court the crime carries such a small penalty as to give little disincentive.[10] Friends of the Earth is promoting changes in the legislation governing SSSIs to ensure adequate legal protection for these sites.[11] Effective changes in the law would go far towards achieving the target for protected area.[12]

Habitat restoration and expansion schemes are needed for key habitats if we are to achieve acceptable levels of protection. This has begun with projects aimed at the Caledonian Forest and the lowland heathlands typified by the Dorset Heaths made famous by Thomas Hardy (see Box 6.1). But these are only a beginning.

# BOX 6.1 *EXAMPLES OF HABITAT RESTORATION SCHEMES*

*Caledonian pine forest*

There are roughly 12,000 hectares of Caledonian pinewoods in Scotland today. These pinewoods once dominated Scotland, covering 1.5 million hectares. Grazing, felling for timber and clearing for farming reduced this area to 16,000 hectares by 1950; since then a further 25 per cent of this has been lost through clear felling and under-planting with exotic conifers. Over the last 20 years the Royal Society for the Protection of Birds (RSPB) has acquired the Abernethy Forest Reserve, in Speyside, which includes 15 per cent of the remaining native pine in Scotland.[a] Yearly culls of the large red deer population have given all vegetation types the chance to recover, and seedlings and saplings have been increasing, leading to a recovery of the existing pinewood. It is expected that in the long term the area of pinewood should increase to its former extent in the reserve.[b]

*Lowland heaths*

The UK has only 30 per cent of the area of lowland heathland it had in 1800 (58,000 hectares remaining of over 190,000), but still holds an important proportion (about 20 per cent) of the world total of this habitat. The restoration action plan aims to maintain and improve existing lowland heathland and also encourage re-establishment of 6000 ha of heathland by 2005 to link existing separate heathland fragments. There are 67,000 ha of recently modified heathland with the potential for restoration. The target represents a modest attempt to restore degraded heath area equivalent to approximately 10 per cent of the existing lowland heathland resource.[c]

Sources: *a* Newton, I and Moss, D (1977) Breeding birds of Scottish pinewoods *Native pinewoods of Scotland Symposium* 1975; *b* Beaumont, D, Dugan, D, Evans, G and Taylor, S (1994) Management of deer for the regeneration of Caledonian Pine Forest at the RSPB's Abernethy Forest Reserve *RSPB Conservation Review* 8; Bain, C and Bainbridge, I (1988) A better future for our native pinewoods? *RSPB Conservation Review* 2; *c* Her Majesty's Government (1994) *Biodiversity: the UK action Plan* London: HMSO

There are other measures which will help ensure that the UK adequately protects its best habitats and rarest species. Under the European Habitats directive, the British Government is obliged to designate Special Areas of Conservation (SACs): these should afford nature sites better protection as the legal mechanisms for their protection are stronger. The area of SACs and Special Protection Areas designated under the Birds Directive – which have a more or less equivalent level of protection – would be a good indicator of progress against the 10 per cent target. At present only 1,182,500 ha or 5 per cent of the UK area is so designated, or proposed for designation. To meet a simple target for adequately protected area should be easy, even by 2010. The mechanisms largely exist to deliver a larger and better protected area for habitat and biodiversity conservation: SACs designation and tougher SSSI protection. But without policies and practices to promote biodiversity protection in the wider countryside, protecting key areas of natural or seminatural habitats will not be enough. The idea of targets and action plans for specific protected species and habitats at risk in the UK has already been officially accepted, but the mechanisms to implement them in the face of countervailing policies and practices threatening biodiversity, promoted by other government departments such as the Ministry of Agriculture and the Department of Transport, are still largely absent.

For the UK to contribute fairly to the global target of protecting at least 10 per cent of land of all major ecological types does place some constraints on our agricultural systems, principally in terms of the management practices required. However in some areas, the restoration of grassland, heathland or woodland ecologies may require the return of arable land to other uses. Assuming that no more than 10 per cent of total increase in protected area will be achieved through such restoration schemes, this implies a net shift from arable to protected land of about 50,000 hectares.[13] Our global calculations for land use are based on the assumption that additional land for biodiversity protection will not reduce the net area of agricultural land, but this cannot hold strictly for the UK, where land is already more intensively used, and many of our protected sites are often already islands in a sea of intensive agriculture.

# LIVING SPACE FOR AN URBAN RACE

Whether we are discussing cities or modern intensive farms, specialised land uses are increasingly dependent on external inputs, especially of energy. The provision of food, energy and materials for our cities effectively takes up many times the land area occupied by roads and buildings. Film-maker and writer Herbert Girardet has estimated that London's 'ecological footprint' is 125 times its area.[14] While such a reliance on external inputs is not necessarily unsustainable – we would almost certainly find ourselves using even more resources if we spread the population of London out over 125 times the current area – it is a helpful indicator. And while the costs of transport are so much less than its true environmental costs, those external inputs tend to travel much further than is necessary, consuming yet more energy in the process.

In fact, urban sprawl – the expansion of urban areas – is not just a concern for lovers of the UK countryside. The physical size of cities in developing countries is expected to double between 1980 and 2000. Around certain cities, urban land expansion is occurring even faster. In Sao Paulo, Brazil, the urban core grew from an area of 180 square kilometres in

1930 to more than 900 square kilometres in 1988.[15] Estimates suggest that as much as 476,000 hectares of arable land in developing countries is being transformed annually to urban uses.[16] And it becomes ever more critical; as natural frontiers close, as less new land is available for conversion to agriculture, the loss of the best and most fertile land to essentially irreversible urban development is a deeper loss. Similarly, now that there is little if any wildlife habitat unaffected by humans in the UK, the destruction and fragmentation of what remains by road building such as at Newbury or Twyford Down, or for housing and other urban developments, is not only more controversial but also a greater threat to biodiversity.

Encroachment onto productive land or valued habitats is not the only criterion to judge the sustainable use of land for urban development. The built infrastructure of our urban areas accounts for much of the stock of materials in our economy and for around 30 per cent of the flow of materials through our economy (excluding water).[17] Patterns and forms of urban development which reduce its energy and material intensity are, virtually by definition, more sustainable.

## Sustainable Cities in the UK

There has been wide debate, and some research on the relationship between urban form and energy, and to a lesser extent, materials use. Most of the evidence suggests that forms of development that utilise traditional three to four storey terraced building types, typical of much Georgian and Victorian housing, are the most energy and materials efficient. Building higher than this is more energy intensive in construction and requires lifts for access. It is also generally more materials intensive, requiring steel frames and more substantial foundations. On the other hand, low density, one to two storey development is less energy efficient in use, both because it has more outside walls increasing heat loss, and because lower densities increase car use, as they support fewer local services.[18] Low-rise development is also more material intensive because there are fewer shared walls, and more materials required to provide roads and other infrastructure. In simplistic land consumption terms, medium to high densities are clearly more efficient.

This evidence helps create a set of arguments for urban forms generally termed 'compact cities'. They complement and reinforce arguments about quality of life. To optimise quality of life in cities we need safe and largely traffic-free streets, good local facilities, including street markets, shops, parks, formal and informal education facilities for all ages, arts and cultural venues and healthcare facilities. Many of these can only be provided efficiently in the compact city form. Both empirical and modelled evidence supports the argument that higher urban densities can reduce the need to travel, and 'there is no evidence to show that high

densities are necessarily associated with disbenefits in energy use in buildings, in mental or physical health, or in terms of crime, equity or quality
of life'.[19] There are those who argue against policies to promote compact
cities. Some, who perversely assume that car use cannot be reduced even
where local services are available and streets traffic-calmed, argue that
such cities would simply become more congested and polluted (and thus
more wasteful of energy too).[20] Others believe that to advocate such
urban forms is promoting uniformity instead of the cultural and historical diversity reflected in our cities now. But one has only to compare the
diversity of thriving urban quarters where the density of population and
services is high with the soulless monocultures of modern car-based
surburbs to realise how ludicrous this argument is.[21]

# Housing in Cities

We cannot simply assume that all need for new development will be accommodated within existing urban areas in the UK. There is a potential need,
identified by the Department of the Environment, to accommodate an
estimated 4.4 million extra households in England alone by 2016. Wales is
predicted to need an additional 200,000 homes, while figures are not available for Northern Ireland and Scotland. We use a UK figure of 5.2 million
by extrapolating simply according to population.[22] If past trends in development patterns continue, England's urban area will have increased to
between 11.5 and 16.6 per cent of the land area by 2012, and by 2050 to
between 12.3 and 20 per cent.[23] Whatever the rate of change, in the long
term, such continuing growth of the urban area is unsustainable. This is
not simply because of the consumption of ever more land, but the fact
that such growth has formed patterns of development – related to high
car-borne mobility – which are highly inefficient in transport terms, and
severely constrain our ability to reduce $CO_2$ emissions from transport.[24]
There will inevitably be continued pressures to expand the urban area and
build houses on greenfield sites. But there is great potential to increase the
efficiency with which we use land and building space in our cities. From
increasing density and regenerating derelict land, to filling empty properties
and converting flats above shops, there are many options which need to be
taken forward more rapidly than at present.

    These options are not being taken up at present. As ever, perhaps
the most influential reasons are economic. The apparent costs of greenfield development are low, with developers rarely meeting the full costs
of associated new infrastructure. To illustrate the point, in 1991 it cost
A$35,000 per house in outer Western Sydney just to provide kerbs, roads,
footpaths, fences, water and sewer services.[25] Although some argue that
the planning system inflates land prices by limiting the supply to that
designated for development in plans, rather than allowing new develop-

ment anywhere, this can be viewed in a very different way. In south-east UK, for example, structure plans allocated 59 per cent more land than required to meet housing projections in 1992, and 34 per cent more in 1993.[26] This effectively depresses the price of land far below what would prevail in a precautionary system which required new developments to demonstrate that they were sustainable before granting permission.

At the same time, while car travel is cheap, demand for such detached and semi-detached country and suburban homes remains high. So new houses on greenfield sites can, all too often, be built cheap and sold dear. And the role of 'housing starts' as a key indicator in our economic mythology means that such new development earns more political weight than refurbishment and improvement activity to fill existing empty dwellings, although it normally carries greater resource costs. While sale prices for new homes in prime urban locations can also be high, the incentive to develop here is lower, as the costs of redevelopment are generally much higher. These include land purchase, site assembly, construction on constrained sites, clearance and possibly decontamination, adding as much as £100,000 an acre to the costs according to British Gas.[27] Moreover, the draining of resources and the tax base from our cities with out-migration has meant that many areas of our cities have become unsafe and unattractive. In such areas, development costs remain high, but sale prices are relatively low, so there is little new private development. A tax or levy on new greenfield development, as proposed by the Round Table on Sustainable Development,[28] might help redirect the attention of builders.

In the social housing sector, investment in city housing has suffered from similar financial pressures, especially as grant settlements from central government have declined. The imposition of value added tax (VAT) on property refurbishment, while new-build is free of VAT, means that housing associations can ill afford to refurbish properties, however much they would prefer to. The same constraint acts on private developers too, but for housing associations the effect was reinforced when grants to housing associations started to be allocated by competitive bidding after the 1988 Housing Act. At this point, many associations stopped refurbishing derelict properties and switched largely to new-build. By 1995, the London Development Control Forum calculated that new-build was more than 25 per cent cheaper than refurbishment.[29] Although there is no longer VAT on conversion of vacant commercial space to housing – a shift that stimulated a mini-boom in such conversion activity – this differential should be eliminated from all conversion activity.[30]

The pattern in housing provision in part reflects expressed public preferences for the 'country life'.[31] Such expressed preferences relate poorly to the reality of rural life: few services, little social contact, limited employment opportunities, need for high car use and high house prices (especially in relation to local wages).[32] Yet the preferences are promoted and reinforced by the advertising strategies of the housebuilders promoting a rural idyll. Changing these preferences requires measures to improve the urban environment and services.[33] A survey by Strathclyde University which set out to find the areas of the UK with the highest perceived quality of life concluded that, given the choice, people would choose to live in a place which has low levels of crime, good health service provision, low levels of pollution, a low cost of living, good shopping facilities and one which enjoys racial harmony.[34] In these terms, Edinburgh came top, demonstrating that a high-quality dense urban environment can clearly provide a high quality of life.

*Empty Properties*

Making more efficient use of the existing housing stock, through reducing the number of empty properties, is the first step. In April 1995, there were 804,000 empty homes (or 3.9 per cent) in England; 28,000 (or 2.3 per cent) in Wales; 35,000 (or 5.8 per cent) in Northern Ireland; and 130,000 (or 5.9 per cent) in Scotland. In the UK as a whole there were almost 1 million empty homes (997,000 or 4.1 per cent of the stock).[35] Amongst property owners, the worst offender, by a large margin, is the Government: its property is 16 per cent vacant. However, the Government owns a relatively small number of homes, so most empty homes are in the private sector. Overall, the vacancy rate in the UK is currently almost 1 in every 25 houses and over half of these have been empty for prolonged periods. This figure can never be reduced to zero because of turnover, but the current level is far higher than necessary.[36] Levels of empty homes vary greatly over the country. London has some of the worst rates for empty houses with an average of 5.86 per cent, 131,128 empty properties. Within London, there are wide variations. If each borough were to achieve Harrow's rates for the private sector, Barnet's for local authority housing, and Sutton's for Housing Association properties, then there would be just 27,645 empty properties, a rate of just 1.2 per cent.[37] But to achieve anything like this rate will require targeted investment to improve homes and to bring them back into use.

A relatively unambitious target of reducing the rate to 3 per cent in the next ten years has been enshrined in the Housing Act of 1996 which requires local authorities to draw up strategies to fill empty properties. However, there is little money earmarked to help local authorities meet this target. They must use their limited resources to encourage private investment in currently empty property. Reading's empty homes strategy shows how this can work. To date it has returned over 250 empty properties into use, creating around 270 homes, and housing over 700 people.[38] A total investment of at least £4m in private sector funds has been levered in to regenerate empty properties. These 'recycled' properties generate an annual rental income of over £1 million for owners. The Housing Act target amounts to around 70 properties per council per year. This is less than the real potential: Portsmouth has dealt with 200 in the last year and New Forest brought over 100 homes back into use in just six months. These are not places with especially bigger than average housing stocks, they are just doing a better job by focusing resources in this area. Bringing houses back in to use is good for landlords as well as tenants.The average cost to the landlord of keeping a property empty is £5680 a year.[39] Removing or reducing the council tax rebate on empty dwellings would further increase the financial incentive to ensure that homes do not stand empty for long. In the UK as a whole, achieving the Environment Committee's target of 2 per cent vacancy levels would effectively add 516,000 properties to the housing stock before taking account of any scope for subdivision of these properties to create more, smaller housing units.

Several councils, such as Brighton and Portsmouth, use deposit guarantee schemes to help fill empty properties. Such schemes do not only meet environmental objectives, they directly help meet social needs too, by providing homes to those in need. In 1995 the Joseph Rowntree Foundation published research suggesting that over 100,000 affordable homes a year needed to be made available for the next 20 years in England alone.[40] Clearly, a substantial share of the homes provided by new-build, refurbishment and bringing empty properties into use must be targeted at those in housing need. There is also vast potential for increasing the number of homes above commercial and retail outlets, a potential targeted by the Living Over The Shop programme (LOTS).[41] In 1992 the English House Condition Survey found 63,000 vacant flats above shops in England. So far, very few of them have been filled. Yet there are queues of tenants wanting to move in, and queues of landlords wanting rent revenues. Empty homes strategies could be instrumental in bringing them together.

*Increasing Residential Density*

Since the Government issued a revised Planning Policy Guidance Note 13 in March 1994, local authorities have begun to incorporate specific housing density policies into their plans, as promoted by Friends of the Earth in 'Planning for the Planet'.[42] Sunderland is one of many such councils. Their 1995 Unitary Development Plan states:

> *There are also benefits to be gained from locating higher density housing close to shops and community facilities as this also minimises the need to travel by car ... In urban terms, higher densities enable a return to the traditional street rather than suburban-style estates.*

Peter Newman and Jeff Kenworthy, who have studied this issue in cities all over the world, report two density thresholds for automobile dependence. They note that public transport use becomes much more viable at net residential densities over 90–120 persons per hectare and that walking becomes important at net densities over 300 persons per hectare.[43] So to get these benefits of increasing residential densities means raising them from the levels typical of new greenfield development – which rarely exceed net densities of 100 persons per hectare – to 225–300 persons per hectare in urban areas generally and up to 370 persons per hectare in central or especially accessible locations. This does not mean cramming everyone into back-to-back terraces or tower blocks, which deliver net residential densities more in the range of 500–800 persons per hectare. What it does mean is the equivalent of Georgian three to four storey terraced development.

Such planning measures are not without their opponents. The House Builders' Federation and the big volume builders lobby strongly to protect and further their interests through influencing planning regulations and the decisions of local planning authorities, especially through appeals against refusal of planning permission if their more conventional proposals are rejected. However, developers are not solely to blame for the failure of new developments to achieve suitably high densities. Although some development plans are promoting higher densities – and architects too tend to favour such densities in urban locations – many such proposals are rejected in practice. A survey of developers revealed that many believe that development plans should set high maximum density levels, but that high density schemes are often rejected because planners take the view that developers are only interested in trying to extract the maximum level of profit from the site. Moreover, planners still demand high levels of car parking on new developments. Despite recent improvements, the planning system still pivots around the requirements of the car, road capacity influencing development location and parking provision dictating density.[44]

Planners are being over-cautious about car parking issues. Consultants Llewelyn Davies' report to the DOE on providing more homes in urban areas said that in typical housing layouts a similar amount of space is given over to cars, regardless of whether the prevailing rate of car ownership is 0.4 cars per household or 0.8. They concluded that: 'local authority car parking standards appear to be overspecified and insensitive to local circumstances'.[45] According to Llewelyn Davies, if only 40 per cent of homes were to enjoy an off-street space this would comfortably allow a 25 per cent increase in housing density. Even this is too cautious. Overall, land for transport functions, largely dedicated to cars, takes up at least 20 per cent of our urban areas; this figure excludes off-road parking.[46] Llewelyn Davies concluded that: 'In most new development the equivalent of at least two habitable rooms is given over to cars for each home built'. Car-free areas could allow very significant increases in housing density of almost 50 per cent.[47] Conventional developments typically provide at least one car parking space per house; in the Edinburgh 'car-free' development project there will be one space for every ten dwellings.

## Conversion to Flats

Overly high car parking standards particularly hinder the conversion of houses into flats. This is seldom permitted if the front gardens cannot be turned into car parks. In London, according to Llewelyn Davies, current parking standards rule out up to 70 per cent of the capacity for conversions. Davies examined the remaining potential for conversion by examining three representative urban areas: Newcastle, Lewisham and Cheltenham. About 18,000 of the 25,000 large houses (all with seven or more 'habitable' rooms) in the study areas are under-occupied. Converting all of these could create a net gain of 34,000 houses without affecting the stock of smaller 'family unit' homes. This takes no account of 'their intrinsic suitability for conversion or of the cumulative effects of so many conversions'.[48] But the cumulative effects, if managed properly, could be positive rather than negative: improving the density of and support for local services and thus further reducing the need for car ownership. There are 47 equivalent sets of urban areas in the UK with similar populations. Assuming cautiously that only 50 per cent of the properties would be suitable for conversion would provide a net gain of 800,000 dwellings.

## Converting Empty Commercial Space

There is also great potential for converting empty commercial space into housing, particularly if car parking issues are not allowed to constrain such development. LOTS report that

> *whilst politicians, academics and the media continually declare the need to create living city centres, the reality is that ... under-use is increasing ... [and] despite the widespread concern about the need to repopulate town centres, the level of conversion work is lower than in 1992.*[49]

They estimate that for every existing empty flat there is empty space for ten more, which has never been in residential use or is no longer classed as residential. This suggests that as many as 630,000 dwellings could be provided in this empty space in England alone. There are large empty areas in every city. For example, the centre of Newcastle has 1.7 million sq feet empty (enough for at least 7000 people) and 75 per cent of upper floors in Chester are empty.[50] In the absence of more comprehensive data we assume, conservatively, that in the UK as a whole, 440,000 dwellings could be provided through such conversions by 2010, and 630,000 by 2016. Indeed, the LOTS project has, so far, been more successful in bringing some of this space into use, than existing empty flats.[51]

As well as increasing the housing stock, filling floors above shops offers many other advantages: stimulating and supporting urban regeneration by increasing local trade and providing a livelier and safer town centre. Moreover, over the shop accommodation generally creates small dwellings, and centrally-located dwellings are particularly attractive to small households, so as household sizes decline they will be especially appropriate.

## Using Derelict Sites

There are around 24,000 hectares of derelict urban land in the UK of which approximately 21,660 hectares is potentially reclaimable.[52] As 9500 hectares of derelict land was reclaimed between 1988 and 1993, the rate implied if all this land were to be reclaimed by 2016 seems attainable. Easily half of this land could be developed for residential uses, even accounting for leaving some of it untouched for its value for biodiversity or as open space. Although higher densities would be preferable, raising redevelopment densities to average London densities (170 people per hectare) would be a great improvement over current practice. At such densities this use of derelict sites would provide homes for around 850,000 households.[53]

## Increasing Densities in Redevelopment

Each year 1635 hectares of residential urban land is redeveloped.[54] Even assuming that this land is already at higher than average densities (170 persons per hectare), by 2016 an additional 1,350,000 households could be accommodated by increasing densities by 50 per cent in redevelopment (and assuming an average household size of 2.17).[55] In practice, the rate of redevelopment needs to increase to reverse the slow deterioration of the housing stock, especially in energy efficiency terms. There are large areas in poor condition, especially some of those last redeveloped in the 1950s and 1960s, which account for about a quarter of the current housing stock[56] and offer opportunities for intensification in redevelopment. Assuming that by 2016 the annual rate of redevelopment has been doubled, then a total of almost 50,000 hectares would be redeveloped, providing space for 2,030,000 households. By 2010, just over 30,000 hectares would have been redeveloped, providing space for 1,274,000 households. By 2050, for purposes of illustration, such redevelopment could house an extra 6.6 million households, if such rates of redevelopment were to continue. By 2050 at least another quarter of all houses would be over 60–70 years old, including many of those built at very low densities in the last two decades. By 2016 this implies a renewal rate of around 0.9 per cent of the housing stock each year.[57]

Our estimates are based on 50 per cent increases in net residential densities. This might seem a lot, but it can be achieved even in refurbishment of typical city houses. Innovative rehabilitation techniques can increase floor space by 50 per cent, and provide 4 dwellings and 17 bedspaces in houses that if conventionally rehabilitated would provide three dwellings and ten bed-spaces.[58] The technique, although more materially intensive, as it renews everything apart from the facade, scores highly on energy efficiency, able to achieve scores of 8–10 on the National Home Energy Rating Scheme, in comparison with scores in the order of five for traditional rehabilitation. There are limits to intensification. The failed experiments of 1960s tower block living show that very clearly. But these density levels do not approach them. High density, high-quality car-free development could free-up space for public spaces, allotments and gardens. In other words, we can achieve densities that seem unrealistic to those used only to conventional development patterns and preferences expressed in today's constrained market.[59] Moreover, densities at the levels we advocate are not bad for mental health. Similarly, crime will not increase simply because densities are increased. In fact density tends to have a negative effect on crime, due in part to the effects of greater surveillance by others.[60]

## Housing and Other Environmental Space Resources

Affordable shelter is a basic need and indeed a basic human right. If sustainable development is to meet needs, then it must provide homes for us all. In this chapter we have focused on the use of land. But our homes also account for much of the stock of materials in our economy and a significant share of energy and water use. New buildings can save land, and incorporate green design principles: using less, but more-environmentally sensitive, materials in construction, and minimising the need for electricity and energy use through a range of measures. For example, in energy terms, up to 50 per cent improvements can be achieved simply by building in flats or terraces rather than free-standing detached houses.[61]

## Conclusions on 'Living Space'

Current urban land use is 1.8 million hectares. In theory this could be reduced to a more optimal level by increasing population densities and reducing the area given over to cars. But there are other pressures. By 2016, as we saw earlier, the average household size is expected to fall to 2.1 persons, but millions of new households will form. If England is typical of the UK as a whole – a cautious assumption – then we need to provide some 4.6 million new dwellings by 2016, or 3.1 million by our interim target year of 2010.[62] We have presented estimates of the potential to provide additional homes through use of derelict sites, unoccupied

**Table 6.1** *Providing Dwellings for 4.6 Million Additional Households*

| Policy measure | Additional households (2010) | Additional households (2016) |
|---|---|---|
| Reducing vacancy rates for housing | 516,000 | 516,000 |
| Conversion of large houses to flats | 560,000 | 800,000 |
| Conversion of empty commercial space | 440,000 | 630,000 |
| Reusing derelict land | 590,000 | 850,000 |
| Increasing densities in redevelopment | 1,274,000 | 2,030,000 |
| Total | 3,380,000 | 4,826,000 |

buildings and various forms of conversion which are summarised in Table 6.1.[63]

In total, the figures suggest that the UK can deliver the additional homes that we expect to need, and a few more besides to help relieve 'hidden' homelessness too, and that this can be done within our existing cities, towns and villages without 'towncramming' and worsening quality of life. So we need not take up more land for urban development. But it's a very big political nettle to grasp and it will take a stronger land use planning system than we have now. In looking to the future, our sustainability scenario will assume no significant increase in urban land area, in comparison with 'business as usual' which would take around 80,000 hectares of greenfield sites to provide new homes for the new households expected to form by 2016.[64]

## SUSTAINABLE FOOD SUPPLY

Underlying our approach to environmental space for food production is the concept of food security – not primarily at a national but an individual level.[65] The basic human need is not simply for food, but for a secure, predictable and nutritionally balanced supply. This need is not always met, either in the North or the South. In both regions poverty threatens food security, as does the process in which control over food production and distribution has passed to non-local companies, mainly transnationals. The mechanisms of distribution do need to be addressed, but our focus is upon establishing what a fair distribution would mean in quantitative terms. The food–land–population equation is at the heart of the classic Malthusian argument that while population and therefore consumption tend to increase exponentially, agricultural production, on the other hand, could only increase geometrically. Now, over 200 years after Malthus, we know that this simplistic analysis was wrong. Overall agricultural production has more than kept pace with demand, by a combination of expansion of the productive area, and increasing yields through the application of new technology. Even in recent years overall global food production has grown faster than world population.[66] However, there are at least three threats to sustainability in the current model.

First, the distribution of food is such that eating disorders and health problems from overconsumption are growing alongside malnutrition; each affecting millions of the planet's people. Eight hundred million people on this planet do not have enough food to meet their basic nutritional needs.[67] Sixty-seven per cent of under-fives in Bangladesh are malnourished, as are 53 per cent of Indians.[68] Yet about one-third of all Americans are officially obese. In the UK 16 per cent of adults are obese, while up to one in five parents and one in ten children occasionally go without food because of poverty.[69] Second, production techniques geared to increase the productivity of land in use are unsustainable.[70] Modern agricultural systems are heavily dependent on external inputs of energy and materials, which are themselves limited in availability. The wastes and pollution – including pesticides and fertilisers which leach into rivers, groundwater and seas – resulting from specialised intensive agriculture have a major impact on natural systems. Third, there is a finite limit to the expansion of productive agricultural land. Table 6.2 shows the current distribution of global land use, and a prediction of the situation in 2010 based on estimates for likely trends in land use change.[71] These figures provide the basis for broad estimates of agriculturally productive land per capita: at present, 0.83 ha per capita, and in 2010, 0.71 ha per capita (assuming a world population of around 7 billion). Figure 6.1 shows the broad pattern of land use in Britain.

**Table 6.2** *Global Land Use Patterns*

| Land Use | Current area (billion hectares) | Predicted – 2010 (billion hectares) |
|---|---|---|
| Global land area | 13.08 | 13.08 |
| Forests and woodland | 4.18 | 3.88 |
| Agricultural land | | |
| cropland | 1.44 | 1.51 |
| pasture and rangeland | 3.36 | 3.49 |
| Other land | 4.09 | 4.2 |

Source: Postel, S (1994) Carrying Capacity: The Earth's Bottom Line.
In Mazur, L (ed) (1994) *Beyond the Numbers* Washington: Island Press

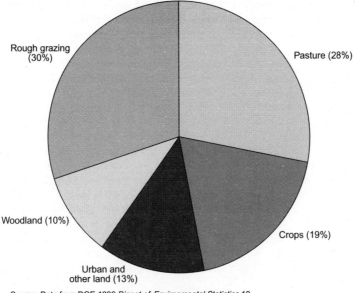

Source: Data from DOE 1996 *Digest of Environmental Statistics* 18

**Figure 6.1** *UK land use*

Some of these trends are clearly unsustainable. The net conversion of forest to agricultural land must be halted, while the increase of 'other land', due to erosion and degradation, and conversion to urban uses, must be minimised. In addition, a significant area needs to be dedicated to biodiversity conservation. At present around 5 billion hectares of land are in agricultural use including pastures and rangelands. Even assuming that the majority of additional land protected for biodiversity comes from forests and from 'other land' we cannot assume that there is significant scope for a substantial sustainable increase in world agricultural land, although there may be scope for some transfer of rangeland and pasture to cropland, which could increase overall productivity.

Even the small increases in agricultural land predicted in Table 6.2 would be won at high cost, based, as they are, on other unsustainable trends. The most optimistic estimates suggest that almost 4 billion hectares are cultivatable and that over 4 billion hectares more could then be available as pasture or rangeland for livestock. But this would mean taking large areas of forest or savannah into cultivation. Moreover, there are other, opposite trends. Cities in developing countries are growing fast: Karachi, Lahore, Lagos and Kinshasa are expected to grow by 3 per cent a year for the next 20 years.[72] Land-take for urban development in developing countries is running at around half a million hectares a year,[73] and seems set to grow. Also, much land already in use has proved liable to

**Table 6.3** *Estimates for Per Capita Availability of Environmental Space of Productive Agricultural Land in 2050*

|  | *Low population (7.9 bn)* | *Medium population (9.8 bn)* | *High population (11.9 bn)* |
|---|---|---|---|
| No increase in area available (4.8 bn ha) | 0.61 | 0.49 | 0.40 |
| Small increase in area available (5.2 bn ha) | 0.66 | 0.53 | 0.44 |

Source: Increased land availability based on Postel's estimates to 2010 and a falling rate of conversion of forested land thereafter, resulting in a total increase in availability of agricultural land in 2050 twice that predicted by Postel for 2010. Postel, S (1994) Carrying Capacity: The Earth's Bottom Line. In Mazur, L (ed) (1994) *Beyond the Numbers* Washington: Island Press

erosion and degradation. We do not believe that any major expansion could be undertaken sustainably. For the purpose of our calculations of environmental space, we assume that there will be no net increase in agricultural area by 2050. Table 6.3 shows our estimates for per capita availability.

These figures must be put in perspective. First, we have to take into account productivity. Even at current global average productivity, the land available in 2050 could feed a global population of 10 billion if the food it produced were to be fairly distributed. Famine and malnutrition are not a result of absolute food shortages, but of inequitable distribution of food, and perhaps more importantly in most areas, of access to land to grow food. In practice an assumption that average productivity in 2050 could be at the current world average is in fact very cautious. During the 1980s per capita food production in developing countries as a whole rose by 14 per cent.[74] The adoption of more sustainable practices will not reduce such gains, but reinforce them.[75] We are not basing our estimates for changes in productivity on further substantial increases in yields in already intensive agricultural systems, so the estimates are not affected by concerns over physiological limits to crops' response to fertiliser.

To estimate sustainability targets we explicitly treat land as a global resource. We believe that in a sustainable future there is no place for the nationalist politics of land resources. For centuries the UK has exploited land all over the world, and treated it as its fair share. Now we are in a position where we must estimate what a fair share really is. This means aiming for a net balance of trade so that our total use of land, wherever it is in the world, is no greater than our fair share. To do this we use a measure of average productivity under sustainable practices to reflect the varying quality of land and climate.

# FOOD AND LAND IN THE UK

To estimate sustainable land requirements for food production we must be confident that our estimates of yields are based on sustainable production techniques.[76] The combination of subsidies for food production in developed countries, alongside inappropriate agricultural development aid focused on modern intensive techniques and cash-cropping for export has actually done as much to undermine food security in many developing countries as it has done to improve it. In the UK, although it seems likely that productivity per hectare will fall in the short term as a result of a reduction or cessation of intensive inputs, there is growing evidence that a whole range of more sustainable, low-input forms of agriculture can reach almost as high output levels as industrial high-input agriculture achieves now. Critically, such practices can go on achieving such yields indefinitely, while providing a decent living for farmers. Generally, the loss in yield per hectare is no greater than some 5–10 per cent for crops and 10–20 per cent for livestock.[77]

These levels of output are being achieved even with the currently poor levels of research and development and other support that such techniques receive in comparison with conventional techniques. Moreover, this yield 'penalty' is only a problem if it is viewed from a single-minded perspective of maximising food output in the short term. This is, of course, now far from the case in the UK. As European Union and individual state policies are now targeted to reduce output through the use of the set aside mechanism, this yield penalty can be seen as an alternative, and more sustainable, means of achieving this goal. Currently, the amount of UK land under rotational set aside is 328,000 hectares.[78] There are 4,469,000 hectares of cropland in use in the UK. Adding in the set aside land would increase the area by 7.3 per cent. So changing to sustainable agriculture on all the arable area (with a yield drop of 5–10 per cent) would have little effect on the amount of food produced. In developing countries, the picture is, if anything, even brighter. Time and time again, researchers are finding that sustainable and regenerative techniques using few external inputs are increasing yields in a sustained fashion. Pretty cites figures from Brazil, Senegal, India and Honduras, to name but a few, where cereal yields were increased by 2.5 to 3 times.[79] These figures contrast with many of the conventional intensive attempts to increase yields which lasted only until the new 'wonder variety' of rice or maize proved vulnerable to a previously unregarded pest or disease or until the problems of soil erosion or water shortage proved unbearable.[80]

There is not just one sustainable system. Pretty explains how the range of techniques and technologies which he describes as 'regenerative agriculture' incorporate natural processes, reduce use of external inputs, reflect local climate, ecology and cultures and remain productive and profitable.[81] Sustainability of agricultural systems can and should be measured in wide terms, including people's diets and health, and the number and quality of work opportunities they provide. A fundamental feature of unsustainable policy making is its failure to consider the multiplicity of goals and outcomes relevant to the issue at hand. Modern techniques may have achieved efficient food production, but only if, for example, we disregard dependence on external inputs of energy and materials, the degradation of soils, the erosion of genetic diversity, the declining quality of diets, the cruelty imposed on animals in factory farms, and the hardship and poverty of the displaced and unemployed agricultural labourers. A sustainable society would require an integrated policy for agriculture which took account of these different factors; what could be described as 'multifunctional agriculture'. The extent to which one more sustainable system – organic farming – meets many of these wider objectives is outlined in Box 6.2.

For the purposes of this report we have assumed conversion of UK production to organic agriculture. But this is only for simplicity of calculation. At present we see organic agriculture as the clearest example of a proven 'sustainable technique', but this should not be taken as excluding the possibility that other production techniques could meet appropriate aspects of sustainability. If anything, other sustainable techniques may incur smaller short-term yield reductions.[82] We have assumed, conservatively, that conversion to sustainable production will reduce crop yields on average by 10 per cent in 2010 but that by 2050 this penalty will have been reduced to 5 per cent. Some figures for relative yields in organic production are much poorer. However, this is, at least in part, the result of such produce falling foul of unnecessarily high cosmetic standards of appearance for fruit and vegetables that result in perfectly edible produce being rejected, especially by supermarkets.[83] Current organic yields imply a decline of 21–31 per cent, although this takes no account of the factors mentioned above.[84]

## Livestock and Factory Farming

In many parts of the country stocking levels are kept high, especially in dairy systems, by high levels of use of chemical fertiliser. But even where this is not the limiting factor, such as in many upland areas, stocking densities may still have to be cut.[85] Concerns have also been raised by the official agencies responsible for nature conservation, who report that the cause of the largest area of damage to the UK's Sites of Special Scientific Interest is overgrazing.[86] So, for the purposes of our estimates of land use requirements under sustainable agricultural systems we can assume that yields per hectare for most livestock systems will fall by the 10–20 per cent suggested above. Aside from questions of yield, some livestock systems have no place in sustainable agriculture. Friends of the Earth believes that

# BOX 6.2 *BENEFITS OF ORGANIC FARMING*

*Biodiversity*

Of the 59 butterfly species in the UK, 25 are threatened. Organic farms have twice as many butterflies as conventional farms.[a] Other pollinating insects such as bees are also threatened by the use of pesticides and loss of habitat principally due to intensive farming.[b] Also, more birds are found on organic farms. A British Trust for Ornithology study found all bird species at higher densities on organic farms. Both hedgerow birds, like the yellowhammer and blue tit, and field dwelling birds like skylark flourished.[c] Greater diversity in crops is also typical of organic systems. In Austria, the amount of maize grown has decreased from 80 per cent to 35 per cent and there is now a greater variety of alternative crops, including Indian millet, buckwheat, sunflowers, white poppy safflower, medicinal plants and spice plants.[d] Where traditional varieties are included, such living gene banks are a far better guarantee for genetic diversity than seed banks in laboratories.

*Human Health*

Organic food has not had pesticides sprayed on it, and contains no pesticide residues. This means that there should be no pesticide health problems, either for the farmworkers growing the food, or for the people eating it. There is continued debate about whether the pesticide residues found in conventional food cause ill health effects. However, the Government recommends through the Department of Health that people should eat carrots because they are good for us, and yet, through the Pesticides Safety Directorate recommends that carrots should be washed, peeled and topped because of the high levels of insecticides that can be found in them. The irony here is that the goodness in carrots is found on or near their surface, but so are the organophosphorus insecticide residues.

*Employment*

Organic farming is good for jobs. In Austria, the number of people working on the land per hectare is 10–50 per cent higher on organic farms,[e] and in Germany data suggest that organic farms employ 10–19 per cent more people than conventional farms.[f] Transition to organic agriculture could also help to stop the drain on jobs caused by the set aside policy. Set aside has led to 4000 lost farming jobs.[g]

Sources: *a* Feber, R (1996) *The effects of organic and conventional farming systems on the abundance of butterflies* London: SAFE Alliance and Butterfly Conservation Trust. Two types of butterfly – the large white and small white – are pests for cabbages and sprouts, but these white butterflies are not found in greater abundance on organic farms; *b* English Nature, cited by Leake, J (1996) Vanishing bees threaten plants *Sunday Telegraph*, 28 July; *c* British Trust for Ornithology and Institute for Arable Crops Research (1995) *The effect of organic farming regimes on breeding and winter bird populations*. Parts I-IV Research Report 154. Rothamsted: BTO and IARC; *d* Pirklhuber, W and Gruedlinger, K (1993) *Der Biologishe Landbau in Oesterreich. Ein Beitrag zur umweltvertraeglichen Landbewirtschaftung* Vienna: Federal Environment Agency; *e* OEKO-WIRT Information service for farmers and consumers. Wartberg, Austria; *f* Jenkins, T and McLaren, D (1994) *Working Future?* London: Friends of the Earth; *g* Ansell, DJ and Tranter, RB (1992) *Set-aside: in Theory and in Practice* Reading: Centre for Agricultural Strategy, University of Reading.

# BOX 6.3 *FEEDING SOUTHERN PEOPLE NOT NORTHERN ANIMALS*

In the last three decades, soya cultivation in Brazil expanded from 200,000 hectares to 26 million hectares. Smallholder producers have been displaced to make way for giant mechanised soya estates, which have triggered massive soil erosion on the Cerrados Plateau, the country's main soya producing area. Many of those displaced have been resettled in the north-east of Brazil, where they have become unwitting instruments of rainforest destruction. Trade in soya has brought Brazil major foreign exchange gains, but it has 'proved considerably more efficient at feeding European cattle than maintaining the livelihoods of poor Brazilians'.[a]

In 1995 the UK alone appropriated over 400,000 hectares of land for soya imports, over half of it in Brazil.[b] Overall, each kilogram of beef produced in Europe requires 5 kilograms of high-protein feedstuffs. In the mid-1980s the supply of feedstuffs diverted over 9 million hectares of land in developing countries, much of it in countries with large populations of rural landless, and where mechanised cultivation of soya is ecologically unsustainable. Despite this the World Bank has continued to support the expansion of soya cultivation in countries such as Bolivia.

Sources: *a* Watkins, K (1995) *The Oxfam Poverty Report* Oxford: Oxfam Publications;

*b* Based on UK government trade data for oil-cake, and Food and Agriculture Organisation yield figures

sustainable agricultural systems should not rely on cruel or unnatural treatment of animals in intensive livestock farming systems. This is not simply because we share many Britons' concern for fair treatment of animals, but because of a range of health and environmental reasons too. BSE is only the latest food scare to arise from the obscene practices of the intensive livestock industry.[87] The UK has net imports each year of 4.29 million tonnes of feeding stuffs for animals – our calculations suggest this is equivalent to an import of 17,500 km$^2$ of land (see Table 6.4). This is an issue for two reasons. First, production of crops for feed can undermine food security in the exporting countries (see Box 6.3), and second, the wastes produced by such intensive systems are a disposal problem and source of pollution – rather than a nutrient resource – because they are concentrated in the wrong places. In the UK, the total national pollution load from livestock excreta is equivalent to that of 150 million people, and there are typically around 1000 pollution incidents from livestock slurry reported each year to the Environment Agency.[88]

Intensive cattle raising brings another problem. Globally, cattle are responsible for about 15 per cent of emissions of methane – a potent greenhouse gas[89] and energy use per kilo of meat is estimated to be some 60 per cent higher in intensive systems.[90]

**Table 6.4** *Net Import of Land into the UK (hectares, 1995)*

| | | | |
|---|---|---|---|
| Animal feed stuffs | 1,750,000 | Rice | 61,000 |
| Oils | 650,000 | Bananas | 53,000 |
| Cocoa beans | 430,000 | Groundnuts | 48,000 |
| Pork | 320,000 | Malt | −46,000 |
| Natural rubber | 240,000 | Potatoes | 44,000 |
| Wheat | −180,000 | Tobacco | 31,000 |
| Barley | −180,000 | Sugar | 19,000 |
| Coffee | 180,000 | Grapes/dried grapes | 14,000 |
| Cotton | 150,000 | Molasses | 13,000 |
| Beef | 140,000 | Oranges | 13,000 |
| Lamb/mutton | 110,000 | Vegetables | 7000 |
| Maize | 80,000 | Other citrus fruits | 5000 |
| Tea | 73,000 | Coconuts | 4000 |
| Cashew nuts | 67,000 | Others | 7000 |
| | | Total | 4,110,000 |

Notes: Sum of elements may not equal total due to rounding.

Animal feed does not include sugar or fish imports used for feeding animals. Oils includes soya oil, groundnut oil, palm oil, palm kernel oil, sunflower oil, and rapeseed oil.

# Establishing Environmental Space Targets for Productive Land

First we will try to estimate how much land we actually take up at present.[91] Table 6.4 shows the areas used by the principal agricultural crops imported and exported by the UK. Net imported area has been calculated from data on tonnage of foodstuffs and other major agricultural crops traded, and data on food yields in each country.

This includes trade with all countries, for all crops. Data for trade with other EU countries are from 1994. Data for trade with other countries are from 1995. Figures include re-export of finished products where possible, ie the cotton figure is not just cotton seeds, but includes cotton fabrics as well. Similarly, tobacco includes import and export of manufactured as well as unmanufactured tobacco. Timber and paper products, accounting for a net national land import of 7 million hectares, are considered separately in Chapter 7.

Using as a base the figure for UK agricultural land given by the Food and Agriculture Organisation of 17.175 million hectares, the above table implies that the UK currently uses, including 'net imported land', some 21.3 million hectares.[92] To estimate the UK's fair share of agricultural land in 2050, first we need to calculate the average availability of agricultural land per head. With a total world population of 9.8 billion, there is just

**Table 6.5** *UK Environmental Space Targets for Productive Agricultural Land*

| Rest of world yield increase | Low population (7.9 bn) (%) | Medium population (9.8 bn) (%) | High population (11.9 bn) (%) |
|---|---|---|---|
| 25 | −20 | −36 | −46 |
| 50 | −9 | −27 | −40 |
| 75 | 0 | −20 | −33 |

Note: This table shows the change in net use of land appropriated by UK consumption of agricultural products required to meet environmental space targets for productive agricultural land in 2050 under various scenarios.

0.489 hectares per capita.[93] We cannot simply allocate the UK a share of this according to our population, as the land we use is mainly in the UK, and is of much higher average productivity than land elsewhere. The UK's average quality agricultural land will be 1.88 times more productive than the world average.[94] Our fair share of land in 2050 is 29.1 million hectares of world average quality land – simply multiplying UK population by per capita land availability. After applying the quality factor, this equates to 15.5 million hectares of land of British average quality. This compares with our current use of land, 21.3 million hectares, used not only for basic food needs, but for a range of luxury foods and fibre crops. Table 6.5 shows the effective reductions in use of land necessary under different population forecasts, and with different levels of improvement in yields under sustainable agriculture in the rest of the world.[95]

For an interim target for 2010, we apply the same approach as for other resources: achieving one-quarter of the total reduction. This is equivalent to a 7 per cent reduction, or reducing net effective imports of land by about one-third. Our central figure for 2050, a 27 per cent reduction in the UK's total use of productive land, implies a shift from being a net importer of land to the tune of 4.1 million hectares, to a net exporter of some 1.7 million hectares as shown in Figure 6.2.

The challenge is to achieve this, adopt sustainable practices, and continue to feed our own population. We need to minimise the irreversible loss of productive land to urban development, to protect our existing agricultural base. And there are many efficiency measures for increasing the effective yield of sustainable agriculture. Rebalancing our diet, reducing wastage, reversing land degradation and enhancing yields through targeted crop-breeding and a host of other sustainable technologies can all help us obtain more food from the same land in a sustainable manner.

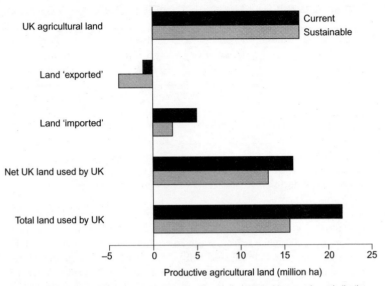

Note: The absolute size of the land imports and exports under the sustainable scenario are indicative of one feasible pattern which would meet the target and include adequate imports to meet our needs for non-temperate products.

**Figure 6.2** *UK agricultural land use – current and sustainable patterns*

# What We Eat

Even without assuming any major changes in land use patterns for agriculture, simply reducing the area available for each product in line with the overall reduction given above, and reducing yields to account for the adoption of sustainable techniques, gives the per capita availability of food shown in Table 6.6.[96] Comparing these figures with the current average diet shows that in most respects this availability would easily provide a diet similar to our current needs. And where this is not possible, either shifting land between crops, or trading could easily achieve the desired end. For example, our deficit in fruit is much less than our surplus in cereals or dairy products.

This leaves us with a surplus over our current diet, roughly equivalent to 2.5 million hectares, even after accounting for the previously mentioned export of 1.7 million hectares.[97] This arises because, first, imports of animal foodstuffs are eliminated, substantially reducing our demand for land for this use. Second, UK crops are no longer used to feed animals. These changes, resulting from the adoption of sustainable livestock farming and the elimination of livestock products surpluses, increase food availablity for people, yet in total, less land is required.

**Table 6.6** *Feeding the UK in 2050*

|  | 2050 availability (g per person per day) | Current diet (g per person per day) | Diet based on current health recommendations (g per person per day) |
| --- | --- | --- | --- |
| Cereals | 564 | 205 | 275 |
| Vegetables | 148 | 178 | 275 |
| Potatoes | 237 | 258 | 275 |
| Fruit | 19 | 104 | 225 |
| Meat | 124 | 195 | 54 |
| Dairy products | 512 | 359 | 290 |
| Fish | 28 | 21 | 32 |
| Oils and Fats | 55 | 55 | 40 |

Source: EU Commission (1995) *Agricultural situation in the EU, 1994 report* Brussels (figures for 1992/93)

Third, there are two implicit assumptions in the calculations which would have the effect of increasing the apparent surplus. These are that no account is taken of foodstuffs used to feed pets, and more significantly, that there is zero wastage in the processing, marketing and consumption of food. Current levels of wastage, estimated at £18 million-worth of food per week, could easily be reduced.[98] But counterbalancing these factors, no account is taken of food grown in gardens or allotments, which currently provides a substantial part of the diet for many people, and could easily be increased even in compact urban areas.[99]

These figures also do not take account of luxuries, and non-food crops, especially those which cannot be grown in the UK. They are based on the assumption that UK production feeds British people. If we want to grow flax for fibre, or oilseeds for chemicals, then this will supplant food production. If we want orange juice, coffee, tea, chocolate, cotton, tobacco and so forth, we will need to trade for these goods. Table 6.7 shows current imports of agricultural products that cannot be grown in the UK, in terms of areas occupied.

This totals 1.4 million hectares. Even if we assume that this land is of the same average quality as UK land, this still leaves a potential surplus of land of around 1.1 million hectares. In other words, we could achieve a 33 per cent reduction in agricultural land use. This would allow for increased protection of natural habitats for biodiversity by restoration of agricultural land (estimated earlier at 50,000 hectares). It also allows some margin for unavoidable wastage of food in processing, marketing and consumption. It may also allow for further development of energy, fibre and chemical crops to reduce the pressure on other aspects of environmental

**Table 6.7** *Area Occupied by Current Imports of Non-domestic Goods*

| Crop | Hectares | Crop | Hectares |
|---|---|---|---|
| Bananas | 53,000 | Cocoa beans | 430,000 |
| Grapes | 14,000 | Cotton | 150,000 |
| Cane sugar | 19,000 | Figs | 500 |
| Cane molasses | 9,600 | Coconuts | 4,000 |
| Orange juice, oranges | 13,000 | Cashew nuts | 67,000 |
| Mandarins | 1,500 | Groundnuts | 48,000 |
| Lemons and limes | 1,600 | Palm oil | 111,500 |
| Grapefruit | 2,000 | Natural rubber | 240,000 |
| Coffee | 180,000 | | |
| Tea | 73,000 | Total | 1,418,000 |

Source: Authors' calculations based on UK trade data and FAO yield data for originating countries

space, or allow the expansion of our forest and woodland areas by about 40 per cent. It would also give us some breathing space if the impacts of past urbanisation and land degradation proved more substantial and significant than we have assumed. However, the land use needs for imports in Table 6.7 are based directly on the areas occupied at present. Some of these are crops whose yields may increase under the adoption of sustainable practices. But most are already rather intensively grown, cotton being a key example. So to sustain current cotton consumption the land area dedicated to cotton may need to increase significantly.[100]

All of this suggests that it may be difficult for us to meet the 2050 targets for agricultural land use without dietary changes. With lower reliance on meat and dairy products as recommended for our health by the government's official advisers, the land area needed would be significantly lower than that needed to provide our current diet. The effective shortage of cropland (10 per cent) would be more than balanced by our surplus of grassland (46 per cent) to provide a net surplus of over 4 million hectares.[101] Although this does assume a rebalancing of our diets to consume less meat and more vegetables, grains and pulses, a deliberate shift of land use from pasture to arable in the UK is not necessary to achieve these goals. A regime in which the UK exports the products of upland pastoral agriculture and imports arable products, especially vegetables from elsewhere in Europe, would remain acceptable, within the targets proposed.

# FOOD AND FISHERIES

We cannot reduce pressure on agricultural land by increasing fish yields; fishery pressures already desperately need reducing. Fisheries all over the world are in decline, including those in UK and European waters. In the North-East Atlantic, the main North Sea 'demersal' stocks harvested for human consumption purposes (cod, haddock, saithe, whiting, sole and plaice) continue to be intensively exploited.[102] On the basis of dietary recommendations of 32 grams of fish per day, a global population of 9.8 billion would consume 114 million tonnes a year. The global fish catch has increased 4.5 fold since 1950 to a record in 1994 of 109.6 million tonnes.[103] But at least 13 of the world's 15 fisheries are now in decline. The FAO's analysis suggests that a catch of much more than 100 million tonnes cannot be considered sustainable.[104] This currently equates to about 47 grams of fish per day per person. By 2050, with a larger population it would be equivalent to approximately 28 grams. Current UK consumption on average is 21 grams per day.

The current catch is not used efficiently. A decreasing share is actually feeding people. In 1994, 34.7 million tonnes, or 32 per cent, was used as fishmeal to feed livestock and other fish in fish farms. This share is growing; the 1994 figure was the highest ever.[105] Globally, it is estimated that 27 million tonnes of fish are discarded each year, a fifth of the total catch.[106] Production of fish by aquaculture – mainly for consumption in Northern countries – has been on the rise: up from 6.9 Mt in 1984 to 18.3 Mt in 1994.[107] But fish need around two kilograms of feed (mainly fishmeal) per kilo of live weight gain, so the overall production of fish for human consumption is reduced as a result.[108] Even though the ratio of fishmeal to fish at 2 kg per kilo is better than that for other livestock, this does not reduce the burden on the fish stocks exploited for fishmeal.[109] Aquaculture also creates additional environmental problems.[110]

Many of the problems are exacerbated by the practice of governments worldwide of subsidising fishing fleets to the sum of US$54 billion a year.[111] This magnifies the problems that arise because fisheries are effectively 'common property resources', in other words, it is not in the interests of individual fishers to limit their catches. This problem is also reinforced by management practices which set maximum quotas for total catch, rather than limiting the fishing effort which can be applied. This means that if stocks begin to decline, catches will be maintained by increased fishing effort, thus accelerating the decline of the stock. Measures that limit the fishing effort, by limiting or reducing the fleet size, give stocks more chance to recover, as falling stocks then mean smaller catches.[112]

In conclusion, the UK may not need to cut its consumption of fish, but we have a clear role in making the industry more sustainable for the future. So although globally we need to both cut environmental impact and feed more people, major gains can be made by not using fish as meal for other fish, and cutting back on wastage.

**Table 6.8** *Soil Degradation in Europe*

| Cause | Proportion of affected area (%) |
|---|---|
| Deforestation | 38 |
| Overgrazing | 23 |
| Agricultural activities | 29 |
| Industrialisation | 9 |

Source: GLASOD cited in World Resources Institute (1992) *World Resources 1992–93: A Guide to the Global Environment* Oxford: Oxford University Press

## LAND DEGRADATION

We are optimistic about future yields and land availability in the UK, but if our soils are degraded, then this optimism may be misplaced. Globally, in the last 45 years over 1200 million hectares of land has suffered moderate to extreme soil degradation due to human activities.[113] This is equivalent to an area the size of China and India. Moderately degraded land (900 mha) takes more resources to restore than the average farmer can provide. The main causes of this degradation in Europe are shown in Table 6.8.

Despite the widespread extent of this soil degradation, agricultural yields have increased due to high yield crops, irrigation, and increased chemical inputs. But, as the World Resources Institute says: 'Although technology often sustains yields, it only temporarily masks the effects of soil degradation; the yield increases might have been even greater if the soil had not been degraded'.[114] It has been estimated that about 10 per cent of the UK's soils are suffering irreversible damage.[115] Research by soil scientists suggests that yields may be depressed by about 2.5 per cent on as much as 40 per cent of arable land as a result of past erosion and intensive use.[116] Around 25 per cent of soils are presently at moderate to high risk of erosion.[117] These effects are largely obscured by yield increases achieved by intensive chemical use in conventional agriculture, but as low organic matter levels increase susceptibility to erosion, this will be particularly significant given the increasing likelihood of a drier climate in the arable parts of the country in the next century, as a result of climate change.

Improved soil protection is essential. However, for the purposes of our target scenarios we have assumed that such soil degradation problems can have been largely eliminated by 2050 as a result of the widespread adoption of sustainable or regenerative techniques such as organic production. Such techniques not only rely on enhanced soil fertility and organic matter content, but incorporate a range of measures designed to improve soil status in these respects. This will leave only the severely contaminated land unavailable for agricultural use. There is no contaminated land register in the UK although 100,000 sites, estimated to cover 100–200 thousand hectares are thought to be contaminated.[118] Given that this area is largely included in the built-up area figures at present, this has no effect on our food production estimates for 2050, although it does hamper increased growing of food within cities.

We also need to consider the impacts of mining. According to the Department of the Environment there is around 19,000 ha of derelict rural land in England,[119] mainly the result of abandoned mineral working. Even where quarries and other mineral workings have been ostensibly restored for agricultural or other uses, soils have been degraded as a result. Although the industry and some of the research it supports argues otherwise, the balance of evidence suggests that severe soil disturbance during opencast mining or quarrying causes effectively permanent damage to soil. After attempted restoration, soils are massively depleted of nitrogen and thus made more infertile[120] and the disturbance creates a weak soil with poor hydrological conditions.[121]

# INCREASING YIELDS WITHIN SUSTAINABLE SYSTEMS

As research has begun to develop and improve low-input techniques, experimental yields have improved. Pretty cites a range of positive findings, concluding:

> *What is clear from the evidence in the USA and elsewhere in Europe is that performance improves over time. In the USA, the top quarter of sustainable agriculture farmers now have better yields and much higher gross margins than the top quarter of conventional farmers. But these changes have taken at least 5–10 years to make.*[122]

Similarly, as the quest for new varieties and genetic diversity focuses on crops suitable for sustainable agriculture in a future where climate change is certain, it seems likely that higher-yielding varieties will be developed. This requires, however, more attention to the maintenance of the genetic diversity of crops and livestock. Currently, there is a widespread decline in the number of varieties grown, paralleled by a decline in the number of companies involved in seed production.[123]

Moreover, low-input does not necessarily mean 'low-tech', and there is great potential in techniques developed to manage and minimise inputs by computer technology, for example. Many would also add the potential of biotechnologies or genetic engineering to this list. Despite the hype, at present there seems little potential for biotechnology to feed the world by increasing yields. The current focus of biotechnology is on supporting intensive production methods. Genetically manipulated organisms

(GMOs) involve risks of gene transfer, interbreeding and mutation, and could include increased use of resources, water, or increased pollution from herbicide use. For example, by 1990 at least 27 corporations, including the world's eight largest pesticide companies, had initiated herbicide-tolerant plant research.[124] Fundamentally, the release of GMOs should be constrained by the precautionary principle. More recent concerns about GMOs include the risk that in gene transfer, undesirable characteristics such as human allergens or antibiotic resistance could be transferred into other species. Thus there is a critical need for full labelling of products containing GMOs.

Biotechnology also represents a commercialisation of biodiversity. This creates pressure to reduce the practical availability of diversity in the competition for market share where each individual product represents a substantial investment, the return from which has to be maximised. This commercialisation is already threatening the interests of indigenous people in natural biodiversity and reducing the incentives for conservation of varieties and indigenous knowledge.[125] We have to conclude that relying on biotechnology as a means of increasing yields is not only highly risky, but likely to undermine the wider sustainability of agricultural systems.

## Less Meat, More Crops

It takes over 300 hectares to produce 100 tonnes of beef each year, including land used for fodder crops, and only 2.5–20 hectares to produce the same weight of grains, pulses or vegetables.[126] Yet about half of the European grain crop is used to feed livestock.[127] The UK's net imports of feed for livestock take up more land in other countries than our total net imports of fruit, nuts and vegetables together. As shown in Table 6.6, nutritional guidelines suggest that the average UK diet is low in vegetables and fruit, but too high in dairy products, and especially in meat.[128] In general terms, a shift to lower meat diets, easily justifiable on health grounds, would reduce the land area needed to feed the same population. Nevertheless, livestock production will remain an integral part of UK agriculture. Even in the UK, there is much pasture land unsuitable for crop production, on which sustainable meat production is practical and even ecologically desirable. And the efficiency of many low external input systems can be boosted by the recycling and reuse of animal wastes as fertilisers.

## From Field to Plate

It has been estimated that around 1.5 per cent of the factory output of major grocery manufacturers is written off and food retail waste is less than 1 per cent, but greater losses occur between farmer and processor, and in the home.[129] There are several potential measures to cut wastage. One existing project, which could be expanded, uses otherwise waste food for charitable purposes. 'Provision' is a charity which is supplied with a range of goods – such as discontinued lines, goods with incorrectly marked packaging and under or over filled tins – by manufacturers and retailers in the grocery industry. Provision then distributes these goods to centres in ten major UK cities, who deliver to residential hostels, Salvation Army groups, children's centres, homeless groups and other charities.[130]

# THE FEASIBILITY OF SUSTAINABLE AGRICULTURE

The amount of land under organic farming in the UK is already increasing: 47,901 hectares in 1996, 47 per cent more than in 1995, and 140 per cent more than in 1990. However, the total percentage of agricultural land which is organic is only 0.3 per cent, one of the lowest in Europe (see Figure 6.3) and MAFF has only a modest target for 75,000 hectares (less than 0.5 per cent). Moreover, the rate of growth in the UK, while ostensibly impressive, is far below that achieved by Austria over the same period (see Figure 6.4). This suggests a significant unfulfilled potential. Even within the UK, there is wide variation with Wiltshire, for example, having five times more organic acreage than the average.

MAFF's low target reflects the problem that, within the current framework of support, and at current levels of demand, organic producers in the UK occupy a 'premium product' niche, selling their lower production at higher unit prices – even though we import over two-thirds of the organic food sold in the UK. This situation is largely dictated by the imbalance created by the subsidies given to conventional agriculture – direct subsidies of price support and area and headage payments, as well as indirect subsidies – for example, cheap fertiliser which doesn't reflect the environmental costs of the energy used in producing it or its impacts as leachate into water. To achieve the transition from current intensive agricultural systems to sustainable and regenerative techniques requires various incentives. One principal option is to directly reduce use of nitrogen fertiliser by some mechanism such as a tax or a quota system. This would provide an incentive for farmers to take up the potential for reduced fertiliser use that already exists, although careful timing and appropriate compensation would be needed.[131] Nitrogen restraint would help encourage use of manures and green wastes for their fertiliser value. Such recycling of nutrients could reduce overall waste flows, while replacing mined inputs. It would also stimulate the return of nutrients in manures and sewage.[132]

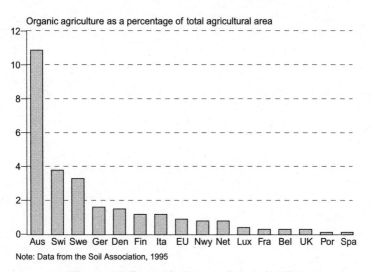

Note: Data from the Soil Association, 1995

**Figure 6.3** *Share of land organically farmed in Europe*

# The Potential for Organic Farming

Even with high prices, demand for organic produce is growing, and outstrips supply.[133] According to MAFF:

> *Demand for organic produce has grown steadily and the UK market has risen in value from £40 million in 1987 to over £150 million in 1994, an average annual growth of 25 per cent. Imports from Europe and further afield account for much of the supply. All the available evidence suggests that for the foreseeable future the UK organic market will continue to increase.*[134]

Retailers seeking to specialise in organic produce are finding it impossible to meet demand from UK sources. Weak distribution networks mean that economies of scale are rarely obtained, so retail prices remain high. MAFF sees economic potential for many farmers converting to organic systems given these price premiums.[135]

However, recent research suggests that, at least for specialist dairy farms, MAFF's view is still too cautious and that such farms can maintain yields and increase margins per cow, even in the conversion period, before premium prices can be obtained.[136] Official policy in the UK has been ostensibly sympathetic to increasing organic areas[137] but this has not been reflected in great support. Not only is the UK among a handful of European states that does not give targeted support to existing organic producers, but organic conversion payments for various crop types in the

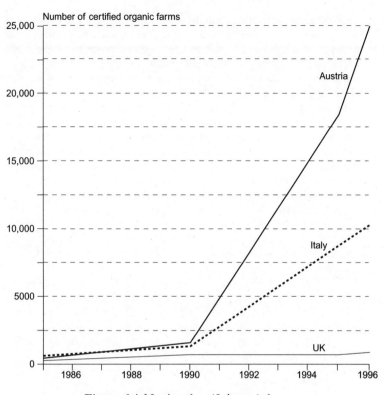

**Figure 6.4** *Number of certified organic farms*

UK are just 15 to 43 per cent of the EU average while payments in Austria are generally 50 per cent higher than the average.[138] But the biggest obstacle, and one that is not exclusive to the UK, is that conventional production continues to receive unwarranted subsidies. Also, compared to the majority of our European partners, the availability of advice is poor. In the UK, the organic sector relies almost entirely on the input of a very limited number of private sector consultants, with only occasional and inadequate assistance from state-owned extension agencies.[139]

The true future scope for organic production is not seen in MAFF's policies, nor in the supermarkets, but in the virtual explosion of informal distribution schemes. 'Green Box' and other buying schemes which provide cheap organic produce by cutting out the 'middle men', with consumers dealing directly with local farmers, have spread and grown like wildfire over the past few years. Over the past four years, the growth in box schemes for the marketing of vegetables has been spectacular. By mid-1996, one-third of British organic farmers were involved in marketing directly to 35,000 households.[140]

This is similar to the beginning of the growth phase in organics in Austria. Austrian production expanded rapidly because the Austrian rural development programme established professional, profit sharing regional development agencies which saw promoting organic production as a way of meeting their aim of job creation. Austrian farmers have also been offered special funds since 1989 if they are converting or are farming organically, whilst chemical fertilisers have been taxed.[141] The last strand in this environmental success story is the cooperation between organic farmers' associations and retailers which led to several main supermarket chains heavily backing organic produce and organic production methods. It is this cooperation that has led to organic produce becoming a mainstream product rather than the specialist area that it remains in the UK.[142] These factors have combined to produce a 20-fold increase in the number of organic farms in Austria in the ten years to 1995. In the UK the same period, from a similar base, saw little more than a doubling to 715.[143] The Austrian example suggests that organic or other sustainable, regenerative production techniques could become the 'mainstream' form of agriculture in the right conditions.

The growth of informal schemes in the UK will not bring about such a change alone, but with the right policy framework for farmers and retailers, organic really has potential as a 'staple' rather than premium product. Breaking into the mass markets of processed food would change the economics of the entire sector. However for sustainable lower intensity farming to become the norm in the UK, the whole of the food industry needs to change; something that would have to be driven, as in Austria, by the government.[144]

## Targeting Social Benefits

The Austrian example illustrates one further point: like all financial support schemes for agriculture, in providing money for organic practices Austria sought to support rural society. In this too it would appear to have been far more successful than we have been in the UK. In Austria many jobs on small farms and in rural food processing have been retained; in the UK employment in these sectors has fallen rapidly. Most financial support has been directed at highly intensive farming on large farms with high labour productivity. The multiplier effects of the additional income have been limited – much of it flowing into the coffers of the multinational agrochemical, seed and machinery companies, rather than circulating in rural local economies.

There is a related issue of land ownership, which has particularly disadvantaged rural communities in Scotland, where the present system could even be characterised as feudal.[145] Studies comparing ownership patterns in Scotland and Norway (a country with similar climatic and soil conditions to the Highlands of Scotland) have shown that a more equitable system of land ownership could have considerable benefits for the economic and social viability of rural communities.[146] Friends of the Earth is supportive of moves to extend ownership and economic access to the land. For the long term viability of rural communities to be sustained, the law regarding the buying and selling of land should be altered as necessary to favour the retention of ownership and control within those communities, rather than, for example, Scottish estates being sold to the highest bidder regardless of whether that person lives in the area (or even in Scotland), which is presently the case.[147]

## SUSTAINABLE AGRICULTURE AND ENVIRONMENTAL SPACE INPUTS

The uptake of more sustainable systems would reverse the trend within the farming system towards specialisation of use. We can expect the revival of mixed farming in which manures and wastes can be used effectively for their value as fertilisers. This will be one factor reducing material and energy inputs into agriculture. Based on the British Survey of Fertiliser Practice, we estimate that around 2 million tonnes of inorganic fertiliser (nitrogen, phosphate or potash) is used in the UK each year, of which around two-thirds is nitrogen.[148] A widespread conversion to sustainable techniques would be expected to reduce these inputs substantially. Total conversion to organic agriculture would reduce inorganic fertiliser use to a tiny fraction of current levels. The absolute energy consumption of agriculture per hectare has increased in OECD countries by 39 per cent in the 20 years following 1970.[149] Sustainable systems perform almost six times better than modern high input systems in terms of yields per unit of energy input (see Table 6.9). In other words, energy use could be cut by around 80 per cent.

Other environmental space resources are not only used in food production, but also in distribution. We need to consider what have been dubbed 'food miles'. In needlessly transporting food thousands of miles, there are not only implications for land use, but for energy use as well. For example, importing 64,550 tonnes[150] of butter a year from New Zealand is rather unnecessary when the European butter mountain is 129,000 tonnes.[151] Many products are involved, many of which could be grown in the UK: for example the average UK supermarket now boasts chillies from Zimbabwe, mangetout from Guatemala and apples from the United States. Food miles are not only clocked up by long-distance international imports. The distances have increased dramatically within the UK too, where food miles are estimated to have increased by over 50 per cent since 1978 with products trucked up and down the country via processors and centralised depots before reaching the shops.[152] The

**Table 6.9** *Kilograms of Cereal Produced per MJ of Energy Input (including indirect or embodied energy for fertilisers and pesticides)*

| Country and system | Modern, high input systems (kg cereal/MJ energy used) | Sustainable and low input systems (kg cereal/MJ energy used) |
|---|---|---|
| USA – maize (high and low input) | 0.25 | 0.67 |
| USA – wheat (high and low input) | 0.45 | 1.09 |
| Philippines (high input irrigated compared with sustainable) | 0.22 | 0.79 |
| Mean of six countries | 0.26 | 1.44 |

Source: Pretty, J (1995) *Regenerating Agriculture* London:Earthscan

implications for environmental space resources can be significant. Increased transport leads to greater emissions of carbon dioxide, making it harder to meet our energy targets. Protecting food in transit requires processing and preserving (often energy intensive) and heavy packaging – increasing materials use. Worse, preservatives can be environmental threats in their own right. For example, ozone depleting methyl bromide is widely used as a fumigant on food before transport.

There can be associated environmental and social impacts in exporting countries, too. Long distance trade in foodstuffs tends to encourage specialisation in agriculture, and the allocation of resources to production for export, rather than to local needs and self-sufficiency. For example, in Bangladesh, shrimps rank as the country's third largest export earner. Yet the country is unable to feed its own population: a clear conflict over the use of resources for local food needs, as opposed to export production.[153] It would be simplistic to conclude that food exports are necessarily bad; they can earn valuable foreign exchange for example, and cash-cropping provides incomes for many in rural areas. But where land is taken from production of food for local consumption and the profits accrue almost entirely to the traders and supermarket dealers, food security for the poorest in such countries can easily suffer for the sake of all year round variety on our supermarket shelves. One of the major reasons why food miles are growing so quickly is that transport does not reflect its true environmental and social costs. Higher fuel duties are part of the solution, but so is promotion of 'fair trade' products where the benefits of trade are seen by those actually growing the crops. Overall, we can conclude that the uptake of sustainable systems will have beneficial side effects in terms of the use of other environmental space inputs.

# CONCLUSIONS

Globally, humankind must be able to feed between 8 and 12 billion people sustainably by 2050, with a central estimate of 9.8 billion. With sustainable or regenerative production methods, such as organic agriculture, it should be possible to raise world average yields for cropland by almost 50 per cent, even though yields in areas with already intensive agriculture may fall – but by no more than about 5 per cent in the long term. As a result, we estimate that the UK will need to reduce its use of agricultural land by about 27 per cent to provide environmental space for others. By 2050, even accounting for a 5 per cent reduction in yields of crops and a 15–20 per cent reduction in yields of livestock products in the UK as a result of the adoption of sustainable agricultural practices, this fair share of the world's productive land can easily feed us all. The main reason this is possible is that sustainable production significantly cuts the feeding of grain and other crops to livestock as feed and fodder. This provides substantially more food for human consumption. However, it may require cutting livestock yields below the level needed to support our current diet and adjusting our diets closer to those officially recommended for good health: consuming less meat but more vegetables. More broadly, with the adoption of the efficiency strategies suggested in this chapter, there should be adequate land available for production of 'luxury' food crops such as chocolate, and non-food crops such as cotton – as part of the land we will still 'import' and for fibre crops in the UK. However, there is not much margin for error, and further loss of agricultural land to urban development cannot be accepted within a sustainable land use strategy.

Yet the UK has no framework targets for land use to reflect such an analysis. In agriculture, there are significant targets for set-aside, but only a minuscule target for organic production. There are also targets for Environmentally Sensitive Areas and Nitrate Vulnerable Zones, but these will help direct agriculture towards more sustainable practices only in small specific areas. These are all very limited in scope in comparison with the objectives of achieving sustainable production on all agricultural land in the UK, and reducing our claim on land to a fair share. As well as reducing our overall use of agricultural land by the various measures suggested earlier, we can set other helpful targets for the future based on the analysis of this chapter. If we do not deliver on the following, then however much we cut the land area we exploit, we will not achieve sustainability in land use.

First we must increase the area protected for biodiversity. The reasoning behind protecting 10 per cent of major ecological regions is that diversity in habitats and species all across the world is of ecological value. We cannot therefore seek to preserve natural habitats elsewhere and not in the UK, even if this were morally or politically feasible. And if our future projections are correct, and pressure on land is increasing everywhere, then strong protective measures will be needed to ensure that in the UK there is no further loss of high quality seminatural and natural habitats, and more widely that humankind does not further damage the biodiversity that its long-term future depends upon. So by 2010 the UK should have increased the area designated and improved protective legislation to ensure that 10 per cent of our land area is adequately protected. Existing targets will not achieve this. The statutory nature conservation agencies have a broad indicative target for coverage of Sites of Special Scientific Interest of approximately 10 per cent of the land area. Whilst this area is of the right magnitude for biodiversity conservation, this target is not endorsed by the Government, and the level of protection granted to these sites is inadequate.

Second, we can and should minimise further any increase of urban areas and use the land to ease the pressure on other environmental space resources; not just indirectly by limiting urban growth, but directly by using land for non-food crops which can substitute for other limited resources, such as biomass for energy, fibre for paper production or oilseeds for chemical feedstocks. Such an approach will also help us support the role of sustainable agriculture as the foundation for sustainable rural society. At present Government targets do exist, but push in contradictory directions. Although the last Government set a target for providing 50 per cent of new homes on land already in urban use (not including vacant land such as open spaces), it also set targets for provision of land for new homes in development plans, generating pressures for land allocation outside exist-ing urban areas. In the absence of strong policies promoting compact cities, this exacerbates pressures for urban sprawl.

Third, we must reverse the trends of soil degradation by erosion, acidification and organic matter decline. Soil in good condition is an essential prerequisite for sustainable agriculture which cannot rely on vast external subsidies of chemicals and energy to substitute for natural fertil-ity and productivity. At present there are no explicit targets for reducing the areas of soils affected by these problems.

Fourth, we should aim to have converted entirely to organic or sustainable agriculture by 2050, with an interim target of 25 per cent organic by 2010. This is not unrealistic, as the Austrian example shows, but although the UK has targets, they are tiny.[154]

# Chapter 7
# Wood

## INTRODUCTION

Although the production of wood could be seen simply as another use for land, it is important enough to merit a separate chapter. Wood and paper products in one form or another are a significant resource in all economies. In particular, wood is in widespread use as a construction material, even in the richest countries. But the more important reason for a separate chapter on wood is that forests have such significant environmental functions within the hydrological cycle and the carbon cycle, and in biodiversity conservation, that ensuring sustainable consumption of wood is a critical issue in global sustainability. Forests also enhance soil stability and protect watersheds.

As timber is a renewable resource we can interpret any net loss of forest area as a reduction in the potential supply to future generations; a case of consuming the stock of capital, rather than the flow of income it provides. One doesn't have to believe the most extreme figures for potential species loss to realise that loss of tropical forest, much of it species rich, old growth forest, at a reported rate of 15.4 million hectares (an area greater than the size of England) or 0.8 per cent of the remaining area every year is a reason for worry.[1] Loss of old growth forests has not just been something that has happened in the tropics. In the UK humans cleared the primeval forest centuries ago, but in North America and northern Eurasia, there are still vast tracts of relatively undisturbed forest. In recent decades, loggers have felled hundreds of thousands of hectares every year, often to replace them with single-species plantations mainly to feed the voracious appetites of the developed countries for paper, pulp and timber products. Such changes have serious implications for both biodiversity and the carbon cycle. Secondary and plantation forests not only hold less species of wildlife, but generally create a smaller carbon store, so replacing old growth forest by plantations does not help stabilise the greenhouse effect.[2]

# FORESTS AND BIODIVERSITY

Forests are critical to biodiversity. Some foresters have developed ways of harvesting which do much less damage to diversity than clear felling, including various types of selective and coup felling (logging small groups of trees).[3] Where such techniques are practised, the wildlife which thrives on disturbance and the creation of 'edge' habitats can be conserved alongside that which survives best in largely undisturbed woodland. The best estimate available suggests that almost a quarter of the area of forest which existed undisturbed by humans until the development of agriculture, still survives.[4] This is larger than the IUCN figure of 10 per cent of area for biodiversity protection suggested in the last chapter. But forests are an especially valuable reservoir of biodiversity. A precautionary basis suggests that, to protect biodiversity, no logging should be permitted in old growth primary forest. As our management techniques improve, we may be able to use some of the protected area without damaging the other valuable functions it provides. Until then, we assume that a sustainable supply of timber will be reduced to account for the exclusion of old growth forest from the productive base. To ensure that these areas of forest are protected effectively requires several practical measures.

Effective labelling and certification provides reliable, credible information about wood products and their origin and has grown rapidly over the last four years under the auspices of the Forest Stewardship Council (FSC). The aim is to establish a worldwide system for identifying and labelling wood products from well managed forests, based on environmental, social and economic criteria. Setting out the minimum criteria for good forest management, accredited certifiers are required to evaluate forest management using detailed forestry standards which take account of specific national or regional forestry issues. In practice, if the standards set by the FSC are to be met, it is critical that adequate resources are made available to ensure compliance and that certifying bodies are free of commercial vested interests. Trade rules, under GATT, must be sympathetic to such initiatives. Current debate over whether such labelling constitutes a barrier to trade must be resolved in favour of such schemes. Other standards currently being considered by the International Organisation for Standardisation (ISO) could undermine the FSC guidelines, because ISO standards look at management processes rather than the actual forestry practices. Foresters practising sustainable forest management could actually be penalised under the ISO scheme.

The industry has justified old growth logging on various grounds. Now, as the economic and employment arguments so long promoted are being disproved, as in the case of the spotted owl versus logger debate in the Pacific North West of the USA (see Box 7.1), the industry is supporting and employing publicists to promote the idea that it doesn't matter what type of forests we have, as long as there are lots of them. This is a

# BOX 7.1 *OLD GROWTH FORESTS AND THE SPOTTED OWL DEBATE*[a]

The ancient forests of the Pacific North West are the last relatively intact old growth ecosystems in the United States.[b] However, extensive logging has reduced its extent from 7.6 million hectares to below 1 million hectares or 13 per cent of what once was. Since the implementation of the Endangered Species Act of 1973 and the listing of the Spotted Owl as an endangered species in 1991, the forests have become the focus of a debate between timber companies and environmentalists. The economically and politically powerful timber industry argues that it must have access to the virgin forest to stay in business and maintain employment. The environmental movement on the other hand argues that these forests are unique, fragile and support many species that are threatened with extinction.

*Environment or Jobs?*

According to the US Government, 28,000 jobs could have been lost by the year 2000 under proposals for the preservation of the spotted owl. Under a new plan only 6000 jobs are expected to be shed. Even these estimates are exaggerated. To suggest that jobs will be lost as a sole result of protecting trees is misleading. Over the past 20 years the industry has become more automated. In Oregon, for example, production increased 4.3 per cent while the number of timber-related jobs declined by 14.3 per cent between 1977 and 1987. Cutting old growth forests remains attractive partly because an old growth mill employs ten jobs per million board feet cut, whereas an automated second growth mill employs only four jobs per million board feet. So these jobs will be shed anyway when the virgin forest is all felled.[c] More recently, the *New York Times* and the *Oregonian* have reported that, in practice, the diversified Washington economy has been little affected by the court order in 1991 which halted logging of old growth forests. Even Oregon, the leading producer of lumber in the US, has thrived economically, in both rural and urban areas, since then, despite an overall decline in rates of logging.

Sources: *a* Kerasote, T (1991) Old Growth: More than just owls and jobs *Sports Afield* July 1991; Egan P (1994) Oregon, foiling forecasters, thrives as it protects owls *New York Times* 11 October; Hill and Hamburg (1994) High tech prepares to topple timber *Oregonian* 1 September; *b* Such old growth forests, over 250 years old, contain large trees, fallen logs and large dead trees in a mixed and multi-layered canopy broken by occasional light filled gaps. This fast dwindling forest area has provided a suitable environment for many varied and rare species; *c* Similarly the timber industry has been unsustainable in its harvesting of secondary growth. Some research shows that during the first half of the 1980s, the industry over-harvested its own lands in the Pacific Northwest by as much as 256 per cent and the national forests by as much as 61 per cent, putting long-term employment under threat.

practical example of one of the most pernicious misinterpretations of sustainability: the idea that we can trade off valuable environmental assets such as our old growth forests for something else – in this case a combination of the timber and a plantation on the same land.

The extent of this fallacy can be seen from the case of eucalyptus plantations which, although extending forest area, are often severely environmentally and socially damaging. In Portugal, eucalyptus plantations have led to increased soil erosion, natural chemical inhibition of the germination and growth of other species and, most seriously in such a drought prone country, falling ground water levels. Farmers in surrounding areas have complained of wells and streams, often the only source of water, drying up. Some Portuguese farmers have taken to uprooting new saplings. One farmer in Agua Travessa has said, 'If things continue as in recent years our children and grandchildren will have to feed on eucalyptus.'[5]

A parallel story can be told of Finnish forests. Forestry in Scandinavia has been portrayed by the industry as an example of the sustainable use of natural resources. However the expansion of commercial forestry has replaced natural old growth forests with uniform plantations, threatening many species, disrupting the livelihoods of indigenous peoples and increasing carbon dioxide emissions. According to one estimate, less than 3 per cent of Finland's primary forest remains, yet the National Board of Forestry still plans to fell around one-sixth of this old growth forest.[6]

The draining of wetlands for forestry during the last few decades has been by far the most rapid project of large-scale environmental destruction ever carried out in Finland. Over half of the 10.5 million hectares of peatland in Finland have been drained, mostly for tree plantations. Drained mires now cover more than a fifth of the country's land area. By the year 2000 about 15 per cent of Finland's wood production will come from drained mires. Drainage has increased nutrient and humus loads in waterways, worsening water quality and reducing fish populations; worsened spring floods; reduced the amount of summer pasture available for reindeer; and led to vast net carbon emissions to the atmosphere. In Finland, forests contain on average about 10 times and peatlands about 100 times more carbon than the atmosphere above them. When peatlands are drained, the organic material stored in them decomposes much quicker than before, and peatlands are transformed from carbon sinks to important sources of atmospheric carbon dioxide. The annual net carbon production is between 3 and 4 tonnes per hectare. If this is representative of the whole country, in Finland the draining of mires is already a greater carbon dioxide source than the country's burning of fossil fuels.[7]

# SUSTAINABLE WOOD CONSUMPTION

Total global production of wood stands at 3430 million m$^3$ each year, but more than half of this is used for fuel purposes, largely in the South. Fuelwood is not considered further as it is assumed, first, that this does not come from productive 'industrial forests', and second, that renewable energy technologies, such as solar ovens, designed to replace unsustainable fuelwood use, will become widely available.[8] The area of productive forest we use below is much smaller than the global total forest area, allowing for both biodiversity protection, and continued use of fuelwood, albeit at sustainable rates. Global industrial roundwood production in 1989–91 stood at 1661 million m$^3$ per year.[9] But this rate of production is not sustainable. It relies on felling of primary or old growth forests, which represent a key haven for wildlife, and on forestry practices which, like modern agriculture, depend on external inputs of energy and chemicals.

We can estimate sustainable production rates for both tropical and temperate forests. In the tropics sustainable yields range from 0.26 to 0.46 m$^3$/ha/year, and in temperate regions from 2.2 to 3.6 m$^3$/ha/year.[10] Excluding the 1.3 billion hectares of remaining primary forest as well as existing areas already excluded from production to protect biodiversity, soils and watersheds leaves around 1.2 billion hectares of productive secondary and plantation forest. Applying the sustainable yield estimates to these areas allows us to derive estimates of sustainable production that range from 1187 to 2336 million m$^3$/year.[11] These provide baseline figures for 2010 assuming that the same area of forest will be 'productive' by then. In other words, forest planted since 1990 is not considered as productive by 2010. This does imply that the stock can be increased by 2050 (or even sooner) but, with some exceptions, only at the cost of alternative uses of land.[12] For now, we assume no net increase in land under productive forestry by 2050, as new afforestation is still relatively insignificant at a global scale – although increasing in many Northern countries – and we foresee continued pressure to take land from forestry for conversion to agriculture in many Southern countries.

These figures are based on estimated sustainable yields. The conservative estimates of sustainable production are already exceeded by current global consumption of industrial roundwood (1691 million m$^3$ in 1990). Three-quarters of this is consumed by the Northern industrialised countries,[13] and overall consumption is projected to increase. Food and Agriculture Organisation (FAO) figures for the year 2010 forecast an increase in demand for roundwood by almost 60 per cent from 1990 levels, to 2700 million m$^3$. Our optimistic estimates of sustainable yield above suggest that at most global roundwood consumption can increase by 35 per cent. The conservative estimates suggest a cut of around 30 per cent.

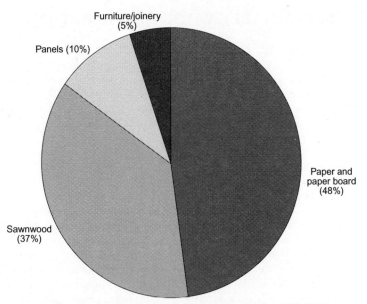

Sources: Paper Federation of Great Britain 1995 *Industry Facts*; UN/ECE and FAO 1994 *Forest Products Statistics 1990–1994*; FICGB *Forest Industry Yearbook*, various years

**Figure 7.1** *UK use of primary industrial wood products*

# WOOD CONSUMPTION IN THE UK

The UK is a major consumer. Using conservative estimates, current UK consumption of primary wood products is 51.5–52.8 million m³ Wood Raw Material Equivalent (WRME), equivalent to 0.88–0.91 m³ per capita, compared with a world average of 0.32 m³ per capita. UK consumption is equivalent to around 3 per cent of current world consumption, even though the UK has only 1 per cent of the world's people. Consumption of wood increased steadily from 1970 onwards and accelerated in the latter half of the 1980s. Figure 7.1 and Box 7.2 show the main uses.

# THE ENVIRONMENTAL SPACE FOR WOOD

The figures shown in Table 7.1 suggest that the UK needs to cut consumption of wood by between 67 and 89 per cent. For this study we will use the figure of 73 per cent as our target reduction. This is based on a medium population, and optimistic yields. We choose 'optimistic yields' because by 2050 we would expect sustainable forestry techniques to have improved average yields.[14] So if we are to use only our fair share of global sustainable production, the UK will have to cut use of primary wood

# BOX 7.2 *WOOD PRODUCTS – USE OF, AND TRENDS, IN THE UK SINCE 1970*[a]

*Paper and paperboard* form almost half of the total demand for wood products in the UK. Consumption increased from 19 million m³ wood raw material equivalent (WRME) in 1970 to 25.1–25.5 million m³ in 1994. Domestic production, imports and exports have all increased significantly.[b] By 2010 the UK's consumption of paper is forecast to have increased by 63 per cent over 1990. In 1990 packaging accounted for 40 per cent of paper consumption and printing and writing paper for 32 per cent.

*Panels* have seen a steady increase in demand. In 1994 they accounted for 4.8–5.4 million m³ WRME. Plywood represents a third of the wood consumption by panels, and by 1992 the volume of UK production had become insignificant. Fibreboard accounts for 15 per cent of panel consumption and has changed little over the past 20 years, although here, UK production has increased as imports have fallen. Particle board accounted for over half the panel consumption by 1992, having increased from 20 per cent in 1970. This demand has been met by both imports and domestic production. Panels are used mainly in construction, but also in furniture (particularly in the form of fibreboard).

*Hardwood sawnwood* consumption has fallen substantially. Although domestic supply has halved, imports have remained stable over the long term. The construction and joinery industry accounts for between 35 and 38 per cent of hardwood consumption. Furniture accounts for 24–41 per cent. Consumption is not growing in either sector.

*Coniferous sawnwood* consumption has varied cyclically, but remains much the same in 1992 as in 1970. Proportionally however, its share has decreased as consumption of other products has increased. The share of demand met by domestic production has increased from 7 per cent in 1970 to 22 per cent in 1992 and imports have decreased. The construction and joinery industry accounts for 42 to 67 per cent of softwood consumption in housing; civil engineering; repair, maintenance and improvement and other building. The total consumption of hard- and coniferous sawnwood was 18.7–19.0 million m³ WRME in 1994. Furniture and joinery products accounted for a further 2.9 million m³ WRME.

*Pitprops and other industrial wood* is a diminishing and minor sector supplied primarily by domestically produced wood.

Source: *a* Bevan, T and Rice, T (1995) Overview – Wood Consumption in the UK. In Rice, T (ed) *Out of the Woods* London: FOE. Wood can be classed into two sources: primary sources (products manufactured from the raw material) and secondary sources (products manufactured in whole or part from residues, alternative fibres or recycled material). This box and Figure 7.1 are based on the amounts of primary wood consumed in the UK in 1994, having taken account of imports, exports and recycling. All amounts have been converted into wood raw material equivalents (WRME), and corrections made to minimise double counting where products appear twice in the statistics, eg as sawnwood and as joinery; *b* Exports grew to 3.7 million m³ WRME in 1993

**Table 7.1** Environmental Space for Wood (m³/capita) 2050

| | Low population 7.9 billion | | Medium population 9.8 billion | | High population 11.9 billion | |
|---|---|---|---|---|---|---|
| | Global target m³/capita | UK reduction (per cent) | Global target m³/capita | UK reduction (per cent) | Global target m³/capita | UK reduction (per cent) |
| % cut required (conservative production) | 0.150 | 83 | 0.121 | 86 | 0.099 | 89 |
| % cut required (optimistic production) | 0.295 | 67 | 0.238 | 73 | 0.196 | 78 |

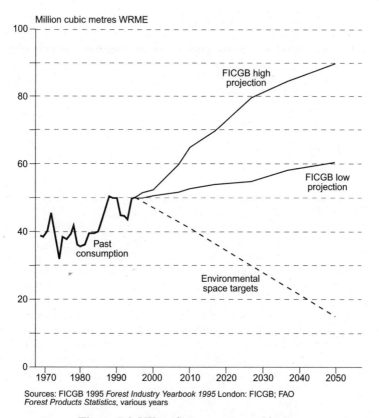

Sources: FICGB 1995 *Forest Industry Yearbook 1995* London: FICGB; FAO
*Forest Products Statistics*, various years

**Figure 7.2** *UK wood use – projections and targets*

products by 73 per cent to 0.24m³ per capita.[15] Only a small amount of timber is traded globally, but because of the important global functions of forests, and the fact that the trade between North and South is particularly damaging to tropical forests and their indigenous people,[16] we will treat wood as a global resource.[17] The International Institute for Environment and Development estimates that the UK per capita consumption of timber products is 66 per cent higher than the permissible global average or 'ecological fair share'.[18] This is of broadly the same order as our figure of a 73 per cent reduction.

Our target for reduction contrasts with a forecast increase in consumption in the UK, driven mainly by increased use of paper and board, of 30–90 per cent by 2050 (see Figure 7.2).[19] These forecasts, as in many other sectors, do not reflect any assessment of increasing need, but are mainly driven by the past relationship between consumption of wood products and economic growth. However, in one area we foresee potential increasing needs: wood for construction to meet the needs for new housing and housing renewal and refurbishment. But even if the need for additional homes was met entirely by new build, then this would require only 1.4 million m³ WRME per year, or around 7 per cent of current sawnwood consumption.[20] In Chapter 6 we set out ways in which the need for about one-third of these new homes could be met by conversion, refurbishment and reducing vacancy rates. This would reduce the additional demand for wood.

# UK Production

The environmental space approach does not require us to produce all our own timber, any more than it requires us to produce our own oil or aluminium. However, at present the UK imports a net area of land of 65,000 km² (6.5 million ha) as a result of its imports of wood products.[21] It is therefore a worthwhile exercise to review UK production and the scope for increasing our forest estate in a sustainable fashion. The UK has had production targets for timber since the First World War, after which self-sufficiency in timber became a national policy goal. In theory new planting adds to the sustainable harvest of timber. In practice, inappropriate location of planting has damaged other components of environmental space, such as biodiversity value or the carbon sink in our upland peatbogs.[22] The scope for extending our forest area is limited. The House of Lords report on sustainable development agreed that a single planting target is not desirable, but suggested indicative targets reflecting the multipurpose objectives of forestry.[23]

Sustainable production of timber in the UK in 2010 is estimated to be 14.6 million m³. This is the predicted output of 16.2 million m³,[24] less 10 per cent to account for an increased area in the UK protected for biodiversity conservation. Even if the UK increases its forest area substantially – and the last Government proposed a target to double woodland area in England by 2050[25] – we would fall far short of being able to provide for current levels of consumption. A doubling of woodland area in England would increase the UK's forest area by about 40 per cent to 3.4 million hectares, in comparison with the total of 8 million hectares or more used to meet our current demands. This might increase sustainable production to around 20 million m³.[26] We do not consider the scope for increasing sustainable production in the UK any further here, as we are considering wood as a global resource, so such an increase would simply increase the total available globally, rather than all being available to the UK, unless the land converted to woodland was part of the UK's share of productive agricultural land. However, there are ways to increase, sustainably, the productivity of our existing trees to contribute to meeting our environmental space targets.

# REDUCING WOOD CONSUMPTION

## Pre-consumer Wastes

Thinnings, or wood that is removed during woodland management to ensure optimum growth, constitute up to 50 per cent of the annual forest crop, therefore their use is important to reduce waste.[27] The aim of thinning is to improve the quality of the remaining crop and, as part of a sustainable forestry industry, is essential. At present the potential for use of thinnings is underutilised. Today the process of thinning is only economic where the material can be sold and much of it is used in particle board manufacture, but thinning could be undertaken more widely without damaging the long-term crop or the forest ecology. As well as use in board manufacture, thinnings are being exploited – although not widely – by various other organisations, using small diameter timber (50–200mm) as a structural building material to build anything from sheds to very large buildings, or for furniture production. Coppicing of broadleaved hardwoods provides a more constant supply of wood, and can produce a greater yield of wood in volume terms, but virtually all in smaller diameters. Short-rotation coppice can produce up to five times greater maximum yields than conventional broadleaved hardwood forestry. The revival of coppicing along with use of thinnings from conventional forestry could create up to 1000 additional jobs in, for example, charcoal production, and construction material supply[28] and traditional coppicing would bring benefits to wildlife.[29]

The scope for increased use of thinnings and coppicing to replace primary industrial wood products is clearly substantial, but it is very difficult to quantify. Using other forest residues: stumps and roots; tops and branches; bark; and harvesting losses, principally sawdust; is less easy. The Forestry Commission has developed technology to collect forest residues, but the economics of its use depend on the markets for its produce: paper, particle-board and soil improvers in horticulture. At present only horticultural uses appear economic. Moreover, not all residues should be removed, as dead and decaying materials form a vital link in forest ecology. Remarkably, at present, effectively exploiting such residues becomes easier in urban surroundings where waste disposal is expensive. The London Borough of Croydon produces 400 tonnes of timber a year, alongside charcoal and compost from its timber and green wastes, in a scheme made financially feasible by the combination of recycling credits and avoided disposal costs (see Box 7.3). At present there is very little wood recycling carried out by local authorities. More widespread adoption of similar schemes could produce around 185,000 m$^3$ WRME.[30]

The potential savings from better use of urban tree wastes serve to highlight just how much could be saved by improving the efficiency of use of thinnings and other pre-consumer wastes. Rice estimates that in

## BOX 7.3 *THE LONDON BOROUGH OF CROYDON*

The London Borough of Croydon has 800 acres of woodland and 37,000 street trees. The Borough has developed an efficient infrastructure for recycling the green waste from its parks and streets. The council stipulates in its management contracts that all green waste arisings are its property and contractors are obliged to deliver them to its 'tree station'. Also the Council encourages non-council contractors to participate by offering lower tariffs than at other disposal sites.

The timber and green waste is dealt with at a 'tree station' by a variety of means.

- A sawmill makes timber products such as fencing and posts, which are sold back to the council at discount prices.
- Charcoal is produced using timber unsuitable for the mill.
- 16,800 m³ per year of compost is produced from lower grade residues.

The scheme reduces landfill costs, reduces transportation and produces local products for local needs. However, it relies on a significant capital invest-ment that will take a number of years to be recouped financially. Other local authorities have stressed that future prospects for tree stations are currently constrained by their poor financial position.

Sources: London Borough of Croydon (1994) *Croydon Waste Minimisation Project* London: LBC; Rice, T (ed) (1995) *Out of the Woods* London: FOE, Chapter 6; Personal Communication with London Borough of Croydon's Recycling Officer, August 1996

total some 1.75 million m³ (WRME) could be saved by measures in this sector (including secondary processing) by 2010, even allowing for appro-priate levels of retention of wastes in the forest ecology.[31] One of the main markets for such wastes is particle board and other wood-based composites. These are increasingly widely used in the construction indus-try where they are replacing sawn timber not only in non-structural areas, but also for structural purposes.[32] This opens up opportunities to make much greater use of wastes, not only from the pre-consumer stage, but also through recycling of post-consumer wood wastes.

## Post-consumer Wastes

### *Paper Recycling*

Recycling and reuse can also be applied to post-consumer products from structural timber to waste paper. Localised examples demonstrate the possibilities. The London Borough of Sutton is one of the leading local authorities in the UK for recycling and has achieved a 25 per cent target for paper recycling. In 1991 a fortnightly door-to-door kerbside collection service for paper and card was introduced. By 1993 this had been increased to a weekly service in all parts of the borough. Paper banks were also provided in the 32 neighbourhood recycling centres, approximately one site for every 5000 people. Community groups in the 'adopt-a-bank' scheme maintain the sites in return for payments for every tonne collected. In 1995 book banks were introduced, in partnership with Oxfam. The Council now aims to recycle 50 per cent of all domestic waste by 31 March 2001 and 80 per cent by 31 March 2006.[33]

Sutton has been so successful in its recycling programme partly because the community was involved from the outset. Council officials feel that a decrease in paper prices, and associated poor publicity, is the only thing that may constrain future increases in recycling.[34] Sutton collected 5912 tonnes of waste paper from domestic households in 1994/95 (or 0.034 tonnes per person).[35] If the same percentage (25 per cent) of paper from the waste stream was collected in all UK towns and cities of over 100,000 population, 0.91 million tonnes would have been recycled.[36] This equates to 2.6 million $m^3$ WRME or 10 per cent of total UK paper consumption (25.2 million $m^3$ WRME).[37] Achieving 50 per cent recycling in these larger towns and cities would save 5.2 million $m^3$ WRME, and, less conservatively, throughout the UK, 10.5 million $m^3$ WRME. Achieving an 80 per cent target would save 8.4 and 16.8 million $m^3$ WRME respectively (see Figure 7.3). For the purposes of this book we have assumed that the target of 50 per cent is achievable throughout the UK by 2010 (almost ten years after Sutton expects to achieve it) delivering 10.5 million $m^3$ WRME savings and that by 2050 the 80 per cent rate will be the norm.

Increasing recycling provides a balance of payments benefit, from cutting imports. Peter Jones of BIFFA[38] cites a figure of £216 per tonne for using recycled fibre. Moreover, the amount of waste going to landfill or incineration will be cut. Employment opportunities will be created as recycling is more labour intensive than waste disposal. Extrapolating from findings in the Netherlands where collection rates are nearer 75 per cent it is possible that 4500 jobs could be created in the UK if similar rates were achieved.[39] But there are several obstacles in the way of such a scenario. For various reasons, the economics of recycling are still marginal and unpredictable, discouraging investment. Supply and demand for waste paper is very unstable.[40] There are a series of options open to government to help stabilise and increase demand (see Box 7.4). Also, much of the paper collected at present cannot be recycled due to contamination by, for example, glue or food. Effective separation between high and low quality paper is needed so that high quality paper can be recycled back into high quality products, which would help stimulate demand.
There is a link between the costs of landfill disposal and the rate of recycling. Recycling should become more attractive with the introduction

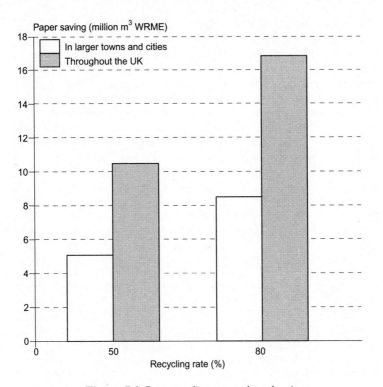

**Figure 7.3** *Paper recycling rates and wood savings*

of the landfill levy, but this will depend largely on the treatment of incineration in the waste system. At present incinerator operators actively seek waste paper because it has a relatively high calorific value. Some are signing long-term contracts with local authorities that commit the authorities to providing a certain amount of waste for 25 to 30 years.[41] As a result support for recycling in many such local authorities is being cut back. Yet a ten-fold energy saving over incineration is possible by recycling paper, for example.[42] Incineration must be covered by an extended waste disposal levy to maintain a strong incentive for recycling.

*Timber Recycling and Reuse*

The potential for recycling of timber and use of recycled wood is great. In St Edmundsbury a pilot furniture recycling scheme is estimated to have reduced 'bulky household waste' for disposal by 10 per cent.[43] It is expected that the scheme will prove cost effective for expansion as the landfill levy raises the cost of waste disposal. Waste timber which cannot be reused can be chipped and recycled as board. Caberboard, in Scotland,

## BOX 7.4 *POSSIBLE MEASURES TO STIMULATE DEMAND FOR RECYCLED PAPER*

- Government procurement – the government is a major user of paper. If all government departments and local authorities were to use recycled paper and paper products, investment in collection and production would be encouraged.
- Stringent, legally binding targets for recycled content, supported by regulations. Voluntary targets of 40 per cent by the year 2000 exist for newspaper and have already been achieved on average, but much higher levels of recycled content are practicable.
- Clear labelling – clear, concise and visible labelling, complying to an external standard, is needed to end the confusion over recycled products.
- Virgin fibre tax – a tax on use of virgin wood fibres would make it more economic to use recycled paper and board in products instead of using primary sources.

produce particle board/chipboard and medium density fibreboard (MDF) from woodchips or fine particles of wood held together by resins. At present 60 per cent of their raw material intake is from wood residues from sawmills and other timber processors and 10 per cent is waste timber, 50,000 tonnes of it each year.[44] Bark is sold for horticultural use and other residues are used to fuel the plant's driers. Although the production of boards is energy-intensive, the use of waste in this way reduces total energy demand.[45] Caberboard achieve a higher than average use of waste inputs. The average recycled content for fibreboard and particle board is between 40 and 60 per cent. Increasing this to the 70 per cent recycled content used by Caberboard, would mean that in the UK as a whole a total of 2.7 million $m^3$ WRME of timber residues and waste could be recycled as useful board. This would mean a net saving on primary wood of approximately 0.4–1.02 million $m^3$ WRME: a saving of 8–20 per cent in primary wood consumption for the production of panels.[46]

As yet timber products are rarely designed with ease of reuse or recycling in mind. But improved design is possible which could help overcome such problems. For example, Crocodile Packaging, a Swindon based company, produce collapsible reusable packaging boxes. Traditionally large items such as furniture and car parts are packaged for transit in a framework of softwood nailed around the goods, which is discarded after one use. Crocodile's reusable boxes are made from plywood or chipboard and can be reused 40–50 times.

These are only a few of the potential opportunities for recycling of post-consumer wood wastes. In his more wide ranging review, Rice estimates that the total potential for recycling of such wastes by 2010 would save two million $m^3$ (WRME).[47]

# Substitution by Non-wood Fibres

Millions of tonnes of waste residues are generated every year in farming practices throughout the world. They are underutilised and often discarded. However these agricultural byproducts, residues and non-wood fibres could substitute for primary wood consumption in diverse uses such as paper, particle boards and building materials. For example, paper can be made from non-wood fibres such as hemp, grass, kenaf, flax, cotton, bagasse (sugar cane waste) and straw. These fibres already make up over half the virgin pulp production in some developing countries and are currently experiencing a revival in interest in developed countries too. At present they are competitive on price, but market penetration is limited as a result of familiarity with existing products and concerns over the reliability of supply.[48] Non-wood fibres have traditionally been used in paper making and are still used to make the highest quality papers such as banknotes.[49] Because all fibres degrade with repeated recycling, a proportion of virgin fibre is required in the paper cycle as a whole. The use of non-wood fibres could therefore further reduce the demand on virgin woodpulp for paper.

Significant amounts of paper or board could be produced without additional cultivation. Almost 63,000 tonnes per year of non-wood fibre (excluding straw) could currently be used for paper making in the UK. At present most is not utilised or is sold abroad.[50] If the woody material from non-wood fibres such as linseed and flax had been utilised, 120,000 tonnes of board material could have been produced.[51]

In addition, the UK currently produces 13–15 million tonnes of straw (see Table 7.2). Although about 5 million tonnes of straw is already ploughed back into the soil as a soil conditioner, and more may be needed in organic production, less than 2 million tonnes diverted to produce straw-based board would cut wood use in particle board manufacture by 4 million $m^3$ WRME. Such straw-based board can meet or exceed the standards achieved by woodchip board.[52] A further 2 million $m^3$ WRME could be substituted for by woody material produced from increased fibre crop cultivation at yields of up to 4 tonnes per hectare.[53]

Similarly, increased cultivation of fibre crops could further substitute for wood use in paper. At present the UK only has the pulping capacity to produce around 47,000 tonnes of pulp from non-wood fibres: just four small pulp mills. The Bioregional Development Group estimate that 30–40 mills, each producing 125,000 tonnes of paper a year from non-wood and recycled fibre, could supply our entire current printing and writing paper consumption: 3.75–5 million tonnes (over 13 million $m^3$ WRME) per year. This would require 1.8 million tonnes of non-wood pulp. Because of the high quality of fibres, non-wood fibres can be recycled many more times than wood based paper. Assuming, conservatively, that 45 per cent of inputs are from non-wood fibres and 55 per

**Table 7.2** *Potential Fibre Yields from Crops Grown in the UK (1995)*

| Non-wood fibre | Hectares grown or total produced (pa) | Straw yield tonnes/ha | Fibre yield (25%) (thousand tonnes) | Woody material yield (50%) (thousand tonnes) |
|---|---|---|---|---|
| Linseed | 62,000 | 2 | 31 | 62 |
| Fibre flax | 17,000 | 7 | 30 | 60 |
| Hemp | 1000 | 7 | 1.75 | 3 |
| Sub total | 80,000 | | 62.75 | 125 |
| Oil seed rape straw | 2 million tonnes | | 900 (45% fibre yield) | |
| Wheat straw | 11–13 million tonnes | | 4620–5460 (42% fibre yield) | |
| Totals | 13–15 million tonnes | | 5520–6420 | |

Source: Desai, P (ed) (1996) *Local Paper – waste paper and non-wood fibres for a sustainable paper cycle in the south east* London: Bioregional Development Group

cent from recycled paper waste, then 350,000 ha of hemp could produce approximately 4 million tonnes of paper.[54] Such a shift to hemp production seems feasible, within our estimates for agricultural land availability in Chapter 6, and we therefore include a figure for such substitution in our total savings for 2010.

Overall, we estimate that the potential for primary wood product replacement by non-wood fibres is at least 8 million m³ WRME per annum and this could be achieved by 2010.[55] To achieve such levels will require active stimulation of markets for non-wood products, and planned investment in dedicated processing and localised production facilities, as adding non-wood fibres into wood-pulping processes is relatively complex and energy-intensive. Localised production is preferable as straw and other non-wood fibres are bulky and transport costs and pollution would otherwise be excessive.

## Cutting Wood and Paper Use

The potential to cut wood use is significant. A best practice project in the USA cut timber use in housing by 80 per cent. Simply reducing 'over-specification' could save 10–20 per cent of timber in construction uses. Modern structural timber-based composites can cut use of wood in, for example floor, construction by 50 per cent. Even excluding gains from increased longevity of timber by designing and maintaining joinery such as doors and window-frames for durability, we estimate, based on earlier research reported by Rice, that an overall 25 per cent cut in timber use in construction is feasible, equivalent to 2 million m³ WRME.[56] The potential to reduce paper consumption is at least as large. Primary paper and paperboard consumption in the UK is almost half of total primary wood consumption. This includes printing and writing paper, but also sanitary paper, newsprint, and packaging.

## Over-packaging

The packaging industry is the largest paper-using sector in the UK. It consumed 3.6 million tonnes (9.1 million m³ WRME) in 1990.[57] Even though the recycled content in UK produced packaging is high[58] there is still scope both for reducing initial demand and for increasing collection of packaging waste for further recycling, as only about 40 per cent of paper in packaging waste is collected for recycling.[59] Use of paper packaging is expected to increase by 11 per cent between 1991 and 1999 due to, for example, increases in sales of pre-packed meals. According to the German Department of the Environment, one study showed that 98 per cent of all secondary packaging, such as boxes around toothpaste and shampoo, is unnecessary and can be dispensed with.[60] However, packaging is not categorised in this way in the UK, so we cannot say what proportion of packaging is 'secondary'.

Albert Heijn, a large chain store in the Netherlands, was among the first to challenge the problem of overpackaging. It has introduced minimalist packaging for a number of products. For example, chocolate packaging trays were replaced by more simple separators. This reduced the overall size of the box, making savings of 43 per cent, equivalent to 3.4 tonnes of raw material per year, some of which is plastic. Similarly the store's rice is now sold directly in a cardboard box without the paper bag previously used inside. This change has resulted in a 26 per cent saving of paper or 148 tonnes annually. Whole cheeses were previously packaged in cardboard outer boxes for transport and export. A standard reusable container was produced for transportation within the Netherlands. This resulted in savings of about 140,000 boxes or approximately 57 tonnes of cardboard annually.[61]

Although the figures above are small, they are only for one chain and a handful of products. If similar savings of around 25 per cent in packaging could be made throughout the economy then over 2.1 million m³ WRME of – mainly already recycled – material could be saved to be used in other products.[62] Bigger relative cuts in packaging can be made in the commercial and public service sector. The city of Bjorneborg in Finland abolished unnecessary packaging in municipal canteens. Yoghurt is now delivered in tanks, eliminating 345,000 plastic cups each year. Milk comes in 13,000 25-litre cartons, rather than 320,000 one litre cartons, and bread comes unwrapped.[63]

The EC Directive on Packaging and Packaging Waste has set targets for recovering 50–65 per cent and recycling 25–45 per cent, with a minimum of 15 per cent of each material by 2001, but the mechanisms to implement this in the UK are still under discussion. Most packaging waste currently goes to landfill. Paper and board packaging represents 5–6 per cent by weight of household collected waste. If targets towards the higher end of the ranges in the Directive were to be set and met, then this would add to our suggested savings for the sector. Broad waste reduction targets as high as 25 per cent by the year 2000 have been set in some countries such as Canada but the UK currently has no target for waste reduction. Despite producing a national Waste Strategy in 1995[64] it postponed setting a target for waste reduction until 1998.

*Towards the Paperless Office*

In the past 25 years the volume of paper used in offices has soared by 600 per cent. Today's staff often spend 60 per cent of their time working with printed documents. But there is potential to reduce the amount of paper we use in offices with the advances in technology to create a 'paperless office'.[65] For example, Aetna, a large insurance corporation in the US, has in the past three years converted 435 underwriting manuals in its property and casualty division into electronic files, eliminating 87 million pages of paper, 10,000 three ring binders and US$4 million in printing and distribution costs. This is equivalent to a saving of 14 tonnes of paper. The potential for many insurance companies, local authorities, banks, publishing houses and national government departments may be as big or even bigger. However, in the UK, printing and writing paper use increased by 10 per cent between 1990 and 1993,[66] despite the amounts invested in new technologies. We are supplementing technology with paper. Several barriers to change need to be overcome to release the potential for the paperless office. These include improved screen technology to make prolonged VDU use less unhealthy; and improved compatibility of information technology. The rewards for overcoming these barriers are greater than just the paper savings. For example, the United Services Automobile Association now use an imaging system to store their data. It saved 35,000 square feet of office space that used to be taken up by paper files. Developing integrated computer networks could also facilitate homeworking and thus travel savings too.

Overall, measures to cut paper and paperboard use could probably save several times more than the 2.1 million m$^3$ estimated above for packaging. However, to take a conservative approach, we will apply the estimate of Rice that, overall, by 2010, 5 million m$^3$ WRME could be saved by cutting use of wood and paper, of which around three-fifths would be paper and two-fifths wood.[67]

# IMPLICATIONS FOR OTHER RESOURCES

Increasing recycling generally has positive implications for other resources. Recycling rates of 50–80 per cent would not only deliver savings in wood use, but lower energy and chemical requirements and reduced waste and sludge disposal because recycling paper is more efficient in these terms than producing it from virgin fibre. The World Resource Foundation have calculated that recycling can reduce water use by nearly 60 per cent and energy consumption by 40 per cent.[68] Air pollution can be decreased by 74 per cent and water pollution by 35 per cent in comparison with producing paper from virgin pulp. These figures are dependent on specific factors such as the transport distances involved in taking collected waste paper to mills for reprocessing, the methods used to de-ink the paper and so on. The recycling rates suggested above would cut $CO_2$ emissions by 0.4-0.7 million tonnes.[69] The other major area with implications for other resources is the production of non-wood fibre. This would, as discussed above, require the conversion of significant areas of agricultural land to fibre production. This has been taken into account in Chapter 6. There are offsetting benefits from using non-wood fibres for energy and chemical use however. The fibres of hemp and flax are lower in lignin, higher in cellulose, stronger and finer than wood fibres. Therefore they can be pulped using less energy and fewer chemicals to produce a higher quality paper and most of the cropped material can be used in this way.

# TOTAL WOOD CONSUMPTION SAVINGS

For this study we have adopted a consistent approach with the other resources considered, to suggest an interim target for 2010, and a longer term objective of reducing consumption to within environmental space by 2050. The 2050 target is therefore the 73 per cent reduction calculated earlier. According to this methodology, the interim target for 2010 would be just 18 per cent, or an absolute reduction of 9.5 million $m^3$ WRME. However, the continued damage to old growth forests in Scandinavia and elsewhere, resulting in part from UK demand for wood and paper, means that a much stricter interim target is merited. In such circumstances, the more rapidly we can get within the environmental space limits the better. A stricter interim target will increase the pressure and incentive for developing further savings towards the full environmental space target. As an aspirational target Friends of the Earth has advocated a 65 per cent reduction by 2010.

This is ambitious, but as FOE's previous in-depth study of this area has shown,[70] a 65 per cent reduction in wood consumption by 2010 could be achieved through vigorous action in certain sectors, including rapidly increased use of non-wood fibres. Further reductions are possible but

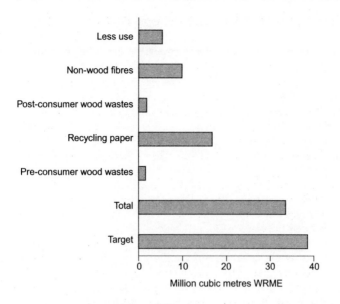

**Figure 7.4** *Potential for cutting UK wood consumption*

dependent on concerted action from government and industry; for example, to stimulate the development and uptake of new technologies and greater resource efficiency. Table 7.3 and Figure 7.4 show the total amount of savings that can be made in the UK by widespread adoption of the best practice represented by the case studies and estimates presented above. We must note that the recycling contribution means that the last Government's target of 25 per cent by 2000[71] must be exceeded, at least for paper, by a large margin in subsequent years.

Our estimates of potential savings for 2010 are equivalent to 48–52 per cent of current consumption. However, achieving the 65 per cent that we have previously advocated will be more difficult, especially as consumption is still on an upward trend. We need to reverse this, and reach the full environmental space target as soon as possible, to prevent as much irreversible damage to the forests of the planet as possible. Reaching that target appears realistic, if challenging. Our estimated savings for 2050 are equivalent to 60–66 per cent of current consumption, while the target requires a 73 per cent cut. All these figures for potential savings are conservative, as there are several exclusions where it has proved difficult to quantify the potential. The real savings from increased use of coppicing and thinnings and reducing paper use, especially in businesses, may well exceed our cautious expectations. The opportunities for reducing timber use by increasing the longevity of timber products is even more difficult to quantify, so no estimate has been included. However, there is potential

**Table 7.3** *Summary of Savings: Wood*

| Measure | Saving by 2010 (million m³ WRME) | Saving by 2050 (million m³ WRME) |
| --- | --- | --- |
| Increasing use of pre-consumer wood waste | 1.75 | 1.75 |
| Recycling paper (2010: 50% recovery; 2050: 80%) | 10.5 | 16.8 |
| Less wood and paper use, including packaging | 5 | 5 |
| Increasing use of post-consumer wood wastes | 0.4–2.0 | 0.4–2.0 |
| Use of non-wood fibres for board and paper | 8 | 8 |
| Total | 25.65–27.25 | 31.95–33.55 |

for savings in increasing the lifespan of components such as doors and windows through design and finishing improvements, and in increasing the average lifespan of the buildings themselves.

## Chapter 8
# Water

## INTRODUCTION

Water is unevenly distributed within and between countries. In many countries shortage of fresh water for drinking and irrigation is reaching critical levels.[1] As we saw in Chapter 2, water is a source of political and even violent conflict in some parts of the world, and water resources are not just a resource for humans, they are critical for biodiversity too.

## WATER AND ENVIRONMENTAL SPACE

Unfortunately, water fits uncomfortably into the 'environmental space' methodology. Water is bulky and expensive to transport, so is rarely carried over regional or natural watershed boundaries, except when embodied in other products (see Box 8.2). For this reason, even though it raises some moral concerns, we will treat water, not as a global resource, but as a regional or national one. As water is traditionally a regional resource, it makes sense to deal with sustainability issues for water broadly at a regional level. Artificially creating a standardised European environmental space with transport of water from the Danube to Portugal, or even a UK environmental space implying transfers of water from lochs in Scotland to farms in Suffolk, is a notion that should be rejected. So here we start from uneven regional consumption figures and do not assume that consumption should be equal everywhere. Nonetheless in this chapter we will set a national percentage target for reductions in water use based on current and predicted impacts of abstraction of water. We believe this is appropriate for three reasons: first such a national target would be a suitable staging post towards detailed regional targets; second a precautionary approach is demanded, if nothing else, by the threat of climate change; and third, many of the practical measures that can save water, and we discuss these later in the chapter, are most effectively promoted at a national level.

# BOX 8.1 *WATER QUALITY*

Despite recent improvements, 3650 km (or 9 per cent) of our rivers and canals still have 'poor' or 'bad' water quality.[a] Our rivers and groundwater are polluted by agricultural and industrial practices. The number of water pollution incidents in the UK increased every year from 1986, reaching 25,425 in 1994 (in England and Wales).[a] This is affecting our valued wildlife too.[b]

Pollutants released to water can be toxic and persistent – but many that fall into this category are emitted legally. Fish from the Mersey Estuary have been found to contain over 300 different industrial chemicals, many of which are not regulated or even normally tested for.[c]

Recent concerns regarding freshwater have focused on the presence of oestrogenic hormones and oestrogen-mimicking compounds. These have been shown to trigger 'sex-changes' in fish, where male fish develop female characteristics. They have even been linked with the widely reported decline in human male fertility.[d]

Underground water reserves, or groundwaters, have also been contaminated. Abundant use of cheap fertilisers and pesticides in agriculture has raised pollution levels in much of our groundwater. In several areas, boreholes now produce water unfit for drinking due to high nitrate levels. Yet the worst quality groundwater is found under our cities where decades of poor industrial management have allowed contaminants such as organic compounds which do not occur in nature to leach into the ground. At worst the water has become unusable.[e]

Sources: *a* Department of the Environment (1996) *Digest of Environmental Statistics* 18, 1996 London: HMSO; *b* For example, English Nature, one of the Government's statutory advisers on nature conservation, has investigated 102 Sites of Special Scientific Interest (SSSI) which have been damaged by eutrophication caused by phosphate pollution from sewage works and farms. According to English Nature, in 85 of these SSSIs (84 per cent), the site is so badly damaged that the very reason for its designation is threatened. Carvalho, L and Moss, B (1995) The current status of a sample of English sites of special scientific interest subject to eutrophication *Aquatic Conservation: Marine and Freshwater Ecosystems* 5(3); *c* Department of the Environment (1991) *Chlorinated organic pollutants in fish from the North East Irish Sea* London: DoE; *d* There are still differing views on the causes and sources, including industrial processes involving alkylphenol ethoxylates, domestic sources of hormones, including the birth control pill, and sewage treatment processes. Warhurst, M (1995) *An environmental assessment of alkylphenol ethoxylates and alkylphenols* Edinburgh: Friends of the Earth Scotland; *e* Rivett, M, Lerner, D, Lloyd, JW and Clark, L (1989) *Organic Contamination of the Birmingham Aquifer. Report WRC PRS 2064-M* Birmingham: University of Birmingham Water Research Centre. A recent survey by the Environment Agency, which is thought to identify only the 'tip of the iceberg' of groundwater contamination, found over 1200 sites causing groundwater contamination, of which almost 100 were classed as likely to have caused 'gross contamination of a major aquifer' *ENDS Report* 260 (1996) Aquifer pollution inventory sets the scene for tussles over clean-up, pp15–18

## BOX 8.2 *EMBODIED WATER*

All our figures exclude imports of water embodied in produce. For example our imports of orange juice alone embody 3.3 million cubic metres (equivalent to 9 megalitres per day), while our net cotton imports embody 1.5 billion cubic metres, equivalent to more than 4000 megalitres per day! We have not been able to estimate what total volume of water is embodied in our net imports, but it remains an important consideration even when the environmental space for water is being calculated nationally. It cannot help sustainability if we import crops with a high water content, or which require high water use in their production, from areas where water availability is limited.

However, as we saw in Chapter 6, sustainability in land use will require a shift to being a net effective exporter of land through exports of agricultural products. This will make it much less likely that we will import significant net amounts of water, even though our imports will probably remain more likely to be irrigation-intensive crops than our exports.

Source: Environmental Challenge (1994) *Environmental Measures. Indicators for the UK Environment* Sandy, Bedfordshire: RSPB

## SUSTAINABLE SUPPLY

Even in our equable climate, where complaining about the weather is a national pastime, our use of water is not sustainable. The quality of our surface and ground waters is the first reason for concern (see Box 8.1).

In terms of environmental space, sustainable management of water resources means ensuring its quality both for human use and for biodiversity. This requires effective regulatory and market measures in a range of sectors. As well as quality, quantity is an issue. Even though water is a renewable resource, the amounts we can use are limited. Although we have a lot of rain, we have a lot of people too. The UK is a densely populated country, so, per capita, we have little water. A US think-tank, the World Resources Institute, has graded countries according to water availability per capita, as 'very low', 'low', 'medium' and 'high'. The UK is classed as 'low', in the same category as South Africa.[2]

In Yorkshire in 1995, water shortages required a major tankering operation, costing £47 million to move millions of gallons of water to the areas most in need. While there are good reasons to believe that with better management and appropriate advance investment to reduce leakage in the system this problem could have been avoided, it can be seen as a first warning. If we stretch our supply system to the limit in seeking to meet demand, any future shortage could cause similar or even worse problems. And with climate change threatening to dramatically increase the frequency, intensity and duration of droughts – in the last 20 years we have had three droughts which, on the basis of the records, we might expect only once in 200 years or more[3] – it is clear that we cannot go on seeking to meet all demand.

# THE CURRENT SITUATION

The Environment Agency collects detailed information on water use in England and Wales. Water comes from three sources: surface water, ground water and tidal water. Over 90 per cent of tidal water use is by the electricity supply industry. Excluding tidal water and water used for 'through cooling', UK water abstractions in 1994 were approximately 28,800 Ml/day, equivalent to around 500 litres per person per day. The amount of water put into the public water supply has increased slightly over the last ten years, with some fluctuations, and the amount of water delivered to consumers has similarly increased. For overall water use, increased use in the household and commercial sectors has been largely counterbalanced by reductions in the use of surface water by industry as a result of improved water management and economic recession.

Even in the absence of climate change, demand is expected to grow with more smaller households, and increased ownership of dishwashers and other water-intensive household equipment. The NRA predicted that even a 'medium growth in demand' would create a deficit in supply in the Severn Trent, Thames and Anglian regions by 2021, even after local resource options had been developed (see Table 8.1). With high growth in demand, the Wessex region would also be in deficit by then.[4] The figures for water consumption exclude embodied water (see Box 8.2).

Scotland is self-sufficient in water. Average per capita demand varies from 584 litres per day in the central region to 324 litres per day in the Borders but no region is expected to suffer from a deficit of supply in the foreseeable future.[5] The NRA estimated that 'total available yield' – using all of which, as we will see, is unsustainable in several respects – exceeds average demand in all regions of England and Wales. But Thames and the North-West have only a 9 per cent margin, Yorkshire – recently severely afflicted by drought – 10 per cent, Severn Trent 13 per cent and Wessex 16 per cent.[6] These figures, rather than being a reason for complacency, imply only a small – if any – margin for manoeuvre.

## Water Use in the Future

The NRA looked in detail at levels of water use, following and preceding the 1995 drought. It concluded that 'with reasonable success in achieving demand management the need for new strategic water resources such as major resources or transfers can be delayed for 20 years or more'.[7] Its demand forecasts have been reduced by proposed demand management measures, mainly expected leakage reductions and the increasing penetration of household metering. It still expects growth in demand from households (+12 per cent) due to population increases, falling occupancy rates and growth in per capita consumption.[8] But this is expected to be largely offset

**Table 8.1** *Water Use and Supply*

| Public water supply | Current use (1994) | | Growth scenarios. Increase in demand to 2021 as a proportion of 1991 demand (%), and predicted deficits (megalitres per day) | | | | | |
|---|---|---|---|---|---|---|---|---|
| | Megalitres per day | Litres per capita per day | High | | Medium | | Low | |
| Anglian | 1760 | 319 | 37 | 128 | 27 | 72 | 18 | 0 |
| Northumbria | 1013 | 385 | 16 | 0 | 10 | 0 | 6 | 0 |
| North West | 1771 | 257 | 15 | 0 | 0 | 0 | −6 | 0 |
| Severn Trent | 2494 | 298 | 28 | 252 | 12 | 4 | 3 | 0 |
| Southern | 1359 | 329 | 31 | 0 | 15 | 0 | 6 | 0 |
| South West | 588 | 378 | 43 | 0 | 27 | 0 | 19 | 0 |
| Thames | 3980 | 331 | 28 | 629 | 7 | 66 | −2 | 0 |
| Welsh | 1787 | 565 | 18 | 0 | 5 | 0 | −1 | 0 |
| Wessex | 766 | 287 | 32 | 84 | 15 | 0 | 6 | 0 |
| Yorkshire | 1217 | 261 | 23 | 0 | 8 | 0 | 0 | 0 |
| Total (mean) | 16735 | (324) | | 1110 | | 142 | | 0 |
| Scotland and Northern Ireland | 2952 | (440) | n/a | n/a | n/a | n/a | n/a | n/a |

Sources: National Rivers Authority (1994) *Water, Nature's Precious Resource* Bristol: NRA. The table also shows current use per person (from the public water supply), which averages 324 litres in England and Wales. This compares with 445 litres per person per day for Scotland and 427 litres per person per day for Northern Ireland. Department of the Environment (1996) *Digest of Environmental Statistics 18, 1996* London: HMSO

by reductions in company leakage levels (−21 per cent) and falling industrial demand (−5 per cent). In other words, water used can increase, while water abstracted remains constant or declines, particularly as a result of reductions in leakage. Beyond 2010, the NRA predicted that pressure on resources will continue to grow: becoming potentially severe in the Thames region, and of increased concern in the Anglian and Southern regions.[9]

One reason for the current inefficient use of water is that water has been underpriced. Increasing water charges to companies can trigger remarkable reductions in waste, as has been seen in other countries. If we assume that similar incentives are introduced in the UK, this would result in a much increased uptake rate for known and practical cost-effective demand management options. If we account for this in the assumptions underlying the demand forecasts, it would create an 'ultra-low' alternative in which total demand would be expected to decrease. At present such a scenario is not considered by the Agency, because the pressure for increasing demand management is assumed to be growth in demand, rather than the unsustainability of current abstraction rates. As a result, low growth forecasts include only low uptake of demand management measures.

# SUSTAINABILITY AND SCARCITY

Absolute shortages of water for human use are only the tip of the iceberg as far as a sustainability analysis is concerned. In the same way as the environmental limits on using fossil fuels are far more pressing than the absolute supply, the environmental impacts of water abstraction bring us to sustainability limits long before we have exploited all the water we technically could. Even in regions where no deficits are forecast, the environmental impacts of overabstraction are already being felt.[10] At present, seasonal variation in demand is a threat to rivers in many regions, leaving flows too low to sustain wildlife populations. The NRA identified a 'hit-list' of 40 low flow rivers where damage to ecological and fishing interests are resulting.[11] The low flows are almost exclusively the result of authorised abstractions rather than drought, although drought exacerbates the problems. The NRA list covered simply priorities for action, rather than a comprehensive analysis of where damage is resulting from overabstraction. Regional NRA branches also conducted low-flow studies: for example, NRA South West alone identified 109 sites where environmental damage occurred due to upstream or groundwater abstraction.[12]

To illustrate the problems, in the Anglia region, East Rushton Site of Special Scientific Interest's diverse ecology is home to two rare species of spider, but it is drying out. The NRA reported that the drying is alleged to be the result of groundwater abstraction for the public water supply by Anglian Water Services at East Rushton. Similarly, a report for the NRA confirmed that increased abstraction mainly from public water supply boreholes is the cause of lowered groundwater levels and flow in the River Hiz near Hitchin, also in the Anglian region. Options proposed to resolve the problem include relocation of public water supply abstraction, river support, river recirculation and replacement of public water supplies from Grafham Water. The proposed solutions are complex and the total cost for a comprehensive scheme is estimated at up to £7.1 million.[13]

These are simply a few examples: similar problems can be found in all regions of England and Wales, although there are more of them in East Anglia, the Midlands and the South West than in other regions. They even occur in parts of Scotland despite the much higher levels of rainfall in comparison with demand in Scotland. For example, Loch Tarff in Scotland has been subject to falling water levels due to water abstraction. This has affected the breeding success of black throated divers and Slavonian grebes, as the abstractions have left nests stranded above the water's edge, making them vulnerable to predators.[14] An English Nature survey suggests that in England, almost one in ten freshwater wetland Sites of Special Scientific Interest may be threatened by water abstraction.[15] Friends of the Earth, along with other NGOs in the 'Biodiversity Challenge' group, has identified over 250 SSSIs in England and Wales alone which are affected by or currently threatened by overabstraction. Over 100 more are expected to be at risk in the future. More widespread impacts beyond SSSIs are not covered in this survey.[16] Catering for increased demand for water will inevitably worsen these impacts. As Matt Phillips, Habitats Campaigner for Friends of the Earth, says:

> *Water resources are now a matter of biodiversity policy, not just a resource to be managed for humans. Government, every department and minister, is signed up to the [Biodiversity Action] plans which aim to reverse the decline of species and habitats. That means a transformation in the attitude taken to the amount and quality of water used by people.[17]*

# Facing up to Climate Change

Although climate change is expected to make the UK warmer and wetter overall, rainfall is likely to be reduced in the South and East, while likely demand for water will increase. Moreover, rainfall is expected to be further concentrated in the winter months, adversely affecting river flows in summer. Overall, according to the Department of the Environment,

> *climate change might add an additional five per cent onto the 12 per cent increase in demand for public water supplies expected in Southern England between 1990 and 2021, largely due to increased usage in gardens. The increase in peak demands could be much greater. Demands for spray irrigation [in agriculture] are predicted to rise by 69 per cent without climate change, and could rise by 115 per cent if temperatures were to rise.[18]*

Increasing agricultural demands would reflect drier summers and planting of new irrigation intensive crops in response to raised temperatures.

Because of the continuing uncertainties about the exact impacts and their distribution, such forecasts demand a precautionary approach to manage demand for water. A broad package of reforms is needed to ensure that the current problems can be addressed, and that new problems are prevented from arising. At present, although new abstraction licences incorporate provisions for regular review, the Agency cannot revoke licences without having to pay compensation to the licensees. The system should be overhauled and all existing licenses reviewed by 1999 to identify damaging impacts on wildlife. Furthermore, planning authorities should be required to adhere to catchment management plans to ensure that overabstraction does not become likely due to developments granted planning permission. The Environment Agency should be given powers to implement a sustainable water resource strategy, including legal powers to require agreements to protect river flows, rather than having to rely on voluntary agreements. We also need to take a precautionary approach to defining the environmental space for water. At present we suggest that a general reduction of 15 per cent in water consumption would be an appropriate target, equivalent to a cut in abstraction of 4810 megalitres per day to 20,840 for England and Wales (the cut for the UK is 5430 megalitres per day).[19] This would not wholly eliminate the need to undertake additional targeted remedial action for low-flow rivers. Figure 8.1 contrasts this target with recent trends in consumption and the forecasts made by the Agency.

A general reduction would relieve pressure on the environment, which has suffered from years of overabstraction, and in effect, establish a buffer in case of unexpected changes in our rainfall or other parts of the hydrological cycle as a result of climate change. Such a reduction will also have economic and social advantages, not least because water conservation is better for local economies and employment than increasing supply.

## THE POTENTIAL FOR REDUCTION

In practice there are four ways in which we can meet needs for water. The conventional method is to invest in supply infrastructure to collect, store and distribute water. More recently, attention has been given to the reallocation of existing resources by transfer schemes. Alternatively we can use and reuse water more effectively, or reduce demand by introducing techniques that meet the same needs with less water. In general, the first two options will increase the already excessive environmental costs of water supply, whilst the last two will potentially allow us to meet needs with less abstraction of water from the environment. Transfer schemes do not only involve new infrastructure to divert water flows from one catchment to another, they create ecological risks too. The recently publicised proposals by Yorkshire Water to transfer water from the Kielder reservoir in Northumberland via rivers in Yorkshire, provide a good example. One of the threats of the proposed transfer is the spread of the American signal crayfish. This is a vigorous invasive species which out-competes the native white-clawed crayfish. It also carries a fungal plague which is fatal to native crayfish. The ecological implications of this are considered so serious that under the Wildlife and Countryside Act 1981 it was made illegal to introduce signal crayfish to the wild.[20]

The privatised water industry has focused its proposals for investment on ways to increase supply to meet demand, such as building new

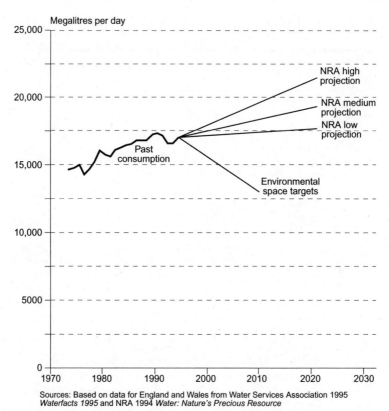

Sources: Based on data for England and Wales from Water Services Association 1995
*Waterfacts 1995* and NRA 1994 *Water: Nature's Precious Resource*

**Figure 8.1** *UK water use – projections and targets*

reservoirs, and water transfer schemes to shift water from areas of surplus into areas of shortage. But, as the House of Commons Environment Committee concluded recently, their arguments for such investments have not been convincing.[21] Demand management can be expected to bring wider benefits. Research by Environment Canada has compared water conservation with infrastructure expansion for meeting demand in the Halton region of Canada.[22] Their results are shown in Table 8.2.

The average cost to householders is Can$550. As water is already metered, this would pay for itself in 3–4 years. The researchers say:

> *Unlike infrastructure expansion, water conservation programs actually leave money in householders' pockets – money that would have been spent on water bills and energy costs associated with pumping and heating water ... These savings increase the amount of household income available for other things, and the spending of cost savings generates the larger economic impact shown in the charts.*

**Table 8.2** *Economic Implications of Water Saving*

|  | *Water conservation* | *Infrastructure expansion* |
|---|---|---|
| Job years in Ontario | 3000 | 2300 |
| Job years in Halton | 1200 | 800 |
| Income generated locally | Can$82 million | Can$54 million |
| Household savings | Can$33 million | Can$0 |

Source: Environment Canada (1995) *The Economic Impacts of Water Conservation. Research Summary* Burlington, Ontario: Environment Canada

> *Conversely, expanding infrastructure typically reduces disposable household income because higher water and wastewater bills are required to pay for the additional expense.*[23]

The attention given by the companies to demand management has been limited, although some companies have pursued the possibility of water metering which the last Government also strongly promoted. In general, proposals for demand management have only been considered as short-term measures, as a stopgap before new supply can be developed. In reality, there is significant potential in the UK for cutting water use, particularly in control of leakage, and in increasing the efficiency of domestic and industrial use. As the Environment Committee says, there is too much waste.[24] However, the water companies have little incentive to reduce long term water consumption by domestic households, commerce and industry, particularly if metering becomes widespread. Metering only provides an incentive for customers to save water. While there are cost and practical obstacles to investing in water efficiency, this will be less effective, and more inequitable than approaches focused at the level of the supplier. Rather than merely being given duties to promote efficient use of water by their customers and to achieve efficiency in supply, the companies should be placed under a legal duty to conserve water and use it efficiently and, where appropriate, companies should be given targets for reducing water consumption. Such measures should be reinforced by giving the Environment Agency powers to oversee companies' resource planning. The Government should adopt a policy of demand management which would emphasise the need to conserve water as an alternative to expanding supplies.

In some states of the USA, water companies are given a duty to reduce per capita consumption. For example, in Arizona, Tucson Water is now required by law to reduce per capita consumption. Failure to reach specified targets results in fines of up to US$10,000 per day.[25] The Dutch water supply company association (VEWIN) has drawn up a programme aimed at reducing consumption of drinking water by 10 per cent by the

**Table 8.3** *Relative Cost of Demand Management Options*

| Demand Management Option | Demand management costs (p/m³) | Ratio to resource development costs |
|---|---|---|
| Efficient washing machines | 0 | 0 |
| Controllers on urinals | 9 | 0.1–0.3 |
| Leakage Control | 13 | 0.2–0.4 |
| Convert WCs (option 3) | 18 | 0.3–0.6 |
| Convert WCs (option 1) | 28 | 0.4–0.9 |
| Domestic metering (universal) | 89 | 1.3–2.7 |
| Shower installation | 94 | 1.4–2.9 |
| Low volume shower heads | 102 | 1.6–3.1 |
| Replace WCs (option 2) | 172 | 2.6–5.2 |
| Domestic recycling | 321 | 4.9–9.8 |

Source: National Rivers Authority (1995) *Saving Water – the NRA's Approach to Water Conservation and Demand Management* Brsitol: NRA

year 2000. Information campaigns and promotion of products such as water saving shower heads seem to be producing positive results.[26] In California, local ordinances require new development to be accompanied by a package of investments that will reduce total water demand in the area by the same amount as the new development will increase demand.[27] These examples show that imaginative regulatory approaches can help control water use efficiently.

# Reducing Leakage

OFWAT, the water industry regulator, has recently estimated that 30 per cent of water put into distribution systems leaks away. To illustrate the extent of losses, in the Thames region, enough water is lost to leakage for every household in the region to have ten showers a day![28] Leakage from Scotland's ageing Victorian water supply system may be as high as 40 per cent.[29] The potential for satisfying increases in demand through leakage control is therefore considerable. The Environment Agency has estimated that 2340 megalitres a day could be saved by leakage control alone, at one-third of the cost of developing new resources. This figure is based on reducing leakage to the equivalent of 120 litres per property per day. In our calculations we have assumed, conservatively, that this average will be achieved across all households, rather than the addition of new households reducing the average leakage figure still further. In the Environment Agency's calculations, leakage control is the third cheapest option, after efficient washing machines and fitting controllers to urinals, and it offers by far the largest potential for water savings (see Table 8.3).

The Environment Agency notes that: 'even within a 40 year time horizon, where the expenditure on leakage control has to be maintained to keep leakage at a specified level, it is still significantly cheaper than developing resources.'[30] Recent failure to deal with leaks has been very costly: Yorkshire Water's £47 million tankering operation should be seen in the context of its total leakage rate of over 36 per cent.[31]

Reducing leakage to much less than 120 litres per property per day is not unrealistic: Anglian and Southern regions are already below it. The main companies at fault are Dwr Cymru, North West, Thames, Wessex and Yorkshire, whose leakage rates are between 225 and 241 litres per property per day. Although the water companies have set themselves targets for leakage, to be achieved by between 2000 and 2005, these are rarely ambitious. At best the targets aim to halve losses, but even if they are achieved, leakage will range from 10 per cent in Southern to 25 per cent in Dwr Cymru (see Table 8.4). Although the best rates will be achieved in the drier parts of the country, this is no protection against water shortages, as the case of Yorkshire showed. The published targets are scarcely inspirational: for two companies – Thames and Yorkshire – they are less demanding than those in the companies' confidential Strategic Business Plans. Worse, in practice, between 1992–93 and 1994–95 although targets were already in place, leaks increased in several regions: Yorkshire, Wessex, Thames, Severn Trent, Northumbrian and Anglian. Much better rates are possible. For comparison, leakage rates in Denmark average 7 per cent, and Friends of the Earth in Denmark is promoting a target of 2 per cent.[32]

According to OFWAT's recent report on leakage, environmental costs and benefits should be calculated when assessing what level of leakage control should be put in place.[33] Once environmental concerns are accounted for, the relative merits of reducing inefficiency over increasing supply will make even higher levels of leakage control justified. Leakage control will also help increase the take-up of domestic demand management options. The last Government, in its paper 'Water conservation – Government Action', judged that customers would be more likely to take action to reduce water consumption if they can see that water companies are making similar efforts.[34] Of course, leakage control is not 'free' in environmental terms, but its impacts on ecology and the wider environment are much more limited than the development of new supply. The most significant impacts come from the consumption of materials – especially plastics – and energy, in renewing underground pipes.

## Reducing Domestic Demand

Houses use 62 per cent of water delivered to the public water supply.[35] Traditionally, water companies have taken a 'supply to meet any demand'

**Table 8.4** *Leakage Targets*

| | Distribution losses as a proportion of distribution input | | |
| --- | --- | --- | --- |
| | *1994–5 leakage level (%)* | *Revised target (%)* | *Target year* |
| Anglian | 13 | 11 | 2002–03 |
| Dwr Cymru | 29 | 25 | 1999–00 |
| North West | 30 | 22 | 2002–03 |
| Northumbrian | 17 | 16 | 2014–15 |
| Severn Trent | 24 | 12 | 1999–00 |
| South West | 24 | 15 | 1999–00 |
| Southern | 14 | 10 | 1999–00 |
| Thames | 28 | to halve distribution losses | 2004–05 |
| Wessex | 27 | 15 | 2004–05 |
| Yorkshire | 30 | 20% in the longer term | – |

Source: OFWAT (1996) *Leakage of water in England and Wales* Birmingham: OFWAT. These figures are for water lost in the water companies' pipes only: total leakage is on average one-third higher

approach, and consumers have paid an annual charge for the service, which varies according to the size of the property, but not with the amount actually used. This means there has been little incentive for the adoption of water-saving products and techniques. Not surprisingly, there is a lot of potential for water use savings in homes. Figure 8.2 shows the share taken by different uses of water in the average home.

It might appear rational to suggest that water metering would be the most effective measure here, creating a general incentive for water saving by allowing unit pricing of water. However, there are even bigger obstacles to its effectiveness than there are to increasing domestic energy prices in an effort to reduce domestic energy use. Fitting water meters to existing homes falls low in the list of cost-effective measures. Nonetheless, the introduction of domestic metering of water use, and volume-related charging, has been promoted by many water companies. Small-scale metering trials have suggested savings of around 11 per cent,[36] which if achievable at a UK scale, would equate to savings of 1000 Ml/day. However the National Rivers Authority's demand management strategy,[37] shows that leakage control, and a number of technologies including efficient washing machines, controllers on urinals and low-flush toilets are all more cost effective than metering, and together could achieve savings of over 3400 Ml/day in England and Wales alone. Domestic metering

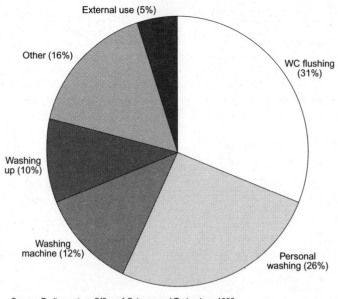

Source: Parliamentary Office of Science and Technology 1992
*Environmental and Technical Aspects of Water Shortage* London: POST

**Figure 8.2** *UK domestic water use*

also raises significant equity implications risking the creation of 'water poverty', and significant health implications from reduced water use or even disconnection where users cannot afford water bills.[38] The British Medical Association has called for disconnection to be made illegal in England and Wales, as it already is in Scotland and Northern Ireland.[39]

The incentive for the companies to invest in water saving measures is reduced by metering, while the installation of meters is relatively costly at up to £200 per home. The equity concerns are no less real. Up to 8 per cent of households suffered 'hardship' as a result of introducing meters in relatively affluent trial areas in the UK.[40] According to an independent tax think-tank, the Institute of Fiscal Studies, if metering were introduced, the poorest in society would be £18 worse off per year, middle income groups £8 worse off and those on high incomes £1 better off.[41] These issues must be overcome as meters are introduced even in new properties, if not before. There are good reasons for creating an incentive for water companies to make the investments in water saving. This requires only limited reform of the regulatory framework for the industry in England and Wales, where it is privatised. In Scotland, where the industry is still publicly owned, an appropriate policy framework could be directly set in place. Currently the unit price for water charged to water companies by the Environment Agency is low, as it just covers the cost of issuing licenses providing the incentive. By working in collaboration with OFWAT, the Environment Agency could raise the price of water to the companies at least tenfold,[42] while OFWAT continued to put a price ceiling for water from water companies to customers. This would create a strong incentive for water companies to increase efficiency. The measures that could then be introduced by water companies, cost-effectively, include low flush toilets, low volume shower heads, pressure butts for water reuse, and rain collection water butts for garden use.

## Low Flush Toilets

In houses, 35 per cent of water is used for flushing toilets.[43] As toilets therefore use 20 per cent of all water in the public water supply, measures to save water here will have a major effect on total levels of water use. Currently the Environment Agency estimates that 90 per cent of all toilets have an average flush of 9.83 litres. The rest are either dual flush (9 and 5 litre) or have a 7.5 litre flush. Best practice designs used in parts of the USA have flushes of as little as 2–3 litres.[44] There is a great deal of scope to save water here. The Environment Agency has calculated that converting high flush toilets is a good deal more cost-effective than developing new resources. There are various different ways of reducing water use in toilets. One of the simplest and cheapest are Hippo bags which have been tested recently by some water companies, including Wessex Water and Thames. The latter is now distributing them free to its customers. Hippos are heavy duty plastic bags which are put into the WC cistern: on average they save 19.4 litres per property per day,[45] including any need for extra flushes. Applied to the 90 per cent of high-flush toilets in the UK, Hippos would save around 480 megalitres a day.

The Environment Agency has calculated that replacing all toilets with dual-flush systems would save 850 megalitres a day.[46] Although such conversion is around half the price of building new resources to meet demand, it would take a long time to convert all of these toilets and in the interim, Hippos should be used. They are simple to install – it could be done by householders themselves – and they are very cheap (if installed on a wide scale, they cost 13 pence each), so they are a very useful short-term measure to quickly save large amounts of water, while a medium term conversion programme is put in place to give even greater savings. In new homes dual flush toilets should be the norm.

## Showers

On average, baths use 80 litres of water, and showers 35 litres. It would seem that installing showers would be a good demand management option. However, showers are used more often than baths, and shower installation costs around £200. But shower installation is at least as cost-effective as retrofitting meters. It is difficult to assess exactly how much water could be saved, although for metered households, financial savings would be noticeable at around £10 per year. If in the next 20 years another quarter of existing homes got showers – this is fairly likely just because showers are a modern convenience, rather than for water saving reasons – and all new homes had showers fitted, then the total water saving would be 250 megalitres per day.[47] If low volume shower heads are fitted to old showers, additional savings can be made. These cost around £10 each, and reduce shower water use by 10 per cent. Attached to existing showers this would save 12 million litres a day.[48] This is also a measure that would be more attractive to people with a metered supply.

## Reuse of Water

Water from baths and showers can be reused as grey water for flushing toilets. The UK company Water Dynamics have developed a pressure butt, which collects used bath and sink water, and treats and filters this water so it can be used on gardens or for toilet flushing, using a pump and separate header tank. Water use from baths and sinks is enough so that all toilet flushing could use grey water. Assuming that a house had a low-flush toilet, this pressure butt would save 65 litres per household per day.[49] However, such pressure butts are not cheap. The payback period for metered households is around ten years. As production volumes increase and prices fall, it is expected that the payback period would be around 3–4 years.[50] Currently 40 pressure butt units have been installed. Trials in the Isle of Wight have received good feedback from householders, and production is increasing. For metered houses they are a good investment. If water companies were to provide grants to support installation, reuse schemes could become more popular. If just 1 million households installed pressure butts, there would be a water saving of 65 million litres/day.

## Gardens

Raindrain in Dewsbury have developed a 'Rain-Sava', a simple device which is attached to drainpipes to divert rainwater into a rain barrel or other storing tank. On average 3 per cent of water for houses, or 13.2 litres per day, is used outside.[51] As the average roof gets around 124 litres of water a day on it, the Rain-Sava device can completely remove the need to use tap water for gardens. Their cost is £13, and installation can easily be done by the householder. This is a very cost-effective unit. If half the households in England and Wales with gardens installed a Rain-Sava, this could save 104 million litres a day.[52]

## Washing Machines

Washing machines use 12 per cent of domestic water consumption. The best cut water use by 38 litres per wash – almost by half compared with the average machine's water consumption – and their widespread adoption could reduce UK water use by 708 Ml/day.[53] Even though the extra expense may not be cost effective for the water savings alone, the water-efficient machines are also more durable and energy efficient. Water companies under a duty to implement least cost planning or demand management should be able to offer grants to encourage uptake of water efficient machines.

*The Domestic Sector – Summary*

The scope for savings in the domestic sector, according to the conservative estimates used above, add up to 884 megalitres per day in England and Wales. For the UK this figure becomes 962 Ml/day.

# Commercial and industrial water savings

In the commercial sector, water use has been declining, but there is still much more cost-effective potential. The total water used by industry and commerce is 7864 Ml/day.[54] As we will see below, users in this sector can typically save 20 per cent or more.

*Urinals*

Uncontrolled urinals waste large amounts of water. Flushing 24 hours a day, every day of the week, urinals use water very inefficiently. Controllers can be fitted to urinals which ensure that water is only used when needed: this results in large reductions in water use and hefty financial savings. One device on the market is UK firm Chess Industries' SmartFlush, which uses infrared detectors and a timer to control when urinals flush. For every urinal, this device saves 220 m$^3$ of water a year.[55] The Government has installed SmartFlush in its Cabinet offices: it is estimated that this saves 3500 m$^3$ of water a year, and saves £2600 per year. These savings overtook the cost of installation in little more than one year, taking running costs and maintenance into account. There are 2 million urinals in the UK. The NRA estimates that 75 per cent of these are uncontrolled. It is now mandatory for new urinals to be fitted with some form of controller, but this does not apply for old urinals. There is a strong economic justification for retro-fitting old urinals, as most of them are in commercial buildings with water metering. Retrofitting 1.5 million urinals would save 328.2 million m$^3$ a year, or 900 megalitres each day, as well as delivering cash savings to businesses. There are also potential knock-on benefits for employment. If each fitting takes on average 1hr (including travel) this is 1.5 million hours, equivalent to 190 jobs for five years.[56] This does not include the jobs created in manufacturing the devices. If take up of controllers for urinals is slow, even though the capital costs are recouped after such a short period, water companies could be proactive and install these devices for compa-

# BOX 8.3 *WATER SAVING IN INDUSTRY – SOME EXAMPLES*

*Carlsberg-Tetley's Burton Brewery*
Redesigning processes and equipment in cask-washing has reduced water and energy use and lowered maintenance costs. Total annual savings of £86,900 were achieved, with a payback period of 13 months. Each year 43,000m$^3$ of water is saved – a reduction in use of 65 per cent – bringing down annual costs for water by £23,000.

*Goldrite Metal Finishing Ltd*
Goldrite fitted a counter current rinsing system in place of an old dip-tank system, to save and recycle chemicals in its metal plating processes. Goldrite now use well under a fifth of their previous consumption of nickel, and have eliminated the discharge of toxic metals from this process. This also saved large amounts of water: consumption was down by 70 per cent, with 4370m$^3$ saved, worth £3600 a year. Overall, the payback period for this expensive technology was 2.4 years.

*Project Catalyst*
This regional waste minimisation club covering the Mersey Basin has had some spectacular results, especially in water savings. Project Catalyst identified over 100 opportunities (amongst just 14 companies) to reduce water use. The potential savings totalled 1.9 million cubic metres of water per year. Two of the many examples from Project Catalyst are:
*Pilkington Tiles* spent £20,000 on new pumps and water recycling equipment at their tile plant at Clifton Junction, Manchester. There were no financial savings for Pilkington, as their water abstraction is not related to use, however their plant now runs more efficiently, and wastewater has been reduced by 100,000m$^3$ a year.
*Colgate–Palmolive* made savings which highlight the large cumulative effect that lots of small measures can have. One leaking tap may not be much on its own, but when it is fixed along with dozens of other little things, the savings soon mount up. The site uses 190,000m$^3$ less water each year, saving Colgate £186,000 a year. The payback on individual projects ranged from immediate to two years. It was noted that: 'It was clear that most problems could be solved by raising the overall awareness of water costs, ie overcoming the "water is free" syndrome.'

Sources: WS Atkins, March Consulting Group and Aspects International (1994) *Project Catalyst: Report to the project completion event* Warrington: WS Atkins North West; Leicestershire County Council (1995) *Leicestershire waste minimisation initiative project report* Leicester: LCC, March

nies and get their investment back in the first year by simply charging companies for the water they would have used. Urinal controllers are a definite win–win option, and the potential savings are very large.

*Industry*

Despite significant gains in recent years, many companies can still save huge amounts of water through simple water audits highlighting areas of inefficiency. The cost-effective potential for industrial water efficiency is probably much greater than the reductions forecast by OFWAT of 5 per cent.[57] As industry's water use is usually metered, these water savings result in large financial savings as well. Box 8.3 shows some examples of current good practice. These not only demonstrate the scope for water saving, but the frequent synergy between water efficiency and energy and materials efficiency.

These and other examples show that there is great potential here, and that it makes economic sense, too, to reduce water. Average savings in Project Catalyst (see Box 8.3) exceeded 20 per cent. But here we take a conservative estimate of a 20 per cent saving being possible: this would save 1315 Ml/day in England and Wales.[58]

# WATER: TOTAL SAVINGS

In England and Wales, the public water supply uses 11,845 Ml/day; an additional 4888 Ml/day leaks away. Sixty-two per cent of the public water supply is used by households. In addition, water is delivered to industry and agriculture, including almost 400 Ml/day for spray irrigation and other agricultural uses, and nearly 4000 Ml/day for fish farming: not counting tidal water or water used by the electricity supply industry for 'through' cooling (in other words water that is returned directly after use).

Total water abstraction is currently 24,521 Ml/day. The various measures outlined would save 5500 million litres of water a day, 23 per cent of current abstraction (see Figure 8.3 and Table 8.5). But by 2010, growth in the number of households would have increased demand (before these savings) to 25,650 Ml/day. The net reduction over current levels of abstraction would be 18 per cent. This would achieve our target if demand growth as a result of changing lifestyles stayed within the low expectations of the Agency – which is plausible given the cultural shift towards water saving that this strategy would promote. Much of this saving would also save money within a relatively short period. According to OFWAT, environmental costs and benefits should be taken into account when balancing resource development against leakage control. Based on the NRA's calculations, the vast majority of this water saving, over 5000 megalitres, is also already cheaper per litre in financial terms than developing new resources to satisfy demand,[59] even *without* taking into account the detrimental environmental costs of developing new resources. With so much inefficiency and wastage in the water system, no new infrastructure can be justified when the costs of reducing inefficiency are so much lower and the damage to the environment from water abstraction is so high.

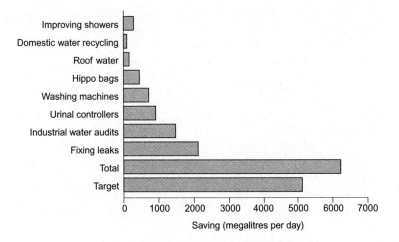

**Figure 8.3** *Potential for cutting UK water use*

# IMPLICATIONS FOR OTHER RESOURCES

Achieving such levels of water savings is not without environmental costs. For example, street trees may be put under stress as water obtained from leaky pipes is reduced. But the net effects on energy, timber and land use are negligible. Indeed, water efficient appliances and practices in homes and businesses are likely to be more energy efficient too, proving a reinforcing beneficial effect. On the other hand, there may be short-term increased demands for construction materials and plastics in achieving lower levels of leakage. But the savings in construction materials from not developing new reservoirs seem likely to outweigh these costs.

# CONCLUSION

For reasons set out above, we have set an environmental space target based purely on national data for water supply and use. That target, of a 15 per cent cut in comparison with current consumption, is based on our best analysis of the current situation, and the likely future stresses imposed on sustainable water supply by climate change. We believe that the target should therefore be achieved as soon as possible, and in any case no later than 2010. But we have not set a general 2050 environmental space target. By 2050 we need to have developed specific regional targets to supplement the 15 per cent overall cut. In Scotland, as Friends of the Earth Scotland report,[60] a precautionary approach may only require ensuring no net increase in total abstraction, alongside local

**Table 8.5** *Summary of Potential Savings in Water Use*

| Measure | Water saving (megalitres each day) England and Wales | Water saving (megalitres each day) United Kingdom |
|---|---|---|
| Fixing leaks | 1920 | 2170 |
| Audits for industry | 1320 | 1490 |
| Fitting controllers to urinals | 800 | 900 |
| Efficient washing machines | 630 | 710 |
| Hippo bags for toilets | 430 | 480 |
| Using roof water on gardens | 100 | 120 |
| Recycling water in the home | 65 | 75 |
| Installing showers, and making current showers more efficient | 260 | 290 |
| Total | 5500 | 6240 |

Note: This table incorporates adjustments for the predicted increase in households to 2010, where appropriate. Data for Scotland and Northern Ireland are less complete. We have assumed that the savings for the UK are 1.129 times those for England and Wales, as the UK's population is this factor larger than that for England and Wales. The ratio based on numbers of households is almost identical. Leakage rates in Scotland are possibly as high as 40 per cent, so savings based on leakage control could be higher. Figures have been rounded, so columns may not add exactly.

targeted reductions. Such a stabilisation of use could easily be achieved through leakage control alone.

But unlike the Netherlands, where there is a target to cut potable water consumption by 10 per cent by 2000, the UK has – as yet – no overall target for cutting water use. Yet the water savings we have identified here can all be achieved by 2010, and indeed virtually all are cost effective within that period. To coordinate the different policies and measures needed, a national body to promote the sustainable management and use of water – a 'Water Savings Trust' as proposed by the House of Commons Environment Committee[61] – would be helpful. Achieving these savings will achieve our environmental space target if underlying demand growth is low, or at a medium level, although further savings will be needed if underlying demand continues to grow after 2010. However, an underlying high level of demand growth seems unlikely in a scenario where objectives for water saving are widely pursued, and thus individual awareness of water scarcity is much higher.

# Chapter 9
# Metals, Minerals and Chemicals

## INTRODUCTION

Humankind is overloading ecological systems with the waste products of extracting, processing and using mineral resources. And human health is being threatened by a host of chemical hazards resulting from the extraction, processing, use and disposal of non-renewable raw materials. Between 1900 and 1990, use of non-renewable raw materials grew from 50 per cent of materials use to 75 per cent of a much a larger total.[1]

Sensing that scientists and industrialists were focusing on minor details, such as the safe concentrations of particular effluents, the Swedish oncologist (cancer scientist) Karl Henrik-Robert began a remarkable process of achieving scientific consensus over environmental threats. After two years, in 1991 he was able to publish a paper endorsed by 50 of the country's most prominent scientists. This paper – the basis of the Natural Step movement for sustainability – argues that in any sustainable economy there will be no systematic accumulation of materials such as metals and fossil fuels in the biosphere. To achieve this, the only acceptable source of materials js the recycling of those already extracted. In other words, according to the Natural Step, mineral extraction should be completely phased out.[2] The radical proposals of Natural Step have since inspired similar initiatives in several other countries including the UK. Of course, not even the most ardent advocates of the Natural Step are arguing for an immediate phaseout, but this long-term goal sets the general direction for the economy and policy.

At the same time, research in Germany by Friedrich Schmidt-Bleek was coming to a more modest, but broadly similar, conclusion. Schmidt-Bleek believes that we can broadly correlate the increasingly parlous state of the global environment with the period in which many flows of materials caused by humankind have begun to exceed the quantities moved in nature, by erosion and sedimentation, for example.[3] He argues that we should at least reduce this effect back to below the levels moved naturally and suggests that this broadly equates to at least a 50 per cent reduction in the current level of materials inputs into the global economy. For example, flows of copper from the earth's crust to the ecosphere are today 24 times larger than the corresponding natural flows.[4] While there is nothing intrinsically unsustainable about exceeding natural rates of flow of such materials, these figures are indicative of the scale of the interference with natural processes that has resulted from humankind's exploitation of materials.

# THE IMPACTS OF MATERIALS USE

## Mining the Earth

Communities all over the world – from Costa Rica to the Czech Republic, from Madagascar to the Philippines, and from Finland to Australia – are fighting for their local environment, their homes, their health and even their lives against multinational mining companies. Environmental impacts arise from extraction, including exploration, prospecting, survey, mining, and spoil disposal, tailings; and the landscape and productive value of the land are often still damaged long after the mine is exhausted, even if landscape restoration is undertaken.[5] The costs of remediation are, all too often, not borne by the polluters. For example, at Summitville in the USA, worked intermittently for gold from 1870 to 1992, most of the costs of remediation – more than US$100 million – were borne by the Environmental Protection Agency (EPA), funded by the American tax-payer.[6]

Modern mining generates many more tonnes of waste than useful product. During 1991, more than 1000 million metric tonnes of copper ore were dug up to obtain just 9 million metric tonnes of metal. Industry in the US alone devours nearly 2.7 billion tonnes of raw material a year, not counting stone, sand and gravel. The extraction process creates 6.9 billion tonnes of solid waste annually, in addition to 7.7 billion tonnes of solid waste from metal and mineral processing.[7] As ore grades have declined, the impacts become greater. Copper ore is now normally between 0.5 and 2.0 per cent by weight, so for each kilogram of copper, between 50 and 200 kilograms of waste are produced, excluding any overburden that has to be moved to access the copper ore. Making 1 tonne of aluminium produces over 50 tonnes of waste.[8]

As the examples in Box 9.1 show, there are social impacts too. In many cases tribal lands are mined, with concomitant cultural damage. And there is little evidence that mining companies have helped developing countries develop further. Resource economist Judith Rees concludes that the minerals sector performs best when judged against the criteria of supply security objectives for the consumers of its products, and poorly against objectives of economic efficiency, development or equity.[9]

# BOX 9.1 *THE IMPACTS OF EXTRACTION*

*The Ok Tedi Mine*
The Ok Tedi Mine in New Guinea is the South Pacific's largest mining project. This gold and copper mine has been a social and environmental disaster. The suspended sediments and heavy metals from the mine have threatened fish, turtle and crocodile populations. The local Wopkamin people have lost 7000 hectares of their land. A barge overturned on the Fly River in June 1984 losing 2700 60-litre drums of cyanide, the single largest loss ever of one of the world's most dangerous poisons. Five days later a bypass valve was left open, releasing 1000 cubic metres of concentrated cyanide into the river, resulting in dead fish, prawns, turtles and crocodiles.[a] The pollution was so bad that the health of islanders in the Torres Strait between Australia and New Guinea was affected. The metals were contaminating the seafood that the islanders were eating.[b] With more than 80,000 tons of mining waste going into the river daily, the damage now is considered to have destroyed the ecosystem upon which 30,000 tribal people depend for their livelihoods. Now mine supporters are pushing through a law that would make it a criminal offence to sue the Ok Tedi Mine.[c]

*Freeport in Irian Jaya*
The Carstenz mountain chain in the Lorentz nature reserve in Irian Jaya, Indonesia, is unfortunate in being rich in copper. Although it is in a very isolated area, right in the middle of Indonesia's largest national park, the first mining concession was granted in 1967 to the American company Freeport. In 1972 the company started open cast mining at a height of 3600 metres. This continued until the mine was exhausted in 1989. In 1991 Freeport was able to expand its concession to cover an area of no less than 25,000 square kilometres (two-thirds of the size of the Netherlands). Freeport and RTZ are working together with the Indonesian army to suppress critics. As a result, no information is available from the area. The effects from outside the area are visible to everyone, however: rivers are silting up and overflowing their banks; trees, fish and birds are dying; people are becoming ill; the number of miscarriages is inexplicably high. The local population are bearing only the burdens of mining, personnel are largely brought in from elsewhere. The tax income disappears to Jakarta. In order to be able to work without disruption, Freeport moved 1000 inhabitants from the area in 1988 with the aid of the army. In order to carry out its new developments, another 2000 people will have to relocate. A number of local inhabitants have paid for their resistance with their lives.[d]

Sources: *a The Ecologist* (1988) Ok Tedi: New Guinea's Disaster Mine 18(1); *b New Scientist* (1989) Polluted prawns on paradise islands, p19, November 18; *c* Friends of the Earth US (1995) The Ok Tedi mine not Okay *Friends of the Earth International Link* October/December; *d* Friends of the Earth Netherlands (1996) *While stocks last* Amsterdam: Milieudefensie. In addition to 650,000 tonnes of copper, 220 tonnes of silver and 14.5 tonnes of gold were also extracted A hole measuring 350 metres in diameter and 250 metres deep was left behind

# The Impacts of Processing

Forty years after the Japanese Minamata tragedy, the impacts of processing minerals are still significant.[10] The metals industry accounts for around 26 per cent of the current global total of toxic emissions of 19 million tonnes, and the chemical industry for 37 per cent.[11] And many of the toxic products of the chemical industry will be dispersed into the environment in use, so the share attributable to chemicals may be even higher. Moreover, despite major improvements in efficiency, these industries are still substantial energy users.[12] Aluminium smelting accounts for 1 per cent of world energy use. The Valco smelter in Ghana produces 1 per cent of the world's aluminium. The Akosombo dam on the Volta river simply provides power to the smelter; it turned 5 per cent of the country (an area the size of Lebanon) into the world's largest artificial lake.[13] The dam and smelter project have forced the relocation of 80,000 people. The incidence of waterborne diseases in the area has escalated, while the new reservoir has impeded rather than enhanced the mobility of average local Ghanaians. Many local industries and agricultural practices were adversely affected or eliminated by the dam. Local benefits have been few; early promises of rural electrification and spin off industries remain long unfulfilled.[14]

# The Impacts of Consumption

The environmental impacts of the use of many materials depend on the extent to which those uses are 'dissipative', how far they disperse the substance into the environment directly, or in the form of wastes or pollutants. Good examples of the former are propellants and pesticides, whilst fuels are the classic example of the latter: they are consumed in use, releasing combustion byproducts as pollution. Tim Jackson, of the Centre for Environmental Strategy at the University of Surrey, suggests that: 'almost all the environmental problems of the industrial economy arise from dissipation of materials through the economic system'.[15] Indeed, it is easy to see how many of our biggest environmental concerns come from highly dissipative uses. Climate change and ozone depletion are the result of dissipated losses of $CO_2$ (and other greenhouse gases) and CFCs (and other ozone depleting chemicals) respectively. Some of our concerns over chemicals in food, water and air are the result of inherently dissipative uses of fertilisers and pesticides.

A particularly worrying concern is being raised in recent debate over the risks to human health of micropollutants in the environment from dissipative chemicals. Some fear that a serious decline in human fertility has begun – a human equivalent of the 'Silent Spring' – because of exposure to synthetic hormone mimicking chemicals, some of which are released in dissipative uses, including toiletry products such as shampoos.

Others – including the chemical industry and its apologists – note that there are many natural chemicals, including such hormones, in the environment at higher concentrations. But human sensitivity may be higher where the artificial versions are concerned, and especially where mixtures of such chemicals combine. It is known that chemicals in combination can have additive effects; there is still dispute whether there can be more than additive effects.[16]

Of course new compounds receive increasingly intensive scrutiny before release into the environment, thus lessening the risk of new sources of environmental damage, but, as a DOE study has pointed out:

> *most of the regulatory information required for the licensing of new materials has been based on short term, acute toxicity tests and formal measurements of properties such as solubility coefficients, leaving the most dangerous properties of long term accumulation and biological impact largely untested.[17]*

A precautionary approach would be less relaxed about the release of potentially damaging chemicals, known, for instance, to change gender in fish.[18]

Progress towards sustainability, for Robert Ayres, Sandoz Professor of Environmental Management at INSEAD in Paris, requires that dissipative uses decline, and where feasible the proportion recycled increases.[19] This analysis lies at the heart of the concept of industrial metabolism. Dissipative losses not only damage the environment as pollutants, but for the industrial system as a whole, these losses are made up by replacement from virgin sources. Industrial metabolism looks at industrial systems like natural systems, seeking to minimise wastes and maximise recycling and reuse in the system, with firms turning wastes (whether their own, or others') into useful products – in the way that animals and plants interact in natural systems. With such an approach it is difficult to separate the impacts of materials use from those of materials disposal.

Jackson examines the strategies for materials disposal and concludes that neither 'dilute and disperse', nor 'concentrate and contain' are reliable strategies for dealing with wastes.[20] Neither can guarantee replicating the conditions in which equivalent approaches work in nature. Dilute and disperse is particularly suspect as natural systems can cycle and accumulate materials in ways that increase the risk to humans and other lifeforms. But attempts to concentrate and contain chemicals and metals wastes have also led to severe impacts. Perhaps the best known example is that of Love Canal in New York State in the USA. The site was used as a dump in the 1940s and 1950s; more than 40,000 tonnes of toxic chemical wastes were dumped. Although the likely effects were known, the company sold the site (along with liability) to the local board of education. Twenty years later, after a school and housing had been built, the site was found to be leaking. In 1978, 240 families were evacuated in response to the declaration of a 'state of emergency' by the federal government.[21]

Such problems cannot be disregarded as the product of outdated technology and techniques; even the most modern landfills are expected to leak eventually,[22] and even the best controlled incinerators still emit dioxins, heavy metals, particulates and acid gases. In part, these problems are the result of poor standards and weak enforcement. But they also result from a fundamental failure to consider the underlying laws of physics. The law of the conservation of matter means that material inputs will end up in the product or waste, or dissipated in pollution. Unless we can prevent contamination by, for example, heavy metals in the first place, or recover the heavy metals in a usable form, they will end up as environmental pollution. The only conclusion is that reduction in use, recycling and reuse are the best strategies for managing such toxic and hazardous materials flows where emissions must be reduced to zero to ensure the protection of public health and the environment. The impacts of extraction add weight to this conclusion. For other materials such as construction wastes, paper and glass, reuse and recycling still sit at the top of the waste hierarchy, especially because of impacts in extraction and processing, including energy use. If we control dissipative uses and disposal methods, then we can create a greater potentially recyclable stock. This also brings benefits in how we respond to resource scarcity as it is a demand side measure which reduces pressure on virgin resources.

# IS SCARCITY AN ISSUE?

There is no doubt that the environmental resources which are damaged or depleted by mineral extraction and use are becoming increasingly scarce. On the other hand, the practical, economic availability of mineral resources can increase as investments are made in exploration and development. Real scarcity will only arrive as the absolute resource starts to run out. This trend should trigger rising prices and therefore investment in efficiency and alternatives. So is real scarcity increasing? The price indicator cannot tell us, as it is influenced more by short-term fluctuations, political factors and demand factors, than by supply.[23] In practice, it would seem that the key influence on scarcity has been demand – as technological changes have enhanced or reduced demand, so prices (and investment in supply) have followed. For example, real timber prices in the USA rose significantly when demand for construction, railroads and mining uses was highest in the period 1870–1957, and fell later as various substitutes, including imported timber, came to dominate these markets. All this variability inherent in the price indicator means that, as Rees concludes, we cannot rely on markets to deal with minerals and environmental scarcity. Her view is that virtually all the imperfections in the system, and there are many, tend to reinforce the bias towards present consumption. She concludes:

> *it is just possible that the technological changes and other forms of*
> *adaption generated by the market to avert stock resource scarcity will*
> *prove compatible with the maintenance of critical bio-geo-chemical*
> *cycles, but it would be an act of supreme faith (or extreme folly) to*
> *rely on such a happy coincidence of interests.*[24]

The key question in practice is whether these distorting effects have masked any price impacts, for example from declining ore quality and increasing exploration costs, which would be amongst the first signals of increasing scarcity. Most conventional economic analysts suggest that the average real costs of these resources have consistently fallen, with the exception of the effects of the oil price shocks of the 1970s, which are discounted as of political origin, rather than resulting from actual scarcity. But one very detailed analysis has shown that the real and financial energy costs of getting resources will inevitably rise in the long term, even though to date this has been entirely offset by falling labour and capital input costs.[25] As long as the resource is plentiful, and new exploitable reserves can be found cheaply, then consumption can easily increase while prices remain low. But as easily accessible reserves are exhausted, more time and effort is needed to find new reserves. This can be seen in proposals to exploit more remote reserves such as west of Shetland oilfields, or Alaskan oilshales. Exploration becomes more costly, development becomes more costly, prices rise and consumption falls. When this starts happening substitutes tend to be developed, so, for example, copper has been replaced in many uses by optic glass fibres.

But when the scarce resource is fossil fuels, it will affect the whole economy, not just one sector. Although real energy costs increase with declining ore quality, improvements in extraction and processing technology can overwhelm this trend for a long time. But these gains will eventually reach the thermodynamic limit and there is now generally scope only for further improvements by a factor of two to three in smelting processes, for example, in comparison to improvements of a factor of ten over the last century.[26] In such circumstances, the increasing energy cost of declining ore quality creates a positive feedback loop with further increases in energy requirements (and further increases in extraction costs for energy).

We can conclude, first, that the energy costs of obtaining minerals impose real limits, especially given the need for cuts in $CO_2$ emissions. Reducing material flows in industry will inevitably reduce energy use too, not only in extraction and refining, or mining and smelting, but also in the transport of goods and wastes. In Japan, improvements in energy efficiency have been broadly paralleled by improvements in materials use efficiency.[27] Second, trends in mineral extraction are increasing the environmental costs of obtaining mineral resources. This is in turn exacerbated by the fact that the environmental goods being degraded are themselves getting scarcer (and more valuable) as a result. This damage to environmental resources is not reflected in any economic indicator of scarcity,[28] except to the limited extent to which regulations are used to limit environmental impacts. And because these materials are largely globally traded commodities, there is great pressure for such standards to tend to the lowest common denominator. We should not rely on economic indicators of scarcity, but should take precautionary steps to conserve the natural resources we value. Within the period covered by this book, up to 2050, if we pursued business as usual, there would be good reasons to be concerned about scarcity. However, by reinforcing the operations of the market with policies to restrain demand for materials as proposed below, we should have little need to worry about the onset of absolute scarcity.

# SETTING ENVIRONMENTAL SPACE LIMITS

In the Netherlands, the original advocates of the eco-space approach, Weterings and Opschoor, have been trying to elaborate a method based on the lifespan of known reserves at current rates of use. Using Weterings and Opschoor's figures, the Business Council for Sustainable Development has concluded that the targets mean that business needs to achieve an average 20-fold improvement in 'eco-efficiency'.[29] Weterings and Opschoor's global criterion for sustainability is the maintenance of a stock for at least 50 years (see Table 9.1). The figures in the table reflect only the global limits, but they argue that in addition we should follow an equity scenario which means that Northern industrialised countries bear the brunt of these cuts.

This approach suggests that as long as we balance use with additions to reserves, or reductions in the rate of use, and thereby keep a 50 year reserve at current rates of use, our use is sustainable. This might be adequate to deal with the approach of absolute scarcity, even though the reserves figures themselves do not measure absolute scarcity.[30] If this approach was adopted in practice, then where absolute scarcity is not approaching, an increased rate of use will be reflected in increased search and development effort to bring new reserves on line. If absolute scarcity is approaching, then the only way to meet this criterion would be to continually reduce the rate of use by developing substitutes or increasing efficiency. The reserves criterion does not take account of the environmental and social impacts of mineral extraction, processing, use and disposal outlined above, but Weterings and Opschoor also argue for national sustainability criteria for deposition of metals which suggest greater reductions in the Netherlands (of 90–95 per cent).[31] This work

**Table 9.1** *Examples of Global Sustainability Limits for Some Materials*

|               | *Predicted level, 2040*              | *Desired reduction (%)* |
|---------------|--------------------------------------|-------------------------|
| Fossil fuels  |                                      |                         |
| Oil           | stock exhausted                      | 85                      |
| Gas           | stock exhausted                      | 70                      |
| Coal          | stock exhausted                      | 20                      |
|               |                                      |                         |
| Metals        |                                      |                         |
| Aluminium     | stock for more than 50 years         | none                    |
| Copper        | stock exhausted                      | 80                      |
| Uranium       | depends on use of nuclear energy     | not quantifiable        |

Source: Weterings, RA and Opschoor, JB (1992) *The ecocapacity as a challenge to technological development* Rijswijk: Advisory Council for Research on Nature and Environment

adds further weight to the arguments for substantial reductions in consumption rates in Northern countries.

It is clear that current rates of use are disrupting our ecological systems and threatening human health.[32] We do not believe that there is enough evidence yet to promote the goal of zero extraction as advocated by the Natural Step, or even the concept of maximising recycling rates (say, 95 per cent to allow for minimal losses in the recycling process),[33] in the period covered by this book, although we agree with the principles on which such arguments are based. So we have adopted a 50 per cent reduction, and to ensure consistency we have based the target on 1990 levels of use for which comparable data are available.[34] A few key resources make up most of the volume of non-renewable material inputs to our economies. As long as we do not assume that substituting another material is a sustainable way of reducing their use, we can treat them as representative of the economy as a whole.

To apply equity in materials use we need to consider the current distribution of consumption. As of 1991, seven countries – the US, South Korea, Japan, Germany, Italy, France and the UK – hold 11.6 per cent of the world's population and consume 59 per cent of the world's aluminium, 43 per cent of the world's crude steel and 58 per cent of the world's copper.[35] Once we take this distribution into account, as we will see below, it makes little difference for the UK in the short term whether we base our strategy on a global cut of 50 per cent or simply stabilisation of extraction at the current level. The North–South inequity in consumption may not be so great as these figures suggest as, on balance, Northern countries import raw materials and export finished goods, which embody some of these raw materials. It is difficult to be sure how significant this effect is.[36] However, it can be looked at in a different way in terms of the balance of trade in manufactured goods, to take account of increasing exports of manufactured goods from the newly industrialised countries. Recent figures for the UK suggest that overall such trade is largely in balance, while we are a net importer of major consumer manufactured goods: white goods and cars. This effect therefore does not systematically bias the calculation of targets for the UK. Like oil and coal, most other resources – metals and chemicals for example – are traded internationally. Many construction materials are not so widely traded, but international trading is increasing even in the UK, despite our very limited land borders. The 'super-quarry' operated by Foster Yeoman in Glen Sander in Scotland regularly exports aggregates to Germany, and on occasion has exported as far afield as Texas.

# CONSTRUCTION MATERIALS

Consumption of cement in the UK is declining. In 1990 apparent consumption was 282 kg per capita. By 1992 this had declined to 219 kg per capita[37] or about 12.5 million tonnes each year of which about 12 per cent is imported. However, the Government's demand forecasts predict an increase in demand for cement of between 60 and 120 per cent between 1991 and 2011.[38] Brick and crushed rock aggregates are more typical materials in the UK construction sector. The use of aggregates in the UK has grown rapidly over the past decades, reaching 281 million tonnes in 1994 of which 259 million tonnes were 'construction aggregates' (excluding aggregates for cement). In 1991, 240 million tonnes of construction aggregate were used.[39] Yet the construction industry categorised as most would understand it – building houses, industrial and commercial buildings – uses only about 110 million tonnes per year;[40] more goes into road construction and other infrastructure.

## Sustainability and the Aggregates Industry

Demand for construction aggregates for all purposes is forecast to rise to between 330 and 365 million tonnes by 2006.[41] This would mean quarrying or mining on 3100–3500 hectares of land each year.[42] Such forecasts of increases in demand for aggregates have, until recently, driven increases in supply. This is because of a planning system in which public authorities were expected to maintain a 'land-bank' of reserves with planning approval which could meet demand for a period of ten years. This in turn has kept the price of aggregates low, discouraging efficiency in use and promoting consumption of virgin aggregates rather than reuse of buildings and recycling of demolition and mineral wastes. So the demand forecasts were largely self-fulfilling. Although the Government finally decided in 1994 that the forecasts should not be treated as targets, in practice, land-banks, although only for seven years, are still required, so the industry dynamic is little altered.

The industry has become increasingly concentrated, developing very large quarries, often in remote locations. Generally, aggregates can only be quarried in areas where the geology provides outcrops of hard rock. These areas are normally attractive upland landscapes, highly valued for aesthetic, recreational and wildlife reasons. As a result, many proposals for new or extended quarries have faced strong local and political opposition. So the industry has begun to assess alternative sources, especially marine-dredged aggregates from the seabed, and so-called 'super-quarries' in remote locations, even outside of the United Kingdom. The most biggest debate over a super-quarry so far relates to the proposal by Redland to quarry in a designated National Scenic Area at Roinebhal on the Outer Hebridean island of Harris. Locals see this proposal directly as environmental colonialism: the dumping of activities not acceptable in the consumer market into a poorer economy where the bribe of new jobs is expected to outweigh environmental and social concerns.[43]

Sustainable aggregate supply, therefore, depends on decreased use of virgin aggregates, even though technically there are reserves for hundreds of thousands of years. Increasing the price of virgin aggregates to depress demand and stimulate recycling is a clear first step, although a similar effect could be achieved with a high tax on disposal of construction waste.[44] A modest increase in prices would increase secondary use by 48 million tonnes; more than the target established by the last Government, as we will see later.

# The Construction Industry

The Department of the Environment predict continued increases in construction materials demand with economic growth. Although the UK road building programme, a major aggregate user, has been heavily cut back in recent years, the increasing number of households will mean a strong continued demand for construction materials. The quarrying and construction industry disingenuously argues that unless we allow continued expansion of quarrying, we will not be able to have the homes, schools and hospitals that society demands. However, there are practical options for reducing the materials intensity of construction. Box 9.2 outlines one option for reducing materials use in housebuilding.[45]

As of 1990 the annual average rate of housebuilding stood at around 180,000 new dwellings per year.[46] This is very similar to the annual addition needed over the next 15–20 years, according to our estimates in

## BOX 9.2 *MATERIAL-EFFICIENT CONSTRUCTION – AN EXAMPLE*

Azurel house construction systems use panels made of a high insulation 80 mm Styrofoam core with a double timber frame glued on each side. This material is used for roofs, floors and walls. It achieves improved levels of energy efficiency over the current average, although it does not perform as well in use as the high-efficiency houses considered in Chapter 5. It is, however, cheaper than normal construction materials, quick and simple to assemble, and uses much less material.

Azurel houses use only 24 tonnes of material (including timber). This compares with figures for typical houses in France, where the new system is being developed, of 163 tonnes in a masonry house and 95 tonnes in a timber house. These figures cannot strictly be translated to British houses which have different specifications, but indicate that building Azurel houses would use far less construction materials. The table below shows the potential gains accounted for over the entire lifetime of the house. There are also apparent gains in the overall energy intensity of construction, achieved through, for example, lower transport energy use, and lower waste generation.

|  | Masonry house | Timber house | Azurel house |
|---|---|---|---|
| Construction materials used (tonnes) | 163 | 95 | 24 |
| Lifetime energy use (gigajoules) | 3453 | 3252 | 3045 |
| Waste to landfill (tonnes) | 150 | 85 | 18 |

Source: ECOBILAN (1995) *LCA of the 'Azurel house' and comparison with two traditional houses* Paris: ECOBILAN

Chapter 6.[47] In fact, if our suggested rates and patterns of redevelopment suggested are achieved, then two factors could act to reduce the rates of use of materials. First, building to our suggested densities is more materials-efficient per dwelling than construction of conventional suburban housing. Second, the opportunities for recycling of construction materials will be high, as demolition and rebuilding will be happening in the same areas. Recycling rates of 80 per cent are achieved in Denmark for all construction waste.[48] A similar rate could be achieved in the UK in such a redevelopment programme.

Current levels of recycling of building materials are very low. According to a recent report for DOE, only 4 per cent of the estimated 70 million tonnes of demolition waste produced in the UK is processed and recycled as secondary aggregates and at least two-thirds of all wastes are disposed of.[49] The remainder is used as low grade aggregate on or near the site of arising. This, and a large proportion of that disposed of, could be recycled. At least 8 million tonnes of brick and concrete, 7 milllion tonnes of sand and gravel and 2 million tonnes of bituminous material could potentially be diverted from landfill.[50] The key to increasing recycling rates is changing the relative costs which in turn will help encourage segregation of wastes at source. The landfill levy will have added to the costs of disposal, but while primary aggregates remain underpriced, the incentive will still be limited. Increased recycling could create jobs. A study for Scott Homes suggests that just raising the recycling rate from 1 per cent to 5 per cent could create 13,000 jobs in Scotland.[51] Increased recycling will also reduce the land required for quarrying of building materials. Use of 48 million tonnes of secondary aggregates a year would save 540 hectares of land annually from the damage caused by aggregate quarries.[52]

Note: Based on data from BACMI 1995 *Statistical Yearbook 1995* and Department of the Environment library.

**Figure 9.1** *UK aggregates use – projections and targets*

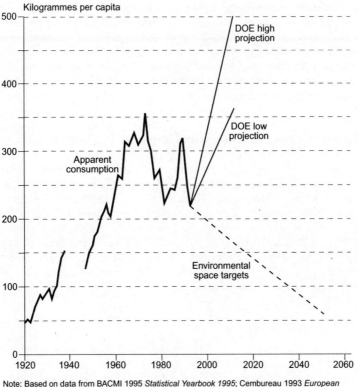

Note: Based on data from BACMI 1995 *Statistical Yearbook 1995*; Cembureau 1993 *European Annual Review* 15 Brussels: Cembureau; and Department of the Environment library.

**Figure 9.2** *UK cement use – projections and targets*

## Environmental Space for Construction Aggregates

For illustration we calculate an environmental space target based on a 50 per cent reduction in use of primary aggregates by 2050 and a national supply (see Figure 9.1).[53] This suggests a target for 2050 of around 140 million tonnes per year, and an interim target for 2010 of 245 million tonnes. Road construction spending is expected to fall by 28 per cent by 1998/99. If this equates to a 28 per cent reduction in construction materials, this would result in a reduction of 15.4 million tonnes. There are also official targets set for the use of recycled/secondary aggregates: 40 million tonnes per annum by 2001 and 55 mt per annum by 2006.[54] Current recycled use is no more than 10 per cent[55] or 32 mt, so meeting the 2006 target would save a further 25 mt of primary aggregates. Thus a 2010 target of a reduction of around 35 million tonnes is easily practicable if overall demand does not grow substantially. We do not believe that it is appropriate to use past trends from a situation where aggregates have been cheap and supply subjected to self-fulfilling demand projections as a guide to future needs. Overall, we would judge that in a market where materials profligacy is no longer encouraged by low prices, then the underlying trend of demand would no longer be increasing, and measures to promote efficiency and, in particular, recycling should be able to cut actual demand for aggregates.

## Environmental Space for Cement

Environmental space targets for cement have also been calculated, based on a 50 per cent cut in global consumption (see Figure 9.2).[56] The 2010 interim target for cement is 210 kg per capita: a reduction of 20 per cent over the 1990 consumption rate of 282 kg per capita. As long as the downward trend of cement consumption in the 1990s is not reversed, the UK will reach this target with some ease. However, the 2050 environmental space target for cement of 3.45 mt (or 58 kg per capita) is more challenging. Put in a different way: the UK, with only 1 per cent of the world's population is consuming 3 per cent of the world's sustainable production of cement.

## METALS
### Steel

UK steel demand has not shown a consistent trend in the past two decades. Currently it is rising after low points in the mid-1980s and in the early 1990s. Industry commentators believe that demand is unlikely to exceed 15 million tonnes per year during the 1990s unless major construction projects are started. UK steel consumption in 1994 was 14.04 million tonnes of crude steel equivalent or around 1.8 per cent of world production. UK consumption of steel is less than production: we export 3–4 million tonnes per year. But a proportion of UK steel comes from recycled scrap. Apparent primary steel consumption in 1994 was just 8.9 million tonnes or 153 kg per capita.[57]

Over 90 per cent of steel is bought by manufacturing industry either as plant, or as raw materials for products, notably for use in vehicles and domestic white goods. Around 5 per cent of steel and 7 per cent of all metals by value is used by the construction industry.[58] Net imports of steel in semi-finished and finished products have not been included in this study, because to attempt to do so would make our UK figures incomparable with those estimated by other countries. However, to illustrate the scale of this effect, we present figures on the UK's net imports of the main white goods and cars (see Table 9.2). This shows that the total net

**Table 9.2** *Imports of Embodied Steel into the UK*

|  | Net import (tonnes) | Net import (million ecus) |
|---|---|---|
| Fridges and freezers | 55,577 | 179 |
| Washing machines | 54,374 | 140 |
| Dishwashers | 18,426 | 76 |
| Televisions | 12,618 | 69 |
| Cars | 384,134 | 3171 |
| Total | 525,129 | 3636 |

Source: EUROSTAT, figures for 1995

import of steel is around 0.5 million tonnes and even assuming that there is some wastage associated with the production of these goods, the net effect on current levels of consumption is negligible. However if

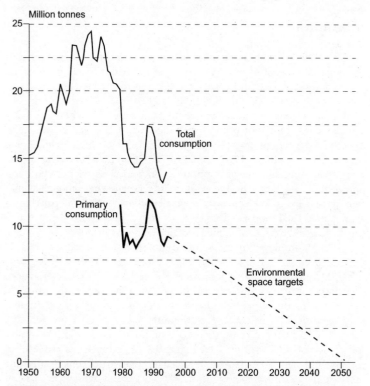

Note: Figures in crude steel equivalents. Based on data from Iron and Steel Statistics Bureau and DOE 1996 *Digest of Environmental Statistics* 18. The industry does not forecast demand for more than two years in advance.

**Figure 9.3** *UK steel use – projections and targets*

consumption is to be reduced to the environmental space target of 25.7 kg per capita, or 1.53 million tonnes for the UK (see Figure 9.3),[59] then such net levels of embodied imports would clearly be significant.

The interim target for 2010 is 116 kg per capita of primary steel: a reduction of 24 per cent over current consumption. The main measures for reducing primary steel use are increased recycling, and greatly improved product durability, along with some continued substitution by more modern materials, especially in uses where weight is at a premium. To achieve the interim target by increasing recycling would require a recycled share of steel inputs of 49 per cent. This in turn would imply recovery of 6.94 million tonnes of steel waste, an increase of 1.82 million tonnes.[60] For 2050, the target is 1.53 million tonnes of primary metal. With the same total consumption, 89 per cent recycling would be needed. We return to other measures to cut consumption, such as increasing product durability, later in this chapter.

# Aluminium

Consumption of aluminium is growing fast, but because recycling of aluminium is so energy efficient in comparison with primary production, much, but not all current growth is accounted for by increases in use of recycled or secondary aluminium. In 1990 apparent consumption of primary aluminium products was 7.90 kg per capita.[61] In 1993 the UK's apparent consumption of primary aluminium was 8.21 kg per capita, equivalent to 2.5 per cent of world production.[62] Including secondary aluminium, consumption was 10.88 (1990) and 11.81 (1993) kg/cap.[63] Over the last ten years total aluminium consumption has increased by 54 per cent, and primary use by 47 per cent. Increases in the recycling rate, although significant, have failed to keep pace with overall growth. Around 35 per cent of aluminium is used for packaging, 18 per cent in construction, 11 per cent in engineering and 6 per cent in transport, including car manufacture.[64]

The interim target of 6.1 kg per capita represents a reduction of 22 per cent over 1993. The environmental space target for the UK for 2050 is 59,000 tonnes, or 0.99 kg per person.[65] To achieve this requires a cut of 88 per cent in the use of primary aluminium. Once again, the principal measures for reducing aluminium use are increasing recycling and durability. Currently, 31 per cent of aluminium was sourced from recycled scrap.[66] The 2010 target for primary aluminium use is 373,000 tonnes (down from 477,600 in 1993) (see Figure 9.4). To achieve this by recycling alone would mean an increase in recycled input to 46 per cent, an absolute increase of just over 100,000 tonnes.[67] This seems achievable. Use of secondary aluminium increased by 87,000 tonnes between 1983 and 1993. Yet large amounts of materials, including 80,000 tonnes of aluminium cans[68] are not recycled yet. To achieve the 2050 target through recycling

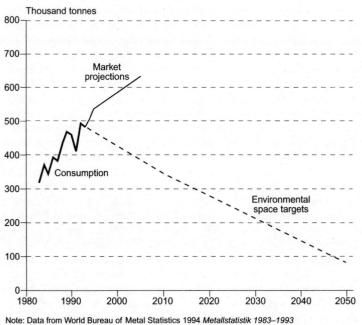

Note: Data from World Bureau of Metal Statistics 1994 *Metallstatistik 1983–1993* and CRU International Ltd.

**Figure 9.4** *UK primary aluminium use – projections and targets*

alone would mean recycled inputs making up just over 90 per cent of aluminium produced: or recovering and recycling almost 630,000 tonnes of aluminium scrap each year.

To summarise for metals: the UK with just 1 per cent of the planet's population is consuming over 3.5 per cent of the world's sustainable steel production, and 5 per cent of sustainable aluminium production.

# CHEMICALS

In this section we look at some of the largest volumes involved in the chemicals industry. The first of these is somewhat exceptional within the environmental space approach but serves to illustrate a wider point.

## Chlorine

Many chlorinated products raise environmental concerns. Chlorinated organic compounds are virtually absent from natural material cycles, and many of them are highly toxic, but because of their organic nature are easily assimilated by organisms. Increasingly these concerns are being reflected in a precautionary call from a range of governmental and professional bodies for the complete phasing-out of chlorine.[69] US President Clinton announced in 1994 that he would ask the US Environmental Protection Agency to introduce a national strategy to 'substitute, reduce, or prohibit the use of chlorine and chlorinated compounds'.[70] The call for a chlorine phase-out has been widely misrepresented by the chemical industry as an attempt to banish salt from our tables. This is not so. Campaigners' concerns are with the more complex organic forms of chlorine which are widely implicated in threats to human and ecosystem health. We would anticipate completing the phase-out of chlorine before 2050. Greenpeace argue that 97 per cent of chlorine use could be phased out within 30 years.[71] Here, for the sake of consistency, we present figures based on a phase-out by 2050, with a quarter of the reduction achieved by 2010. The target used for 2010 is 12 kg per capita, a reduction of 25 per cent over 1990, and for 2050, virtual elimination, treated here as a 100 per cent reduction.[72] Apparent consumption of chlorine in 1990 was 16.0 kg per capita and in 1991, 15.4 kg per capita.[73] These figures are subject to some uncertainty, as they refer to pure chlorine only,[74] and do not include chlorine embodied in other chlorine compounds, for example in poly-vinyl-chloride (PVC). In 1991, total chlorine production in Europe was 9 million tonnes, most of which was used to make products such as plastic, particularly PVC.

The main uses of chlorine are as an industrial feedstock in a variety of different sectors. It is used in disinfection of water supplies, as a bleaching agent in the paper and pulp industry, in the manufacture of various plastics, polymers, vinyls, solvents and resins, and in the formulation of various refrigerants, propellants, insulators, preservatives and pesticides. Phasing out chlorine is easier in some of these sectors than others. However, alternatives are now available and in use in many countries for all major uses of chlorine: oxygen-based compounds for paper bleaching; traditional materials or chlorine-free plastics instead of PVC; mechanical or water-based cleaning and coating methods for chlorinated solvents; ozone, ultraviolet light, or effective sand, carbon, or membrane filtration methods for water disinfection (see Box 9.3). Because of the reasons driving the target reductions for chlorine, substitution seems likely to play a more significant role in achieving them, rather than recycling.

## Other Chemicals

The most important chemical feedstocks, in volume terms, are oil, phosphates, potash and sulphur. These are all subject to similar concerns as non-renewable resources in general. There are alternatives from renewable sources such as straw, oilseeds and even potatoes[75] but to shift to

# BOX 9.3 *TACKLING CHLORINE USE – SOME EXAMPLES*

*Non-solvent dry cleaning*

In the UK, 85 per cent of dry cleaning uses organic solvents. The main cleaning chemical is perchloroethylene: the average system uses 260 litres of this solvent every year. Perchloroethylene is a highly toxic chemical. However there are alternatives to dry cleaning, which use water based. Aquatex is the leading non-solvent dry cleaning system in the UK with 95 per cent of the market, and 10–15 per cent of all dry cleaning. It has been shown to clean a wider range of clothes than systems using perchloroethylene (including, for example, duvets and wax jackets).[a]

*Water purification*

Alternatives to chlorine based systems for decontamination of water include various options based on oxygen chemistry, and substances such as hydrogen peroxide and sodium percarbonate can be used as disinfectants in some applications. A different technological route uses ultraviolet light to decontaminate water. But the most important measures to eliminate this use of chlorine relate to the prevention of such contamination of water by protection of water sources and delivery systems, and by improved sewage management, such as the use of low-water sewerage systems.[b]

*Paper bleaching*

Totally chlorine free (TCF) bleaching involves a series of treatment stages. Enzymes are used to enhance the bleaching process as well as hydrogen peroxide. TCF technology is improving, but as yet paper whiteness achieved by this method is only ISO 70–86 per cent (full brightness is ISO 90 per cent+). However, there are very few uses where this difference is more than cosmetic. In the UK at present, 11.7 per cent of pulp consumed is TCF and the rest uses chlorine at some stage. In Scandinavia, almost 30 per cent of production is already TCF, and the rest is 'elemental chlorine free' (ECF). This shift was triggered, at least in part, simply by the threat of a tax on chlorine bleaches by the Swedish Government.[c] Converting to chlorine free bleaching processes in the North American pulp and paper industry has been estimated to save the industry US$185 million and US$370 million in chemical costs and between US$108 and US$189 million in energy costs plus increased savings in other areas such as water use and sludge disposal.[d]

*Use of PVC*

PVC is widely used, but the experience of the IKEA chainstore suggests that in many uses it is relatively easy to substitute for. Not only has it eliminated use of chlorine bleached paper, but over the past four years it has reduced the number of products it sells that contain PVC from 350 to 38, using a range of substitutes including polypropylene and wood.[e] The Body Shop has already removed PVC items from its retail products.

Sources: *a* As Aquatex and other water systems do not use toxic chlorinated solvents, and offer as good a performance over a wider range of clothes, it is not surprising that JLA, Aquatex's manufacturers, aim to double their market share to 200 machines over the next year. If all 1000 machines in use were converted to water-based systems by 2010, this would save 370 tonnes of chlorine a year, and reduce chlorine use in this application by 100 per cent. Use of perchloroethylene is 5 litres per week per machine (which processes 500 kg of garments). So average annual use of perchloroethylene is 260 litres. On the basis of 1000 machines and a density of 1.6311 kg/litre the saving is 260 x 1000 x 1.6311 = 430 tonnes of perchloroethylene. Perchloroethylene is 86 per cent chlorine, so chlorine weight saving is 370 tonnes. JLA (1996) *Aquatex News* Issue Two Ripponden: JLA; *b* Jackson, T (1996) *Material Concerns: Pollution, Profit and Quality of Life* London: Routledge; *c* Sterner, T (1994) *Environmental tax reform: the Swedish experience. Studies in environmental economics and development* Goteborg University; *d* Greenpeace (1990) *The Greenpeace Guide to Paper* London: Greenpeace; *e ENDS Report* 260 (1996) Strategic alliances for environmental solutions – the Greenpeace recipe for business success, pp19–22

these would require dedication of land to such crops. At present we would assume that rates of use need to be cut. A clear example is the case of chemical fertilisers – nitrogen, phosphorus and potassium, in particular – where environmental problems arise principally because of the dissipative nature of their use. The adoption of organic or other sustainable farming techniques could easily reduce use of artificial chemical fertilisers to a fraction of current levels. In other cases, savings in chemical feedstock uses can be achieved by increasing recycling rates, for example of plastics. But at present, Western European recycling rates for plastics have dropped as waste generation has increased by 29 per cent between 1990 and 1994, outstripping the 13 per cent increase in volume recovered. In 1994, 76 per cent of plastics waste went to landfill.[76]

# MOVING TOWARDS SUSTAINABILITY

Efficiency with all materials involves a strategy of product-life extension, aimed at getting the maximum possible use out of material products.[77] There are four key elements: reuse, repair, reconditioning of the product and recycling of raw materials (see Figure 9.5). Each tends to require more energy and material inputs than the preceding option, but also more opportunity for effective upgrading of the product. Recovery of materials to close the material cycle still requires additional energy (and materials), but at present it generally requires less energy than mining new materials. Thus it is more 'eco-efficient'. At present the need for such inputs is not the limiting factor on our attempts to close these cycles: labour costs, and technical and institutional obstacles are far more significant. However, in the long run this requirement will prevent us from absolutely closing materials cycles.

As Jackson says, 'zero-emissions of *all* materials ... The concept of a "no-waste economy" is just an illusion [emphasis added]'.[78] But he goes on to point out that this limit is still far off. So prevention is the key to minimising waste: through efficiency, and where toxic or otherwise dangerous

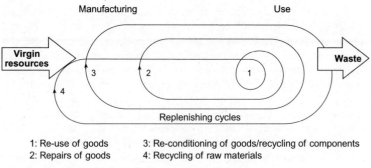

1: Re-use of goods     3: Re-conditioning of goods/recycling of components
2: Repairs of goods     4: Recycling of raw materials

Source: After Jackson 1996 *Material Concerns* London: Routledge

**Figure 9.5** *Industrial ecology – closing the cycles*

materials are concerned, through substitution. Reducing mixing of wastes is also necessary to support recycling. Returning to the ecosystem analogy, mature ecosystems may recycle far more than half the materials they use (but never 100 per cent), but they generally achieve rates far higher than our economic systems do. So as our systems mature, we should seek to imitate the best practice of natural systems: creating material cycles; improving material and energy efficiencies; reducing dissipative consumption; and improving the utilisation of our natural solar inheritance.[79]

## Waste Minimisation in Industry

Jackson identifies six key strategies for industrial waste minimisation and pollution prevention:[80] waste reduction audits (good housekeeping); internal recycling; process modifications, to optimise material flows or separate waste streams for example; cleaner process technologies, such as electrolytic rather than thermal smelting; input substitution, principally to replace hazardous materials; and product reformulation, such as the introduction of non-CFC propellants to help control particularly damaging dissipative uses. But often the most effective ways of reducing material consumption can come from redesigning products by looking even further upstream in the industrial process: starting from the demand for products and services.

In the US one waste reduction project examined opportunities in 29 organic chemical companies. The first study in 1985 identified 44 cost-effective waste reduction possibilities, accounting for 7 million pounds (weight) of waste (or 1 per cent of the total). The follow up study in 1992 found 181 reduction activities with an average reduction per waste stream of 70 per cent. Average savings were US$3.50 for every dollar invested in waste reduction with an average payback time of only just over one year.[81] In the UK several waste minimisation projects have been undertaken in specific regions, sponsored and supported by the Department of Trade and Industry. The best known are the Aire and Calder project in West Yorkshire which was initiated in 1992, and Project Catalyst on Merseyside which began in 1993. Both projects were designed to help companies identify cost savings through waste reduction. The projects have revealed massive potential for companies to reduce waste (particularly focusing on emissions to water) in cost effective ways.[82] If UK industry as a whole followed the example of the Aire and Calder project then the savings could total £1 billion.[83]

Sadly, data on such schemes are rarely gathered in such a way as to be able to estimate what percentage reduction in materials use such figures imply.[84] Information has not been gathered on resource flows reflecting the fact that energy and material inputs are rarely perceived as important costs by industry at present. This in turn suggests that the potential savings identified by such projects are likely to prove highly conservative in the long term. At present, beyond these focused projects, the Government has done little to increase the incentives for companies throughout the economy to exploit this potential, with the exception of voluntary information schemes. Partly as a result, 44 per cent of UK companies do not even know how much the current costs of their waste are.[85] In such circumstances, voluntary schemes cannot overcome the other obstacles to uptake of cleaner technologies.[86]

## Durability in Consumer Products

Greater product durability is officially recognised as a key tool for waste minimisation.[87] The question of durability is especially relevant to cars, and to 'white goods' (for example washing machines and fridges) and 'black' goods (such as hi-fis and TVs). In the UK we buy over 3.5 million TVs each year, 2.2 million washing machines, 880,000 fridges, 840,000 fridge-freezers and 760,000 freezers.[88] Throwaway attitudes and cheap, shoddy products are factors increasing resource use. People are increasingly reluctant even to seek repairs of such products. According to a recent Norwich Union survey, about one-tenth of consumers will throw out even a cooker or washing machine, rather than attempt a repair at all.[89] Shifting to a repair culture would be good for local economies, as most repairs, reconditioning and other service work would be carried out locally and almost certainly within the UK. Worse, many products these days have a predetermined design life which is controlled by the manufacturer.

As Tim Cooper writes in his report 'Beyond Recycling':

> *The main obstacles to increased product life are not technological ...*
> *As society has become increasingly acquisitive, people have come to*

*expect that certain consumer durables will need to be regularly replaced, whereas once they were regarded as long-term investments and lasted for several decades.*[90]

At present companies which manufacture products intended for above average life spans are more often found at the premium end of the market. But Cooper reports that things are beginning to change:

*volume manufacturers such as Philips, Braun and Miele have stated publicly in recent years that they intend increasing their products' life spans. They have evidently concluded that there will be net benefits from such a strategy, and that gaining a competitive advantage through increasing quality will outweigh any loss of replacement sales.*[91]

John Cridland, the CBI's director of environmental affairs, considers product durability to be 'one of the key issues emerging on the environmental agenda for business'.[92]

Durability can sometimes be a disadvantage where the majority of energy and materials use is incurred in use of the product, as is the case with cars or washing machines. Information on the full life-cycle impacts is essential to achieve optimum lifespans, rather than maximum ones.[93] In such cases there are two strategies to obtain the material benefits of durability without sacrificing the gains from technological progress. First is the approach of design for technological upgrading within the product lifespan. But second, and with far greater potential is the strategy of shared use; in car pools and launderettes respectively, more durable cars and washing machines can be used until they wear out and resource gains come from there being less of each in use at any one time.

More widely, product lives can be extended by finding ways to separate hardware from software, and function from fashion in ways that allow the latter elements (software and fashion) to be upgraded without replacing the material base. Lunz-Gunther Scheidt of the Sony Corporation advocates 'moving from hardware to software and from single products to modular systems' as business strategies for sustainability.[94] Walter Stahel, Director of the Product-Life Institute in Geneva argues that such changes can be profitable too. Products like office chairs designed to be easy to reupholster, or single use cameras that are recycled offer the chance to 'make more money selling one product six times than selling six different products to six different clients'.[95]

Durability is also a key issue for construction materials. The lifespan of buildings and infrastructure varies widely. Building regulations and government incentives in the housebuilding market act to discourage high standards, and discourage repair – for example by charging VAT on repair activities, but not on new-build – and have left the UK with a deteriorat-

---

# BOX 9.4 *CREATE*

Create is a new charity in Liverpool which aims to train long-term unemployed people to repair and reconstruct old fridges, washing machines and other white goods. It acquires end of life and traded-in products from rental companies and from local council waste collections.

Create currently has 12 trainees: and plans to expand to 24 in 1997. The project aims to provide breakthrough opportunities for the long-term unemployed in Liverpool's inner city, by providing a two year training and development course to National Vocational Qualification level 2. The work is waged after three months. The scheme takes products which would have gone to landfill, and rebuilds and repairs them to a high standard, such that all products are given a 12 month parts and labour guarantee. The finished machines are sold through charity shops in Liverpool, and at factory shops.

Source: CREATE (1996) *Press Pack on Community Recycling and Training* London: Lexus Public Relations. Create hope to expand to other towns and cities in the UK. Currently, throughput is one machine per person per day: for 24 people in each of 100 towns and cities, this would be around 550,000 units a year. Assuming that these would be half washing machines (61 kg steel) and half fridges (24 kg steel, two kg aluminium), this would save 23,000 tonnes of steel, and 550 tonnes of aluminium (equivalent to 14,800 tonnes of primary steel and 380 tonnes of primary aluminium)

---

ing housing stock with much higher proportions of energy inefficient and poor quality dwellings than our European neighbours.[96] In the long term the design lifespan of houses can be raised substantially from the 60 years now typical. The potential improvements for commercial buildings, currently renewed even more frequently, are even greater. In parallel to increasing product durability, lifetimes of products can be extended by ensuring that they can be repaired rather than thrown away. There are many benefits to changing direction: extra jobs and skills, and money circulated within local economies. Box 9.4 describes one charitable scheme set up to deliver such local benefits. However, there is wider evidence that repair, like recycling, generates more jobs than the one way 'manufacture, use, dump' approach to economics, as well as saving materials.[97]

Shifting taxes from labour to energy and raw materials would help stimulate a repair rather than a replace culture. In Canada, one innovative scheme has used a levy to create jobs specifically for people with disabilities in product repair[98] but the scope is much wider than this.

# Recycling

Environmentalists have been campaigning for years to increase the recycling of useful materials. As the impacts of extracting and disposing of materials in our linear economy have become clear, many scientists and researchers in industry have adopted a similar position. This is not to say that every last product and every last kilo of waste must be recycled, but just that there should be a presumption in favour of reuse or recycling, rather than disposal. This idea of a 'waste management hierarchy' has been widely supported.[99] At the top of the hierarchy is waste reduction, achieved by, for example, increasing the material efficiency of the production process, by increasing product lifespans or miniaturisation. Then comes reuse, for example by designing for repair and reuse of products and components. Recycling is next in the hierarchy, followed by disposal with some form of energy recovery. Of course, in increasing recycling of wastes to supplant use of virgin products, we need to take care that we do not expose workers in the recycling industry to increased hazards from toxic materials, or indeed to dirty and unhealthy working conditions in general. At worst, stricter regulations on waste management in the industrialised North have so far stimulated exports of hazardous materials to countries with lower standards for disposal or 'recycling'. For example an incinerator for US waste tyres was recently proposed in El Salvador. Fortunately, in this case CESTA, a member of Friends of the Earth International, was able to successfully coordinate opposition to the proposal, but others have not been so lucky.[100]

Increasing recycling is also important as a means of reducing wastes going to landfill or incineration (both industrial and household). The low cost of landfill is a major disincentive to recycling. Although a levy has recently been introduced to increase landfill costs, this is only at the rate of £7 per tonne, with a lower rate for so-called 'inert waste'. In comparison, the landfill tax in Denmark is equivalent to £27 per tonne with no lower rate. Denmark's landfill tax has proved very effective at increasing the recycling of construction waste.[101] In the UK construction waste counts as 'inert' and is only taxed at £2 per tonne. Perhaps unsurprisingly, according to EC data, the UK construction sector is responsible for the largest demolition waste arisings in Europe.[102] Secondary aggregates use was just 32 million tonnes in 1992 although more than 130 million tonnes are produced as byproducts or wastes from other processes every year.[103] There are no good reasons why use of secondary materials should be so low.[104]

*Domestic Recycling*

Effective recycling of post consumer wastes is more challenging. This source of secondary materials is more dispersed and often mixed or contaminated with other materials. Although post-consumer waste comprises a smaller proportion of the total material wasted, it is more significant than the crude figures would suggest. Household waste accounts for only 5 per cent of all waste in the UK. But it is often highly manufactured or processed rubbish. Estimates by FOE Scotland suggest that Scottish households throw away enough quantities of metals, plastic and other

## BOX 9.5 *INCREASING RECYCLING – AN EXAMPLE*

The City of Bath, in collaboration with Avon Friends of the Earth, runs a separated collection system based on 'Green Boxes' which keep recyclable materials separate from other waste. Cans, foil, clothing, car batteries, sump oil and oil filters are collected weekly from homes throughout Bath, and mini-recycling centres for paper, glass and cans are provided at large blocks of flats. The service covers 35,000 households, and employs 23 staff. This approach means that Bath has already met the 25 per cent target, with rates for glass at 72 per cent and paper at 63 per cent, although only 20 per cent of aluminium cans are recycled. Every month 234 tonnes of paper, 141 tonnes of glass, 18 tonnes of steel cans and 6.8 tonnes of aluminium are collected. This adds up to 2.5 kg per person of steel, and 0.96 kg per person of aluminium each year. If the UK were to reach Bath's recycling levels this would save 120,000 tonnes of steel, and 47,000 tonnes of aluminium. But the potential to go beyond 25 per cent is clear. In Bath, little waste is rejected because of contamination (less than 3/4 of a tonne each month). The key need is to increase participation rates still further.

Source: Bath and North East Somerset Council (1996) *Green boxes and partnership: keys to successful recycling in Bath* Bath: B&NESC

materials to make all the new cars that Scotland imports every year.[105] If recovery of post-consumer wastes for reuse or recycling replaces primary materials, then a substantial reduction in total waste can be achieved. For example, if an aluminium product is made from primary metal, 50 times more waste will be produced than in recycling or reusing it.

The last Government established a target for recycling 25 per cent of domestic waste by 2000. This falls well short of what is technically feasible: in practice almost 70 per cent of waste is recyclable, including those things which could be composted. The main recoverable materials are paper and card, metals, glass and plastics. Achieving the target could create up to 6600 additional jobs.[106]

But progress towards the target has been very slow. Only one in ten authorities recycle more than 10 per cent, and just two authorities have exceeded 20 per cent (see Box 9.5). Current levels of recycling average just 5.6 per cent, and increased by just 0.6 per cent over 1995.[107] In a quarter of local authorities rates fell between 1995 and 1996.[108] This is not because people do not want to recycle: 94 per cent think recycling is 'very or fairly' important to the environment.[109] It is because the obstacles to recycling are so large at present. The disincentive given by cheap waste disposal costs is exacerbated for local authorities as incinerator operators are seeking to make long-term contracts, committing the authority to provide set amounts of combustible waste.

The Government target is not a statutory requirement and no one is under any obligation to ensure that it is achieved. Waste collection authorities have a legal duty to write a Recycling Plan. But they are not actually required to meet any commitments made in the Plan. Furthermore, local authorities' finances are strictly limited by central government, and recycling is not included in their duties, merely their discretionary powers. Not surprisingly, many find they lack the money needed to invest in recycling schemes. And to cap all these problems, there are, as yet, no stable markets for recycled materials. Prices fluctuate widely over time, and in the UK there are no mechanisms, such as futures markets, to help stabilise them. The landfill levy needs to be increased, and supported by more substantial measures to support separated recycling collections, build markets for recycled materials, to encourage waste avoidance, and to give producer industries, including the packaging industry, responsibilities to avoid waste, reuse and repair items, and recycle them.

For certain materials recovery and recycling performance is better. For example, 28 per cent of aluminium cans are recycled. The benefits from recycling aluminium are substantial. But there is a great deal of further potential. The UK has by far the biggest aluminium can market in Europe. We consume 6.79 billion cans, the next biggest being 1.46 billion in Italy. Cans account for about 13 per cent of our aluminium use.[110] On average, Britons get through 117 aluminium cans each and every year. Only 33 of these will get recycled. The average Swede uses 108, and recycles 98. In the last ten years the proportion of aluminium used which is either scrap or recycled has not increased. Although we are recycling more aluminium, our consumption is growing faster.[111] This has a considerable environmental effect: the 80,000 tonnes of aluminium cans we threw away last year generated over 4 million tonnes of waste in countries such as Jamaica, Canada and Guinea. And making aluminium from bauxite uses 20 times as much energy as recycling it.

There is plenty of potential for improvement. Compared with other European countries, the UK's recycling performance is middling (see Figure 9.7). The UK could achieve 90 per cent aluminium can recycling by 2010.[112] Assuming that total consumption of aluminium cans is the same in 2010 as in 1995, increasing the recycling rate from 28 per cent to 90 per cent would save 71,000 tonnes of primary aluminium each year. The key issue for aluminium recycling is collection. Recycling the material is not the problem, nor is creating markets, say the Aluminium Can Recycling Association.[113] There is more reprocessing capacity than there is scrap aluminium. While it is true that recycling aluminium makes economic and environmental sense, it would be better still environmentally either to reuse aluminium or to use a less environmentally destructive material. There is nothing inevitable about high can use; the average French person uses just ten aluminium cans a year. Glass bottles could be used more, and more efficiently. With a comprehensive reuse scheme

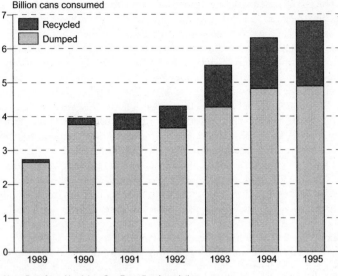

Note: Data from Aluminium Can Recycling Association.

**Figure 9.6** *Treatment of used aluminium cans in the UK*

glass bottles would be a more sustainable option. The apparent benefits of lightweight packaging such as aluminium, plastic or 'tetra-pak' identified in several industry sponsored 'life-cycle analyses', although real enough in the current situation, do not hold where distribution distances are short and reuse of containers is the norm.[114] The leaders in this area are the Danes: beer and soft drinks can only be marketed in returnable containers in Denmark.[115]

As a general principle, there are significant energy savings to be made by recycling, rather than using more primary materials. Table 9.3 shows one estimate of savings that can be made, even once energy use in collection is taken into account.

More recent analysis of waste streams has concluded that even if the waste materials are incinerated with energy recovery, the energy costs of replacing those materials from primary sources are so great that recycling is the more energy-efficient, as well as materials-efficient, waste management technique.[116]

## Product Design

Products of widely different designs and material intensities can perform exactly the same function. The design and redesign of products to be

**Table 9.3** *Energy Used in Processing Virgin and Recycled Materials*

| Material | Energy needed to process (BTU/pount) Virgin ore | Energy needed to process (BTU/pount) Recycled material | Amount of energy saved by recycling (per cent) |
|---|---|---|---|
| Steel | 8300 | 7500 (40% scrap) | 10 |
| | | 4400 (100% scrap) | 47 |
| Aluminium | 134,700 | 5000 | 96 |
| Aluminium ingot | 108,000 | 2200–3400 | 97 |
| Copper | 25,900 | 1400–2900 | 88–95 |
| Glass containers | 7800 | 7200 | 8 |
| Plastics | 49,500 | 1350 | 97 |
| Newsprint | 11,400 | 8800 | 23 |

Source: Hayes, D (1978) *Repairs, Reuse, Recycling – first steps toward a sustainable society* Worldwatch Paper 23. Washington, DC: Worldwatch Institute

more profitable goes on continually. We need to redirect that ingenuity towards making products more efficient in their use of environmental space. The simplest way to do this is to increase the costs of using those resources, so that designing to cut costs also cuts environmental costs. Here, as an example, we briefly examine the redesign opportunities for the product that symbolises Western consumer society – the car. In 1994 the UK produced 1.46 million new cars, and 1.91 million new cars were registered on the roads. Cars are made primarily from steel, plastics and aluminium. It is still true, as it was in the 1930s, that 'as a consumer of raw material, the automobile has no equal in the history of the world'.[117] The 1.46 million new cars coming out of UK factories use 810,000 tonnes of primary steel and 39,000 tonnes of primary aluminium each year. The 24 million cars in use in the UK produce 74 million tonnes of $CO_2$ each year. This is 9 per cent of all steel, 8 per cent of all aluminium, and 14 per cent of all $CO_2$ emissions, for this one product.[118]

Currently, fuel efficiencies are improving only slowly, car weight is increasing, miles travelled per car are increasing and car numbers are increasing. Cars are a major global problem. But there are at least partial solutions. The Rocky Mountain Institute in the USA has developed the hyper-car concept. By combining ultra-light construction with a hybrid-electric engine and a number of energy saving devices, design synergies offer 'order of magnitude' reductions in fuel and metals use.[119] This hyper-car would be roughly a third of the weight of the average car, and mainly substitutes carbon and glass fibre composites for steel. Hyper-cars would contain 58 kg of steel, and 53 kg of aluminium. It is conservatively

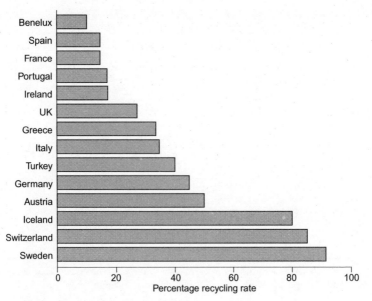

Note: Data from Aluminium Can Recycling Association.

**Figure 9.7** *Aluminium can recycling rates in Europe (1995)*

assumed here that use of recycled metal would not increase over today's level.[120] There is a corresponding tenfold reduction in fuel use: this is treated here as a tenfold reduction in $CO_2$ emissions also, although hyper-cars are designed to be powered by different energy sources, and non-fossil power sources are currently being developed. The gains made by building cars with less steel and aluminium are apparent immediately. Only 57,000 tonnes of primary steel and 29,000 tonnes of primary aluminium are needed: reductions of 90 per cent and 26 per cent. The $CO_2$ emissions savings will arise more gradually, as there will be many conventional cars still on the roads.

Amory Lovins of the Rocky Mountain Institute, the designer of the hyper-car, says: 'There's no doubt that today's automakers have the technical skills to make excellent hypercars quickly. Whether they are culturally able to remains to be seen'.[121] One of the fundamental aspects of the hyper-car is weight reduction. In today's pressurised car market, manufacturers selling almost identical products compete with each other by offering more and more gadgets such as ABS, side impact bars, stereos and even air conditioning. So the trend is for car weight to increase. While progress is being made to improve engine efficiency and prevent air pollu-tion, without a concomitant reduction in car weight the order of magnitude savings needed will prove very difficult to achieve. Given past

## BOX 9.6 *PRINCIPLES OF SUSTAINABLE PRODUCT DESIGN*

*Replacing products with services* which minimise resource and energy use, such as car sharing schemes, rental products, or nappy laundering.

*Strategic life-cycle design* that considers all the interrelated environmental impacts and ensures that products are more sustainable in production, consumption and disposal.

*Optimised design – multi-functional and upgradable products*, such as the all in one printer, fax, scanner and photocopier.

*'Dematerialisation' to replace products*, for example, virtual libraries, and teleworking systems.

*Longevity and durability* – design of products and components for an optimal lifespan, and to allow for repair.

Source: Working Group on Sustainable Product Design, UN Environment Programme (1996) http://unep.frw.uva.nl/unephome/text/seven-ways.html

failures with 'green' cars, hyper-cars will have to look smart and sexy and be aggressively marketed for them to succeed.[122] Car manufacturers are unlikely to develop these cars unless they are forced to. Strong financial incentives to develop very fuel efficient cars might do the trick, giving car manufacturers reason to take the risks in developing new products.

Reducing materials use, as seen in the example above, is just one objective of 'sustainable product design'. The UN Environment Programme's Working Group on Sustainable Product Design has suggested several broad principles for sustainable products (see Box 9.6).

As the US National Academy of Engineering has pointed out: 'Design should not merely meet environmental regulations; environmental elegance should be part of the culture of engineering education'.[123] Designs allowing upgrades rather than replacements would show environmental advantages. Miele washing machines have an update function which can alter the amount of water used if technology reduces the amount needed. This method of combating obsolescence is being used in the computer industry too. The PC industry has been notorious for turning state-of-the-art machines into second best within months. Increasingly, however, the main body of the computer can be upgraded by adding new computer chips. Currently, new products may meet one or two of these criteria: a long-lasting washing machine, or a computer which just needs a new chip to upgrade it. The challenge is to build products which meet several of these criteria.

# Sharing Resources

A commonly accepted principle for efficient materials use is the idea of life-cycle responsibility for products and materials; in effect making the manufacturer responsible for impacts generated in the disposal of their products, and providing a strong incentive for dematerialisation and design for reuse and recycling. The development of leasing approaches offers a step towards this, and towards fuller sharing of products and resources, even in the private consumer sector. At present the scope of leasing is relatively small; for example, companies are increasingly leasing cars for their employees, rather than buying them (and similar practices are being introduced in the private car market). Many companies lease office services such as photocopiers, or computer hardware. The practical impacts of such schemes are small, but the implications could be vast. Because the products are leased, maintenance, upgrade, reconditioning, reuse and the recycling of the equipment or its components remain the duty of the supplier. Xerox, for example has been taking back old photocopiers since the 1960s, but in 1990 it redesigned the machines, replacing screws and welding with snap-together parts and making the components more durable. Now the components can be easily recovered and reused. Xerox now says that it sells the service of guaranteed performance – not a product – and claims that the shift has saved it money, too, US$4.2 million in 1995.[124] Of course, leasing schemes need to be encouraged within the right regulatory framework to ensure product durability and upgradeability otherwise there is a real risk that leasing will increase turnover of equipment, as lessees trade in equipment before its useful life is over.

The car is particularly amenable to sharing through leasing arrangements. The average car is used for only 314 hours per year. It is claimed that in Bremen each shared car replaced five private cars[125] and we can conceive of going further than car sharing or leasing to the development of travel service companies which combine long-distance public transportation with short-distance taxi services or car rental.[126]

An innovative approach to resource sharing has begun with LETS, local exchange trading systems. These are trading networks in which people use a local currency – the Bobbin in Manchester, the Exe in Exeter, for example – to pay for goods and services offered by other members. There are around 350 LETS in the UK, and perhaps another 50 across mainland Europe.[127] LETS systems positively encourage sharing of equipment and resources. Manchester LETS say: 'We have two wall-paper strippers in circulation, which is about right for the moment with 500 members. This shows purchasing according to need within a community rather than as an individual'.[128] LETS also focus on provision of services to meet needs, rather than consumption of material goods, and at the same time, strengthen bonds within communities. People offer to baby-sit, loan their video recorder or repair bicycles in return for having their kitchen painted, their hair cut or getting the use of a computer. LETS thus work as another way to reduce consumption of resources. More rapid expansion of LETS throughout the country will reduce the need for individual consumption, preventing damage to the environment and saving money for households. Such trading systems are growing rapidly in the UK, and they have a large potential for reducing consumption of resources through simply sharing equipment and tools.

Beyond product leasing or sharing, we can conceive of materials leasing. Tim Jackson explains how this can operate, with the example of kerosene used as a degreasing agent. Kerosene is supplied on a use and return basis. The degraded solvent is reprocessed for reuse and the grease recovered is sold as a commercial fuel.[129] At present various products are collected already, such as motor oil, because dispersed disposal is considered too damaging. This creates the stimulus for reuse. A similar scheme has been suggested for sheep-dips to prevent disposal of used dips into the environment. Such schemes are a step on the way to material leasing. More widely it is clear that a stronger product liability regime would act as a powerful stimulus to such strategies.

# CURRENT POLICY

In the UK environmental policy and practice with respect to non-renewable resources is very poorly developed. It has not previously been perceived as an important environmental issue. However, there are signs of positive change towards demand management with respect to some materials, notably construction aggregates, as a result of the impacts of growing demand for quarrying. More generally, however, waste and pollution issues have provided a driving force in this area with government support for a number of waste minimisation schemes in industry, and increasing development of recycling schemes for domestic waste by local authorities. The main UK initiative in this policy area has been to establish a recycling target. The 25 per cent target compares favourably with the cuts in consumption of steel and aluminium of over 80 per cent by 2050, as an interim target for 2010 would suggest around a 20 per cent cut in use of these primary resources. However, the recycling target does not fall within a waste reduction framework and applies only to household waste, which is only a tiny fraction of total waste.

In minerals planning, the guidance on aggregates now sets targets for use of secondary or recycled materials. The target is equivalent to around 15–17 per cent of forecast demand by 2006. However, the forecasts are demand-led, and although the weight given to the forecasts has been reduced, they still underlie the provision of land for primary aggregate extraction, running directly counter to the considerations of an environmental space approach. Overall it is clear that, for resource use, stringent and clear targets are needed urgently.

**Table 9.4** *Summary of Targets: Representative Non-renewable Resources*

|  | 2050 target | | | | | |
|  | Low population | | Medium population | | High population | |
|  | Global target kg/capita | UK reduction (%) | Global target kg/capita | UK reduction (%) | Global target kg/capita | UK reduction (%) |
|---|---|---|---|---|---|---|
| Aluminium | 1.23 | 85 | 0.99 | 88 | 0.82 | 90 |
| Cement | 73 | 66 | 59 | 72 | 48 | 78 |
| Steel | 32 | 79 | 26 | 83 | 21.2 | 86 |

Note: 2050 target based on world 1990 figures, reduction on current UK consumption

# CONCLUSION

Table 9.4 summarises the targets for this chapter. It does not include chlorine, as a phase-out is not sensitive to population levels, or aggregates, which we have calculated a target for at the national scale.

It has proved more difficult to quantify the scope for practical measures to meet the environmental space targets for materials use. This reflects the low priority given to this issue by governments and business. However, it is clear that putting the right incentives in place can promote major increases in recycling and materials efficiency. Moreover, the same reforms would stimulate companies and communities to seek out ways of meeting needs by supplying services rather than material products. We return to many.of these issues in Chapter 10. Nonetheless, we have seen that increasing recycling rates could meet our interim targets for metals, with sufficient investment in recovery and recycling. For aluminium, an increase in proportion of recycling inputs from 31 per cent to 46 per cent would deliver the target, and for steel a similar increase from 36 per cent to 49 per cent would do so. Similarly, for aggregates, increased recycling, along with reduced road construction could save around 40 million tonnes, more than the 35 million tonne reduction required by 2010. Clearly it will be more difficult to achieve the 2050 targets, but the measures reviewed in this chapter offer much, at present largely unexplored, potential.

# Conclusions

Figure C.1 and Table C.1 below summarise the environmental space targets derived in the preceding chapters. They demonstrate the scale of the challenge for the UK. We must reduce our use of these key resources by between 15 and 100 per cent. In all cases, whether the resource is limited at a global level, or at a national one, the UK is clearly overconsuming. However, in general the degree of overconsumption is far worse for globally traded resources of which we take a very unfair slice of the pie.

The table also shows the interim targets and the results of our attempts to quantify the possible measures for reducing use of environmental space. These suggest that meeting the interim targets for 2010 is largely achievable with a range of measures, generally already demonstrated in practice, and often already cost effective. To put these measures into practice will involve starting major transitions in how we deal with wastes, improve our technology and even in the role of consumption in our society. Because of this we have been less able to quantify the possible achievements by 2050, and where we have been able to estimate the potential of existing practical measures, this often falls somewhat short of the environmental space targets. So they will be tough to meet. However, we do not see this as a gloomy situation. There are several reasons why not, most of which have been introduced already.

Our ability to predict the development of technology and social and economic practice that far into the future is limited. Our ability to quantify the effects of trends and changes that are easy to identify – such as 'dematerialisation' – are even more limited that far ahead. Moreover, we are confident that in a culture where environmental resources are adequately valued, many more opportunities for saving on their use will emerge from technological and social innovation.

It comes over loud and clear from many of the case studies in this book that knowledge and ideas are not in short supply, even now. A great many things can be changed which would benefit the environment, the economy and people. They predominantly stem from the same idea: be less wasteful, and do better with less. This is not some ascetic crusade, but common sense: there is little point building a new reservoir when instead we can simply reduce the excess water being flushed down everyone's toilet, or any point building nuclear or fossil-fuelled power stations when energy efficient lightbulbs can do the same job whilst saving money for householders too. Worse, the cost of many of these mistakes goes on for years: installing an expensive air conditioning system because the

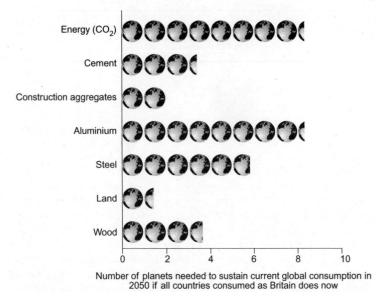

**Figure C.1** *UK overconsumption of environmental space*

office has been badly designed, or having to buy a new washing machine every five years because the old one wasn't made to last.

Unfortunately, at present, mainly because of the inertia of our economy and the power and influence of vested interests that benefit from the continued exploitation of environmental resources, we are not taking up the energy, water, paper and metal saving opportunities that exist, and as a result, we are all losing out. But we need to beware the risk that we will exploit efficiency gains simply to consume more. It won't help having Azurel houses if we then expect to have a second one out in the country, or in the south of France; or having hyper-cars if we use them to drive around the corner instead of walking, and jet off around the world by aeroplane at the drop of a hat! The real question is not so much 'how can we be that much more efficient', but, 'how can we ensure that the gains from our efficiency strategies are used to deliver real environmental improvements through real cuts in our use of environmental space?'

The final section of this book turns to the political, economic and social changes that would redirect our ideas and initiative towards sustainability not just through technological efficiency improvements but by recognising sufficiency and the need for social and cultural innovation too. As William Rees, the originator of the ecological footprint concept, says, we need cooperative, social solutions. There is no alternative: 'On a

**Table C.1** *Summary of Achievable Gains in Comparison with Targets for 2010 and 2050*

| | *Target 2010 (%)* | *Achieveable reduction 2010 (%)* | *Target 2050 (%)* | *Achieveable reduction 2050 (%)* |
|---|---|---|---|---|
| Energy | −30 | −25 | −88 | −79 |
| Land | −7 | n/q | −27 | −33 |
| Timber | −65 | −39–52 | −73 | −53–72 |
| Water | −15 | −18 | −15 | 2050 target achieved by 2010 |
| Aluminium | −22 | −22 or more | −88 | n/q |
| Steel | −21 | −21 or more | −83 | n/q |
| Cement | −18 | −18 or more | −72 | n/q |
| Construction aggregates | −12.5 | −15 | −50 | n/q |
| Chlorine | −25 | n/q | −100 | n/q |

Note: n/q – not quantifiable

finite planet, at human carrying capacity, a society driven mainly by selfish individualism has all the potential for sustainability of a collection of angry scorpions in a bottle'.[1]

# Part 3
# Towards a Sustainable Society

# Chapter 10
# Economic Sustainability – 'Ten Times Better'

## INTRODUCTION

In this section of the book we address some of the opportunities and obstacles to sustainability that lie in the economic, social and political spheres. As we have shown, it is within our practical and intellectual abilities to make the reductions in consumption necessary to meet the targets outlined in Part 2. The key obstacles to achieving sustainability are not technical or practical, but economic, social and political. It is in these arenas that the battle for the planet will be fought. These domains also offer opportunities through policy integration to deliver economic and social as well as environmental goals. In doing so, we can turn the potential of Part 2 into practice, and turn our vision of a sustainable future into reality. We are not offering a political manifesto, more of a practical programme for government. The policies we recommend are not predicated towards any single political philosophy; they should be attractive to those realists from all parts of the political spectrum who can see the growing public awareness, as yet only barely politicised, of the nascent sustainability agenda.

In this chapter we raise two fundamental questions. First, can our economy continue to create wealth and employment, and go on supplying us with the goods and services to meet our needs, on significantly reduced material inputs? And second, assuming that this is possible, can such a restructuring occur without major economic disruption and hardship for specific regions or groups in society? To answer these questions, we must look at sustainability from two perspectives: for companies, and for the economy as a whole.

## COMPANIES AND THE ECONOMY

Most new employment is created in small, new or expanding companies, not in old established ones. It is important that any restructuring of the economy offers opportunities for new firm formation and for existing firms to expand, even if others can be expected to decline. Ensuring that the UK is an attractive location for 'eco-efficient' and sustainable businesses in the twenty-first century is critical for our future economy. The environment will inevitably become one, if not the, main dimension of competitiveness. Those who move early will gain bigger market shares in this future. If instead, we listen to the losers – the dinosaur companies who still rely on intensive use of energy and materials – and delay, then the UK will lose markets to the more foresighted. We are already losing out in Europe. Germany has taken the lion's share of the pollution prevention technology market – estimated to be worth some US$200 billion globally – and Denmark is beginning to corner the market in wind turbines. Yet UK firms are all too often under-represented at European meetings on business and the environment, where many of our European competitors are already planning for the changing markets of the next century.

As the European Commission says, 'we should not confound the interest of specific [sectors] with the overall economic interest of our economies'.[1] In other words, the losers may not be representative of our overall economic interests. In practice, the potential problem is even bigger. Europe is poised to take a world lead in these areas – a lead which could bring serious economic returns – but at the Council of Ministers, the UK has been amongst the nay-sayers, pleading the 'special interests' of its dinosaur industries to block progress on environmental taxes and fiscal reforms that would provide a continuous incentive for our industry to get better and better.[2]

## Winners and Losers

Who will be the winners and losers if we cut inputs to meet environmental space limits? Are the fears of UK industry correct? The short answer is no. In part these fears are illusory, based on the traditional experience of costly end-of-pipe environmental technology. The economics of preventative environmental management can be radically different, as industries all over the world have already found. In part they are real; much of industry will face a real challenge, and undoubtedly, some companies will go under. But the UK economy is already largely based on the service sector, especially financial services – which almost doubled its contribution to gross domestic product in the decade from 1979 to 1989. Table 10.1 shows the broad sectoral use of the different environmental space resources we reviewed in Part 2. It also shows the contributions of those sectors to gross domestic product and employment for purposes of comparison.

Even the financial sectors rely on some material and energy use; the economic basis for financial services is speculation on commodity prices and trading in investment capital. The former requires material flows (although it is value-based, not volume based) and the latter requires physical investment (although this need not be in material-intensive industry). The financial services industry will therefore also need some reconceptualisation, but a dematerialised economy will require innovative new investment tools. The opportunities for such businesses to redirect investment to less energy and material intensive sectors are very real. More conventional material intensive industries are not doomed, although they face greater challenges. However, many of our remaining companies in the heavy industrial sectors – such as chemicals and steel – have undergone, and continue, a shift towards higher value added products and niche markets where quality and unique product characteristics are the stuff of competitiveness. This shift means they already tend to use a smaller volume of material; value is added through clever application of ingenuity and technology. So many UK companies, and certainly the most innovative ones, should find the transition to environmental space targets relatively easy and even an opportunity for obtaining competitive advantage. With careful policy design, many will profit from it.

However, potential short-term losers have remarkable political influence, whether through MPs on their boards, through donations to political parties, or, in the case of organised trade unions, through sponsoring MPs. Those who will gain are often less well organised; there is no trade union for those who might get a job handling leasing and servicing of products in the future. There is only a nascent organised parliamentary lobby for the existing environmental technology companies and the many more that will inevitably form to take up the new opportunities that policies to promote sustainability and eco-efficiency would create.

# BUSINESS SUSTAINABILITY

Yet particular business practices can become unsustainable when public values shift against them. The recent controversy over the export of live animals for slaughter abroad, which caught several companies (and not just the exporters themselves) by surprise, illustrates this well. It shows how issues which are not related to traditional consumer concerns over quality or value for money can become highly significant to company survival. More broadly, the public believes that business should take its environmental and social responsibilities more seriously. In 1995, twice as many of the British public said they would choose to protect the environment at the expense of the economy than vice versa.[3] What is happening in such cases, is that the public – one of the 'stakeholders' in any company – too long ignored, is flexing its muscles. In practice the privilege of incorporation granted to companies by the state, principally

**Table 10.1** Sectoral Use of Environmental Space – UK

| 1990 | GDP (%) | Jobs (%) | Water (%) | Steel (%) | Wood (%) | Aggregates (%) | Energy as $CO_2$ (%) | Aluminium (%) | Land (%)[2] |
|---|---|---|---|---|---|---|---|---|---|
| Agriculture | 1.86 | 1.3 | 18 | 0 | n/a | 0 | 1.3 | 0 | 76.8 |
| Transport | 10.63 | 8.5 | n/a | 0 | 3.2 | 36 | 24.2 | 3.1 | 1.5 |
| Energy supply | 4.95 | 1.8 | 4.3 | 0 | n/a | 0 | 6 | 0 | 0.1 |
| Industry | | | | | | | | | |
| Total | 20.69 | 18.5 | 34 | 51.4 | 37.2 | 26 | 31.2 | 79.3 | |
| Chemical | 2.40 | 1.3 | n/a | | | | 5.6 | 0.1 | |
| Paper | 0.74 | 0.5 | 0.3 | | 16.4 | | 2.2 | 0 | |
| Steel | 0.69 | 0.5 | n/a | | | | 6.4 | 0 | |
| Construction | 7.21 | 4.9 | n/a | 24.5 | 38.6 | 23 | 1 | 14.2 | 6 |
| Services | | | | | | | | | |
| Total | 54.27 | 64.9 | | | n/a | 0 | 6.3 | 0 | |
| Tourism | 2.78 | 5.4 | 43 | | | | n/a | 0 | |
| Households | 0.39 | n/a | | 24.1 | 9.6 | 0 | 26.7 | 3.5 | |
| Other[1] | – | – | – | 0 | 11.5 | 15 | – | 0 | 15.6 |

Notes: 1 Other includes uses which cannot be allocated to a specific sector due to poor definition. 2 Land-use figures are very uncertain. The share for transport has been estimated as 20 per cent of all built-up land.[a] The share for energy use is based on the area of land affected by coal mining. Water used by the electricity supply industry for through cooling is not included. Water used by the paper industry is based on water used per tonne of pulp production. Housing starts are counted under construction for aggregates. Steel and aluminium trade statistics attribute much consumption to industry, when the final end-use will be households (fridges, knives etc.).

Source: a Transport and Environment Studies (1991) *Wrong side of the tracks?* London: TEST providing for limited liability, has long since been seen as a right. But as American business writer Paul Hawken has argued, this need not be so.[4] Companies require at least a metaphorical licence to operate. And that licence is issued by the public. As public values shift they will be reflected in patterns of consumer demand, in political regulation, and where the shift outstrips conventional responses, in protest. Continued protests against road building expanded into growing protests against the car industry in 1996, partly in response to its blinkered self-congratulatory attempts to celebrate the 'centenary of the car' in ways which failed to account for the shifting view of the public against its environmental and social impacts.

## The 'Stakeholder Economy'

The idea of 'stakeholders' is older than Prime Minister Blair's recent conversion. The modern conception of a stakeholder is distinct from that of a shareholder, who holds a financial stake in the company. There are five other principal groups of stakeholders in any company, besides the shareholders or financiers: its employees, its customers, its suppliers, the local or wider community and the government. Much has been written in recent years on the recognition and balancing of the different interests of the different stakeholders by successful companies. Management guru Charles Handy notes some similarities in the successful Japanese and German traditions in this respect.[5] Both rely on close, often localised, business networks, explicit recognition of the various stakeholders, and a balanced approach to them, including works councils and a long-term perspective on investment.

In other senses however, at present the successful company is the one that, in a more Anglo-American tradition, best manages not the stakeholders' interests, but their expectations. In other words, the company effectively uses its power and influence to divide and conquer its various stakeholders. This view explains the strength of the myth that there is a conflict between jobs and the environment. This position is promoted by many companies, often through threats to disinvest and other propaganda, to divide opinion in local communities and help them minimise their costs in dealing with environmental concerns expressed by community stakeholders. Companies can influence all their stakeholders in one way or another, including governments, as David Korten suggests.[6] Their influence over local or national governments grows with their size and wealth, which helps them access political processes, and with the openness of the local or national economy to mobile capital, which increases their ability to threaten disinvestment.

The Japanese traditions are, in part, being more widely adopted in the Eastern Asian economies. As Christopher Hampden-Turner of the

Judge Institute of Management Studies in Cambridge reports,[7] such corporations do more for their employees – for example, providing credit unions – and their employees repay them with higher productivity. His view is that this convention has contributed significantly to the productivity and recent growth of these economies. A 'stakeholder' economy in this sense offers great potential for increasing sustainability generally, as well as increasing the sustainability of individual companies, although it cannot guarantee either. For example the overall sustainability of the Asian Tiger economies – doing well out of engaging their employee stakeholders better – is most doubtful.[8] In a detailed study of the Korean case, Jong-Il You documents widespread pollution and contamination of air, water and soil, and notes that the interests of economic growth have consistently overridden environmental concerns and civil rights, with persecution of environmentalists and non-enforcement of environmental regulations.[9]

## Stakeholders and the Environment

Our interest in a stakeholder approach is not just that it can help ensure that some of the social and economic interests of the wider stakeholder group are met. We also see an opportunity for carrying environmental concerns into the corporate decision making process in a far more comprehensive way than is the norm today. But this requires the right framework of accountability for companies and real transparency, so that the stakeholders know exactly what the company is doing. For any individual company, even at present, recognising the interests of all stakeholders is critical; any one of them can seriously damage it. However, at present, some stakeholders – particularly the local community, but also employees – have such opportunities only infrequently. For example, when a company is seeking planning permission the opinions of the local community can be very influential, and for major developments companies spend a lot of money and effort in persuading local people that their environmental and social credentials are good, whether or not this is really the case. But once the development is in place, the local community has little influence over the company.

Environmental concerns can be, and increasingly are being, expressed by many of the different stakeholders, although most importantly by the wider public or community. Companies are increasingly finding that 'sound' science and legality are not adequate defences against the deepening environmental concerns of the public.[10] Shell found this to their cost over the Brent Spar incident. In the realm of values, sound science and legality are simply a basic minimum standard. In such cases companies need to manage the process of dialogue with stakeholders effectively. But few organisations, as yet, run proactive and inclusive dialogues. And even then, it is rarely a case of a dialogue of equals; communities and NGOs can rarely match the resources available to companies.

The key question for us now is, how can the market framework be reformed to make it easier, and more profitable, for companies to balance the interests of all their stakeholders in practice, rather than simply in rhetoric? David Korten has suggested that the process of globalisation has left company managers with no chance of taking such an approach.[11] He sees no choice but to decline to the lowest common denominator: if managements don't pursue the highest short-term profits, then they will be outcompeted by those that do, asset stripped by corporate raiders, or replaced by shareholder action driven by fund managers. Despite the elements of truth in his analysis, this a very bleak conclusion, and flawed in several respects. First it does not recognise that preventative environmental management can pay financial dividends for companies. Second, governments can still exert power over corporations; in practice most companies still keep the majority of their operations in their home country, however often they might threaten to leave. Third, the market has more niches and diversity – driven at least in part by growing concern over environmental and social standards – than Korten recognises. Finally, as Korten himself admits, companies can act as 'citizens' too, seeking a high standard of 'level playing field' through regulation.

## Corporate Greenwash

In many cases, however, companies do not act as citizens. There are big differences between the best practice and the worst practice between and within sectors and even within big companies. Companies are not monolithic, and different parts of the same companies act in different ways. Nonetheless many companies and their trade associations are still more likely to obfuscate and confuse the debate than to act as citizens. They do the former through public relations activities, marketing, subsidising contrarian research and writing, establishing 'front' pressure groups; the whole arena of 'greenwash', from green product labelling and tree-planting sponsorship to the more insidious 'wise use' movement in the US.[12]

While companies will do many things to appear greener, most will never question their levels of investment and activities as such, even though this question lies at the heart of business sustainability. In the words of an employee of the Billiton-owned Trombetas mine in the Brazilian part of the Amazon, during a visit from the Netherlands Committee for the IUCN: 'We are willing to discuss every part of the operation process, but we are not going to discuss the existence of the operation itself'.[13] This conclusion is supported by the findings of a survey of members by the Institute of Environmental Management (IEM). Despite senior management commitment to minimising the environmental impacts of existing activities, the IEM reports that 'it is not evident that this commitment extends to the acceptance of the need to evaluate and consider environmental issues at the core of business development and evolution'.[14] Indeed, even though these firms could be considered 'leading-edge' as they all have environmental managers, the lack of senior management commitment is seen as the main obstacle to progress by almost three-quarters of those managers.

Rather than taking the current state of play as given, we must ask how we can increase the rewards companies get for acting as 'citizens', by enforcing environmental and social standards more rigorously, for example. As Madeline Grulich, Director of the Pacific Northwest Pollution Prevention Research Centre notes: 'regulation forces companies to act, and the results [financial savings] motivate them to go on'. Says Grulich, with companies that present themselves as pro-environment 'good guys', 'if you probe more deeply, you often find something like a major fine within the past few years that really shocked the company'.[15]

### Sound Science?

Sound science is a minimum standard needed to ground debates over values. Naturally, science commissioned by a business will be directed towards meeting the company's goals. But in the current market framework the science commissioned to meet a particular business goal will not necessarily be directed towards meeting needs. Nor can it be assumed that it will be used rigorously and objectively. It is therefore absolutely essential that the research, and the way that it is used, is set out in a fully transparent way so that it can be subjected to scientific peer review and public scrutiny. Otherwise there is a real risk that people's needs will be compromised by peremptory 'science' pursued to meet public relations objectives rather than genuinely address unresolved scientific uncertainties. A topical example is the lengthy and costly Nirex science research programme. Due to plans to dump foreign waste in the UK, the company were under pressure to build a nuclear dump quickly. As a result the scientific work that they commissioned was not fully peer reviewed or properly used. Its weaknesses were exposed by Friends of the Earth at a public inquiry, and ultimately Nirex's scientific case was rejected by the Inspector and the Secretary of State.

More generally companies and some governments – such as the UK's last Conservative Government – have begun to use the concept of sound science as a shield against precautionary action. This is one reason why public values have increasingly been expressed in protest. Nowhere is such abuse of the concept of sound science more worrying than in the effects of pollution on human health. There are so many confounding factors that it has taken decades to demonstrate even something as obvious as that smoking is bad for your health (and even this is still disputed by some tobacco companies). When it comes to air pollution from industry and traffic it is easy to show a broad correlation with increased respiratory illness, but difficult to demonstrate the pathways by which it takes effect. Yet only several years after figures were first published estimating additional mortality and illness caused by traffic pollution, did the UK Government accept the need for action. In the interim, it accepted the arguments of the auto industry and oil companies that to impose extra costs on them would be unfair and premature. So the public has had to go on bearing the costs of ill health and environmental degradation.

Even where scientific consensus is almost complete, such as the case of climate change, parts of industry – notably the American fossil fuel lobby – have supported, endorsed and publicised the work of the few scientists who dispute the Intergovernmental Panel on Climate Change's assessment.[16]

In other cases, companies have been found to abuse the scientific process more directly, withholding or, at worst, falsifying data to ensure that their products can enter or remain on the market. For example, scientific evidence on pesticides has been withheld from the public on several occasions at least.[17] Dow Chemicals, who have recently publicly championed business sustainability arguments, just three years ago received the largest ever US Environmental Protection Agency fine for withholding adverse data on effects of pesticides drifting onto schools.[18] At worst, laboratories have been discovered to have falsified test data for pesticide firms.[19] These are examples of companies seeking short-term benefits by trying to mislead some of the wider stakeholders in their activities. There are two ways in which government action, endorsed and supported by companies acting as 'citizens', can help prevent this. First, it can alter the framework of financial incentives so that it encourages longer-term, and more environmentally responsible activities. Possible measures include tax reform to alter the relative price of companies' inputs and the establishment of long-term industrial development banking with tax incentives for long-term investment.[20] Second it can impose a regulatory framework that ensures greater transparency over corporate activities, and greater accountability for them, through an effective liability regime, and strong enforcement of environmental regulation. We would not go so far as to suggest following the example of China, which has made certain environmental crimes punishable by death,[21] but we would support much stricter personal liability for directors.

## The Failings of Voluntarism

The interaction of public attitudes and values with government action is critical if we are to achieve greater sustainability. The previous British government, in recent years, had adopted a voluntary approach to business sustainability in several areas, arguing that companies can respond directly to public attitude, where the incentives to change are reinforced by 'bottom-line benefits' and the threat of regulation.[22] In practice, without the appropriate regulatory framework companies find it hard to do this, especially in the short term. Indeed the 'Producer Responsibility Initiative' in which businesses were asked to come up with a strategy for increasing recycling of packaging turned into a long-running farce. Even after changing the aim of the policy from increasing recycling, to reducing landfilling (opening the door for increased incineration) the businesses involved had to repeatedly demand government intervention because otherwise less conscientious companies would be able to free ride. The Industry Council on Electronic Equipment Recycling also says that the voluntary approach is 'open to abuse and evasion' in this way.[23] Similar weaknesses have been found in labelling schemes. For example, recent tests of fridges by the Consumers Association found that 11 out of 15 models tested used more electricity than their labels claimed.[24]

These problems are even worse where the product concerned is not sold directly to the public. While the public has shown an increasing preparedness to pay more for more environmentally sensitive products, companies purchasing inputs or components rarely look beyond the bottom-line of cost. The cases of companies such as B&Q (the DIY and garden store), IBM, BT and even Rover, which have begun to 'green' their supply chains – in effect passing their customers' demands back onto their suppliers – are the exception rather than the rule, and only effective where the supplier has few alternative outlets for its products. To facilitate this more widely, better information on the environmental impacts of products and processes needs to be consistently available through some form of accredited and transparent environmental auditing procedure. Company reporting, even under the new European Eco-Management and Audit Scheme (EMAS) is still often sketchy and inconsistent.[25] Worse, current voluntary eco-labelling initiatives and environmental management systems standards such as BS7750 and ISO14001 fall short of imposing more solid requirements.

Regulations alone will not be enough in the modern fast-moving marketplace. The OECD has estimated that based on present trends, 50 per cent of the products that will be in use in 15 years' time do not yet exist.[26] Many of these new products will involve environmental innovation. This can be fatal for companies producing the conventional alternative product. The more companies focus on needs, and the services to meet those needs, the less likely they are to miss the opportunity for a market shift. The more far-sighted automobile manufacturers – such as Volkswagen and Volvo – are already positioning themselves as transport companies, rather than car makers. Volvo, for example, see themselves as 'a natural partner when it comes to providing complete transport solutions for cities' including buses and traffic planning,[27] whilst Volkswagen have recognised for many years that car use may need to decline and that 'we need improved public transport as well as technical [vehicle] improvements'.[28] Power companies, such as Pacific Gas and Electric in California, are already rediscovering themselves as energy service companies (see Chapter 5).

# MATTER MATTERS – DEMATERIALISING THE ECONOMY

Here we address the scale of process and product innovation needed to meet environmental space targets. To economists and business people money is the bottom line, or in other words, what matters is what something is worth (in cash terms). All too often, this means that if something is worth nothing in cash terms it doesn't matter. But in environmental terms monetary value is not the bottom line; physical reality is the bottom line. In other words, matter matters, not just money. Environmental space is based on this insight. It sets targets according to actual flows of materials and energy. But when we came to gather information for these studies, all over Europe, it always proved more difficult to obtain data on physical flows, than on value flows. This is symbolic of the blinkers of conventional practice which need to be removed. Fortunately, the emerging science of industrial ecology is filling the void economists have left largely untouched. Industrial ecologists like Robert Ayres (of INSEAD) are examining the firm like an organism, and the economy like an ecosystem, in terms of flows of energy and materials, not simply in terms of flows of money (or value). Other analysts are building mass-balance models of the economy, quantifying inputs and outputs in material terms.[29] Businesses too are getting interested in such approaches, recognising that every pound of waste or emissions is one they have paid for as a useful input!

The Business Council for Sustainable Development (BCSD) established in 1990 by Stephan Schmidheiny to prepare a global business perspective for the Earth Summit, and now merged with the World Industry Council on the Environment, to form the World BCSD (WBCSD) is one hard-headed business organisation which has begun to promote radical targets. In summary they suggest that on average 20-fold 'eco-efficiency' gains will be needed to 'meet the needs of a growing population fairly within the planet's ecological means'.[30] This is even more ambitious than the goal of a collaborative initiative by a group of scientists and business people who in October 1994 founded the 'Factor 10' club to seek a ten-fold 'dematerialisation' or reduction in our use of environmental resources over the next 30–50 years.[31] But before we turn to the strategies companies will need to adopt to achieve these cuts in inputs of materials and energy, we must address the misplaced but common belief that 'dematerialisation' is happening anyway.

Some analyses of evolution in economies have suggested that over time, the material intensity of economies is falling anyway, as in some natural evolutionary process.[32] This view is misleading. First, insofar as it is real, it is simply a result of changing geographical patterns of industry and services facilitated by low transport costs and the drive for free trade. Migration of extractive and manufacturing industries has reduced our apparent materials use in Northern countries. But the service sector and households continue to consume material products, although more of these are imported. As a result, economies like the UK appear more sustainable, but in practice we are exporting our unsustainability.[33] Second, there is little evidence for the inevitability of this process; so far, substitution has accounted for a lot of the decline in use of specific materials, and in many cases synthetic materials have replaced organic ones.[34] The trend can be partly attributed to changing resource prices resulting from political price manipulation – the oil price 'shocks' of the 1970s.[35] Third, and most significantly, dematerialisation so far has generally done no more than cut material intensities per unit of GDP, rather than cutting total material use.

## Achieving Eco-efficiency

The BCSD define eco-efficiency as

> *the delivery of competitively priced goods and services that satisfy human needs and bring quality of life, while progressively reducing ecological impacts and resource intensity throughout the lifecycle,* to a level at least in line with the Earth's estimated carrying capacity *(emphasis added).*[36]

This definition encapsulates four critical elements: an emphasis on services, a focus on needs, a life-cycle view and the 'eco-capacity' imperative, as the BCSD terms it. Despite increasing adoption of environmental management systems to increase efficiency, the BCSD does not expect 'business as usual' to deliver the needed improvements in eco-efficiency. Instead, it argues, the strategic pursuit of labour saving technologies must be redirected to nature saving technologies. Companies need dynamic systems which will allow continuous improvement in environmental performance to keep within environmental space targets. This reflects a wider consensus that business sustainability must be a strategic goal. Only strategic vision can help a company avoid the risks to economic sustainability of the business that we noted earlier: scarcity of key resources; competitive innovation; and changing customer or wider public values. Business analyst Stuart Hart, writing in the *Harvard Business Review* sees such 'sustainability vision' as a key component of the 'Sustainability Portfolio' for companies alongside commitment to cleaner technology, product stewardship and pollution prevention.[37]

# Making the Change

So how can businesses do 10 or even 20 times better to meet our sustainability targets? At the heart of the strategic vision needed lies the concept of preventative environmental management. Preventing environmental damage starts at the very point where a market opportunity is identified, if not before, with the type of opportunity sought. So, sustainable business will start with needs. But at present, corporate scorecards measure success in terms of throughput and volume sold rather than services delivered or needs met. Of course, business responds to effective demand in the marketplace, not needs alone. Social and economic reform which allows the poor to back their needs with purchasing power is also necessary, as the BCSD recognises. But the BCSD do not cynically use this argument to pass the ball to government, and then sit back to wait for the opportunity to profit from such stimulation of demand. They recognise that business has the marketing techniques to shape and create demand for the products it wishes to supply. Business has applied these techniques irresponsibly in the past (see Box 10.1) but we can't put all the blame on business. Governments have pursued economic growth without questioning the value of what makes up that growth. And we consumers can't play innocent either. Very few of us can resist the better, newer or simply more, that the marketplace offers us on a daily basis. As the BCSD conclude, a needs-focused corporate strategy therefore requires businesses not only to listen to customers, but also to learn more about the psychology of consumption.[38]

From needs, the sustainable company moves to product conceptualisation, with a presumption in favour of a service-based way of meeting that need. Tim Jackson, of the Centre for Environmental Strategy, talks of the need to 'reinvent the service economy'.[39] The economy is intended to be a provider of services that meet needs. Some needs can be met by buying material products which provide those services, but only occasionally is this the only option. The challenge is to extend it to other areas, where at present the service sector generates more use of material goods rather than substituting for them.

This is not to suggest that we can or should eliminate the material and manufacturing sectors of our economy, but by taking such an approach, companies in that sector can enhance their long-term sustainability. Companies have evolved remarkably in recent years. Modern modes of production, based on lean production, just-in-time supply

## BOX 10.1 *CONSUMERISM GONE MAD*

'People use money they don't have, to buy things they don't need, to impress people they don't know'[a]

Some European mass producers of beer (eg Heineken) export bottled beer to the USA, rather than licensing local production. This permits a premium price to be charged because the beer is imported, and therefore considered exotic by US consumers. Similarly, Europe imports 'speciality' beers from Mexico for reasons of fashion.[b]

One company which accepts discarded telephones for reprocessing estimates that more than four in every five phones they receive are in perfect working order, simply discarded in favour of new, or different coloured models.[c]

Some products test the bounds of believability. For example, recently marketed in the UK: a spray-on odour to make tumble dried clothes smell as if they had been dried in the fresh air, and a smoke can to test your smoke alarm with the strap line: 'Spray today for a safer tomorrow'!

The UK imports some remarkable products. Research for Chapter 6 revealed that Mauritius exports 4500 tonnes of bovine offal to the UK every year; the UK imports 481 tonnes of rabbit meat each year, 99.4 per cent of it from China; and that the UK imports more fish which is unfit for human consumption than fish which is fit.

Sources: *a* Oystein Dahle, cited in Bank, H (ed) (1995) *Sustainable Production and Consumption: An Agenda for Change* Oslo: The Norwegian Forum for Environment and Development; *b* Weaver, PM (1993) Synergies of association: Ecorestructuring, scale, and the industrial landscape *Paper for United Nations University, Tokyo, Symposium on Ecorestructuring* 5–7 July; *c* World Resource Foundation (1996) *Electrical and electronic waste* Tonbridge: WRF

chain management, Total Quality Management, flexible automation, skilled, flexible workforces, and computer integration, can all be called on to deliver environmental benefits if the incentives are right. New product development is a much more rapid process; old environmentally harmful products could be quickly phased out. Modern quality management reduces reject rates, saving materials and energy. Plant flexibility and the scope to work with small batch sizes could be redirected to meet more localised demands and reduce freight transport. Just-in-time techniques, although potentially requiring more transport, also require less floor space, and lower inventories. However in the past, with cheap transport, these industrial trends have led to rapid growth in transport use of energy: freight traffic in terms of tonne-km increased in OECD Europe by 40 per cent between 1970 and 1987.[40]

Modern management techniques are in many ways essential for the application of preventative environmental management in the product design and manufacturing process. The adoption of preventative techniques is analogous to the shift many companies have already undergone, from quality control systems in which substandard products are picked out after manufacture, to quality assurance, in which potential problems are spotted earlier. As a result far fewer duff products make it to the factory gate, and wastage can be substantially reduced. Of course, preventative approaches also involve the adoption of cleaner technologies which are more efficient.[41] Firms which have taken a preventative approach are, almost without exception, more competitive as a result. For example, waste minimisation could save millions of pounds for UK industry. And these direct financial savings at present factor costs do not include the value of the wider environmental improvements delivered. If environmental costs were internalised in the prices of resources, then the bottom line savings would be even bigger.

## Zero Emissions

The motivating power of 'zero defects' in total quality management has inspired some companies to set goals of zero emissions, especially in response to bad public relations because of their toxic emissions. The major chemical manufacturer Dupont established its target after publication of the Toxics Release Inventory showed it to be the biggest polluter in the USA. The idea of zero emissions, however scientifically impractical at heart, has inspired many companies and developers to adopt the principles of industrial ecology and seek uses for things that are currently waste products. In the USA, DuPont's zero emissions goal led them to open a carpet reclamation plant in Chattanooga that recovers the nylon for use in making car parts. Overall, by 1994 the company had cut plastic wastes disposed of by 25 per cent over late 1980s levels. In Japan, some fifty corporations have established zero emissions divisions and there are even plans for a 'zero emissions' city.[42] Over 300 corporations, mainly in the USA and Japan, financially support the Zero Emissions Research Initiative of the United Nations University.

There are now 50 companies in the USA, all formed since 1980, who match 'waste' chemicals with other companies' input needs. But it's not economic to transport most waste materials very far, so the quest for reuse opportunities is leading to proposals for industrial agglomerations or so called 'zero-emissions' industrial parks. Industrial ecosystem plans are being developed in the USA – one in Chattanooga which in 1969 was dubbed the most polluting town in America – and in Canada, Namibia, Fiji, the Netherlands and Indonesia.[43] But ahead of all these plans, industrial symbiosis is already real. The small Danish town of Kalundborg has become something of a Mecca for would-be industrial ecologists. Here recovered heat from the power station is used in an oil refinery, a drugs company, a fish farm and for domestic heating. Gypsum created in the coal-fired station's desulphurisation 'scrubber' is sold to a local plasterboard manufacturer, which also uses the refinery's light gas, normally burned off as waste, to fire its ovens for drying the board. The refinery also pumps its cooling water to the power station as boiler feedwater. Organic sludge from the fish farm and the drugs company, where microbes are cultured, provides fertiliser for farmers' fields. These links evolved over 25 years, not simply because of the environmental benefits, but because they were economically viable and beneficial.

To create something similar from scratch would 'take some kind of godfather' says Robert Ayres, meaning a major company or investor committed to the project.[44] So far, the 'godfathers' are more often local authorities, but even strapped for cash and limited in powers, local authorities can make key investments in assembling sites and providing supporting infrastructure, as well as identifying and approaching potential partner companies. The system needs to be simple enough for the participating companies to work in easily and predictably, yet have enough redundancy built in, so that one company going bust would not bring down the entire local economy. But many companies have been loathe to provide 'commercial information' on their inputs and wastes. So even designing the system, let alone assembling appropriate companies, has been a challenge. Bringing companies on board also means getting them to look beyond their 'core business'. The question of how tightly companies should focus on their core business is not new. Too tight a focus, and opportunities are missed, too loose, and the whole company is put at risk. For example, the problems of Hanson in recent years have been attributed to its excessive diversification, and in the USA, companies breaking themselves up has been described as the 'great corporate fad of the Nineties'.[45] We aren't suggesting that companies should follow the route of diversification to extremes, merely that they should not be so focused on a particular product that they fail to see the opportunities in selling their waste products, for example, or worse, that they don't see what the business consultancy Sustainability describes as 'the big wave' – changing public values – until it is too late to catch it, and their whole business goes down with their 'core product'.

There are other factors more encouraging to the strategy of industrial ecology by agglomeration, such as increases in waste disposal, raw material and transport and logistics costs, and trends fostering a leasing and service based economy; in turn these factors can be expected to increase the power of local community stakeholders as companies are more tightly bound into their location.[46]

In theory, zero emissions, even if achievable throughout manufacturing industry, would not necessarily meet our environmental space targets, as the concept says nothing about the material and energy throughputs in products themselves. However, in practice, the only ways to even approach zero emissions will involve the strategies set out above for preventative environmental management and dematerialisation: delivering energy and material-efficient services to meet needs. Although the more foresighted companies, including some of those in the WBCSD, are beginning to investigate the benefits of such strategies,[47] they will not be able to deliver on their own. Later we examine the role of government, but first we consider the role of the financial sector and the nature of investment in the development of our economy.

# INVESTING IN THE FUTURE

Current patterns of investment are widely criticised as being too short term even to maximise our purely economic interests. Will Hutton, for many years economics editor of the *Guardian* newspaper, believes that the UK economy suffers from an endemic problem of short-termism in investment.[48] He argues that there is a vicious circle in operation: investors expect rapid and large returns, so employers cannot invest in the long-term development of their employees and businesses. Companies that do so make themselves ripe for takeover and asset-stripping, which brings short-term returns but long-term problems. But as short-term investment returns get higher, the more investment they attract, and the less sustainable our economy becomes. The fiduciary duty of company executives to their shareholders is a powerful factor reinforcing such patterns of behaviour. Korten similarly argues that globalisation has freed major companies from constraints of other stakeholders and made them increasingly accountable only to the global financial system. He notes that the 'S&P' top 500 largest corporations have been increasing their profits at 20 per cent per year on average, defining a high-growth norm.[49] Such short-term profits are achieved by passing costs onto the community, for example, by reducing employment or evading environmental standards.

With short-term returns critical, the euphemistic process of downsizing (sacking people) offers an easy way to make a fast buck, but leaves the company's long-term profitability prospects low. This, unfortunately, doesn't matter to shareholders and top management as with little loyalty to other stakeholders in the business, they can move on, having reaped their reward from inflated share values and share options. Takeovers, mergers and acquisitions also obtain profits for shareholders at the expense of other stakeholders. Takeover targets are often those who have invested in employee training, product development and quality improvements; investments which can be turned into short-term shareholder profits by the corporate raider. Today shareholders wield too much power. And as the overlap of interests of shareholders and management – who are increasingly shareholders, or who have share options themselves – grows, the other stakeholders are further marginalised. Christopher Hampden-Turner of the Judge Institute of Management Studies says:

> *The truth is that for really successful industries, shareholders come last. This is a quote from the 1943 Credo of Johnson and Johnson, the US pharmaceutical house. The irony is that this company has earned more for its shareholders over the last half-century than any other.*[50]

'Last' simply means that shareholders must wait for the other stakeholders to succeed to reap their rewards. And shareholders are not principally individuals. Despite recent privatisations and political rhetoric about a shareholding democracy, the proportion of shares held directly by individuals has fallen since 1980. The big shareholders are indeed the public, but only indirectly, through pension funds and trusts. As Korten says, although mutual funds, pensions funds and trust funds have become the dominant investment vehicles, rather than shareholders buying into specific companies, this has had adverse consequences.[51] The fund managers are subject to a legal fiduciary duty to obtain the best financial returns for their clients, and are evaluated on the basis of very short term, even daily, results. Their interests should be long term, but the structure of the market pushes them into maximising short term returns, and then moving on, shifting their investments to the next short-term opportunity.

The adoption of cleaner technologies suffers particularly from the short-term perspective of most investment capital. Such technologies, although perhaps more risky, are potentially very profitable, but to get them off the ground needs soft loans and 'patient' venture capital.[52] Even without long-term financial investment available, companies which take a longer term perspective will find it easier to improve environmental performance by working with the grain of capital cycles. Natural recapitalisation – the investment in new technology to replace old or worn-out technology – provides substantial opportunities to invest in new, cleaner production technologies.[53]

## Changing the Investment Culture

We need new instruments to direct investment to support innovation and longer-term sustainable business. There are several key routes to achieve this, some of which are relatively well developed.

The insurance and reinsurance sector is perhaps the most important: it underpins virtually all business investment in some way and is set to bear the brunt of the financial costs imposed on the economy by climate change, through insurance claims for storm damage, floods, drought, subsidence and other so-called 'natural disasters' whose frequency and intensity are set to increase. The reinsurance industry is suddenly getting very interested in environmental concerns. The recent escalation of global warming related claims – natural weather-related catastrophes have quadrupled premium income between the 1970s and 1990s[54] – has stimu-

lated 60 major reinsurance companies to get together to demand precautionary action on climate change. As one leading insurance executive says,
'it is absurd to wait for scientific certainty on global warming when
"serious businesses every day" make investment decisions worth billions
of dollars on the basis of far less than certainty'.[55]

The insurance industry is also set to be very influential on companies'
environmental performance as a result of liability claims. Currently most
insurers cover companies for 'sudden and accidental' pollution under
general liability policies. According to Brian Street at ECS Underwriting,
this is effectively a 'freebie, without any inspection or influence on the
insured party to behave itself'.[56] But this is changing. Insurers are discussing
ways to exclude pollution, and develop separate policies. In Germany and
France the insurance industry has begun to force companies to take out
special environmental impairment liability insurance. Such measures
require companies to provide better information on the likelihood of pollution incidents and allow insurers to threaten to refuse cover where
management of the risk is inadequate.[57] A strong stimulus for wider
adoption of such changes would be to increase the scope of liability for
pollution, making it stricter and retrospective, so that companies could not
evade responsibility for their past performance. This would increase the
financial exposure of insurers under the current regime, but not under a
regime where pollution risks were separately insured at higher premiums.

Although the environmental awareness of many insurance companies is rising, as yet very few UK companies have signed the UN
Environment Programme's 'Statement of Environmental Commitment'
which would, albeit voluntarily, commit them to address the environmental implications of all their activities including investment of funds.[58]
Venture capital investment companies and the mainstream banks are
lagging even further behind.[59] They are beginning to come to grips with
what John Elkington of the Sustainability consultancy calls 'corporate
ecology' – in other words, good housekeeping, such as energy efficiency
in their own buildings – but they are not yet grasping the nettle of
'product ecology', the environmental aspects of their core business of
lending and investment.[60]

On the other hand, some European banks are beginning to see the
market in this way. For example, the Swiss Bank Corporation says:

> *In the future it will be essential to include environmental factors in
> every study and analysis. This is not only the responsibility of an
> environmentally aware bank; it is also in the interest of the bank's
> shareholders and customers.*[61]

Some banks, with a history of social or community interests, have moved
more rapidly to take advantage of new market opportunities. The Triodos
bank in the Netherlands launched its two green investment funds during

the 1980s to support organic agriculture and wind power. By astute political lobbying in the early 1990s it persuaded the Dutch Government to establish tax breaks for such investments, which rapidly encouraged mainstream Dutch banks to follow suit. Seven certified funds now exist. They have proved massively popular. Rabobank's Green Fund had to be closed prematurely. It was oversubscribed more than five times within two weeks of opening, bringing in 430 million guilders instead of the expected 80 million.[62] But mainstream banks in the UK are waiting for a lead from government.[63] Similarly, financial analysts pay only limited attention to environmental performance of companies when advising on investment strategies. A 1994 survey for Business in the Environment (BiE) found that only 15 per cent of firms provided analysts with guidelines on environmental issues and 58 per cent believe that 'non-financial issues' such as the environment are 'unimportant to their clients'.[64]

On a more positive note, there are increasing numbers of ethical or environmental investment funds, a result of the growing realisation that individuals, in the final analysis, can exercise some power through this route, especially through influence over pension funds. And the need to do so is clear: 80 per cent of FT-SE top 100 companies are currently considered unsuitable by ethical investors![65] A Mintel survey suggested that the proportion of the public which would like some form of ethical or environmental screening on their investments was 30–40 per cent in 1992 (and it seems to be growing).[66] Yet only 1 per cent of financial advisers ask clients about such concerns. Fortunately this seems set to change. The economic outlook for ethical and environmental funds is good: a UK survey found ethical pensions outperforming average equity pensions by on average 1 per cent per year from 1988 to 1993, while the longest running UK ethical fund outperformed the average over ten years by more than 6 per cent per year.[67] We can expect their financial and political influence to grow; fund managers in this sector are not afraid to use their influence to promote 'constructive shareholder dialogue'.[68]

Yet these funds face problems which only legislative or regulatory changes can solve. They have difficulties getting accurate information to allow them to 'screen' companies, because information on the environmental and social performance of companies is often not publicly available. The BiE survey highlighted that half the analysts questioned believed that company information on environmental performance was not trustworthy, and that two-thirds of them believed that current environmental reporting and disclosure is inadequate to faciltate company assessment.[69] Stricter right-to-know legislation is needed here. And because many funds are bound by fiduciary duties to maximise financial returns, technically such funds cannot discriminate against companies on grounds of environmental or social performance, even where this is clearly in the interests of the individual investors. This too requires regulatory change to allow fund managers, and indeed company directors also, to consider all the interests of their clients and shareholders, not simply their financial ones. As well as setting the regulatory framework, the government has some direct influence on investment capital for companies. It can directly support certain investments, and by the tax regime it imposes, can help direct the pattern of investment. In the Netherlands, the government allows accelerated depreciation on investments made by companies in approved environmental technology.[70] This measure particularly benefits small and medium sized enterprises which otherwise have difficulty accessing capital at appropriate rates for such investments. Similar measures have been implemented in Germany, the USA and Japan.[71]

Overall, such reforms in the investment system should help reduce short termism, at least where environmental costs are concerned. But other measures may be needed to fundamentally challenge the short termism endemic in the UK, and increasingly in the global, economy. Handy points out that in the German economy, banks are long-term investors in specific businesses. They are not seen as short-term financial helpers as in the UK. Partly, this is the result of close local networks of family businesses and regional banks. One beneficial side effect of the web of such investments is that there are very few contested takeovers. Also, companies in the UK retain less of their profits for reinvestment. Between 1975 and 1993 UK companies retained just 45 per cent of profits for reinvestment, Japanese companies retained 63 per cent, and German 67 per cent.[72] To stimulate reinvestment rather than redistributing profits to shareholders, Handy suggests linking managers' bonuses to the performance of employees, rather than to share performance, as occurs when their bonuses come from share options. Hutton suggests regulating share options to create incentives for managers to hold on to them for longer.

Hutton makes several more far-reaching proposals for tackling short termism in the UK.[73] He advocates a 'republican-style' central bank situated within, and accountable to, regional public banks; and a public agency to act as financial intermediary collecting longer term deposits, like the German bank for reconstruction. He suggests a new regulatory framework for banking designed to reinforce the effect of the 'stakeholder' culture by promoting closer but longer term relations between the company and its investors.[74]

# Local and Regional Investment

Community banking offers the potential for the banking sector to also direct its efforts at meeting people's needs directly, rather than assuming that the best way of doing so is to invest in whatever brings the highest short-term returns. Community banks have no higher loss rates and bad-debt rates than commercial banks.[75] But banking law and the current regulatory framework make it difficult to establish them, especially in Europe.[76] Reform of the regulatory framework for financial institutions, for example giving community banks preferential levels of government guarantee for their loans, as suggested by Korten,[77] would help direct investment into local economies. Credit unions are another key source of investment to meet local needs. There are over 37,000 credit unions worldwide with assets of US$418 billion, serving 88 million members. But they need active support, and the right regulatory framework if they are to develop an effective social or community focus.[78]

Ensuring that investment supports localisation and reinforces the incentives for industrial agglomeration should be a specific aim of that regulatory framework. Financial institutions too would then have to reconnect themselves with their community stakeholders. Community banks and credit unions are an important source of finance for cooperative enterprises, another sector which could contribute significantly to economic sustainability. Cooperatives have innate potential to emphasise meeting needs; like some of the best features of the South-East Asian model discussed earlier, they give the employees much more influence over the company, in theory directing it towards meeting their needs, and the needs of the local community, more directly. It is no surprise to find that cooperatives and credit unions are typical of economically marginal regions such as the Western Highlands of Scotland, and Basque Spain, which are often endemically short of conventional investment and employment.[79]

# IN THE DRIVING SEAT

Industry can deliver sustainability in terms of a factor-10 or further 'dematerialisation', but government has to drive the change. There are many technologies, products and processes which would contribute to such an eco-efficiency revolution, which are available from ordinary companies today, but are largely overlooked. Corin Millais of Greenpeace says: 'These solutions are only prevented from becoming mainstream because they are suppressed, ignored, prevented from competing equally, held back by specific vested interests in business and politics and starved of interest and investment'.[80] The need for government intervention to overcome these vested interests is borne out in many surveys of business interests. However interested industrialists are in environmental improvement, they take most action when given a strong incentive. In a recent survey of UK company directors, nearly two-thirds of directors reported that environmental issues were discussed on board agendas. Of the forces contributing most to companies' concern about environmental pressures the need to comply with UK and European Community legislation was cited as the main reason by 34 per cent of directors and social responsibility and corporate citizenship by 28 per cent. Seventy-one per cent of environment-related investments were stimulated by legislation.[81] Regulation has wider effects too. In 1991 the United Nations surveyed 794 transnational corporations with annual sales over US$1 billion. Of the 163 firms which responded, 57 per cent of them cited home country legislation as the most influential factor provoking company-wide changes with respect to environmental policy and programmes.[82]

Other findings highlight the need for regulation, but also suggest that companies are perceiving the potential competitive advantages that sound environmental practices can give them. A poll of financial directors and chief accountants conducted by Gallup for Coopers and Lybrand in 1992 showed legislation and consumer pressure influencing increased spending on waste and pollution control and environmentally friendly product design.[83] The most up to date figures suggest that industry now spends over £2.3 billion a year on environmental protection. It is interesting to note, however, that for two key sectors; chemicals and electricity, the figures found in this detailed survey were significantly lower than those claimed by the industry associations,[84] reinforcing the case for greater transparency. And of course these are not unproductive costs: every pound spent on pollution control buys services or products from the environmental technology industry, as well as a cleaner environment. More recently a survey of environmental management executives in 300 of the top 1000 UK companies found that a majority of respondents thought that various tax measures to increase the relative costs of environmental inputs would help improve their environmental performance by overcoming constraints based on implementation costs.[85]

Of course, it's not enough just to have strict regulations and better taxes. They must be enforced too. The prosecution rate by Her Majesty's Inspectorate of Pollution is increasing, but there were still only 13 prosecutions in 1993/94. Yet in 1994/95 there were 1200 confirmed pollution incidents. Successful prosecutions by the National Rivers Authority declined to 423 in 1993/94, whilst incidents reported grew to almost 32,000.[86] The impacts of poor enforcement go beyond just greater environmental damage. Environmental technology companies lose out too, to the tune of £2 billion a year, according to a recent report by the industry lobby group, the Environmental Industries Commission.[87] Industry is being given little incentive to work with the environmental technology companies to develop effective pollution control and cleaner technologies.

So far in this chapter, we have repeatedly referred to the role of government to set the right regulatory framework. Aside from the regulation of financial institutions, the need for regulation falls into three main areas: stimulating research and innovation into eco-efficiency; regulating markets to promote the development of needs-based service industries; and reforming tax and subsidy systems to promote eco-efficiency and employment.

# Innovation Towards Eco-efficiency

In recent years, the last UK government sought to reduce its role in funding research and development, cutting direct funding into so-called 'near-market research' and pushing universities and research institutes to obtain more private sector funding. The Environmental Industries Commission have reported that UK public funding for environmental technology research and development in 1994 was worth just £50m, compared to the equivalent of £97 million in Germany and £2.5 billion in the USA.[88] Even at current funding levels, the UK government still has a role in funding pure and pre-competitive research, where the distribution of funding can have significant implications for the development of cleaner technologies.

Ian Christie and his colleagues at the Policy Studies Institute suggest three key government measures to promote innovation towards and adoption of new and existing cleaner technologies, based on their research involving 30 companies in the chemicals and engineering sectors.[89] First, financial incentives are essential, at least to kick-start the process. These need not be subsidies for the new technologies, they could just as easily be taxes on inputs. The European Commission's 'communication on economic growth and the environment', as well as endorsing government support for research and development, and demonstration projects, also stressed the importance of removing market barriers to the introduction of new technologies such as subsidies or tax breaks for conventional approaches.[90]

Second, measures to promote good practice through existing business networks such as supply chains and trade associations are needed: working with the grain of how firms innovate. Training and Enterprise Councils and the Business Links 'one-stop shops' could promote a key route for such information. Government can also act here as a purchaser, influencing the suppliers it deals with. Integrating such measures within a broader framework of environmental targets, such as those in the Dutch national environmental policy plans can reinforce their effectiveness. A recent study revealed that Dutch entrepreneurs related their use of raw materials to the environmental issue of limited resources. This was reflected in greater attention to environmental considerations when making innovations in production processes, in comparison with their German counterparts acting within a policy framework focused on emission.[91]

Christie's third key measure is the big one: 'it must be acknowledged that regulation remains the key driving force behind innovation'.[92] As well as more conventional measures relating to emissions and environmental quality, Christie argues for standards for supplier assessments, environmental reporting and accounting. Effective environmental reporting is especially important. In the USA the introduction of the Toxics Release Inventory, requiring companies to document all emissions of prescribed toxic substances acted to promote rapid improvement by companies. The Environmental Protection Agency administrator William Reilly declared that: 'The impact of TRI has far exceeded our expectations as a tool for improving environmental management [and TRI data] should be considered to be among the most important weapons in efforts to combat pollution'.[93] DuPont claim to have cut emissions by up to 87 per cent after featuring as America's largest polluter on the TRI and to have embarked on a transition from products to services, to 'get to where the public want them to be'. This is the public as stakeholders, not simply customers. Transparency empowers other stakeholders – whether local communities, or shareholders – to influence company performance on such issues. Legislation to ensure a full right-to-know about business environmental and social impacts should be a high priority for any government seriously pursuing a sustainability agenda.[94] In the UK, we have league tables for schools and league tables for hospitals, but not league tables for polluters.

But to really stimulate innovation, such transparency needs to be backed by accountability through stringent enforcement of environmental regulation and a strong and effective liability regime. Tim Jackson argues strongly for product liability to promote materials reuse and even materials leasing. More generally, The Natural Step's promoter, Karl-Henrik Robert, suggests that in effect liability needs to be shifted from the public, to the investor, along with the burden of proof that the process is environmentally safe.[95]

# Regulating the Markets – Supporting Sufficiency

Despite free market rhetoric, all markets run within a particular regulatory framework, whether this is set deliberately, or by default. For example, as we saw in Chapter 5, at present the framework in the energy market acts, on balance, to discourage the optimum uptake of energy efficiency measures. In other countries, it is the energy market that has seen the development of the 'least-cost planning' or 'integrated resource planning' approaches that give demand management a fighting chance.

Forty-three US states have now established forms of utility regulation in the energy sector that use 'least-cost planning' principles to meet the need for energy services with the least costly mix of energy supply and energy efficiency improvement.[96] In several states utilities have, as a result, provided energy efficient lighting to customers alongside low-interest loans for the uptake of other energy conservation measures. They are selling what have been coined 'Nega-watts' to their customers and because of the regulatory framework the local ordinances create, they are profiting from it. In the UK, the regulatory framework fails to create such an incentive, and government measures to promote and subsidise energy efficiency have proved largely ineffectual.[97] In principle, similar approaches could be applied in water supply, and even in road transport. In California, local ordinances require new development to be accompanied by a package of investments that will reduce existing water demand in the area by the same level that the new development will increase demand. Similar principles could be applied to new developments which would generate additional traffic.

There is an obvious opportunity to introduce such measures for energy when the market is fully liberalised in 1998. More widely, Simon Marvin suggests that such techniques could be introduced in the UK through the land use planning system, overcoming one of our biggest implementation problems in the process.[98] It is, at least in theory, relatively easy to insist on high environmental efficiency standards for new developments, but difficult to judge when this imposes an excessive cost burden on the developer, while leaving existing buildings very inefficient. To introduce a least-cost planning approach, allowing the developer to invest in demand management elsewhere in the area, would create a market in which more cost-effective investments will be undertaken first, with the same overall results. Private sector investment could be directed into efficiency investments which would, in addition, be good for local employment.

The regulatory framework would also need to address equity issues directly. Otherwise, to take the example of energy, fuel poverty could be a disincentive to investment, as the energy savings from efficiency improvements in a fuel-poor household may be less than those in a household where energy needs were already met, albeit very inefficiently. One way of doing this is to learn from an example in the South. In Sri Lanka, electricity tariffs are structured in such a way as to reward low users, and keep the costs for the poor as low as possible. There are three price bands, with the highest unit rate being charged to the biggest users.[99] This is the opposite of the situation in the UK, where corporate users are encouraged to consume more energy to qualify for lower unit rates. However, it is feasible to consider even a structure in which households get a free allowance of such basic goods as energy and water, but then pay for profligate use at an accelerating rate, linked to the basic efficiency of their dwelling. All it takes is the political will to use the regulatory framework to that end. However, at present, local authorities lack the powers and discretion to introduce such measures.

## Tax Reform – the Price is Right?

We have repeatedly mentioned the need for the prices of environmental inputs to the economy to rise if businesses and individuals are to be given the right market signals to use them more efficiently. The concept of a gradual integrated tax reform, in which new and increased taxes on resources, waste and pollution are balanced by cuts in other taxes, offers several advantages over simply introducing additional green taxes. First it can increase the incentive for businesses, in particular by adjusting the relative price of other inputs, notably labour. If taxes are reduced on labour through cuts in employers' national insurance contributions, then not only do environmental resource inputs get more expensive, but the cost of labour falls. The incentive to substitute for the former with the latter, where this is possible, is reinforced. Second, the reform means that overall costs for business as a whole can be maintained at a constant level, thus reducing or even eliminating the economic disruption that can arise from increased costs. Tax reform also has a potential benefit in terms of our concerns that increased efficiency is often translated into lower prices and increased demand. Through maintaining an overall cost level through offsetting taxes, this approach, at least in theory, should not suffer from this effect.

The idea of a so-called 'ecological tax reform' is relatively new, but has been around long enough for the European Commission to promote it strongly, and even for the OECD to endorse it.[100] At heart the concept seeks to provide a continual incentive for existing and new firms to move towards sustainability by using less environmental resources, triggered by higher taxes on them, and more labour, as a result of lower taxes on it. Econometric modelling exercises indicate that not only would environmental gains be achieved, but that economic performance would be virtually unaffected, most likely with increased levels of employment. Modelling has been undertaken by Terry Barker, from the University of Cambridge Economics department, for a package of taxes: a commercial and industrial energy tax, gradually increased to the equivalent of US\$9 per barrel of oil equivalent by 2005; an increased and extended waste tax, reaching £25 per tonne in 2005; a higher road fuel tax escalator, at 8 per cent in real terms every year; a tax on virgin aggregates, also increasing gradually to £9 a tonne in 2005; an office parking tax and an end to company car tax breaks. According to Barker's E3 model, the most sophisticated economic model of energy, environment and economy linkages in the UK, by 2005 this would reduce carbon dioxide emissions by 9 per cent below the base scenario, and waste disposal by 16 per cent. And if the revenues were recycled in reduced labour taxes, employment would rise by over 700,000, cutting jobless figures by around 300,000.[101]

Even if the UK implemented such a reform unilaterally, the net effect on the UK's international competitiveness would be negligible, as the overall profitability of investment in the UK would remain the same. For some sectors, such as financial services, the reform would enhance their international competitiveness, while for others, such as iron and steel, cement and chemicals, the impact could be more adverse. However, these sectors, where they compete internationally, increasingly do so on grounds of quality in specialised markets, rather than on price alone, so the negative impacts would be lessened. A study of the potential effects of tax reform in Germany suggested similar outcomes: 7 per cent decline in energy use, additional employment of 600,000 and insignificant impacts on growth and competitiveness.[102] Any effects on competitiveness are simply those related to prices of inputs and products. In practice increased prices for environmental inputs have been shown to drive innovation in firms in such a way that they obtain competitive advantages by making even greater efficiency gains. This process partly accounts for the success of the Japanese economy where energy and raw material prices have been relatively high for many years now.[103] However, tax reform does raise some issues regarding trade, as there are currently doubts about whether border tax adjustments, which are accepted for the resources themselves, could be applied to products that embody the taxed environmental resources. If not, tax reform could make imports cheaper relative to domestic production, with a slight negative impact on competitiveness.

In the design of a practical ecological tax reform there are several issues that must be addressed. One can't simply impose any old green tax, and expect it to have the optimum effects. Each tax must be justified in terms of the environmental benefits it is expected to generate. This tends to require close attention to how tax-payers might respond. For example, the tax differential in favour of unleaded petrol was hailed by the previous government as a 'flagship example' of the success of economic instruments. Yet drivers proved remarkably conservative in their fuel choice, and it took over five years for unleaded petrol to exceed 50 per cent of UK petrol sales.[104] The effectiveness of economic instruments can be compromised by market failures, such as barriers to investment or lack of information. These barriers may be closely tied to equity issues, as in the case of fuel poverty. For this reason, any tax on domestic energy would need careful design and parallel action to address fuel poverty concerns.

In the same way as individual taxes do not work in a vacuum, but relate to other policies setting the market framework, tax reform will be undermined if other policies push in the opposite direction. A critical measure to support tax reform is the elimination of tax breaks and subsidies that continue to promote the overuse of environmental resources. This is why the proposals modelled by Barker included measures to eliminate the perverse subsidies for car use provided by tax breaks on company cars and parking spaces. Other environmentally perverse subsidies in the UK include £1.2 billion worth of tax breaks for offshore oil and gas exploration and development; £1 billion plus annual subsidies for 'market support' for agricultural production that provide an incentive for overuse of agrochemicals; support for nuclear power and the tax break given to incineration by excluding it from the waste levy.[105]

The second key issue in the design of green taxes is the question of what level of tax is appropriate. Green taxes or other economic instruments should have clear policy targets and the level of tax should reflect this purpose. We have explained the weaknesses of economic valuation methods already. We cannot rely on such processes to establish tax levels, nor to determine targets for policy. Instead we should use the environmental space targets in this role. To allow valuation measures to determine the objective of policy falsely assumes that all externalities can be fully valued or successfully internalised. As Karl-Henrik Robert says, with a system based on targets, the 'price of nature' becomes what it costs not to systematically destroy or degrade it. The price would be the 'increase in market prices resulting from the investments necessary to achieve these goals, rather than attempts to calculate full cost prices on the basis of contingent valuation or some other dubious methodology'.[106]

# A COMPETITIVE ECONOMY

At the beginning of this chapter we raised two concerns about the likely economic impacts of a sustainability strategy led by environmental targets. Firstly, can the economy as a whole remain competitive in the global economy? And secondly, will the impacts on specific sectors or industries be great enough to cause major regional disruption and hardship? Here we summarise the main arguments.

## International Competitiveness

No country has ever tried to reduce environmental resource consumption in such a dramatic and systematic way. Nonetheless, there are two sets of evidence that give us grounds for optimism. The first is the evidence that suggests that the more energy- and material-efficient economies are, if anything, more economically successful, whether that efficiency has been stimulated by higher prices or stringent environmental regulations. Evidence from analysis of OECD statistics at a national level[107] is supported by studies of the performance of US states. Those with the lowest industrial energy prices generally have the poorest socioeconomic, environmental, business and energy indicators, and can be characterised as being in 'arrested development'.[108] The benefits arise because environmental control costs are not a decisive factor in company or economy competitiveness.[109] Preventative environmental management delivers direct financial benefits from higher environmental standards, the growing global market for environmental technologies and 'environmentally friendly' products offers increased export opportunities to countries which obtain first, or early-mover, advantages by insisting on high domestic environmental standards.

The environmental objectives set out in Part 2 of this book also offer more specific economic benefits. Some of these were reviewed in a recent Friends of the Earth report on jobs and the environment.[110] There are two particular areas where stronger environmental policies would stimulate the economy and potentially create employment. First, the measures necessary to reduce our consumption of resources such as energy and water require investments in plant and infrastructure, notably to improve the energy efficiency of our housing stock. Like any infrastructure investments these could be expected to boost the economy to some degree. These measures are relatively labour intensive, so bring employment benefits. Second, measures that reduce consumption of environmental resources can free up income for spending in other ways. For example, increasing energy efficiency may displace jobs in power generation, but provides financial savings which are spent on goods and services. To ensure that such effects do not result in overall increases in consumption, however, tax reform is essential, to ensure that the goods and services the money is spent on are, on balance, less material and energy intensive.

The second reason for optimism is the results of both theoretical work and empirically-based modelling of the implications of ecological tax reform. As we saw above, these models suggest, at worst only small negative, and at best positive, implications for competitiveness and balance of payments, and for overall profitability, as well as increases in employment, at least in the short term. Modelling at a European scale suggests similar results.[111] So far, we haven't mentioned that great bugbear of current macroeconomic policy: inflation. Yet the UK has been through one of the deepest post-war economic recessions for the sake of maintaining inflation at low levels. Control of inflation and reduction of public borrowing lie at the heart of 1990s consensus economics.[112] Borrowing is unlikely to need to increase more than it has in recent years, especially if tax reform succeeds in increasing employment levels or wages for the low paid, so as to reduce welfare costs. And indeed, reaching the golden rule on public sector borrowing – borrowing no more than we invest – may be made easier by our sustainability strategy which implies a shift from short term expenditure to long-term investment.[113]

While inflation is important, because it can have significant impacts on investment and competitiveness, and distributional impacts which adversely affect savers and the elderly, there is little if any substantive evidence to suggest that it should take pride of place amongst the objectives for macroeconomic policy.[114] This could be taken to suggest that we need not worry about inflation. But this is not the case. Having achieved low and stable rates of inflation it is well worth maintaining them, although not 'at any costs'.[115] There are some implications for the policies suggested above. Clearly, increasing prices of energy and material resources could increase inflation, although offsetting tax reductions on other inputs will temper this effect. The modelling by Barker suggests a net effect of no more than half a percentage point increase in the rate of inflation by 2005 from the substantial increases in resource prices in the tax package he models.[116] The European modelling by DRI suggested even smaller price effects.[117] The impacts for public sector borrowing are equally negligible.[118]

A policy package based on tax reform can, in fact, be designed to simultaneously enhance the employment benefits and reduce the inflationary effect. However, this requires consensus policy making, only possible in a wider 'stakeholder economy' where labour interests can be persuaded collectively to support wage restraint. As the European Commission argues, this would in turn prevent interest rate rises in fear of inflation.[119] In other words the Commission is suggesting that by a social compact of sorts, consumers agree to take lower long-term real wages in return for higher overall employment and a better environment. As Dutch economist Gerrit de Wit shows, this will ensure that tax reform delivers long-term employment benefits.[120] Even without this there is empirical reason to expect short-term employment gains,[121] and both short- and long-term environmental gains.

There is a third area where evidence is growing to support the claim that strategies for sustainability will not harm our economic competitiveness, albeit one not considered by many economists. In these terms, a minimum wage and the social charter are not the disaster some employers would make them out to be. Low wages act as a disincentive to participation in the labour market and to productivity.[122] There is little evidence that minimum wage agreements reduce employment.[123] Tax reform might increase average wages, indeed the belief that this will occur, rather than employment gains, is one of the objections to the idea raised by some economists. In this case then benefits may be seen primarily in better economic performance while higher wages will raise employment by increasing the incentive to work.

This also implies that the last government's infatuation with flexible labour markets, intended to increase competitiveness by driving down costs to attract inward investment, was largely misplaced. Such an approach harms the prospects for long-term investment, especially investment in development of skilled and trained labour forces, as much as it helps. In the labour market, as in the environmental policy arena, driving up standards to enhance investments in quality, seems to be the best strategy for providing the right environment for company formation and growth in the twenty-first century. However, none of these measures will avoid economic disruption if they are introduced too rapidly. That does not mean waiting until we are almost at 2050 before taking steps to meet the targets. But it does mean phasing in new measures, for example announcing new taxes and then slowly increasing them until they reach effective levels.

# Regional Restructuring

The second question, raised at the start of this chapter – of whether severe localised effects will arise – is easier to answer, but also raises challenges for the design of policy. Looked at in one way, economic history is the history of a sequence of restructurings, most of them with significant geographic aspects.[124] Restructuring may be easier to manage if it is foreseen, but it is no less painful for the companies involved and their workers. The social effects are greatest where whole regions depend on a particular industry, as we saw in the 1980s with the run down of the British coal industry. To an extent the UK has already experienced much of the pain of restructuring necessary to set ourselves up for transformation to a less material and energy intensive economy. However, the changing relative prices and demand for certain resources and products is likely to hurt certain industries and regions further, although not as severely as the industrial protagonists concerned like to claim. Again, supportive evidence comes from the modelling of tax reform packages, which suggests that even in the sectors most hit by rising prices of resources, overall employment levels are unlikely to fall.[125]

The most important strategy for reducing the effects of such disruption is to invest in strengthening and diversifying regional and local economies. And there are other good reasons for doing so. Diverse local economies are more self-sufficient, less reliant on transport, and as we saw above, make it easier to close material cycles in industry. In addition, the cause–effect links between consumption and production become more explicit, and thus easier to manage, given adequate local political authority. Localisation of economies can bring employment benefits, especially to poorer areas by creating a local multiplier effect, retaining the respending benefits of money locally. And this can have synergies with our environmental objectives. A recent study in Los Angeles shows that 85 cents of every local dollar spent on petrol leaves the regional economy, much of it leaving the country as well. In contrast, out of every dollar that buys a fare on public transport, an estimated 80 cents goes towards transport workers' wages. The study found that the circulation of those 80 cents in the local economy generated more than US$3.80 in goods and services in the region.[126] Along with support for local authorities embarking on investment strategies to reinforce the local economy, measures to facilitate and support Local Economic Trading Schemes (LETS) would be an effective measure in helping to build local economic capacity.

# Trade and Globalisation

Our evidence clearly shows that globalisation will not undermine the strategy we suggest for reducing the UK's consumption. In any the case, there is evidence to suggest that some of the current concern over global-isation could be misplaced.[127] Analysis by Paul Hirst and Grahame Thompson, academics from Birkbeck College and the Open University,[128] suggests that most national economies are no more open (relatively) than before the First World War. The case of Denmark illustrates that nation states, at least in the developed world, are not at the whim of transnationals and capital markets; there the ratio of government revenue to GDP is 60 per cent, in comparison with 32 per cent in the USA, yet there is no massive outflow of labour or business. In fact, the Danish national savings rate is higher than in the USA, and its net accumulation of foreign capital assets is equivalent to a tiny 1.8 per cent of GDP. So, despite the obvious problems that can arise where countries deliberately open their economies to greater global competition, or are forced to do so, there is much more room for manoeuvre within the global economy, at least for rich Northern countries, than the pessimists would have us believe.

Concern for Southern interests is more valid. Southern economies might suffer, due to their fragility, their need for external investment and their reliance on a small number of commodity exports to earn foreign exchange. If developed world net imports of those commodities were to fall, as a result of the adoption of environmental space targets, then hardship could result in the South. But other factors are involved. Debt is perhaps the strongest driving force behind current rates of commodity exports. Substantial debt relief to reduce this pressure is central because the production of commodities for export is damaging natural environments and community livelihoods in the exporting countries!

We have no argument with trade itself, merely with the unbalanced and unfair version that passes for 'free trade' in the modern world. Indeed, trade underlies our understanding of environmental space, that through trade we can share out access to environmental space more equitably. But at present, the trade system operates to help concentrate access to environmental space in the hands of the rich as a result of the reinforcing effects of pressure for free trade which actually benefits the richer countries more, structural adjustment programmes which open Southern economies to the world market, and the lending and investment programmes of the international financial institutions and their private sector counterparts. As part of the reforms needed in this arena, the trade system must come under the microscope too. Trading can also be a useful tool in allocating environmental space. The idea of so-called 'tradeable permits' for pollution is not a new one. In theory, by allocating a limited quantity of such permits, a market can be established. Those who wish to emit more pollution must buy additional permits from others in the scheme, keeping the overall level of pollution the same. However, if it is cheaper for a company to reduce pollution than to buy permits, then the company (or country) concerned will follow that strategy. In theory it leads to the most economically efficient distribution of pollution control effort for the given level of total pollution.

There are two key issues here: the size and the distribution of the total allocation. In theory the overall limit could be set at the environmental space available – at least in the longer term – and permits distributed according to fair shares in it. Permits should be leased for a specific period, rather than sold on a permanent basis, since this would create a constant income flow, and ensure that the total level of permits could be reduced equitably when necessary. To take a specific example, a tradeable emissions permit system for carbon dioxide designed in this way would be much more radical – because of the basis in environmental space – than any of the current proposals for 'joint implementation' which seek to use similar principles to inform climate change policy. It would give Southern countries, currently with low emissions, some leverage, and something to sell. The World Bank has estimated that at US$25 a tonne, permits for carbon emissions could raise US$70 billion a year for developing countries (at 1988 levels).[129]

But here we focus on the trade system for existing goods, rather than the new markets such permit systems would create. At heart the problems of the current trade liberalisation process arise because it seeks to maximise the welfare derived from trade, rather than total welfare.[130] It thus ignores any non-marketed benefits of environmental resources, including their use for subsistence livelihoods in the South. At the same time, by increasing the mobility of capital, as would be vastly facilitated, for example by the Multilateral Agreement on Investments, currently being negotiated by OECD countries, it makes these non-market, free goods – such as the environment – easier for producers to exploit. In other words, removing one distortion from the market merely emphasises those remaining, in this case, the fact that environmental externalities are, in economic terms, free goods. So we should not be surprised, other things being equal, to see trade liberalisation bringing increased environmental damage and resource exploitation.

The proponents of trade liberalisation at any cost argue instead that the environment will benefit, based on the view that economic growth brings improved environmental protection. While there is evidence that growth can bring improvements in resource efficiency per unit of growth, in practice it has brought overall increases in environmental degradation at a wider and wider scale. For developing countries, increased market access might well benefit producers, but the accompanying changes in GATT's rules on subsidies, and the reduction in GATT's special and differential concessions for developing countries could outweigh any other gains. The only conclusion that can be drawn is that we must avoid simplistic arguments about growth and the environment. Rather we should seek an economic approach that focuses on meeting needs, which we believe will have a side effect of economic growth, at least in the short to medium-term. We must take a similar approach at the international level, seeking trade liberalisation in ways that will help meet our needs, including those which are not currently included in markets.

This should include permitting regulation of trade on grounds of environmental concerns, with a view to influencing processing and production methods. This is underway. The Group of Seven (G7) Environment Ministers meeting in May 1996 called for progress on dovetailing multilateral environmental agreements and eco-labelling schemes into trade rules, and committed themselves to work to ensure that trade rules would not prevent the adoption of eco-labelling schemes which deal with production and processing methods. However, despite UNCTAD's view that environmental policies are generally benign for trade and competitiveness, we share developing countries' concerns that environmental standards could be used as trade barriers by unscrupulous companies and countries, especially in the light of findings that developing countries and NGOs alike have little influence over standards set by the unrepresentative and Northern-industry dominated International Organisation for Standardisation.[131]

We need to ensure that such measures are designed not to discriminate against Southern producers and that they are accompanied by others that would help Southern countries invest in sustainable production methods, and export less at higher prices, such as International Commodity Related Environmental Agreements funded, for example, by generic import levies. Such an approach could be supported by green taxes designed to raise export prices[132] or by a currency exchange tax designed to fund investment in sustainable production, and also to help protect economies from currency speculation. The UK should support positive moves at the European level to establish fair trade preferences and privileged access for sustainable production. We should also support measures designed to ensure that minimum social as well as environmental standards are required to underpin trade. Overall such measures could create a framework in which fair trade can flourish. But it is essential that political momentum is given to this agenda. A strong and independent Intergovernmental Panel on Trade, Environment and Sustainability is needed to ensure that the WTO, with its remit to promote free trade, does not sideline such issues.

There are also trends that will steer trade towards lower volumes and higher-value products. Growing transport costs will combine with some lowering of Northern countries' trade barriers to processed products to encourage developing countries to export less primary raw materials and more processed or finished goods. This could be counterproductive in terms of use of environmental space if the inefficiency and waste typical of current processing technology in Southern countries remains the norm.[133] So effective technology transfer is also an essential component of the new framework for 'free trade'. And that transfer should not just focus on conventional technology; there are vast, and growing, markets in Southern countries for services which meet needs.

# CONCLUSION

As business is increasingly recognising, its own sustainability depends on it meeting the environmental space challenge. To do so it must become accountable to wider groups of 'stakeholders' through an effective economic and regulatory framework, imposed as a result of enlightened businesses acting as 'citizens' to demand such action from government. The levels of improvement in eco-efficiency demanded by environmental space targets are possible, but only with a transition to an economy based on enterprises which provide services to meet people's needs. These shifts demand a long-term view, and thus require an effective regulatory framework to overcome the short termism of investment and financial institutions, and to support direct investment in needs, for example through community development banks. Government must drive these processes, stimulating the uptake of existing cleaner products and techniques and further innovation in this direction by regulatory and fiscal measures, regulating markets to empower demand management and reforming the tax system to provide a continual incentive for economic change towards sustainability. Such strategies will not trigger economic instability, nor undermine the UK's competitiveness in global markets. The obstacles suggested by those who raise such economic concerns can be overcome by effective policy design. But trade will need enlightened reform if the South is to benefit from our cuts in use of environmental space.

# Chapter 11
# Social Sustainability – Meeting Real Needs

## INTRODUCTION

Conventional approaches to reducing poverty and social exclusion in the UK are centred on two measures: anti-discrimination legislation, with all its loopholes and failings, and, underlying that, the assumption that conventional economic growth will provide the resources to give a safety net to the poor and deprived. Yet conventional growth has not reduced inequality, but exacerbated it. United Nations statistics suggest that the UK is now the most unequal country in the western world, with the poorest two-fifths of the population sharing less of the national wealth than in any industrialised country apart from Russia.[1]

In a sustainable economy, the size of the physical resource 'cake' available for material consumption is limited. Environmental resources must be more fairly shared amongst nations. If we want to reduce inequality in the UK, then we must take a similar approach. Athough economic growth might result from the policies advocated in the last chapter, there is little evidence to suggest that benefits for those excluded from mainstream society will naturally result. Instead we must target their needs directly, especially the need for social inclusion. If we fail to restore or create social justice in our communities in the UK, then whatever economic and environmental progress we make towards sustainability will be undermined, in the short-term by the costs of inequality, and in the longer term by the lack of social cohesion that results from inequality. The relationship between equity and sustainability addresses the key issue of investing in people, not simply as a strategy for reducing inequality, but also as a strategy for strengthening our economy, and the chapter concludes with strategies for increasing inclusion and tackling poverty while living within our environmental space.

# EQUITY AND SUSTAINABILITY

The World Health Organisation has shown that more equal societies are healthier, with lower rates of coronary heart disease, and lower incidences of several types of cancer. The healthiest countries are not the wealthiest, but the most egalitarian. Japan, with the narrowest income distribution of any country reporting to the World Bank, has the higest life expectancy in the world.[2] Studies comparing countries across Europe and states across the USA have confirmed the same general principle.[3] In the UK death rates at all ages are two to three times higher among disadvantaged social groups than their more affluent counterparts and the gap is widening with increasing inequality. As a recent study by the King's Fund noted:

> *Death rates in some of the most disadvantaged areas in the UK not only worsened in relative terms between 1981 and 1991... but among some age groups, such as young men, the rates actually rose. As death rates have been declining since the 1930s, this rise signals a new and disturbing development.*[4]

The impacts of inequality on the health of society are yet more insidious. In British society some of the most deprived are ethnic groups in inner cities. Unemployment rates peak amongst young urban black people in virtual ghettos. Such social exclusion is reflected, at worst in rioting, but most endemically in crime. As Jacobs says:

> *In neighbourhoods and among social groups where unemployment reaches 50 per cent and more, where most young people have never had a job and have little prospect of getting one, it is unsurprising that many people feel little stake in society or concern for others.*[5]

Crime, violence and drug abuse are almost natural consequences of social division and the culture of individualism that has permitted it. A major study in the USA related rising crime rates directly to unemployment. Each 1 per cent rise in unemployment was linked to a 6.7 per cent increase in homicides, a 3.4 per cent increase in violent crime and a 2.4 per cent increase in property crime.[6] The same study also correlated growth in crime with growth in wage inequality. On the other hand, in Japan, since 1945, income differentials have narrowed, and most kinds of crime have declined.[7] As crime rates rise, so fears of crime enter our day-to-day lives. In the 1995 British Social Attitudes survey, a quarter of men and a third of women reported that worries about crime affected their everyday life. Fear of crime constrains our children's development and contributes to car dependency. Crime increases insurance premiums and public expenditure on prisons, policing and the judicial system, which has almost doubled in real terms since 1976.[8]

Health inequalities in the USA are paralleled by other social indicators. The states with the highest income inequality also had higher relative prison populations, higher rates of homicide and violent crime, higher rates of unemployment, poorer educational performance, higher school drop-out rates and higher per person medical care and police protection costs.[9] This is not to say that inequality was the cause of all these other problems, merely that it was the best predictor, rather than average income. Clearly there is a nexus of problems. As the gap widens between rich and poor, the health of the nation deteriorates, the social fabric unravels and the cost of maintaining communities goes up. Even more remarkably, both the World Bank and the OECD have tentatively concluded that more unequal societies perform worse economically, turning on its head the received wisdom that inequality drives economic growth in capitalist societies.[10] The Thatcher revolution of the 1980s was based upon inequality, justified by the 'trickle down' theory. Indeed the Prime Minister, as she was then, is reported to have declared 'our job is to glory in inequality',[11] because the rich would spend and invest, so creating jobs for the poor. But the poor's share of the national income fell in the 1980s, for the first time since the Second World War. Worse still, their real incomes fell by up to 20 per cent over the decade, and the numbers living below the official poverty line increased to 14 million, including 3.7 million children.[12] Growth in inequality has been further exacerbated by cut backs in public services, from health to public transport, on which the poor rely more heavily. On the other hand pay rises for the highest paid directors have consistently exceeded average increases by three to five fold.[13]

Falling real wages have not increased employment rates. The OECD recently concluded that there is no link between high inequality and low unemployment and that inequality could even damage the prospects for long-term growth. It admits:

> the future prosperity of OECD countries depends on reducing social and economic exclusion in the forms of high unemployment, non-participation in the labour market ... and in some circumstances, growing inequalities in earnings and incomes.[14]

Now this is something of a turnabout for the OECD, previously a keen advocate of labour market flexibility. But it does not go far enough. Inequality carries yet further costs. It requires higher public spending on social security, it increases the volatility of economic cycles and it even increases the economy's propensity to import as higher income households consume more imports than poorer ones.[15] It reduces the skill base of the labour force at a time when companies are demanding ever more skilled and capable workers to respond to the dictates of flexible production.[16]

The World Bank has analysed the economic performance of a whole range of countries. In both rich and poor countries, greater equality has been matched by greater economic growth.[17] The World Bank concludes from detailed analysis of nine OECD countries over more than 160 years, that the bigger the share of the national cake grabbed by the richest fifth of the population, the lower the growth rate. This is not to say that the nature of this growth is promoting environmental sustainability, of course it isn't. But it does suggest that greater equality could help support the type of growth that we need to see: growth based on dematerialised industry and new community enterprises directly meeting needs. Dr Richard Jolly, principal author of the UN Development Programme's most recent Human Development Report, said, after launching the report in East Asia, that it was taken for granted in that part of the world that greater equality promoted growth: 'They say: "of course equality works. You have to give people a stake in the country. That is what we have done".' The report shows that the 'tiger' economies of East Asia achieved high rates of growth while maintaining or even increasing equality, contrary to the popular view that they have exploited high inequality to achieve that growth. Nor have these economies been economically successful because of low welfare costs and compliant workforces. These conditions have arisen because the corporations provide more for their employees, such as free bus services, day-care centres, and credit unions. Naturally, their employees repay them with higher productivity and greater innovation.[18]

The Human Development Report says that the key to East Asia's economic success was

> a relatively equal distribution of private and public assets – countries there concentrated on redistributing not income but wealth ... a progressive redistribution of assets tends to boost growth because it has a broad positive effect on people's incentives.[19]

Land reform to provide wider access to land, is a central part of the strategy in these circumstances. But as we saw in Chapter 10, the environmental consequences of the Asian model have been no less damaging than those of the conventional Western model, so we cannot rely on such a route to sustainability.

From this rapid review of the arguments it might appear that we are, in some contradictory way, arguing that economic growth is responsible for inequality, yet also that reducing inequality will increase growth. There are two reasons why this is a superficial interpretation of our arguments. First and most fundamentally it assumes that growth is entirely the same, when and wherever it occurs. This is patently not so. As the UN Development Programme says, it is 'ruthless' growth that, for example, reduces equity. Second, we are looking at two different timescales.

Current patterns of growth can clearly maximise short-term economic gains by being ruthless. But the inequalities and degradation of human and environmental capital that result clearly damage the longer-term potential for growth. It is yet another case of the short-term bias of the economic system being self-destructive.

# INVESTING IN PEOPLE

Here we address the central question of human development. How can we enable and empower people to meet their individual and community needs, where necessary with the support of the state? In other words how we can invest in people, in human capital as a resource on which to build sustainability?

## Unemployment and Inequality

Since 1973 total unemployment has risen from 1.7 per cent of the workforce to 8 per cent (or 2.24 million people) in November 1995. Over a million more are not even attempting to seek employment any more (and are therefore not included in these official figures).[20] The social, human and financial costs of unemployment are immense. In the UK unemployment is the principal cause of poverty, which is exacerbated by the redistribution of employment between households. Sixty per cent of households now have two or more earners, while almost 20 per cent have none and most new jobs go to individuals from households with an adult already in work. As a result, for those in 'work-poor' households, the average period of unemployment has also increased dramatically. As well as causing poverty, unemployment also contributes directly to despair, ill health and unhappiness. This is eloquently described by Richard Wilkinson:

> *To feel depressed, cheated, bitter, desperate, vulnerable, frightened, angry, worried about debts or job and housing insecurity; to feel devalued, useless, helpless, uncared for, hopeless, isolated, anxious and a failure: these feelings can dominate people's whole experience of life, colouring their experience of everything else. It is the chronic stress arising from feelings like these which does the damage.[21]*

In general the unemployed lose self-esteem, their range of social contacts declines and they feel excluded from society. Unemployment breeds social alienation and increases crime.[22] Crime costs taxpayers around £23 billion in benefits and lost taxes, and more to pay for its health and social effects. The direct health effects of unemployment are also negative. The unemployed suffer higher rates of mental stress and suicide. They also face other health risks. A study of 30 major metropolitan areas by American economists at the University of Utah found that a 1 per cent rise in unemployment rates is linked to a 5.6 per cent increase in death from heart attacks and a 3.1 per cent increase in death from strokes.[23] Unemployment does not randomly select its victims. The young and single mothers have particular difficulty getting into the workforce. Company 'downsizing' – a major reason for increasing unemployment – has been carried disproportionately by people in their fifties, going into early retirement. This carries wider costs for the economy and for companies. Overall it is desirable to keep older people in the workforce, otherwise the ratio of working to non-working will decline, with greater problems for government budgeting. Although tax reform will help overcome this problem by broadening the tax base, making the welfare system less reliant on labour taxes, there are other costs too. Companies lose some of their most experienced and skilled staff, but pension systems make it advantageous for companies to encourage early retirement.

The last government's response to unemployment was to argue that the labour market wasn't working properly; for if it was, the price of labour would fall, thus encouraging greater employment. So they introduced policies to increase the flexibility and responsiveness of the labour market, including cuts in unemployment benefit, and weakened trade union rights and powers. Combined with economic globalisation and technological trends, such policies have vastly increased insecurity for many of those in a job. Short-term contracts and flexible working arrangements designed to increase labour productivity have replaced secure jobs, and the stress resulting from fear of unemployment is exacerbated by the weakness of the waiting safety net. As Jacobs concludes: 'the long-term effect on productivity is contradictory at best – insecurity damages morale and undermines investment in training'.[24] In fact there is little evidence that greater flexibility has any benefit in employment terms; lower wages tend to reduce productivity by raising employee turnover rates and discouraging investment in training.[25] Higher wages, on the other hand, provide an incentive effect to bring labour into the labour market.

Measures to get the long-term unemployed back into work are critical, as one of the best ways of directly meeting many of their needs. Jacobs suggests a combination of measures to stimulate overall employment, including tax reform, targeted support for employers offering jobs to the long-term unemployed, and investment in community businesses and the third sector to create work opportunities.[26] Tax reform measures could be targeted by focusing the cuts in employers' national insurance contributions onto lower paid jobs. DRI's study for the European Commission suggested that such a strategy could double or even triple the employment benefits.[27]

Will Hutton describes the result of the conventional prescription of lower wages and a more 'flexible' labour market: a 30–30–40 society.[28] There is still some mobility between such groups, and the UK perhaps cannot yet be said to have an 'underclass' although many would argue otherwise. Certainly the impacts of poverty are increasingly being felt by children in ways that reduce their future life chances. The growing evidence of a correlation between deprivation and low educational achievement is illustrated by the case of one inner-city school whose head recently spoke out to highlight that many of her pupils from poor families were 'two inches shorter than average, weighed less and had vitamin deficiencies' and were 'two years behind their contemporaries physically and emotionally'.[29] Such evidence fatally undermines arguments that equality of opportunity already exists, and that innate ability is more important than income or class origin in determining where an individual will end up in the 'income pile'.[30] If the poorest are stunted in intellectual and emotional development, then there is no equality of opportunity for them.

Education is a common factor in all 'development' success stories. Research suggests that a country increases its GDP by 9 per cent for every year of primary education it gives its people. Education also reduces inequality. According to the World Bank, increasing the proportion of the workforce with secondary education is a very effective way of increasing the income share of the poorest half of the population. The same holds true in industrialised countries, says the OECD. A more equitable distribution of education and training prevents skills shortages and inflationary bottlenecks. Country comparisons underline the point. The UN Development Programme ascribes the remarkable long-term growth in Japan and Sweden, in part, to heavy investments in education.[31] The UK, on the other hand, still spends much less on education than most industrialised countries. Sally Holterman, in a review of investment in children, finds that children from poor homes, along with lower life expectancy, poor health and a greater risk of unemployment, also have a lower chance of high educational attainment. She concludes that we are under-investing in our children.[32] The UK needs to become, in the modern jargon, a 'learning society'. Education can nurture the capacities for work and allow individual fulfilment. Lifelong learning must become a reality.

Improving education and training – however essential to any political programme to tackle unemployment – seem unlikely to solve the unemployment problem alone, given its current scale. A neo-Keynesian expansion of conventional consumer demand as advocated by many on the political left, even if not accompanied by inflation, would run into two obstacles: increased environmental impact and the phenomenon of jobless growth. Fortunately, the economic restructuring suggested in Chapter 10 – towards meeting needs through service provision – helps address both of these obstacles. The basic strategy is designed to reduce the environmental impact of each unit of production, while the emphasis on services means that labour-intensive options are likely to be favoured. A greater share of the value added in any service or product will come from labour in the dematerialised economy. Skills and training will be critical to releasing these benefits. These tendencies could be supported and reinforced by ecological tax reform.

## Secure Flexibility

Within the conventional labour market we should not pursue flexibility at any cost. Instead, we need to provide secure flexibility in which security no longer arises from length of service or status, but from employability based on an educational system that encourages life-long learning,[33] and supportive trade unions that help members acquire skills and provide financial support and protection in harder times through some form of social insurance. Most trade unions began as craft collectives to train and skill those entering the profession, and many developed as mutual societies providing financial support for members in times of hardship. As argued by a recent leader in the *Independent* newspaper, unions' 'future lies in returning to those roots'.[34] For example, trade unions could play a catalytic role in the establishment of credit unions for their members.

Jacobs similarly argues that a new approach to work and unemployment is necessary.[35] Rather than simply increasing employment, one of society's key goals should be to enable people – both men and women – to do the variety of kinds of work – including caring and voluntary work – which benefit themselves and society. He argues that particular priority should be given to parenting, especially to enable parents to work shorter hours and take time out to be with their children. The quality of time given to parenting is a key investment in the future, crucial to the education and socialisation of children. Concern is growing amongst psychologists and educators in the USA linking the dramatic rise in childhood depression, delinquency, violent crime, alcohol and drug abuse and teenage suicide with the decline in the time parents were able to spend with their children.[36] Reversing this trend would provide wider benefits for society as well as to family life and family wellbeing.

In the longer term we should be seeking to reduce 'normal' full-time working hours, redistributing work amongst the population. As argued by Jeremy Rifkin, in his unnerving yet exciting book *The End of Work*, we could allow workers to benefit from increases in productivity with shorter working hours.[37] Combined with adequate incomes, increased free time could allow us to renew the bonds of community. This implies some form of voluntary restraint by workers – accepting lower incomes in return for other benefits – including shorter working hours. As we noted in Chapter 10, such a social contract could increase the long-term employment benefits achieved by eco-tax reform.[38] Juliet Schor, of Harvard University, argues that this means breaking the addictive 'work and spend' cycle, so that future preferences for more leisure time, rather than higher incomes, can be met.[39] There are policy measures that could facilitate such a trade-off, particularly in terms of reducing employers' overheads per worker. Yet again, tax reform, by reducing or eliminating employers' national insurance contributions, could contribute positively.

In the longer term, a guaranteed income or citizens' income scheme might provide a realistic option, simplifying the welfare and benefits systems, yet ensuring minimum standards and underpinning flexibility with security. In the UK, social economist James Robertson has long promoted this idea,[40] which is now being seriously debated in some European countries, notably the Netherlands.[41] Its proponents argue that such an approach would actually lower labour costs – as employers would only have to pay a supplement to the basic income – largely eliminate the poverty trap, and would be more effective in supporting flexible patterns of work.

# A New Approach to Social Provision of Public Goods

Some common features characterise those European economies which kept unemployment low during the 1980s.[42] They had some form of 'social contract' in which incomes were restrained in return for employment protection, and they maintained a large public sector, financed by taxes, the level of which is partly offset by the public savings resulting from lower unemployment.

There is plenty of work in the UK too which could be done in a publicly financed employment programme – in caring for children, in building and improving homes, in installing energy and water conservation measures, and in recycling – to name but a few. The case for social provision of public goods is reinforced by the analysis of Dan Corry of the Institute for Public Policy Research who found that the poor rely more heavily on public services, so as they have been cut back or privatised, the relative position of the poor has worsened. Corry calculates that public services such as health, education and housing are worth £3600 a year to the poorest 20 per cent in our society, but only £2000 a year to the richest 20 per cent. In other words, the poor make almost twice as much use of these services as the rich.[43]

We need measures that can create useful jobs, providing such social goods, at small costs – of perhaps £20–30,000 per job – such as investing in energy efficiency in the housing stock.[44] What we don't need is expensive 'job-creation' through unnecessary government spending, such as that on the defence industry, which can cost upwards of £1 million per job.[45] Support for the emerging third sector of community based and voluntary enterprises could help us reduce our use of environmental space and meet needs directly. The French economist Thierry

Jeantet uses the term 'social economy' to describe the third sector and notes that 'its outputs integrate social results with indirect economic gains'. He also argues that 'the social economy is best understood in terms of results that add considerably to what traditional economics does not know how to or want to measure'.[46] Voluntary organisations have arisen from the very human need to love and care for others, as well as to fill service gaps resulting from government and corporate downsizing. As a result, they meet some of the needs of the service providers, as well as those helped. A recent survey suggested that voluntary work was second only to dancing, in bringing joy to people in modern the UK – more significant than sport, religion, and politics![47] Community-based enterprises also strengthen local economies, keeping income circulating locally. In deprived areas where inward investment is difficult to attract, strengthening the community sector, supported by local authorities and local or regional banks or credit unions, could significantly increase incomes.[48]

Many of our recommendations are supported by a major intergovernmental commission. Chaired by former Portuguese Prime Minister Maria de Lourdes Pintasilgo, the Independent Commission on Population and Quality of Life[49] similarly recommends creating new jobs through public partnership with the community and the private sector to meet needs for education, caring and environmental improvement. It also suggests redefining work to encompass and value unpaid activities, worth US$16 trillion a year (equivalent to 70 per cent of recorded output)[50] now overwhelmingly undertaken by women, and to ensure equitable distribution of the wealth generated. One key opportunity to begin valuing unpaid work would be to include it in our indicators of economic success, as is done, for example in the Index of Sustainable Economic Welfare.

# ENVIRONMENTAL SPACE AND POVERTY

Without such radical objectives, the implications of environmental space targets for the poor could be horrendous. If we were to simply impose taxes on environmental resources to reduce their use, then the poor would suffer most. Many are already in fuel poverty or food poverty. Fuel poverty – the inability to buy enough fuel to keep warm – is now thought to affect as many as 7–8 million households.[51] A 1991 survey reported in the *Independent* newspaper showed that one in five parents and one in ten children in poorer households had gone without food in the previous month because they didn't have the money to buy it.[52] More generally, some of the poorest people have the greatest difficulty in obtaining adequate affordable, quality food. Not only do welfare payments have no agreed food elements, the poor are overlooked by our modern food distribution systems, even to the extent of having to pay more for poorer quality food because they may not have a car to give them access to an out of town supermarket.

These circumstances demand two basic responses: first, a package of measures to reduce inequality and poverty, and second, effective compensation for any environmental policy which might worsen the situation of the poor. So, for example, any increase in domestic energy taxes must be accompanied, if not preceded, by improvements in the energy efficiency of the homes of the fuel poor. Increased petrol taxes must be accompanied by measures to compensate the rural poor who remain forced to use their cars, for example by investing in improved public transport, or more directly, by abolishing or reforming Vehicle Excise Duty, which could more than compensate the low-mileage poor drivers, but not the high-mileage rural rich.

There is growing evidence that the poor suffer most from environmental degradation. In the USA, research found that toxic waste dumps, incinerators and other pollution sources were concentrated in poor, and primarily black, neighbourhoods. Similarly, minority groups were found to tend to work in more health-threatening jobs.[53] The interactions of inequality, ill health and poor environmental quality suggest that in the UK too, improving the environment would deliver more benefits for the poor than for the rich. But the government has not shown much interest in this argument. Julian Agyeman asks

> *in the UK, how much research has been done by ... The Department of the Environment on the environmental quality enjoyed (sic) by black people? A Department official, when asked this question, replied 'It's not the kind of research we do'.*[54]

## Healthy, Wealthy and Wise

Inequality is only part of a nexus of issues which are mutually reinforcing. Unemployment, poverty, homelessness or poor housing, and environmental degradation tend to go together, all reflected in poor health, which in turn reduces the likelihood of escaping poverty. A study of poor families with children in Glasgow, Edinburgh and London found that one-third of dwellings were damp, and almost half contained mould.[55] There were almost 1.5 million homes considered unfit for habitation in 1991.[56] It has been estimated that the cost to the NHS from ill health due to poor housing conditions and fuel poverty is £1 billion a year.[57] Professor Hugh Freeman reports that poor housing features in 28 per cent of cases of chronic depression.[58] There are around 30,000 so-called 'extra winter deaths' in the UK every year. These are the additional deaths above the average, resulting from seasonal factors such as cold and damp in poorly insulated homes. Other European countries have far lower levels of extra winter deaths.[59] Ensuring that a major energy efficiency programme targeted at those in fuel poverty is implemented will be a key test of Labour's newly created Minister for Public Health.

Similarly, the poor are more likely to be on the receiving end of traffic noise, traffic danger and severance on heavily trafficked urban roads. Severance of communities by roads has been recognised for many years and the impact of severance on social contacts has been quantified by American researchers Appleyard and Lintell,[60] who demonstrate that the number of social contacts within a street fall rapidly as traffic levels rise. Epidemiological studies have shown that weak social support networks with few contacts are linked to increased mortality rates from all causes.[61] Good social support networks are particularly important for health vulnerable groups such as the elderly. Growing traffic levels have particular impacts on the development of children in all social groups, as a result of the limits traffic imposes on children's independent mobility. This has been quantified by independent transport experts Mayer Hillman, John Adams and John Whitelegg[62] in a study covering five areas ranging from inner urban to rural. They found that between 1970 and 1990 the proportion of seven to 9 year old children allowed to make their way to school unaccompanied fell from 80 per cent to nine per cent, largely as a result of parents' fear of traffic. The authors conclude: 'many children have lost what for adults could be called a basic right'.[63]

These examples clearly show how stronger environmental protection measures – reducing energy wastage, reducing traffic volumes – could have remarkable positive effects on health which are particularly beneficial for, although not limited to, the poorest groups in society. Many will benefit from cleaner air and water, a heathier diet and a stable climate. In global terms the benefits will be even greater: few Britons will starve as a result of changing climates and rising sea levels, but preventing climate change could save millions of lives in those parts of the world where famine is already a fact of life. Similarly, preventing ozone depletion could save a quarter of a million extra cancers a year and millions of additional cases of cataracts.[64] As Friends of the Earth has recently demonstrated, environmental improvements are amongst the best preventative healthcare measures we can invest in.[65] Health strategies are not simply about preventing death or illness; the WHO seeks not only to add 'years to life', but also 'life to years'. The approach of 'investing in people' advocated as a strategy to ensure economic participation can be expected to deliver further health benefits in terms of longer, more fulfilling lives. Moreover, if we meet real needs directly rather than substituting for them with additional consumption, then we can increase real wellbeing. This effect, of course, works in both directions: meeting needs delivers benefits to health, while health improvements are a real need being met! Overall, in direct contradiction to the conventional view – that health improvements (for example) rely upon economic growth to pay for improved medical facilities and care – the case for introducing sustainability policies is only strengthened by looking specifically at their relationship with health.

## Discrimination and Exclusion

We have focused so far on exclusion on grounds of poverty and its impacts. But in many cases the issue is reversed. Poverty, whether financial or spiritual, is the result of exclusion – exclusion by systematic discrimination in educational opportunities, employment opportunities and even housing opportunities. Such discrimination is faced by ethnic groups, by women, and particularly single parents, and to a lesser, but still real, extent by the elderly. Unless this exclusion is tackled, it is unlikely that we will be able to regenerate any sense of community, making it much harder to tackle the environmental, economic and social problems we face. We also believe that inclusion of different groups, and different values will strengthen, rather than weaken our capacity as a society to evolve and meet the challenges posed by sustainability. In particular, equitable inclusion for women in all aspects of our society would facilitate movement towards consensual politics.

This issue is, at heart, a question of rights – the right to freedom from discrimination. While such issues cannot simply be tackled by legislative initiatives, the strengthening of human rights offers a clear opportunity to work towards assuring a basic minimum quality of life for everyone, as recommended by the Independent Commission on Population and Quality of Life.[66] Such a right should be based on a right to a fair share of the Earth's environmental resources. While there is no legislative basis for such rights at present, development and enforcement of existing enabling rights such as the right to know and the right of access to justice could help ensure that citizens could act as stakeholders in the economy and in society in ways that meet their needs equitably. What we are suggesting is no less than a renewal and strengthening of participatory democracy. The governments which signed up to Agenda 21 in Rio in 1992, recognised the central place of participation. It declares that

> *critical to the effective implementation of the objectives, policies and mechanisms agreed to by Governments in all programme areas of Agenda 21 will be the commitment and genuine involvement of all social groups ... One of the fundamental prerequisites for the achievement of sustainable development is broad public participation in decision making... The need for new forms of participation has emerged ... Individuals, groups and organisations should have access to information relevant to environment and development held by national authorities ... and information on environmental protection measures.*[67]

Agenda 21 confirms that a formal and effective right to know and right to participate in decision making are essential to effective democracy. Our last Prime Minister even went so far as to suggest that citizens have a right to information about the environment:

> *Every individual, every group will in future have access to the information they need in order to act as an environmental watch-dog. That information is the citizen's right and the Active Citizen will use that right constructively.*[68]

Sadly, in practice this has not been the case. For example, monitoring data for the discharge of industrial effluents to sewers, the results of operational monitoring of drinking water quality and much information about contaminated land remain effectively secret. The new Labour Government has promised a Freedom of Information Act; it will not necessarily cover all such information.

## An Alternative to the Fortress Society

In modern Britain, the trend is for more exclusion, not less, for more segregation of the poor from the rich. The culmination of such trends would be a fortress society, not just nationally, with the drawbridge raised to repel prospective asylum seekers and immigrants, but locally too, with rich neighbourhoods – with their private schools and private hospitals – fenced in and patrolled by private security guards. But however much the rich could exclude the rest of society, they could not protect themselves entirely from social, and particularly, environmental degradation. Our sustainability 'scenario' offers an alternative to that fortress society by sharing out resources fairly, and offering the scope for a better life to all. To rebuild inclusive communities will take a range of strategic approaches, some of which are being developed by the more forward-looking housing associations, who focus on people and participation to ensure high levels of community support and high management standards.[69]

This book is not the place to elaborate the various ways to set such strategies in motion. But we will outline some opportunities here to illustrate the synergies between such measures and the changes needed to deliver on our sustainability targets. We touched on the scope for sharing work out more widely above. Supporting the community sector in this way would help us increase self-reliance within communities. This is intrinsically empowering (and thus health improving) because it enables people to gain control over their lives. Wilkinson argues that deep-rooted health problems are related to our increasing sense of insecurity resulting in part from the fragmentation of our communities: 'In the pursuit of wealth, we have created a highly transient, fleeting society in which activities or sentiments are not grounded over time and place'.[70]

One way of helping meet social needs simultaneously is to support and encourage the informal economy through Local Exchange Trading Schemes (LETS). LETS effectively provide access to credit for anyone, for 'purchases' which strengthen the local community. It also values all work equally, including work that is presently unpaid and done mainly by women. In a similar vein, Demos suggests fostering a non-money 'voucher sector', and raising the VAT threshold to encourage the cash-in-hand economy as ways of ensuring that valuable work is undertaken, and helping eliminate the poverty trap.[71] This in turn might require delinking benefits from national insurance contributions, both by employers and employees. By shifting taxes to resources and pollution, the Treasury would risk less in promoting informal economic activities such as LETS.

Local Agenda 21 programmes, stimulated in many parts of the world after the Rio Summit, offer a strong vehicle for such local community building. The consultative processes established by many local authorities could be used to focus financial and technical support from those authorities onto meeting locally identified needs in ways that deliver environmental, social and economic benefits at the same time. The environment is a simple and effective place to begin community rebuilding. It is shared by everyone, and comes largely free of political bias and ideology. Examples can be found all over the world, from the Brazilian city of Curitiba, famous for its health care, transport and waste management programmes, to Canada. For example, the Green Communities Initiative developed in Canada aims to stimulate community-based programmes to deliver environmental benefits.[72] In October 1995, The Ministry of Environment and Energy in Ontario said:

> *What do thousands of new jobs, green schools, multi-million dollars of economic activity, ecology gardens, millions of dollars in avoided sewage and water treatment upgrades, neighbourhood composting, lower utility bills, solar water heaters and small business green-ups all have in common? They are the results of communities taking action through the Green Communities Initiative (emphasis in original).*[73]

One of the key benefits of this scheme is that investing in conservation helps reduce spending on imported resources. This keeps money circulating in the local economy.

To truly facilitate such local processes will require bold steps towards political decentralisation, providing the seed-bed for participatory democracy in inclusive local communities. We return to this issue in the final chapter of this book.

## Environmental Space and Cultural Diversity

It has been suggested that meeting environmental space targets would reduce cultural diversity. This is a misinterpretation based on the mistaken view that the targets imply exactly equal consumption by everyone, rather than limits for the nation as a whole. We believe that there is adequate scope within environmental limits for a wide range of cultural lifestyles, within countries as much as between them. Rural lifestyles will inevitably be different to urban ones, but both can be supported by an economy based on environmental space. What may not be supportable is the attempt made by so many commuters these days to live an urban lifestyle in rural surroundings. This illustrates how the targets do not require individual uniformity in consumption, any more than they necessarily imply cuts in individuals' consumption of goods and services. As we saw in Part 2, most of the efficiency improvements will be delivered in industry and the wider economy, so that our lifestyles depend on less material consumption overall. In the same way, the same level of resource use in the economy as a whole can support a wide diversity of lifestyles, all within the same environmental space. In this way, meeting environmental space targets is not about imposing uniformity on different cultures, but more about an opportunity for all cultures to be included in our global society, rather than excluded. This must hold in the UK too.

# CONCLUSIONS

Fundamentally, our approach to equity in the environmental space model is one of equality of opportunity: we are not prepared to see opportunity undermined by the unequal distribution of resources – globally, or nationally. We also believe that sustainability will not be possible to achieve without an inclusive society rooted in local communities, and a society that seeks social justice and wellbeing for all as its goals. As Julian Agyeman says: 'There will only be environmental quality when there is human equality'.[74] Tackling inequality will help improve health, protect the environment, strengthen social cohesion, and as a byproduct, should even help the economy.

   If we are to create the driving forces for our society to focus on real wellbeing, in terms of equity, health and fulfilling work in an environmentally sustainable economy, then we need political systems to achieve it. This is the subject of the next chapter. But before we move on, we must highlight one particular measure that will have a continued and pervasive effect. That is replacing gross domestic product as the principal indicator of the wellbeing of our society. It does not take account of the negative impacts on wellbeing documented in this chapter – inequality, poor health – nor of the positive improvements in health and broader wellbeing that come from unpaid and voluntary activities. Nor does it account for environmental degradation, despite recent attempts to offer limited adjustments. It may have its place as a useful economic indicator, but it is obsolete and redundant as a headline indicator for modern society. It is not easy to decide exactly what should replace it, but almost anything that pointed us in the right direction, rather than one as random as a compass bearing from the South Pole, would be an improvement.

# Chapter 12
# The Politics of Sustainability

## INTEGRATION

At the heart of our interpretation of sustainability lies the need to meet our social, economic and environmental needs. Sustainability cannot be achieved simply by policy in the environmental sphere. The European Community has recognised this: the Maastricht Treaty states that environmental protection requirements must be integrated into the definition and implementation of other Community policies.[1] The same should hold at the national level. Agenda 21 concurs: 'The overall objective is to improve or restructure the decision-making process so that consideration of socio-economic and environmental issues is fully integrated'.[2]

The idea that different goals can be met by the same policy – reducing costs and increasing effectiveness – has begun to penetrate international environmental policy, particularly at the European scale, where complaints from national governments over the costs of meeting prescriptive EU policy objectives has helped foster the idea of an integrated approach to air pollution.[3] But our analysis is of a bigger challenge still: meeting social and economic objectives at the same time as environmental ones. Our political system and politicians tend to treat these as conflicting or incompatible ends. This approach assumes that every pound of government money can only be spent once, so every pound spent on the health service cannot be spent on supporting business exports, and every pound spent on pollution regulation can't be used to improve social services. But the belief is misleading when, for example, a pound spent on improving housing can deliver a more energy efficient property, increasing the health and quality of life of its occupants, and at the same time reducing energy use and stimulating employment.

'Multiple payoff', 'win–win' and 'double dividend' are terms used by various writers to describe the same phenomenon – that we can meet separate objectives with the same policies. The powerful synergy of measures to tackle fuel poverty can be repeated in other areas. For example, 'ecological' tax reform could deliver multiple goals: substantial cuts in use of environmental resources, at the same time as, at least short-term, gains in employment and greater economic efficiency overall.[4] This overturns the infamous economic dictum of 'one problem – one policy measure' in favour of the ecological rule 'you can never do only one thing'. It means recognising the interrelated nature of all things, not for the sake of religious or hippy contemplation, but so we can reap the benefits that arise from well-judged actions.[5]

The European Union's Fifth Environmental Action Programme, *Towards Sustainability*, published in 1992, called for policy integration, but this has yet to emerge from Brussels in many areas.[6] Policy making on agriculture, energy and transport is still dominated by conventional approaches. For example, Commission proposals for road-dominated Trans-European Networks (TENs) became the subject of dispute with the European Parliament, which wanted the majority of funding to support rail networks and other more environmentally sensitive transport alternatives. The principle of integration can be implemented in part by impact assessments which examine the environmental and social implications of projects, plans or policies. By law, environmental impact assessment (EIA) of major projects such as motorways, airports, new towns and such-like has been required in the UK, as in the rest of Europe, since the mid-1980s. Procedures were introduced into various transport and planning regulations as a result of a European Directive. The effects of this have been limited; the most powerful signals in the planning system remain those which facilitate economic development, rather than those which seek to mitigate its potential negative impacts. The assessment of individual projects is of limited value when the overall programme or plan is not assessed in such a way. At the least, integrated ways of meeting needs are rarely considered, and at worst cynical manipulation of the process has been allowed such as by the Department of Transport, which, in developing new road corridors, has shown a strange habit of leaving the most controversial and damaging sections until last when they can be more easily justified because they complete the new route.[7]

# OBSTACLES TO SUSTAINABILITY POLICIES

Our political system is failing to address the issues of sustainability because of the system's infatuation with growth, which leads it to treat economic interests as paramount, and other concerns as costs, to be balanced with or traded off against those economic interests. In other words, in politics the economy comes first. This view is reinforced by the vested interests that benefit financially from the privileged position of the economy in the political hierarchy, and underpinned by a political feedback system that uses indicators of growth as its headline measure of success.

# The Growth Infatuation

Whatever their personal view, politicians have little choice but to accede to this obsession with conventional economic growth. It dominates the language and discourse of politics as nothing else does. The obsession began, quite modestly, as a spade – the spade that Keynesian economics suggested would stimulate employment through increased demand if given to the unemployed to dig holes and fill them up again. Decades later, with today's neo-liberal policies, the obsession has become far worse. Richard Jolly, principal author of the 1996 UN Human Development Report, says: 'Policy-makers are often mesmerised by the quantity of growth. They need to be more concerned with its quality and take timely action to prevent growth that is lopsided and flawed'. The UN cite five damaging forms of growth: that which does not translate into jobs, that which is not matched by the spread of democracy, that which snuffs out separate cultural identities, that which despoils the environment and squanders resources needed by future generations, and growth where most of the benefits are seized by the rich. The UN calls these, respectively, 'jobless', 'voiceless', 'rootless', 'futureless' and 'ruthless' growth'.[8]

We are not 'anti-growth' but simply aware that seeking a higher level of economic growth *per se* will not necessarily deliver on the needs that society wishes to meet. We do believe that in the short term, at least, economic growth may increase under a sustainability strategy, but that the real question is not how much growth, but what sort of growth. We do not believe that it is in the interests of the UK to seek further 'ruthless' or damaging growth. The International Commission on Population and Quality of Life recommend that 'sustainable improvement in the quality of life' should be the chief focus of policy, with a national social development plan with targets and timetables for bringing the poorest and most marginalised groups up to a minimum national standard.[9] Clearly, to do this we need something to measure progress against. But gross domestic or gross national product (GDP/GNP) cannot play that role. The most eloquent condemnation of GDP came from Senator Robert Kennedy, who concluded that it measured 'everything save that which makes life worth living'.[10]

# Better Signposts

The most meaningful indicator would actually be a whole set of disaggregated indicators; one of GDP's main failings is that it tries to be too many different things. Having separate indicators for economic activity, demand, wellbeing, and so on would make it easier to see what was really going on. But neither the policy process nor the political and media debate is geared up to use a wide range of different indicators; at best they are used to using something else as a surrogate for economic performance. In recent years, the rate of inflation has largely taken this 'headline' role. So to replace GDP in a way that would make any practical difference, we need something that can challenge it in the soundbite stakes.[11] There is nothing new about new indicators. In Western societies steel production and rail tonnage were once considered central indicators of economic success: now housing starts, energy consumption and the number of cars produced play this role. *The Economist* magazine, somewhat frivolously, recently suggested fast cars, smart houses, pedigree pets and breast enlargements as indicators.[12] GDP was a creation of its time – the depression of the 1930s and the Second World War – which is now past.[13]

At present the only realistic candidate as a new headline indicator is the Index of Sustainable Economic Welfare (ISEW) that we introduced in Chapter 3. It has a transparent methodology, developed over several years, and work to calculate it has already been undertaken, or is ongoing, in about ten different countries. It provides a measure of sustainable national income which comes much closer to the classic definition given by Sir John Hicks: 'the maximum value a person can consume during a week, and still expect to be as well off at the end of the week as at the beginning'.[14] We recognise the weaknesses of such adjusted measures in the sense of their inability to recognise different critical forms of environmental capital.[15] But the ISEW at least offers a more robust approach to valuing those parts of the environment which we think may be critical in this sense, because it treats the impacts as cumulative. This is ecologically realistic. And we only expect ISEW to help redirect our economy, not to solve all of our problems. We must have strong 'framework objectives' too, based on environmental space targets. Adopting such targets while retaining GDP as the headline indicator would simply generate continued conflicts, and prolong the image that the environment and the economy are not compatible goals.

## Antipathy to Setting Targets

At present the UK is very disinclined to adopt ambitious targets to inspire rapid improvement. It is often argued that the UK does not have a political culture amenable to targets, largely because of its opposition to central planning. However, even the last government accepted the value of target setting in several policy areas: within environmental policy, targets have been set for carbon dioxide emissions and for waste recycling. In economic policy it set a target for the rate of inflation, a practice continued by the present government. In other areas – notably road space and minerals supply – the last government previously operated a system of de facto targets based on forecast demand (predicted as a function of GDP growth). Such targets accepted continuing environmental degradation without regard for sustainability constraints. As a result of growing conflicts with local people and environmental groups over attempts to meet demand by road building and quarrying, the last government had begun to move away from this approach in planning for road infrastructure and minerals supply. But it did not embrace the idea that setting stringent environmental targets may be one way of stimulating the changes needed in society. The combination of apparent conflict with economic growth and influence of vested interests have prevented targets being set.

Target setting is valuable because of its intragovernmental influence in setting a common framework to guide all policy. For example, during the review of the coal industry by the Department of Trade and Industry (DTI) in the early 1990s, the acid emission and carbon emission targets that the Government had agreed were not negotiable in the DTI discussions about future coal markets, even though parts of the industry might have wished otherwise. Target setting provides a clear measure of progress, and if progress is not being made, a stick to beat the guilty party. The European Union's Fifth Environmental Action Programme, *Towards Sustainability* recently readopted after review, recognises environmental limits and stresses target setting.[16] The Programme identified nine key targets which were seen as indicative of broader progress. However, even within this list, not all of the targets have yet been translated into directives or regulations. And progress on relevant targets is still very limited. For example the Programme only sought carbon dioxide stabilisation on 1990 levels by 2000, with progressive reductions to 2005 and 2010. However, the European Environment Agency suggest that achievement of the target for 2000 is unlikely.[17] This should be no surprise; the primary objective of the Union has always been the extra growth it was expected to provide for its members through the creation of a large 'common market'. This is not to deny the opportunities that cooperation at a European scale offer for improving environmental performance, and in particular for ensuring convergence of environmental and social goals if the amended Treaty of Rome's call for sustainable development can be met.

## Vested Interests

In the long term the only businesses that will survive will be those that embrace sustainability. But much of UK business in particular has only a short-term perspective. It can see clearly the short-term risk from higher prices on inputs, from stricter environmental regulation, or from social standards, but because of the blinkers that set objectives principally in terms of increasing returns to shareholders, it cannot see the opportunities that such measures provide to serve wider community needs and turn a profit at the same time. By extension, companies and business interests that have gained most from the single-minded pursuit of growth are those who in one way or another have established effective relations of lobbying and influence over government. And in recent years corporate lobbying strategies have paid increasing attention to the environment. In the USA this process has gone furthest; there: 'overtly and covertly, businesses have responded [to the growing influence of environmental pressure groups] by perverting the democratic process: buying politicians, funding independent think-tanks, forming corporate front groups, and pouring money into public relations'.[18]

Alongside this process there is a growing industry of corporate 'greenwash', using the language of environmentalism to promote consumption as usual. And where the impacts of that consumption are being exposed, the most unscrupulous in the corporate sector are stooping to a range of just-legal tactics: using front groups, scapegoating protestors as anarchists or terrorists, and strategic legal intimidation. This approach is spilling over at a global level, with industry groups lobbying strongly on the climate change agenda. So far proposals for an EU carbon tax have been defeated by the interests of a small group of dinosaur companies, expressed through heavy lobbying by the European Chemical Industry Council, for example. Many of the same companies are involved in lobbying the IPCC through a number of harmless sounding front groups such as the Global Climate Coalition, the Climate Council and the International Climate Change Partnership.[19]

Those investing most heavily in slowing progress on environmental goals are the few losers, in economic terms. They also often dominate business associations, thus giving governments a misleading view of the opinions of business in the round. Gains for the many are being shouted down by the few who will lose most, even though the total gains far outweigh the total losses. But not all the gains are economic, and even those winners who will gain in an economic way are rarely organised in a way that they can be represented. Despite the efforts of the Environmental Industries Commission, it cannot fully represent the business interests of the new firms that will form to meet our needs in sustainable ways. In theory our shared interests as 'winners' should be represented by government. But governments are pursuing deregulation, liberalisation, voluntarism and 'shared responsibility', the mechanisms promoted by free market ideology as the best way to increase economic growth. And the vested company interests in government – MPs' directorships, campaign financing, appointments to 'quangos' – have helped form this climate of opinion, which in turn has further increased the involvement of industry in the policy process, for example, through the influence of the Advisory Council on Business and the Environment, with its advocacy of voluntarism, and other measures designed simply to minimise the financial cost to business. In a fair and open democracy, the involvement of business groups could be positive, helping government choose the best policy options. In practice it has produced worse results.

Such vested interests are particularly good at fighting proposals based on precautionary action. They can easily generate lots of figures to demonstrate their concerns about short-term costs, while arguments in favour of precautionary action are based on more complicated arguments. We discussed the failings of the scientific process to tackle the need for precaution in Chapter 10, but the political process is even worse because of its obsession with balancing such action against the claimed economic costs. To embed precaution in the political process will take improved policy appraisal techniques and processes and better representation of the public interest in the system. The influence of vested interests and lobby groups is as much a symptom of the problem, as the cause. Some commentators on sustainable development such as Paul Hawken[20] and Thomas Gladwin[21] argue that only business can now take the initiative, but in practice we see free-riders and vested interests undermining progress by enlightened industry. The heart of the problem is nothing less than the failure of democracy.

## Breakdown of Democracy

A State of the Nation poll undertaken by ICM in 1996 revealed that most people believe the body politic to be very sick indeed. Fewer than two-thirds of those surveyed believed that the UK is 'democratic' and more than a quarter said that it is 'not very' or 'not at all' democratic.[22] Eight out of ten believed that 'most politicians will promise to do anything to get votes'. Worse, two-thirds believed that politicians are in politics for what they can get out of it. Just four in ten believed that politicians care what people think. Nor did people trust ministers or official government advisory committees to tell the truth: three in four did not expect the truth on food safety, nuclear installations or BSE. The great majority want greater checks and balances on government power. Around three-quarters of those asked supported a freedom of information act, a bill of rights, electoral reform and a written constitution 'providing clear legal rules within which government ministers and civil servants are forced to operate'.[23] Eight in ten agreed that judges should use their powers to ensure that ministers act within the law. Nearly two-thirds believed that government power is too centralised and there were clear majorities for more substantive roles for regional assemblies or local councils.

Current debate on sleaze and standards in public life is a symptom of a deeper malady, 'a political system and a political culture no longer appropriate to the world they govern'.[24] Good governance is hindered rather than helped by our archaic constitution, the clubbiness of Westminster, and the short-term parochial horizons of policy making. And matters have been made worse by the increasing role of appointed quangos. Ministers, especially the Prime Minister, now enjoy powers of patronage unknown in the UK since the abolition of nepotism in the Civil Service.[25] The failings of the system are reflected in falling rates of democratic participation, particularly by young people. In the last but one general election – participation rates are always much higher in general elections than local or European elections – almost half of eligible 18–29 year olds, and more than half of 18–24 year olds did not vote.[26] And only 1 in 20 party activists is under 25. But young people in the UK are not depoliticised, simply disillusioned with formal politics. Opposition to the poll tax, and more recently the Criminal Justice Act, hunting and road building has become intensely political. This crisis of faith in government is representative of a wider global trend[27] reflecting globalisation and the increasing powers of the private sector. But it is exacerbated in the UK by our archaic institutions and processes of government. It is critical that we achieve democratic renewal. Otherwise, even if we adopt environmental space targets it is unlikely that we will ever achieve them.

# DEMOCRATIC RENEWAL

The citizen stands at the heart of democratic renewal. And citizens need not only political rights but also environmental rights. People will take their personal responsibilities to reduce impact on the environment seriously, but only if they know that they share the right to a clean, healthy environment. Being an active citizen does not result simply from living in a democracy. Without effective education we do not learn how to become a citizen, or the personal responsibilities that accompany our rights as a citizen. Without a framework of rights, and wider political reforms to create responsive government, people will not act as citizens to pursue sustainability. And without practical reforms to enable personal action and provide 'a genuine level of personal control and a stake in social, political and economic spheres',[28] rights and citizenship will not be empowering.

The recent Intergovernmental Conference (IGC) stimulated discussion of citizen rights in the European Union. The European Commission wants to see the 'right to a healthy environment, and the duty to ensure it' enshrined in the provisions of the Treaty of Union.[29] The European Parliament similarly wants the Right to Know written into the Treaty to ensure openness in the political process and institutions of the European Union. In parallel, ongoing negotiation of a UN Economic Commission for Europe Convention on access to environmental information and public participation has raised debate about such enabling rights, and in particular the need for access to justice to reinforce participation. Sweden, supported by the Commission, is also calling for provisions for access to justice in the IGC.[30] In the UN process, the idea of a fundamental right 'to live in a healthy environment' raised by Belgium was opposed by three countries including the UK.[31] Mere rhetoric about individual responsibil-

ity, typical of the UK debate over environmental improvement, is unhelpful, even if backed by rights. Leaving the car at home isn't easy if the
alternative is an infrequent, inconvenient and unreliable sequence of bus
journeys. In the final analysis this is blaming the victim and is fundamentally disempowering, rather than enabling.

The concept of a 'stakeholder society' must become more than a
model for our economic system. If the 'stakeholder' concept is not to
become the latest useless political doubletalk, then it must be backed by a
genuine stake in the political system too, based on far-reaching reforms
to establish rights and ensure accountability in the system. Participation
is widely recognised as a fundamental aspect of sustainable development.
At a political level that means a participatory democratic system that
recognises and responds to the needs of its stakeholders. In practice some
existing human rights are under threat in many countries, where environmental protestors allege that they have been subjected to abuse and
violence by police and security guards. Governments have responded to
environmental protest by labelling protestors as 'terrorists' – an approach
which legitimates covert surveillance, harassment and even violence – in
countries as diverse as Nigeria, Canada and the UK.[32]

A Bill of Rights is essential, including not only the right to a clean and
healthy environment, but also to the freedom of information and access to
justice that are needed for citizens to protect and enforce their rights. A more
representative political system, in which the share of seats in Parliament fairly
reflects the votes cast, is equally essential. Reform of the House of Lords to
ensure a democratic second chamber would mean that the vested interests of
the land-owning classes held less sway over our political system. In the
European Union, we must continue the process of increasing the powers for
the Parliament, which in turn will increase interest in voting in European
elections. And in the Council of Ministers we must move towards majority
voting. At present, where it applies, 'the unanimity rule ... either paralyses the
Council or reduces decisions to the lowest common denominator'.[33] Such an
agenda of constitutional reform, far from being the agenda of the 'chatter-
ing classes', is widely shared, as we saw earlier. And it is fundamental to giving
British society the capacity to respond to the challenge of environmental
space. Without truly representative democracy in which the meeting of the
needs of all of us, and improvement in the real wellbeing of society become
fundamental objectives, then action to achieve sustainability will always be
too little, too late; undermined by the actions of vested interests and ideological inertia in the political system.

## Local Democracy

The local level is, if anything, even more critical. Here democratic renewal
goes hand in hand with local sustainability initiatives, community partic-

ipation and regeneration. Regional assemblies are only part of the story; local government at all levels is beginning to rediscover its reason for being in promoting local sustainability. We must take subsidiarity seriously and start rejuvenating political culture and participation at the local level. The local authority associations have prepared an Environmental Manifesto for Local Government[34] to help them involve other key stakeholders in the Local Agenda 21 process. They have called for a power of community initiative and a duty to promote social, economic and environmental conditions and wellbeing of their areas within the overall objective of sustainable development. The new Labour Government has promised such a duty in its manifesto. But alone this is unlikely to be adequate. For example, the land use planning system also needs reform if local authorities are to use it to promote sustainability. At heart it needs a wider remit, so that 'material considerations' in any planning decision can include public health and degradation or depletion of environmental resources. Existing development plans must be revised to recognise the 'primacy of sustainable development in the planning system' and objectors to planning applications given the same rights of appeal against decisions of local planning authorities as developers already enjoy.

But if local authorities are to promote and coordinate action on energy conservation, traffic management and urban redevelopment, amongst other things, they need new and responsive powers and funding. Funding reforms need to facilitate longer term programmes over several years (where environmental improvements have a long payback period). The release of central government funds must be based on realistic assessments of the proposals. For example, many authorities have had trouble obtaining funds for pedestrian and public transport improvements under the 'package funding' scheme because their bids have been assessed using 'cost-benefit' analyses designed for road scheme appraisal that are biased and inappropriate even for that use. Also, local authorities need more discretion in their raising and spending of money. We should provide powers to use green charges, such as domestic waste charges or parking taxes, locally, which could be earmarked for specific expenditure to promote sustainability.

If national regulatory frameworks were appropriately reformed, some of the revenue from such green charges or taxes could be profitably used to support local economies, through direct support for third sector organisations, in support for establishing LETS schemes, or to underwrite local credit unions or regional banks for example. In this way local authorities could help local economies retain more of the benefits of local spending, as well as helping meet social and environmental needs in their area. The more flexibility local authorities have in this respect, the more seriously people will take the local democratic process. However, additional resources designed to strengthen local economies must not be limited to those provided by such local charges; redistributive support provided from national resources is also required.

# THE ROLE OF THE STATE

Effective government action on sustainability depends in turn on democratic renewal. More broadly, such a renewal of state legitimacy through democracy is critical for the provision and protection of public goods and services including the environment.[35] Prime Minister Blair has previously said:

> *we all have a stake in the health and integrity of the environment. If there is any case where collective effort is essential, it is in ensuring that our environment is protected so that future generations are not paying the price for our profligacy.*[36]

There is even sound economic theory now to explain why effective markets cannot emerge in all areas, and why public or community intervention is necessary.[37]

Gerry Holtham and his colleagues at the Institute for Public Policy Research believe that successful capitalism needs collective activity.[38] For example, a flourishing small business sector is often found where the local voluntary sector is strong and active, as in northern Italy. Holtham concludes that a society rich in such social capital reduces the risks of marginalisation, although it cannot do away with the need for safety nets and backstops to underpin participation, like universal education. In other words, sustainability and social justice require a renewal of democracy because they require government. Rolling back the frontiers of the state has been the ideology of recent years, yet market forces alone cannot tackle the critical social and environmental problems we face. Our goals require new forms of economic intervention, regulation, taxation and public spending – at local, national and international levels. Moreover, unless government is truly representative it will never be able to deliver such tools. It must be, and be seen to be, accountable and acting in the public interest. Such a transformation needs the underpinning of formal and inalienable rights of citizenship. In these terms the ideology of deregulation and 'privatisation' can be seen as an abdication of political responsibility. It is not necessarily a question of whether particular institutions and services are provided by the public or the private sector, but of whether the regulatory framework for them acts to protect the public's environmental interest.

It is, however, now the common assumption of both main parties that the public, whatever they say in opinion polls, when push comes to shove, will not pay increased taxes for public service provision. Its consequence is that certain policy tools have been virtually ruled out of bounds. In reality, one of the main reasons for this is the lack of trust in government noted above. We do not subscribe to the view that all taxes are bad, but to that, attributed to Roosevelt, that 'taxes are the price we pay for living in a civilised society'. We believe that there are functions that can only be provided effectively by the state and that therefore justify taxes. Moreover, there is evidence that tax cuts do not necessarily provide economic benefits,[39] while some taxes, such as green taxes, clearly act to increase overall economic efficiency. The 'fear of taxes' that characterises modern political debate is therefore misplaced. As the last Government found, indirect taxes seem to be more acceptable to the public than direct taxes, but these do of course require other measures and spending on 'benefits in kind' – such as education, health and public transport – to compensate for their distributional consequences, otherwise the poor may well pay more. The public does seem more prepared to countenance additional taxes if the revenue they raise is dedicated to a specific need. This does not require formal 'hypothecation' but simply political commitment to link the two, as the last Chancellor of the Exchequer did when he announced the landfill tax – promising to spend the same amount as he expected it to raise, on cutting employers' national insurance contributions.[40]

The most far-reaching approach to acceptable taxation is to use tax reform – changing the basis of taxation. As we saw in Chapter 10 this can deliver a double dividend if the increased taxes are on environmental inputs and wastes. Yet proposals for tax reform are being fought by the same vested interests we met earlier in this chapter. There are growing alliances between NGOs, unions – notably the European Trade Union Congress – and businesses, such as the new business lobby E5, to promote eco-tax reform. Yet other business groups – involving the dinosaurs of the oil and chemical industries – are creating opposition. For example, a new lobby group including Shell, ICI and Rhone-Poulenc has set itself up specifically to block moves towards eco-taxes, and even to influence European Commission research in this area.[41]

# INTERNATIONAL POLITICS

The arguments for a renewal of democracy are reflected at the international level too. There are even more stakeholders in the global environment, and many aspects of international environmental issues concern collective public goods. Nothing less than a new global deal between North and South, brokered and administered by transparent and democratically accountable institutions, will do if we are to achieve sustainability at a global scale. It will not be enough simply to reverse the current flow of financial resources which still runs from South to North, although this is crucial,[42] unless environmental resources are taken into account too, and developing countries are given access to the environmental resources they need to achieve sustainability. In other words we must meet environmental space targets. The new deal must address aid, debt and trade. Most critically it must not follow the conventional 'trickle-down' model which is still promoted by many Northern governments such as the last Conservative administration in the UK. Pursuing tired arguments that we must 'liberalise our economies, minimise the burden of government, and lift all restrictions on the free operation of the market' will not deliver anything new.[43]

Debt relief is the first priority. The UK's approach to debt relief has been typical of most Northern governments. So far, debt relief has been limited, even falling short of the last Government's commitments.[44] Recent 'reductions' in debt – worth about US$5.6bn to about 20 of the poorest countries[45] – agreed by the IMF in Washington in September 1996, are little better. These reductions merely take the form of rescheduling or reduced interest rates, if the borrowing country adheres to structural adjustment policies. True debt relief would take the form of writing off debt, particularly for the world's poorest countries.

Secondly, trade discrimination by the North against the South must be corrected. Free trade must be regulated, so that it does not act as a means of opening up international borders in order to assure a small group of people free access to the world's remaining resources, as David Korten argues, but to permit fair trade that is in everyone's interests.[46] Without regulation, free trade increases the relative significance of failure to internalise environmental costs as it becomes easier for companies to exploit this failure.[47] And as Herman Daly has argued, these costs are missed by trade liberalisation, which seeks simply to maximise welfare from trade, not overall welfare, which depends, so comprehensively, as we have seen throughout this section, on environmental and social goods which are not marketed or traded.[48] Trade, too, needs open and democratic institutions. In the short term, an Inter-Governmental Panel on Trade, the Environment and Sustainability would offer some checks and balances for the highly opaque and undemocratic World Trade Organisation.

Thirdly, aid flows must be increased and targeted to support sustainable development (see Box 12.1). Among other things, that means helping meet unmet demand for fertility control, supporting education, targeting poverty alleviation directly, and financial and technology transfers to assist developing countries in developing their capacity for environmentally efficient value-added manufacture and service delivery. Aid agencies must be transparent and accountable, so that local communities can give 'prior informed consent' for such aid and technology transfer, whether directed via governments, or as is increasingly the case, through the private sector.

The Independent Commission on Population and Quality of Life concluded that the prevailing concept of development – exclusively economic and obsessed with deregulation – inevitably produces massive exclusion inside every society, among nations and on all continents.[49] Its recommendations were that future aid must focus on the poorest people in the poorest nations, and on sustainable human development: education, health (including reproductive health), planning, women and

---

# BOX 12.1 *WHAT'S WRONG WITH AID?*

The UK's approach to overseas aid can be criticised on a number of grounds:

Firstly, quantity: the UK overseas aid budget, at just under £2 billion in 1993/94 is small in absolute terms, especially when compared with the indebtedness of developing countries and the loss of revenue which results from unfair terms of trade. The UK has been retreating from the UN target of 0.7 per cent of gross national product rather than advancing towards it. Despite a stronger commitment to overseas development, the new Labour Government has only pledged to begin to reverse this decline.

Secondly, quality. It has yet to be shown that the UK aid programme is sufficiently targeted to meet the objectives of poverty alleviation and sustainable development. It is far from clear that bilateral aid fully takes into account the views of potentially affected communities when projects are at the design stage. Moreover, as Friends of the Earth's report, *Whose Hand on the Chainsaw?*[a] reveals, such 'assistance' has itself been a factor in environmental degradation and, in particular, tropical deforestation.

Thirdly, aid tying: about 70 per cent of UK bilateral aid is tied to the purchase of UK goods and services.[b] Aid funds are recirculated to UK companies rather than being spent locally or with the most competitive provider.

Fourthly, transparency and accountability: little information about UK funded projects is routinely made available so there is little accountability to Parliament and the public.

*Multilateral aid*
An increasing proportion – around 40 per cent – of the UK aid budget is being channelled through the World Bank, regional development banks, the European Community and United Nations agencies.[c] Many of these multilateral agencies also have a poor record in promoting sustainable development.

Sources: *a* Friends of the Earth (1992) *Whose Hand on the Chainsaw? UK Government Policy and the Tropical Rainforests* London: Friends of the Earth; *b House of Commons Hansard* Oral Answers 26 April 1993. Answer by Lennox-Boyd; *c* Foreign and Commonwealth Office (1993) *Departmental report 1993* CM 2202 London: HMSO, p40

---

environment. To fund such increased support, it recommended a new global charge on all international financial dealings, yielding US$150 billion per year. This is the so-called 'Tobin Tax', a 0.25 per cent tax on the billions of dollars that pass through foreign exchanges every day.[50] Above and beyond even these measures, if such a global deal is to work, then flows of foreign direct investment, mainly the province of the large transnational corporations, must be regulated too. The economic geographer Ray Hudson describes nation states as 'neutered' in their capacities to deal with global capital,[51] and this is certainly true of many Southern nations. A United Nations survey of transnational corporations revealed that less than a fifth of even those corporations which responded supported the creating and strengthening of national regulatory systems in developing countries.[52] The trend is towards less regulation of international capital markets. The solution to this kind of unfair competition is to require, through international trade regulation, transnational corporations to operate worldwide to the highest standard required of them in all their countries of operation.

# CONCLUSIONS

Obtaining societal and political consensus even on the need to reduce consumption of environmental space will be difficult without this democratic renewal, and agreement on the policies needed to implement such a strategy for sustainability well-nigh impossible. In particular the vested short-term interests that so influence policy makers at all scales will continue to delay progress. Without democratic renewal, it seems unlikely that the clear benefits of integrated policies which would meet the economic and social needs of the British people will be implemented in the face of the ideological and cultural obstacles that riddle our current political system. At present it seems that only major shocks will shift political views from the environmental complacency and short termism that characterises what passes for democratic politics in this country. If we are to enter the next millennium with real hope for the human race, nothing less than a sustainability revolution will suffice. It begins here.

# Part 4
# Conclusions – The Longest Journey

# Conclusions

In Part 1 we showed how the scale of environmental damage is increasingly pressing against global limits; and how poverty and inequality in the UK and globally have persisted despite economic growth. We argued that these are not symptoms of the growth model's failure, but of its success. We showed also that the benefits of global economic growth are not always reflected in real wellbeing – partly because at the same time as they provide material benefits, they damage other aspects of wellbeing, by damaging human and environmental capital. Part 1 concluded that we need a fundamental reform of global and national economic systems, with two pillars: keeping within ecological limits and meeting needs.

These pillars are directly reflected in the methods used in Part 2 to set targets for use of environmental resources based on ecological limits to their sustainable use, and equitable distribution of the resources available to meet all our needs. These targets are based on global limits, while allowing access to a fair share of environmental resources for Southern developing countries. Part 2 examined UK use of environmental resources and compared it with the environmental space targets to establish targets for the UK as a whole. These demonstrate the scale of the challenge for the UK. We must reduce our use of these key resources: an 88 per cent cut in emissions of carbon dioxide, an 88 per cent cut in aluminium use, a 73 per cent reduction in wood use, a 27 per cent reduction in the use of productive agricultural land, and a 15 per cent cut in water use. These environmental space targets for the UK clearly provide realistic estimates of the direction, order of magnitude and speed of changes necessary. We do not expect them to be absolutely precise down to a few per cent, but they are a far better guide to a sustainable future than our current indicators of economic growth.

Part 2 also provided a valuable illustration of the possible strategies to meet these targets. It demonstrated how meeting them will be practically possible. Most of the interim targets can be reached through already demonstrated and cost-effective techniques. There are many technologies, products and processes already available, which would contribute to such an eco-efficiency revolution. Many of these are 'only prevented from becoming mainstream because they are suppressed, ignored, prevented from competing equally, held back by specific vested interests in business and politics and starved of interest and investment'.[1] In the longer term, we are confident that in a culture where environmental resources are adequately valued, many more opportunities for saving on their use will emerge from technological and social innovation.

Part 3 dealt with the transition to a sustainable society. As business is increasingly recognising, its own sustainability depends on it meeting the environmental space challenge. To do so it must become accountable to a wider group of 'stakeholders'. Business can meet the environmental space targets by improving 'eco-efficiency', but only with a transition to an economy based on enterprises which provide services to meet people's needs. These shifts demand a long-term view, and thus require an effective regulatory and fiscal framework to overcome vested interests and the short termism of the market. The need for increased economic prices for environmental resources is clear. Government must drive these changes, in particular by reforming the tax system to provide a continual incentive for economic change towards sustainability, matching increases in taxes on resources with cuts in taxes on social goods such as employment.

Our approach to equity is one of equality of opportunity; we are not prepared to see opportunity undermined by the unequal distribution of resources globally, or nationally. The Independent Commission on Population and Quality of Life recently concluded that the prevailing concept of development inevitably produces massive exclusion, inside every society, among nations and on all continents.[2] As Chapter 11 suggested, it will not be possible to achieve sustainability except in an inclusive society rooted in local communities; a society that seeks social justice and wellbeing for all as its goals. Tackling inequality will help improve health, protect the environment, strengthen social cohesion, and as a byproduct, should even help the economy. A focus on real wellbeing and quality of life is necessary to meet non-material as well as material needs. In these ways we can implement 'sufficiency' strategies – ways of increasing wellbeing with less material consumption. If we are to create the driving forces for our society to focus on real wellbeing, in terms of equity, health and fulfilling work in an environmentally sustainable economy, then we need the right indicators and signposts. We must replace gross domestic product as the principal indicator of the wellbeing of our society. GDP is no measure of the progress of society, just as increases in standard of living are not the same as increases in quality of life.

We also need the political systems to achieve a focus on real wellbeing and needs. This means that democratic renewal – at local, national and international levels – must lie at the heart of policies for sustainability. Otherwise, integrated policies to meet the economic and social needs of the British people will be defeated by vested interests and the ideological and cultural obstacles that riddle our current political system. The British Government published a National Sustainable Development Strategy in 1994 in response to the political agenda set by the Earth Summit. That strategy was far from adequate when first published.[3] It is now, with a new government, time for a root and branch revision of the strategy, taking environmental space targets as the starting point, rather than a weak definition of sustainable development dominated by conventional economic interests.

The environmental space approach is at heart pragmatic. It might seem radical here in the UK, but this is not a parochial issue; it's a global imperative. And despite appearances, environmental space starts from where we are – a global economy and an increasingly global society, both of which bring benefits as well as environmental and other costs. We don't reject these benefits, instead we are looking for ways in which modern capitalism can deliver its promises, without bulldozing any culture that stands in its way. This will mean brokering a deal for progress at the global level. The developing countries of the South will accept nothing less than their fair share. That means we in the North can have nothing more, but as we have seen, we could still be better off than we are now. Winning commitment from Southern countries to stop at a fair share, will depend on more than simply freeing up environmental space for sustainable development in the South, it demands real support from the North for truly sustainable development paths.

Meeting the sustainability targets suggested by the environmental space analysis will not be easy, but it is possible, and the economic, social and political reforms needed will bring many benefits for us, for our children and for future generations. Those reforms are simply the first steps towards sustainable development. The *longest journey*, it is said, starts but with a single step. There is no longer, and no more rewarding, journey for humankind than that of truly sustainable and enduring human development – the journey into 'Tomorrow's World'.

# Afterword –
# Values and Sustainable
# development

In many respects this book has taken an unashamedly anthropocentric approach to sustainable development. But this is not to reject the view that a greater 'reverence of nature' rather than simply 'conservation of the environment' is a fundamental foundation of true sustainability. Without a wider context – an understanding that humanity must exist within natural systems – our hopes for sustainability are dashed. Such a reverence must be expressed in a sense of precaution, and respect for the diversity of nature as the foundation of evolution and development. In other words, we must treat our ability to reshape nature with care, balanced by our knowledge that unexpected consequences are, by definition, unknown.

This book has, we hope, offered a foundation for developing values for sustainability, although we are not so pretentious as to think that we know best what those values will be, or that we can impose values on anyone. The foundations we can see are to begin with people's needs, rather than with consumerism-led demands, and to show respect for all other humans and indeed other life on this planet. Only if we build on these can we expect to go from an instrumentalist achievement of sustainability targets to a truly sustainable society; a 'learning society'. As sociologist David Marquand has concluded: 'people change, not because they have been ordered to or given incentives to, but because they have learned to see the world and themselves in a different way'.[4] This learning process has begun, and it challenges the very roots of modern-day life. As one leading journalist put it recently:

> We live in a society which encourages us, almost every second, to believe that we are what we consume. The thought of us actually wanting to earn less and consume less for the sake of the planet, or our mental wellbeing, or both, is one that our political and business leaders simply cannot cope with.[5]

But this is a challenge we will have to cope with. George Carey, the Archbishop of Canterbury, recently commented:

> *We are in danger of becoming a shallow society, focused on consumerism ... We [should be] talking about how we can create again a society based on common values that we all own and all share ....*[6]

Such a sustainable society would be one in which we could all be proud to hold a stake.

# Notes and References

## NOTES TO INTRODUCTION

**1** Cited in International Institute for Environment and Development 1995 *Citizen Action to Lighten Ecological Footprints* London: IIED **2** UN Environment Programme, 1997 *Global Environmental Outlook 1* Nairobi: UNEP **3** Blair, T 1996 Speech to Labour Party Conference, Blackpool, 1st October **4** Jacobs, M 1996 *The Politics of the Real World* London: Earthscan, p11 **5** Wackernagel, M and Rees, W 1996 *Our Ecological Footprint: Reducing Human Impact on the Earth* Gabriola Island BC: New Society **6** Elkin, T and McLaren, D with Hillman, M 1991 *Reviving the City: Towards Sustainable Urban Development* London: Friends of the Earth and Policy Studies Institute

## NOTES TO PART 1 INTRODUCTION

**1** We will generally use the terms 'Southern countries', or 'developing countries' in this book **2** World Commission on Environment and Development, 1987 *Our Common Future* Oxford: Oxford University Press, p8 **3** Her Majesty's Government, 1994 *Sustainable Development: The UK Strategy* London: HMSO **4** UN Environment Programme, IUCN and WWF, 1990 *Caring for the Earth: a Strategy for Sustainable Living* Gland: UNEP, IUCN and WWF **5** Independent Commission on Population and Quality of Life, 1996 *Caring for the Future* Oxford: Oxford University Press **6** Opschoor, JB and Weterings, R 1994 Environmental utilisation space: an introduction *Milieu Tijdschrift voor Milieukunde* 9(5), pp198–205 **7** Beckerman, W 1995 *Small is Stupid* London: Duckworth **8** Kahn, H, Brown, W and Martel, l, 1976 *The Next 200 Years: A Scenario for America and the World* New York: William Morrow **9** Simon, J 1997 *The Ultimate Resource 2* New Jersey: Princeton University Press **10** Cohen, J 1995 *How Many People Can the Earth Support?* London: Norton and Co

## NOTES TO CHAPTER 1

**1** Clay, DC, Byiringiro, F, Kangasniemi, J, Reardon, T, Sibomana, B, Uwamariya, L and Tardif-Douglin, D 1995 Promoting Food Security in Rwanda through Sustainable Agricultural Productivity: Meeting the challenges of population pressure, land degradation and poverty *MSU Bulletin* Michigan State University **2** Bonner, W, Benninghoff, W, Gallardo, V, Kerry, K, Parker, B and Prevost, J 1980 *A Visitor's Introduction to Antarctica and its Environment, Working Group on Biology Conservation Subcommittee Scientific Committee on Antarctic Research* Christchurch: New Zealand Antarctic Programme **3** European Environment Agency, 1996 *Newsletter 8* The Arctic Region – a Global Warming area threatened by pollution http://intwww.eea.dk/newsletter/news8.html **4** Bullock, S 1995 *Prescription for Change: Health and the Environment* London: Friends of the Earth **5** IPCC, 1996 *Climate Change 1995. Impacts, Adaptions and Mitigation of Climate Change: Scientific-Technical Analyses. Contribution of Working Group II to the Second Assessment of the Intergovernmental Panel on Climate Change* Cambridge: Cambridge University Press **6** UN Environment Programme, 1995a *Press Release: Humans Destroying Earth's Biodiversity* November 14 **7** UN Environment Programme,

1995b *Global Biodiversity Assessment* Nairobi: UNEP **8** *Ibid.* **9** *Ibid.* **10** UN Environment Programme, 1995a *Press Release: Humans Destroying Earth's Biodiversity* November 14 **11** The small amount of geothermal energy captured by some living communities in the ocean deeps is negligible in this respect **12** A terawatt is a thousand billion watts. A watt is a unit of power, equivalent to a joule of energy per second **13** Wackernagel, M and Rees, W 1996 *Our Ecological Footprint: Reducing Human Impact on the Earth* Gabriola Island BC: New Society **14** Vitousek, PM, Erlich, PR, Erlich, AH and Mateson, PA 1986 Human Appropriation of the Products of Photosynthesis *Bioscience* 34(6) pp368–73 **15** UN Environment Programme, 1995b *Global Biodiversity Assessment* Nairobi: UNEP **16** Since 1986 perhaps 8 per cent of the tropical forest area has been felled (World Resources Institute, 1996 *World Resources 1996–7* Oxford: Oxford University Press), and global cropland has increased by about 2.5 per cent (Postel, S 1994 Carrying Capacity: The Earth's Bottom Line. In Mazur, L (ed) *Beyond the Numbers* Washington DC: Island Press) **17** Pauly, D and Christensen, V 1995 Primary production required to sustain global fisheries *Nature* 374 pp225–57 **18** World Resources Institute, 1994 *World Resources 1994–95. A Guide to the Global Environment* Oxford: Oxford University Press **19** *Ibid.* **20** Greenpeace, Undated *Fleet Migration Exporting the Overfishing Problem: Seafood Companies React to a Supply Crisis* http://www.greenpeace.org/ ~comms/fish/part8.html **21** Cited in Postel, S and Heise, L 1988 *Reforesting the Earth* Worldwatch Paper 83 Washington DC: Worldwatch Institute **22** World Resources Institute, 1994 *World Resources 1994–95. A Guide to the Global Environment* Oxford: Oxford University Press **23** Myers, N 1995 Environmental Unknowns, *Science* 269, 21 July 1995; World Resources Institute, 1994 *World Resources 1994–95. A Guide to the Global Environment* Oxford: Oxford University Press **24** UN Development Programme, 1996 *Human Development Report* Oxford: Oxford University Press **25** UN Environment Programme, 1995b *Global Biodiversity Assessment* Nairobi: UNEP **26** UN Environment Programme 1997 *Global Biodiversity Outlook* 1 Nairobi: UNEP **27** Smith R, Prevelin, B, Baker, K, Bidigare, R, Boucher, N, Coley, T, Karentz, D, Macintyre, S, Hatlick, H, Menzies, D, Ondrousek, D, Wan, Z, Waters, K, 1992 Ozone Depletion: Ultraviolet radiation and phytoplankton biology in Antarctic waters *Science* 255, pp 952–59 **28** Pearce, F 1996 Deserts of our doorstep *New Scientist* 6th July 1996, pp12–13 **29** Ministry of the Environment, Norway 1987 *Declining forests on acid soils* Http://odin.dep.np/md/publ/acid/Forest.html **30** IPCC, 1996 *Climate Change 1995. Impacts, Adaptions and Mitigation of Climate Change: Scientific-Technical Analyses* Cambridge: Cambridge University Press **31** Wadhams, P (ed), 1996 The development of the Odden ice tongue in the Greenland Sea during winter 1993 from remote sensing and field observations *Journal of Geophysical Research* 101: C8, pp18213–35 **32** Myers, N 1996 *Problems of the Next Century* Paper to UNED UK seminar at Green College, Oxford, 24 June **33** Odum, EP 1993 *Ecology and Our Endangered Life-support Systems* Sunderland, MA: Sinauer Associates **34** Clayton, T and Radcliffe, N 1996 *Sustainability: A Systems Approach* London: Earthscan in association with WWF-UK **35** Houghton, J 1994 *Global Warming: the Complete Briefing* Oxford: Lion Press **36** Sprod, I, Bluth, G, Krueger, A, Walter, L and Schnetzler, C 1993 Comparison of TOMS SO$_2$ data from El Chichon and Mount Pinatubo eruptions *EOS Transactions* AGU, 74 p132, and http://skye.gsfc.nasa.gov/eruptions/pinatubo/pinatubo.html **37** McDougall, CL 1995 *Intellectual Property Rights and the Biodiversity Convention: The Impact of GATT* London: Friends of the Earth **38** Khor, M 1996 *The WTO and the Proposed Multilateral Investment Agreement: Implications for Developing Countries and Proposed Positions* Penang, Malaysia: Third World Network **39** Not In My Back Yard **40** LeQuesne, C 1996 *Reforming World Trade: The Social and Environmental Priorities* Oxford: Oxfam Publications, p25 **41** Independent Commission on Population and Quality of Life, 1996 *Caring for the future* Oxford: Oxford University Press

# NOTES TO CHAPTER 2

**1** UN Development Programme, 1996 *Human Development Report 1996* Oxford: Oxford University Press, p2 **2** *Ibid.* **3** *Ibid.* **4** *Ibid.* **5** *Ibid.* **6** Durning, A 1992 *How Much is Enough? The Consumer Society and the Future of the Earth* Washington DC: Worldwatch Institute **7** Torfs, M 1996 *The IMF Handbook: Arming NGOs with Knowledge* Brussels: Friends of the Earth Europe **8** UN Development Programme, 1996 *Human Development Report 1996* Oxford: Oxford University Press **9** *Ibid.*, p104 **10** *Ibid.* **11** Watkins, K 1995 *The Oxfam Poverty Report* Oxford: Oxfam Publications

**12** Chatterjee, P 1994 *50 Years is Enough* London: Friends of the Earth **13** Torfs, M 1996 *The IMF Handbook. Arming NGOs with Knowledge* Brussels: Friends of the Earth Europe **14** Young, C and Bishop, J 1995 *Adjustment Policies and the Environment: A Critical Review of the Literature* CREED Working Paper No 1 London: International Institute for Environment and Development **15** World Bank, cited in *Ibid.* **16** Gelb, A, Staff Director, World Bank, 1996 Letter to *Independent Newspaper* July 15 **17** Torfs, M 1996 *The IMF Handbook: Arming NGOs with Knowledge* Brussels: Friends of the Earth Europe **18** Oxfam, 1993 *Africa Make or Break: Action for Recovery* Oxford: Oxfam **19** Religious Working Group on the World Bank and IMF, 1995 *Background Paper – Multilateral Debt: A Potential Solution* Unpublished **20** Watkins, K 1995 *The Oxfam Poverty Report* Oxford: Oxfam Publications, p73 **21** Watkins, K 1995 *The Oxfam Poverty Report* Oxford: Oxfam Publications, p108 **22** UN Conference on Trade and Development,1996 *The Least Developed Countries 1996 Report* Geneva: UN **23** Jacobs, M 1996 *The Politics of the Real World* London: Earthscan **24** Watkins, K 1995 *The Oxfam Poverty Report* Oxford: Oxfam Publications, p108 **25** *Ibid.* **26** Torfs, M 1996 *The IMF Handbook. Arming NGOs with Knowledge* Brussels: Friends of the Earth Europe **27** Religious Working Group on the World Bank and IMF, 1995 *Background Paper – Multilateral Debt: A Potential Solution* **28** UN Development Programme 1996 *Human Development Report 1996* Oxford: Oxford University Press p104 **29** LeQuesne, C 1996 *Reforming World Trade: The Social and Environmental Priorities* Oxford: Oxfam **30** House of Commons Environment Committee 1996 *World Trade and the Environment* London: HMSO; OECD, 1994 *The Environmental Effects of Trade* Paris: OECD **31** Cited in Chatterjee, P 1994 *50 Years is Enough* London: Friends of the Earth **32** Watkins, K and Windfuhr, M 1994 *Agriculture in the Uruguay Round: Implications for Sustainable Development in Developing Countries* Gland: WWF International **33** Goldin, I, Knudsen, O and Van der Mensbrugghe, D 1993 *Trade Liberalisation: Global Economic Implications* Paris: OECD and Washington DC: World Bank **34** UN Development Programme, 1996 *Human Development Report 1996* Oxford: Oxford University Press p59

**35** LeQuesne, C 1996 *Reforming World Trade: The Social and Environmental Priorities* Oxford: Oxfam **36** *Ibid.* **37** *Ibid.* **38** *Ibid.* p27 **39** Rich, B 1994 *Mortgaging the Earth: The World Bank, Environment Impoverishment and the Crisis of Development* London: Earthscan; Chatterjee, P 1994 *50 Years is Enough* London: Friends of the Earth **40** Rich, B 1994 *Mortgaging the Earth: The World Bank, Environmental Impoverishment and the Crisis of Development* London: Earthscan **41** Chatterjee, P 1994 *50 Years is Enough* London: Friends of the Earth **42** *Ibid.*; Rich, B 1994 *Mortgaging the Earth: The World Bank, Environmental Impoverishment and the Crisis of Development* London: Earthscan **43** World Bank Internal Report, 1996 *Effectiveness of Environmental Assessments and National Environmental Action Plans: A Process Study* **44** Friends of the Earth, 1994 *Cutting Corners – The IFC and Sustainable Development* London: Friends of the Earth **45** UN Conference on Trade and Development, 1996 *The Least Developed Countries 1996 Report* Geneva: UN; Bowley, G 1996 Prospects Brighten *Financial Times* 27th September, pxiii **46** UN Development Programme, 1996 *Human Development Report 1996* Oxford: Oxford University Press **47** UN Conference on Trade and Development, 1996 *The Least Developed Countries 1996 Report* Geneva: UN; Bowley, G 1996 Prospects Brighten *Financial Times* 27 September **48** UN Development Programme, 1996 *Human Development Report 1996* Oxford: Oxford University Press **49** Friends of the Earth Nicaragua, 1996 *Personal communication* 20 September **50** Mazur, L (ed) 1994 *Beyond the Numbers. A Reader on Population, Consumption and the Environment* Washington DC: Island Press **51** 11.1 gigatonnes of carbon dioxide – see Chapter 5 for more details **52** Milieu Defensie, 1996 *North–South Perspectives on Sustainability: Towards a Global Redistribution of Environmental Space* Amsterdam: Milieu Defensie **53** Speech by the Rev Barry Thorley at the launch of the Black Environment Network, London, 1987 **54** Subak, S and Clark, W 1990 Accounts for Greenhouse gases: Towards the design of fair assessments pp68–93 in Clark, W (Ed) *Useable Knowledge for Managing Global Climatic Change* Stockholm: Stockholm Environment Institute **55** Myers, N 1993 *Ultimate Security* London: WW Norton **56** Helgadottir, B 1996 Maritime court takes brief to rule the waves, *European* 12 September **57** UN Development Programme 1996 *Human Development Report 1996* Oxford: Oxford University Press **58** UN Development Programme 1996 *Human Development Report 1996* Oxford: Oxford University Press **59** Department of Social Security, Government Statistical Service, 1996 *Households below average income 1979–1993/4* London: HMSO **60** Adonis, A 1996 Through a Class System Darkly *Financial Times Report* Britain, the rogue piece in Europe's jigsaw 12 June **61** *The Economist* 1996 Booming Busts 3 August, p29 **62** Hutton, W 1995 *The State We're In* London: Jonathan Cape **63** Leadbeater, C 1996 How Fat Cats Rock the Boat *Independent on Sunday*, 3 November **64** Ball, J and Marland, M 1996 *Male Earnings Mobility in the Lifetime Labour Market Database* London: DSS Analytical Services Division **65** Cited by Mills, H 1996 Life on the brink

*The Observer* 11 August **66** Mills, H and Bright, M 1996 Poverty 'making children shorter' *The Observer* 11 August **67** Cited in Mills, H 1996 Life on the brink *The Observer* 11 August **68** *Ibid.* **69** UN Development Programme, 1996 *Human Development Report 1996* Oxford: Oxford University Press

# NOTES TO CHAPTER 3

**1** Jacobs, M 1996 *The Politics of the Real World* London: Earthscan **2** Beckerman, W 1995 *Small is Stupid* London: Duckworth **3** UN Development Programme, 1996 *Human Development Report 1996* Oxford: Oxford University Press **4** Mintel survey research, cited in Ghazi, P and Jones, J 1996 O, to be a Mexican *New Statesman*, 6 September **5** Cited in Radford, T 1997 The buck stops here *The Guardian* 6 March **6** Heal, G 1997, cited in *Ibid.* **7** Confederation of British Industry, 1995 *The Environment Costs* London: CBI **8** See, for example, Sen, P 1995 Environmental policies and North–South Trade: A selected survey of the issues. In Bhaskar, V and Glyn, A (eds) *The North, the South and the Environment* London: Earthscan **9** *ENDS Report* 258, 1996 Catalysts fail to dent $NO_2$ pollution levels pp6–7 **10** *ENDS Report* 206, 1992 Vehicle emission forecasts pinpoint $CO_2$, $NO_x$, as problem pollutants, p9 **11** *ENDS Report* 209, 1992 Green claims for plastic pouch based on Swiss data p21 **12** Business Council for Sustainable Development, 1993 *Getting Eco-Efficient. Report of First Antwerp Eco-Efficiency Workshop, November 1993* Geneva: BCSD; Greyson, J (ed) 1995 *The Natural Step 1995* Bristol: Natural Step; Factor Ten Club, 1994 *The Carnoules Declaration* Wuppertal: Factor Ten Club **13** Ghazi, P and Jones, J 1996 O, to be a Mexican *New Statesman* 6 September **14** Cited in Rifkin, J 1995 *The End of Work* New York: Tarcher Puttnam p.20 **15** Lebow, V 1950 Cited in Secrett, C 1996 Editorial *Earth Matters* 32 **16** Max-Neef, MA 1991 *Human Scale Development: Conception, Application and Further Reflections* New York: The Apex Press **17** *Ibid.* **18** Jackson, T and Marks, N 1996 *Consumption, Sustainable Welfare and Human Needs – an Examination of UK Expenditure Patterns 1954–1994* Guildford: Centre for Environmental Strategy, University of Surrey **19** Max-Neef, MA 1991 *Human Scale Development: Conception, Application and Further Reflections* New York: The Apex Press **20** Cited in Carley, M and Spapens, P 1997 *Fair Shares: Sustainable Living and Global Equity in the 21st Century* London: Earthscan **21** Hareide, D 1990 *Det Gote Norge* Gyldendal **22** Daly, H and Cobb, J 1989 *For the Common Good* London: Green Print **23** Cobb, C, Halstead, T and Rowe, J 1995 *The Genuine Progress Indicator: Summary of Data and Methodology* San Francisco: Redefining Progress **24** Atkinson, G 1995 *Measuring Sustainable Economic Welfare: A Critique of the UK ISEW* CSERGE Working paper, GEC 95–08 **25** Hareide, D 1990 *Det Gote Norge* Gyldendal **26** Veenhoven, R 1987 National Wealth and Individual Happiness. In Grunert, KG and Olander, F *Understanding Economic Behaviour* London: Kluwer Academic **27** Seabrook, J 1994 Consumerism and Happiness *Ethical Consumer* 27 January pp12–13 **28** Oswald, A 1996 GDP can't make you happy *New Economy* 3(1), pp15–19 **29** Zolatas, X 1981 *Economic Growth and declining social welfare* New York: University Press **30** Jacobs, M 1996 *The Politics of the Real World* London: Earthscan **31** Rogerson, R, 1989 *Quality of Life in Britain's Intermediate Cities* Glasgow: Glasgow Quality of Life Group **32** Schor, JB 1995 Can the North stop consumption growth? Escaping the cycle of work and spend. In Bhaskar, V and Glyn, A (eds) *The North, the South and the Environment* London: Earthscan **33** Cited in Ghazi, P and Jones, J 1996 O, to be a Mexican *New Statesman* 6 September **34** Oswald, A 1996 GDP can't make you happy *New Economy* 3(1) pp15–19 **35** Wilkinson, MJ 1996 Our At-Risk Society: Exclusion as a threat to health and democracy *Journal of Contemporary Health* 4, pp62–4 **36** Jacobs, M 1996 *The Politics of the Real World* London: Earthscan **37** *Ibid.* **38** Home Office, 1996 Home Office Statistical Bulletin 19/1996 *British Crime Survey, 1996* London: Home Office

# NOTES TO PART 1 CONCLUSION

**1** Jacobs, M 1996. *The Politics of the Real World* London: Earthscan p11 **2** Carley, M and Spapens, P 1997 *Fair Shares: Sustainable Living and Global Equity in the 21st Century* London: Earthscan **3** UN Environment Programme 1997 *Global Environmental Outlook* 1 Nairobi: UNEP

# NOTES TO CHAPTER 4

**1** We use a methodology developed by Germany's prestigious Wuppertal Institute for Friends of the Earth Europe. See Spangenberg, J (ed) 1995 *Towards Sustainable Europe* London: Friends of the Earth Europe; Wuppertal Institute, 1995 *Sustainable Europe: The Handbook* Report for FOE Europe, Brussels. For those interested in such things, more detail on the methodology set out in this chapter, and its application to the specific resources can be found on Friends of the Earth's internet site: http://www.foe.co.uk/ **2** HM Treasury, 1997 *http://www.hm-treasury.gov.uk/pub/html/econbf/ eb08/eb2.html* **3** Desai, P (ed) 1996 *Local Paper – waste paper and non-wood fibres for a sustainable paper cycle in the south east* London: Bioregional Development Group **4** Our approach differs in this respect from others based, for example, on 'net primary productivity' (Wackernagel, M and Rees, W 1996 *Our Ecological Footprint* Gabriola Island BC: New Society), solar energy (Odum, HT and Odum, EC (eds) 1983 *Energy analysis overview of nations* Laxenburg, Austria: International Institute for Applied Systems Analysis; Pillet, G 1991 *Towards an inquiry into the carrying capacity of nations* Report to the Coordinator for International Refugee Policy, Federal Department of Foreign Affairs, Berne) or material flows (the 'ecological rucksack' developed by the Wuppertal Institute) **5** For a more detailed analysis of the implications of this, see CAG Consultants, 1995 *Sustainability in Decisions* Report to Scottish Natural Heritage, Edinburgh, which discusses how this can be applied to resources which are critical at different spatial scales **6** Although up to a billion people depend on fish for their only protein, only about 2 per cent of global total food needs are met from fish and other seafood. World Resources Institute, 1994 *World Resources 1994–95: A Guide to the Global Environment* Oxford: Oxford University Press **7** GLASOD cited in World Resources Institute 1992 *World Resources 1992–93: A Guide to the Global Environment* Oxford: Oxford University Press, pp116–17 **8** Rice, T (ed) 1995 *Out of the Woods* London: Friends of the Earth **9** World Resources Institute 1994 *World Resources 1994–95: A Guide to the Global Environment* Oxford: Oxford University Press **10** Jones, P 1995 *The UK Environmental Economy – Do we Value it or Weigh it?* Working Paper. High Wycombe: Biffa Waste Services **11** *Ibid.* **12** World Resources Institute 1994 *World Resources 1994–95: A Guide to the Global Environment* Oxford: Oxford University Press **13** Jones, P 1995 *The UK Environmental Economy – Do We Value it or Weigh it?* Working Paper. High Wycombe: Biffa Waste Services **14** The Dutch pioneers of 'eco-space' define environmental space as the space 'formed by all feasible combinations of environmental services or resource use that represent steady states in terms of levels of environmental quality and stocks of renewable resources'. Opschoor, JB and Weterings, R 1994 Environmental utilisation space: an introduction *Milieu Tijdschrift voor Milieukunde* 9 (5), pp198–205 **15** Ayres, R and Simonis, U 1994 *Industrial Metabolism* Tokyo: United Nations University **16** Jacobs, M 1990 *The Green Economy* London: Pluto **17** A proxy for this approach can be to define sustainability in terms of proven reserves for a constant period at projected rates of use. Weterings and Opschoor attempt this. But the results are still no better than the poor data on reserves on which they rely. To estimate the rate of use which maintains proven reserves is difficult, not least because the rate of exploration activity increases as the rate of extraction increases. And there would be a risk that this criterion may be met by exploiting more environmentally damaging mineral reserves. Weterings, RAPM and Opschoor, JB 1992 *The ecocapacity as a challenge to technological development* Rijswijk: Advisory Council for Research on Nature and Environment **18** Her Majesty's Government 1994 *Sustainable Development: the UK Strategy* London: HMSO **19** Weterings and Opschoor (1992 *Op cit.*) term these 'extension strategies' – extending the boundaries of our environmental space, in contrast to the more significant 'efficiency strategies' with which we use it more efficiently. These latter approaches deliver what they term elsewhere (Opschoor, JB and Weterings, R 1994 *Op cit.*) a '*virtual expansion*' of environmental space **20** For example, we import 380,000 tonnes more cars than we export, a net import of 250,000 tonnes of steel. The steel in these cars is not recorded as 'consumed' in the UK, but in Spain or Germany, as is the energy used to make that steel and the carbon dioxide emissions resulting from its generation (*Eurostat*, 1996). David Pearce, the environmental economist, has also highlighted the problem of 'importing sustainability'. He defines sustainability in terms of maintaining overall capital stocks, including natural capital. A country can appear sustainable in such terms if the environmental capital degraded to provide for current consumption is actually somewhere else in the world. Pearce, D (ed) 1991 *Blueprint 2, Greening the World Economy* London: Earthscan **21** John Hille has attempted to relate typical expenditure patterns in Norway to consumption of environmental resources. His estimates suggest that the damage associated with each Norwegian Crown of spending is widely different depending on the type and source of goods. Hille, J 1995 *Sustainable Norway – Probing the Limits and Equity of Environmental Space* Oslo: The Norwegian Forum for Environment and Development **22** Office for National Statistics, 1996 *Overseas travel and tourism* ONS (96) 87 London: ONS **23** Badger, A, Barnett, P, Corbyn, L and Keefe, J (eds), 1996 *Trading Places: Tourism as Trade* London: Tourism Concern **24** UN Population Division, 1994 *World Population 1994* Department for Economic and Social Information and Policy Analysis, Geneva: UN **25** Ehrlich, P and Holdren, J 1971 Impact of Population Growth *Science* 171 pp1212–17; Ehrlich, P and Ehrlich, A 1990 *The population explosion* New York: Touchstone. There are several variants of this basic equation which use different terms. Weterings and Opschoor (1992 *Op cit.*) refer to wealth (W) rather than affluence and metabolism (M) rather than technological efficiency. The environmental economists, Michael Jacobs and Paul Ekins, use the term consumption (C) rather than wealth or affluence. Jacobs, M and Ekins, P 1995 Environmental sustainability and the growth of GDP. In Bhaskar, V and Glyn A (eds) *The North, the South and the Environment* London: Earthscan. We also prefer to refer to consumption, as it is arguable whether impact is directly related to any real measure of wealth, rather than to material consumption **26** Jacobs, M and Ekins, P 1995 *Op cit.* **27** *Ibid.* **28** Weterings, RAPM and Opschoor, JB 1992 *The ecocapacity as a challenge to technological development* Rijswijk: Advisory Council for Research on Nature and Environment. Taking a similar approach, a World Bank paper has calculated that a 46-fold improvement in technological efficiency is needed to bring developing countries up to current Western per capita incomes without increasing resource consumption and environmental emissions. Goodland, R and Daly, H 1993 Why Northern Income Growth is not the Solution to Southern Poverty *Environment Department Divisional Working Paper no 1993–43* Washington DC: World Bank **29** Oxfam, 1995 *Reproductive Rights and Population Issues* Oxford: Oxfam **30** Other reports have set targets for 2010, based on a projected world population for that year – in the case of work by the Wuppertal Institute, 7 billion. Spangenberg, J (ed), 1995 *Towards Sustainable Europe* London: Friends of the Earth Europe; Wuppertal Institute 1995 *Sustainable Europe: The Handbook* Report for FOE Europe, Brussels **31** See, for example, Factor Ten Club, 1994 *The Carnoules Declaration* Wuppertal: Factor Ten Club **32** Jackson, T 1996 *Material Concerns: Pollution, Profit and the Quality of Life* London: Routledge **33** Karl-Henrik Robert and his co-promoters of the Natural Step also advocate a back-casting approach. They cite Swedish research that suggests it is a superior planning tool in comparison with conventional forecasting, and especially useful when dealing with complex problems which require major change, and where dominant trends are part of the problem, but the scope is wide enough and the time horizon long enough to leave considerable room for deliberate choice. Robert, KH, Daly, H, Hawken, P and Holmberg, J 1995 Methodology. In Greyson, J (ed) *The Natural Step 1995: a collection of articles* Bristol: Natural Step **34** Where consumption has changed significantly since 1990, targets based on the more up-to-date figures will also be presented. However it is important to use 1990 as a base year so that our figures are comparable with those derived for other countries, and so that we can be reasonably confident that the base data will not be subject to further revisions **35** Kamark, A 1983 *Economics and the Real World* Oxford, Blackwell **36** Opschoor, JB and Weterings, R 1994 Environmental utilisation space: an introduction *Milieu Tijdschrift voor Milieukunde* 9(5)

# NOTES TO CHAPTER 5

**1** IPCC 1996 *Climate Change 1995. The Science of Climate Change. Contribution of Working Group I to the Second Assessment Report of the Intergovernmental Panel on Climate Change* Cambridge: Cambridge University Press **2** *Ibid.*; US EPA 1990 *Policy Options for Stabilising Global Climate* Washington DC: EPA. The environmental space methodology focuses on carbon dioxide, but all the scenarios considered assume that at least comparable reductions are made in other greenhouse gases. This is not unrealistic. Indeed in the climate negotiations some countries have taken the position that a 'basket' of gases be used, because the same average reductions would be easier to achieve because their emissions of other gases are falling anyway **3** Department of the Environment 1996 *Review of the Potential Effects of Climate Change in the UK* London, HMSO **4** *Ibid.* **5** Neale, G 1996 Global warming hits house insurance: costs quadruple as weather damage worsens *Sunday Telegraph* 13

October **6** The protected areas covered by this study were principally those listed by the IUCN as category IV or V and wetland sites designated under the Ramsar Convention, rather than all Sites of Special Scientific Interest **7** Tickle, A, Fergusson, M and Drucker, G 1995 *Acid Rain and Nature Conservation in Europe* Gland: WorldWide Fund for Nature. Examples of sites under threat include a number of Biosphere Reserves such as the blanket bogs of Moor House and Silver Flowe, a site with a unique series of seven different mire types **8** Pope, C, Thun, M, Namboodiri, M, Dokery, D, Evans, J, Speizer, F and Heath, C 1995 Particulate air pollution as predictor of mortality in a prospective study of US adults *American Journal of Respiratory and Critical Care Medicine* 151, pp669–74. This research was based on an epidemiological study of 500,000 people in over 150 US cities **9** ECOTEC 1994 *An evaluation of the benefits of reduced sulphur dioxide emissions* London: Department of the Environment **10** Pearce, D and Crowards, T 1995 *Letter to Friends of the Earth* 17 March **11** Bullock, S 1995 *Prescription for Change* London: Friends of the Earth. A standard of 50 $\mu$gm$^{-3}$ for PM10s is too lax to protect public health anyway **12** Greyson, J (ed) *The Natural Step 1995: a collection of articles* Bristol: The Natural Step **13** Fleahy, B 1995 *The decline of the age of oil* London: Pluto Press; Gever, J, Kaufman, R, Skole, D and Vorosmarty, C 1987 *Beyond Oil: The threat to food and fuel in the coming decades* Cambridge, Massachusetts: Ballinger. Fleahy notes that since 1980 there have been almost no major oil field discoveries, despite great technological sophistication. He suggests that globally we are rapidly reaching the oil production peak, and with high and low estimates of reserves, extensions to reserves and new field discoveries, estimates that the peak production year will be between 2003 and 2012 **14** US Coastguard data cited in Marine Oil Spills and Remediation of the Exxon Valdez Oil Spill *Http://bordeaux.uwaterloo.ca/biol447/valdez.html* **15** Deere-Jones, T 1996 *Lost Treasures: the long-term environmental impacts of the Sea Empress oil spill* London: FOE **16** Suggestions for Change 1996 *Position paper of Nigerian and Western Groups working on Shell's activities in Nigeria* Environment Rights Action and Milieudefensie; Bola Olowo 1995 The Shell Factor *West Africa* 27 November – 3 December 1995; Greenpeace International 1994 *Shell-shocked: The environmental and social costs of living with Shell in Nigeria* Amsterdam: Greenpeace **17** World Energy Council 1995 *Global energy perspectives to 2050* London: World Energy Council **18** DTI and the Scottish Office 1995 *The Prospects for Nuclear Power in the UK. The conclusions of the Government's Nuclear Review* London: HMSO, pp29–30 **19** Western, R 1994 *Breach of promise – The public perception of nuclear power* London: Friends of the Earth **20** *Nuclear Engineering International* 1996 Chernobyl's legacy, July **21** *Nucleonics Week* 1990 Tanguy says nuclear safety depends on changes in people, structures 22 February **22** Barnes, M 1990 *The Hinkley Point Public Inquiries Report to the Secretaries of State for Energy and the Environment* Vol 1. London: HMSO **23** Knight, R 1993 *International Commission on Radiological Protection, ICRP 60 and the Uranium Mining Industry* 1993 Uranium Institute Symposium London: Uranium Institute **24** British Government Panel on Sustainable Development 1996 *Second Report* London: Department of the Environment, p18 **25** OECD 1996 *Future Financial Liabilities of Nuclear Activities* Paris: OECD **26** IPCC Working Group 1 1994 *Climate Change 1994. Radiative Forcing of Climate Change and An Evaluation of the IPCC IS92 Emission Scenarios* Cambridge: Cambridge University Press **27** IPCC Working Group 3 1992 *Climate Change. The IPCC Response Strategies* Washington: Island Press; Karas, JHW 1993 *Back from the Brink. Greenhouse Gas Targets for a Sustainable World* London: Friends of the Earth; Krause, F (ed) 1993 *Energy Policy in the Greenhouse* International Project for Sustainable Energy Paths (IPSEP), study for the Dutch Ministry of Housing, Physical Planning and the Environment **28** The environmental constraint for carbon dioxide emissions is based on the understanding that climate change greater than 0.1°C per decade is unacceptable. With a precautionary interpretation – taking account of the high climatic sensitivity scenario – stabilisation at 350–400 ppmv is needed to meet this condition. Assuming no net emissions from changes in land use and the 'most likely' IPCC scenarios for the amount of the carbon budget to 2100 that will have been used up by 2050, we can estimate that global cuts of 50–75 per cent are required. A 50 per cent cut over 1990 levels implies global emissions of 11.1 gigatonnes of $CO_2$, while a 75 per cent cut implies 5.55 gigatonnes of $CO_2$. This gives per capita figures lower than the 1.7 t-$CO_2$ per capita suggested by the Wuppertal Institute, which was based on an optimistic forecast of global population of 7 billion. To obtain UK targets we convert these global per capita figures into a UK total Environmental Space available, by multiplying them by the forecast UK population. This gives a range of 55.6–83.7 Mt-$CO_2$ for the UK in 2050, with a central estimate of 67.3 Mt-$CO_2$ or a reduction of 85–90 per cent, with a central estimate of 88 per cent **29** World Energy Council and International Institute of Applied Systems Analysis 1995 *Global Energy Perspectives to 2050 and Beyond* London: World Energy

Council. Even this might be an underestimate as modelled temperature rises are still faster than may be tolerable **30** Alcamo, J and Kreileman, E 1996 Emissions scenarios and global climate protection *Global Environmental Change – paper 156* Pergamon Press **31** The lower figure assumes low growth in non-Annex 1 countries' emissions, while the higher figure is based on high growth assumptions. The other assumptions of the modelling are based on the same IPCC scenario we have used, and also lead to a 50 per cent or greater cut in global emissions by 2050 **32** European Environment Agency 1996 *Press release 6 September* EEA: Current EU measures insufficient to prevent further increase of $CO_2$ emissions after the year 2000. Copenhagen: EEA **33** ENDS Report 251 1995 Windfall $CO_2$ savings underpin short-term strategy on climate change. The 1990 figure was 576 Mt-$CO_2$ or 10.0 t-$CO_2$ per capita **34** Based on data from Electricity Association 1996 *Information Sheet 1. Generation projects since privatisation* London: Electricity Association. There is already a further 16,000 MW of gas-fired plant in the development pipeline **35** Weightman, F 1994 *Renewable Energy and NFFO3* London: Friends of the Earth. In 1993–94 the levy raised £1,234 million, of which 94 per cent went to the nuclear industry **36** Jackson, T 1993 *Renewable energy – prospects for implementation* Oxford: Stockholm Environment Institute and Butterworth-Heinemann; Independent Commission on Population and Quality of Life 1996 *Caring for the Future* Oxford: Oxford University Press **37** Erlandson, D, Few, J and Kripke, G 1995 *Dirty Little Secrets* Washington DC: Friends of the Earth USA; Kasterine, A and Page, I 1994 *Cutting Corners: The IFC and Sustainable Development* Friends of the Earth International: Amsterdam; Inland Revenue 1996 *Inland Revenue Statistics 1996* London, HMSO **38** Millais, C 1996 Greenpeace solutions campaigns – closing the implementation gap *ECOS* 17(2) pp50–8 **39** Energy Advisory Associates 1996 *Energy Showcase Project – Update, 12 March* Leominster: EAA **40** Worldwatch Institute 1996 *Vital signs 1996* New York: WorldWatch Institute **41** Jackson, T 1996 *Material Concerns: Pollution, Profit and the Quality of Life* London: Routledge **42** Jackson, T 1997 *Power in Balance* London: Friends of the Earth **43** Department of the Environment 1996 *Indicators of Sustainable Development for the United Kingdom* London: HMSO **44** Her Majesty's Government 1990 *This Common Inheritance* London: HMSO; Her Majesty's Government 1994 *Sustainable Development: The UK Strategy* London: HMSO **45** Barker, T 1993 Is green growth possible? *New Economy* 1, pp20–25; Jackson, T 1997 *Power in Balance* London: Friends of the Earth **46** Renewable Energy Advisory Group 1992 *Report to the President of the Board of Trade* Department of Trade and Industry, November **47** Karas, JHW, Roberts, S and Weir, F 1993 *Friends of the Earth Response to the Department of Environment's Discussion Document on Climate Change: Our National Programme for $CO_2$ Emissions* London: Friends of the Earth; Jackson, T 1992 *Efficiency without tears: no-regrets policy to combat climate change* London: Friends of the Earth **48** *New York Times* 1993 Generate Nega-watts says fossil fuel foe 20 April, pB8 **49** *Ibid.* **50** Kidman, T 1996 ESCOs in the competitive energy market *Conference paper at Liberalisation of Gas and Electricity Markets* Newcastle: Energy Action Grants Agency **51** Independent Commission on Population and Quality of Life 1996 *Caring for the Future* Oxford: Oxford University Press. The Independent Commission on Population and Quality of Life recognises this renewable energy research as meriting an international 'Manhattan project' with a network of research laboratories and scientists **52** Hydro-power, although of more limited scope, currently accounts for around three-quarters of UK renewable capacity, most of it in Scotland. Department of Trade and Industry 1996 *Digest of UK Energy Statistics 1996* London: HMSO. Non-hydro renewable electricity generation = 2,365 GWh. **53** The 70.3 mtoe divides as follows: 36.2 mtoe coal, 3.6 oil, 9.1 gas, 20 nuclear, 0.4 renewable **54** Department of Trade and Industry 1995 *Digest of UK energy statistics 1995* London: HMSO **55** British Wind Energy Association 1996 *Switch on to wind power* London: BWEA **56** House of Commons Energy Committee 1992 *Fourth Report, Session 1991–92, Renewable Energy* London: HMSO **57** Flood, M 1991 *Energy Without End* London: Friends of the Earth **58** Gipe, P 1995 *Wind energy comes of age* London: Wiley **59** *Wind direction* XV (3), p5 **60** *Global Environmental Change Reporter* 1996 Denmark unveils new energy plan VIII(8) 26 April **61** According to the BWEA, as of March 1997 there is 260 MW of installed capacity in the UK. At an average load factor of 0.33 this is equivalent to 0.75 TWh, of a total electricity consumption of 300 TWh **62** Flood, M 1991 *Energy Without End* London: Friends of the Earth **63** Department of Trade and Industry 1994 *New and renewable energy: future prospects in the UK. Energy Paper 62* London: HMSO **64** The Government's advisors (Renewable Energy Advisory Group 1992 Report to the President of the Board of Trade Department of Trade and Industry, November) are remarkably cautious about the potential for renewable energy. They say that renewables could meet 20 per cent of the current UK electricity demand by 2050. This is equivalent to 57 TWh/year. But these conservative estimates are based on the current unhelpful policy environment outlined above and 'business as usual' expections of changes in market prices for energy and energy technologies **65** British Wind Energy Association 1996 *Wind energy. Power for a sustainable future* London: BWEA **66** There is a Dartmoor home situated about one kilometre from the electricity distribution network, with all modern conveniences powered by the wind. Before 1992 a diesel generator was used to supply electricity. However this was not satisfactory all year round and the owner installed a 2.2 kW wind turbine near the house. This charges two banks of batteries which provide the house with a 240 V AC supply. The turbine cost £5,000 and it supplies sufficient electricity for lighting, domestic appliances and workshop tools: it also heats some of the water required for domestic heating **67** Accounting for load factors, a 1 MW machine operating in a wind farm on a site with an annual mean wind speed of 7.5 ms–1 at 25 m above ground level should have a net energy output of around 2500 MWh/year. This is about 10 per cent less than that at isolated machines due to clustering effects and electricity transmission losses (based on ETSU 1994 *An assessment of renewable energy for the UK* London: HMSO). From this figure, to provide 55 TWh thus requires 55 x 1 million ÷ 250 = 22,000 1 MW turbines: ie 22,000 MW of installed capacity **68** The $CO_2$ saving from displacing fossil energy is 750–1000 g/kWh – UK electricity on average generates 0.72 kg $CO_2$/kWh, and electricity from coal 1.00 kg $CO_2$/kWh (in Association of Environment Conscious Builders 1995 *Greener building* Coaley: Green Building Press) **69** 1994 figures. The UK used 70.8 mtoe (= 823 TWh) (of which 36.2 mtoe was coal) to generate 300 TWh of electricity. This is a factor of 2.74. Assuming that 2.74 TWh of coal is needed to generate 1TWh of electricity, to generate 55 TWh of electricity from coal needs 55 x 2.74 TWh of coal, ie 151 TWh. This is equivalent to 13 mtoe coal. One tonne of oil generates 45.9 GJ. One tonne of coal to a power station generates 24.8 GJ. The factor here is 1.85. So generating this 55 TWh of electricity from coal requires 13 x 1.85 = 24.1 million tonnes of coal **70** Jenkins, T and McLaren, D 1994 *Working Future?* London: Friends of the Earth **71** Walker, J 1988 A CEGB perspective on offshore wind power *Meeting of the Royal Aeronautical Society: An offshore wind mega-project* London, 29 March **72** British Wind Energy Association 1996 *Policy Statement* October 1996. London: BWEA **73** Anne Marie Simon Planning and Research 1996 *A summary of research conducted into attitudes to wind power from 1990–1996* London, BWEA. Delabole Wind Farm, in North Cornwall, illustrates successful handling of such issues. The first NFFO wind farm to be completed, it consists of ten small turbines with a total rated capacity of 4 MW. The Farm is sited on agricultural land. Land occupied by the turbines is minimal as they are located in the existing, wide Cornish hedges. Farming continues uninterrupted with no measurable loss of agricultural production. A public attitude survey conducted before the windfarm showed that only 17 per cent approved of the concept of a wind farm, 32 per cent disapproved and 51 per cent were not sure. Another similar survey conducted six months after the wind farm had begun operating showed that this had changed to 85 per cent approved, four per cent disapproved and 11 per cent not sure **74** Friends of the Earth 1995 *Planning for wind power* London: FOE **75** 23,649,000/2 (50 per cent) = 11824500. $CO_2$ emissions = 0.35t–1.3 t per year. Therefore a saving of 4.1Mt–15Mt **76** ENDS Report 260 1996 Strategic alliances for environmental solutions – the Greenpeace recipe for business success, pp19–22 **77** Flood, M 1991 *Energy Without End* London: Friends of the Earth **78** Bunting, M 1990 Cited in McLaren, D 1993 Compact or dispersed: dilution is no solution *Built Environment* 18(4) pp268–84 **79** Fuentes, M, Dichler, A and Roaf, S 1996 The Oxford Solar House *World Renewable Energy Congress* Denver, 1996 **80** *New Scientist* 1996 Heat on a hot, thin roof 13 July **81** Flood, M 1991 *Energy Without End* London: Friends of the Earth **82** *Biomass Farmer and User* 1996 Green Energy 3 August **83** Parliamentary Renewable and Sustainable Energy Group 1996 *MORI Opinion Poll on Public Support for Green Energy* London: PRASEG **84** The difference is mainly due to the fact that on average, generating plant runs well below capacity **85** Madrid Summit, May 1994, cited by Jackson, T 1997 *Power in Balance* London: Friends of the Earth **86** ETSU 1994 *An assessment of renewable energy for the UK. ETSU report 82* London: HMSO **87** Labour Party 1994 *In Trust for Tomorrow* London: The Labour Party **88** Association of Environment Conscious Builders 1995 *Greener Building* Coaley: Green Building Press. $CO_2$ emissions estimates depend on the assumed conversion factors for different fuels used in the home. Electricity generates around 1 Mt-$CO_2$ for each TWh/year, whilst fuels used directly in the home are generally less carbon-intensive **89** This figure assumes that electricity is generated from coal. The estimates of cost-effectiveness are based on an 8 per cent discount rate and capital costs at the lower end of the ranges identified **90** The Scottish Energy Study has estimated that, in Scotland, a 50 per cent reduction in domestic energy consumption is cost effective at 1992 prices. AHS Emstar 1993 *Scottish Energy Study* Edinburgh: Scottish Office **91** Cited in *Ibid.* **92** Building Research Establishment 1995 *Information paper, IP 15/95, Potential carbon emission savings from energy efficiency in housing* Garston: BRE **93** At best, such as the new capacity at Didcot, coal reaches around 42 per cent efficiency **94** Combined Heat and Power Association 1996 *Pers comm*, October **95** Based on Association of Environment Conscious Builders, 1995 *Greener Building* Coaley: Green Building Press; Department of Trade and Industry 1995 *The energy report* London: DTI; and Department of the Environment 1996 *Digest of Environmental Statistics* London, HMSO; Figures for 1994 **96** Cited in Friends of the Earth Scotland 1996 *Towards a Sustainable Scotland* Edinburgh: FOE Scotland **97** *Ethical Consumer* 1995 Issue 34, February/March **98** *ENDS Report* 234 1994 Appliance producers hamper EC plans for efficiency standards, pp24–5. Operating costs of fridges surveyed ranging from £10 to £29 per year. Even amongst modern hydrocarbon fridges which do not use CFCs or HFCs there is variation in energy efficiencies. For example the Liebherr KT 1580 model, the second most efficient fridge in the sample, uses 28 per cent less energy than the same sized Siemens KT15RS. But voluntary European ecolabelling measures to improve energy efficiency of fridges have not delivered the scale of improvements possible. Overall, the SAVE programme is only anticipated to deliver about half of its target 20 per cent improvement in energy efficiency. The Candy Aquaviva 1000 uses three times as much energy as the Bosch WFF 2000 for example. The best machines also save water and are more durable and reliable. European Commission 1994 *The SAVE Programme: Overview and Future* Florence, October, 1994; *http://eff.nutek.se/SAVE/ SAVE.html*; Centre for Alternative Technology 1996 *Come Clean: A Guide to Green Washing Machines* Machynlleth: Centre for Alternative Technology **99** Department of the Environment 1993 *Helping The Earth Begins At Home* London: HMSO **100** Flood, M 1991 *Energy Without End* London: Friends of the Earth **101** See for example Energy Efficiency Office, Case studies 177,195, 239 and 249. London: Department of the Environment. For example, renovating a 1940s Manchester housing estate gave a 70 per cent saving in $CO_2$ emissions and heating costs, saving the householders £361 each, every year. The measures pay for themselves in 12 years **102** Department of the Environment and Department of Health 1996 *National Environmental Health Action Plan* London, HMSO **103** Boardman, B 1991 *Fuel Poverty: From Cold Homes to Affordable Warmth* London: Belhaven Press; and Boardman, B 1995 *Personal Communication to Friends of the Earth* 31 May **104** Boardman, B 1990 *Warm homes: Cool planet* London: Friends of the Earth, Neighbourhood Energy Action, Heatwise Glasgow and National Right to Fuel Campaign **105** Jenkins, T and McLaren, D 1994 *Working Future?* London: Friends of the Earth **106** Bullock, S 1995 *Presecription for Change* London: Friends of the Earth **107** Boardman, B 1990 *Op cit.* Similar findings have been made in studies in Scotland. The Scottish Energy Study suggested a £2.5 billion programme could create 40,000 job years. AHS Emstar, 1993 *Scottish Energy Study* Edinburgh: Scottish Office **108** Smith, P and Pitts, A 1993 *Buildings and the Environment. A Study for the National Audit Office* University of Sheffield: School of Architectural Studies **109** *Ibid.* **110** The Energy Showcase project aimed to design a house which uses only 10 per cent as much energy as a normal new house, and obtains 85 per cent of that energy from the sun, so as to achieve an overall saving on fossil fuel consumption of 98 per cent in comparison with the average new home in the UK today. It also sought to do this in a way which is affordable and cost effective. The house, now under construction, will feature: 'super glazing'; 10 m$^2$ of solar collectors; 15 m$^2$ of photo-voltaics on the south-facing roof; with surpluses and deficits of electricity exchanged with the national grid; thermal insulation standards at three to four times normal UK levels; construction in durable and low maintenance materials; energy-efficient lighting and appliances; and heat recovered from waste hot water. Energy Advisory Associates 1994 *The Energy Showcase.* Leominster: Energy Advisory Associates **111** Energy Advisory Associates 1994 *A superinsulated house in 'traditional' masonry construction* Leominster: Energy Advisory Associates **112** Technological advances will make it increasingly easy to achieve such savings. For example, in 1991, the Lawrence Berkeley Laboratory in the States found that super-efficient windows could gain more winter heat than they lost in any US climate, even facing north. These windows are two polyester coated plates of glass with a layer of krypton gas between them. They let in more light and are four times as efficient as triple glazing. *Fine Homebuilding* Annual Issue on Houses, Spring 1991, no 66, USA **113** Rudlin, D and Falk, N 1995 *Future Influences on Housing. Joseph Rowntree Foundation Housing Summary 8* York: Joseph Rowntree Foundation **114** Based on data on energy/GDP ratios from Department of the Environment 1995 *Digest of Environmental Statistics* London: HMSO; and GDP projections from HM Treasury Press Office 1996 *Faxed information and figures* 1 October 1996 **115** It can be estimated that between 2010 and 2050 industrial energy use per unit GDP might not fall by much more than a factor of two. GDP growth at 2 per cent a year would therefore cancel any potential further energy savings **116** For example, the fourth largest Dutch bank had their new headquarters built in 1987. It integrated the most up to date innovations in building design, ventilation, super-efficient glazing and other passive solar technologies. This added US$700,000 to construction costs (for a building for 2400 employees), but as there is no need for air conditioning systems, it saved US$2.4 million a year in reduced energy. Browning, W 1992 Environment – NMB Bank Headquarters. The impressive performance of a green building *Urban Land* June, USA **117** Cited in London Research Centre undated *London Energy Study information leaflet* London: LRC **118** Association for Environment Conscious Building 1995 *Greener Building* Coaley: Green Building Press. A professor of aeronautics is working with the construction consultants Ove Arup looking at ways to use wind on the roofs of buildings to produce electricity and replace air conditioning, with roof funnels and turbines. Professor Graham says: *If you look at the buildings in the Middle East that are a couple of thousand years old you find they nearly all have chimneys to circulate air. Lately, we've gone for direct, immediate control, such as putting fans in a warm area or pumping cool air into offices. But now there is a lot of interest in a more 'green' way of cooling buildings because modern methods use vast amounts of electricity* Hargrave, S 1996 The bible on 'green' air conditioning *The Sunday Times* 4 August **119** Camargue 1996 *The Groundwork ecocentre – The UK's greenest office building* Cheltenham: Camargue **120** The growth in households by 2010 is from 24 m to 27.64. This is an increase of 15 per cent. So assuming a BRE style saving on all houses, domestic $CO_2$ is 150 x 1.15 x 0.58 = 100. This is therefore a saving of 50 $Mt$-$CO_2$. This is a conservative estimate as the additional households will be smaller, and the new properties should meet higher standards. By 2050 we could assume that half of the housing stock has been redeveloped or refurbished to best practice standards, and that the total size of the housing stock has increased to around 30 million homes. The 8 million homes of those in fuel poverty would be included in this figure for redevelopment or refurbishment, so we can assume that the rest of the stock reaches the standards suggested for the average energy efficiency in 2010. Current emissions are 6.25 t per household (150 mt, 24 m h-holds). In 2050, there would be 15 m households at 58 per cent of this (BRE level) or 3.625 t /h-hold, and 15 m households at best practice level, say 20 per cent of current (equivalent to 'lower watts' house) or 1.25 t/h-hold. Total emissions would be 73.2 Mt (achieving an overall saving of 76.8 Mt) **121** Department of the Environment 1996 *Digest of Environmental Statistics* London: HMSO **122** Wolmar, C 1997 *Unlocking the Gridlock* London: Friends of the Earth **123** Air travel causes by far the highest $CO_2$ emissions per person-mile of any mode of transport, and although starting from a lower base, its emissions are growing even faster than those from road traffic **124** Department of the Environment 1996 *Op cit.* **125** Tony May, at the Institute for Transport Studies in Leeds, has analysed the increases in travel. Between 1965 and 1985 the total number of person kilometres of travel increased by 61 per cent, but car kilometres rose by 101 per cent, reflecting a substantial shift to car-use. The 61 per cent increase in person kilometres was accounted for almost entirely by longer journeys (35 per cent), and more journeys (22 per cent). Just four per cent of the increase in travel was accounted for by an increase in the number of people undertaking journeys. May, T 1992 Future lifestyles: transport *Paper to Royal Town Planning Institute conference* Birmingham, 9–11 June **126** *ENDS Report* 259 1996 Greenpeace's fuel efficient car poses challenge to vehicle industry, pp26–7 **127** *Ibid.* **128** Even Audi's aluminium car effectively follows this pattern. Although making the bodyshell out of aluminium has knock-on effects in weight reduction – a lighter shell allows lighter drive systems and transmission, lighter suspension systems and a smaller fuel tank – the car is a prestige model and only 13 per cent more fuel efficient than a conventional car – before accounting for the extra energy used in making it from aluminium **129** Royal Commission on Environmental Pollution 1994 *Eighteenth Report, Transport and the Environment* London: HMSO. Specific targets have recently been suggested by the European Commission and the Council of Environment Ministers which are equivalent to improvements of around one-third, but only through voluntary agreements – which are open to delay and abuse. *Environment Business* 1996 Ministers target road traffic pollution and global warming, 3 July; Jenkins, T 1995 *A Superficial Attraction: The Voluntary Approach and Sustainable Development* London, Friends of the Earth **130** Holman, C 1991 *Transport and Climate Change: Cutting carbon dioxide emissions from cars* London: Friends of the Earth **131** Department of Transport 1994 *Bus and coach statistics Great Britain 1992/3* London: HMSO. A study of deregulation carried out for the Association for Metropolitan Authorities concluded that: 'On the central test of the number of people travelling by bus, the picture across metropolitan areas as a whole was one of failure – patronage had fallen by more than would have been expected without deregulation': Association of Metropolitan Authorities, 1992. *Bus Deregulation – Five Years On* London: AMA **132** The card was first issued in 1984 for a cost of 38 DM/month (the previous monthly pass cost 50 DM). In 1991 this card was replaced with a similar one giving even more incentives. International Council for Local Environmental Initiatives undated Project Summary Series Project Summary #60 Good Practice Guide *http://www.iclei.org/leicomm/lei-060.htm* **133** International Council for Local Environmental Initiatives undated Project Summary Series #56 Transport, Good Practice Guide *http://www.iclei.org/leicomm/lei-056.htm* **134** Metrolink 2000 1995 *Parliamentary Briefing, Number 1* Manchester: Greater Manchester Passenger Transport Authority; Greater Manchester Passenger Transport Authority 1997 *Personal Communication* 25 March. Trams run from early in the morning to late at night, seven days a week with a tram every six minutes. They operate at 80 km/h along former railway lines and at a maximum of 48 km/h on the street **135** 2,500,000 * 0.4 = 1 million tonnes of $CO_2$. Surveys show particularly large transfers from car to Metrolink for journeys between destinations close to the Metrolink stations. In its prime target area – people living within 2 km of the line – between 14 and 50 per cent of car trips to destinations served by Metrolink have switched to the tram. For each trip where the car is not used there is an estimated reduction of 0.2 kg of $CO_2$ per kilometre. Friends of the Earth 1993 *Take the Heat off the Planet* London: FOE **136** Davies, D 1996 *At the crossroads: investing in sustainable transport* London: Council for the Protection of Rural England. Fifty-four per cent of Transport Policy and Programme bids by local authorities for road schemes were successful in 1996/97, compared with 16 per cent for public transport initiatives. Also, only 9 per cent of safety schemes are designed primarily to assist vulnerable road users – cyclists and pedestrians – though 37 per cent of the people who die on the roads are cyclists and pedestrians **137** West Yorkshire Friends of the Earth 1996 *Stemming the Tide* Leeds: FOE **138** Environmental and Transport Planning 1994 *Luneburg: The making of a car-free town centre* Brighton, ETP **139** Department of Transport 1996 *National Cycling Strategy* London, HMSO **140** Assuming that total trip numbers will remain stable, which has been the case in the last decade or so, then this requires around 200 trips to be diverted from car to bike by 2050. Also assuming that only trips under 10 miles in length will be shifted, this will equate to a reduction in car mileage of just over 750 miles per person, or 12.6 Mt-$CO_2$ in total. Achieving a 10 per cent shift by 2010 would save approximately 5.6 Mt-$CO_2$ **141** British Medical Association 1992 *Cycling: towards health and safety* Oxford: Oxford University Press. Mayer Hillman, a Senior Fellow at the Policy Studies Institute, has calculated the scale of this benefit and concluded that 'The benefits gained from regular cycling we estimate to outweigh the loss of life in cycling fatalities by a factor of around 20 to 1'. Hillman, M 1992 Cycling and the promotion of health. PTRC 20th Summer Annual Meeting *Environmental issues: Proceedings of Seminar B* London: PTRC **142** Jenkins, T 1997 *Less Traffic, More Jobs* London, Friends of the Earth **143** Confederation of British Industry 1995. *Moving forward: a business strategy for transport* London, CBI **144** Management Technology Associates 1994 *Telework Based Transport Telecommunications Substitution, 1993–4* Report to the Department of Transport **145** Jenkins T 1997 *Less Traffic, More Jobs* London: Friends of the Earth **146** *Ibid.* **147** A homeworker is defined as someone who works mainly at home using modern communications and computing technology to overcome the constraints which would hitherto require them to work elsewhere **148** Jupp, S 1995 *Digital Communication to T Jenkins of Friends of the Earth* 8 November **149** Gray, M, Hodson, N and Gordon, G 1993 *Teleworking explained* London: Wiley **150** Wright, A, Redford, S and Sharman, F 1995 *Saving Energy Through Homeworking* Chester: EA Technology **151** Cited in Trapp, R 1997 Absenteeism costs industry £13bn a year *The Independent* 3 March **152** Wright, A *et al* 1995 *Saving Energy Through Homeworking* Chester: EA Technology. This translates to a saving of 9.5 kg of carbon dioxide for each homeworker day **153** *Ibid.* There are other potentially beneficial side effects not considered here, such as households choosing no longer to run a car once it becomes unnecessary for commuting, the improvements in home energy efficiency that could arise as homeworking makes this more worthwhile, or the overall reduction in office energy use as offices relocate to smaller, more energy efficient premises. On the other hand, some disadvantages could include: living further away from the urban centre which would increase the length of remaining journeys; having a larger house to accommodate work space which would increase domestic energy use; and making more journeys unrelated to work than previously **154** Rifkin, J 1996 *The End of Work* New York: Tarcher Puttnam **155** *Innovation and Technology Transfer* 1995 10,000,000 teleworkers by 2000? Vol 4, July, p21 **156** Management Technology Associates 1994 *Telework Based Transport Telecommunications Substitution*

*1993–4* Report to the Department of Transport. A sample of 100 teleworkers was questioned, of which 78 were categorised as 'substantive' teleworkers – those who work at home for at least one day each week **157** Management Technology Associates 1994 *Op cit.* **158** Department of Transport 1995 *Transport Statistics Great Britain* London: HMSO **159** Nottinghamshire County Council 1995 *Green Commuter Plans, A Resource Pack for Nottingham's Employers* Nottingham: NCC **160** Bank, H (ed) 1995 *Sustainable production and consumption. An agenda for change* Oslo, The Norwegian Forum for Development and Environment **161** Marvin, S J 1992 Towards Sustainable Urban Environments: The potential for least-cost planning approaches *Journal of Environmental Planning and Management* 35(2), pp193–200 **162** Learman, S 1996 *City of Torrance Innovative Transportation Projects. Nomination for a clean air award* Diamond Bar, California: South Coast Air Quality Management District Management Programs. Torrance, California's transport programme uses measures including a city-wide pool of vans, most running on compressed natural gas; a Child Care Centre; electric buses, public transport subsidies, ridematching services, preferential parking, and support services for cyclists and pedestrians. Companies have seen the benefits of reducing the number of trips in reduced congestion and pollution **163** Levett, R 1996 Business, the environment and local government. In Welford, R and Starkey, R (eds) 1996 *Business and the Environment* London: Earthscan **164** *ENDS Report* 260 1996 'Unsustainable' energy trends in EC road transport, pp6–7 **165** Royal Commission on Environmental Pollution 1994 *Eighteenth Report, Transport and the Environment* London: HMSO **166** McLaren, D 1993 Counter Urbanisation: How do we achieve a trend breach? *Paper to Velocity Conference*, 6–10 September, Nottingham, Nottinghamshire County Council **167** Freeman, H 1984 *Mental health and the Environment* London, Churchill Livingstone **168** *Local Transport Today* 1996 Councils look to Europe for lessons in car-free living, 15 February. The main objective of Bremen's scheme is to remove the need to own a car by ensuring there is good public transport and by providing for community car-sharing. The car sharing scheme was originally set up by environmentalists but now it operates as a self supporting scheme with over 880 members and 48 vehicles. Studies suggest that it can deliver substantial financial benefits too for members of the scheme, reducing their overall transport costs by almost half. This scheme is one of over 230 similar schemes in Austria, Switzerland, the Netherlands and Germany **169** Falkenberg, J 1994 New car free residential areas *Car Free Cities conference papers* 24–25 March. Amsterdam: Ministerie van Veerkeeer en Waterstaat **170** RAC, cited in Lothian Regional Council 1995 *Moving Forward: Car free residential areas* Edinburgh: Lothian Regional Council **171** Department of the Environment and Department of Transport, 1992. *Reducing transport emissions through planning* London: HMSO, p28. A related study showed that the proportion of walk trips was directly related to urban density, being less than 10 per cent in the least dense neighbourhood, and over 40 per cent in the most dense. Further, in the least dense neighbourhood, average journey lengths to the local centre were almost double those in the most dense: Tarry, S 1992 Accessibility factors at the neighbourhood level. In PTRC, 20th Summer Annual Meeting *Environmental issues: Proceedings of Seminar B* London: PTRC **172** Hubbard, A undated What Are Sustainable Communities? Centre of Excellence for Sustainable Development *http://www.sustainable.doe.gov/ articles/what_are/* **173** Jenkins, T 1997 *Less Traffic, More Jobs* London: Friends of the Earth **174** This takes into account the relative proportions of each mode, on the basis of (i) the Government's cycling target (quadruple trips by 2012), (ii) RCEP's recommendation that public transport should account for 20 per cent of all passenger kilometres by 2005, and (iii) RCEP's target to increase freight kilometres by rail to 20 per cent, which implies a fall in road goods kilometres from 63 per cent to 45 per cent. For cars the $CO_2$ reduction is just under 11 per cent, but there is an increase in bus use which counters this. The figures for freight are determined not only by reduction in modal share for road, but also on assumptions of growth in freight travel overall. On balance a 10 per cent reduction in $CO_2$ emissions is a realistic assumption **175** Based on 1.9 million new cars per year, 1.5 million scrapped cars, and phased increases in fuel efficiency to 2005 and 2010 **176** 25 per cent improvement in fuel efficiency and 10 per cent less traffic equals 32.5 per cent less emissions **177** According to the British Wind Energy Association (1996 *Wind Energy. Power for a sustainable future* London: BWEA) 10,280 1.4 MW turbines would occupy 2500 hectares (accounting for the machinery and access roads); so 22,000 would occupy 5350 hectares. 1MW turbines are a little smaller so we round down to 5000 ha **178** Based on Council for the Protection of Rural England (1996 *Campaigners Guide to Minerals* London: CPRE) which gives the area of land directly affected by production of 56 mt of coal in England in 1993–94 as 19,670 ha. 19670*24.1/56 = 8500 ha **179** Trainer, F 1995 Can renewable energy sources sustain an affluent society? *Energy Policy* 23(12), pp1009–26 **180** Department of the Environment 1995 *Climate Change the UK Programme: Progress report on carbon dioxide emissions* London: DOE **181** Denmark, on the other hand, using the environmental space approach, has already endorsed a target of a 20 per cent cut by 2005, as an interim step towards cuts of 50 per cent by 2030. Modelling undertaken for the Danish Government suggests that an even greater target (a two-thirds reduction by 2030) would have almost neglible economic costs – no more than 0.5 per cent of (a doubled) GDP through a package of measures similar to those suggested in this chapter. *Global Environmental Change Reporter* 1996 Denmark unveils new energy plan, VIII(8) 26 April **182** Other things being equal, the Magnox stations will be closed by 2007, the two Scottish stations by 2023, the Advanced Gas-cooled Reactors (AGRs) by 2023, and without policy change the Sizewell B station would close in 2035. Safe Energy Journal, 1997. *Personal communication with the editor* 25 March **183** Department of Trade and Industry 1995 *The energy report* London: DTI **184** IPCC Working Group 2 1996 *Climate Change 1995. The Science of Climate Change. Impacts, Adaptation and Mitigation of Climate Change: Scientific-Technical Analyses* Contribution of Working Group II to the Second Assessment Report of the Intergovernmental Panel on Climate Change, Cambridge: Cambridge University Press; World Energy Council 1995 *Global energy perspectives to 2050* London: World Energy Council **185** World Energy Council 1995 *Op cit.* **186** Glyn, A 1995 Northern Growth and Environmental Constraints. In Bhaskar, V and Glyn, A (eds) 1995 *The North, the South and the Environment* London, Earthscan

# NOTES TO CHAPTER 6

**1** The base data for this chapter (available on FOE's web-page: http://www.foe.co.uk/) proved difficult to establish. Inconsistency of definition has been a constant problem. For calculations of agricultural land we have exclusively used FAO data, which although derived from official UK sources, are adjusted according to their comparable definitions. In general, data for urban land in England appear to be more complete and consistent than for Scotland, Wales and Northern Ireland so we have extrapolated English figures as far as possible to cover these other countries, and used these countries' own figures as guides only. However the figures remain subject to large uncertainty. Sinclair demonstrates the extent of potential errors in the data which may have underestimated rural land-loss between 1945 and 1990 in England alone by 180,000 ha (or 13 per cent). In the absence of comparable data for all parts of the UK, we have chosen to base our calculations on the official figures insofar as possible. This does mean that we may well be being overly optimistic about the availability of non-urban land. Sinclair, G 1992 *The Lost Land* London: Council for the Protection of Rural England **2** UN Environment Programme 1995 *Global Biodiversity Assessment* Nairobi: UNEP **3** Budiansky, S 1995 *Nature's Keepers: The new science of nature management* London: Phoenix **4** Settele, J and Margules, C 1996 *Species survival in fragmented landscapes* Amsterdam: Kluwer **5** Eldredge, N 1993 *The Miner's Canary* London: Virgin, p207 **6** Naeem, S, Thompson, LJ, Lawler, SP, Lawton, JH and Woodfin, RM 1995 Declining biodiversity can alter the performance of ecosystems *Nature* 368, pp734–7; Kareiva, P 1996 Diversity and sustainability on the prairie. *Nature* 379, pp673–4 **7** In the UK, the Government's previous advisory body on such issues, the Nature Conservancy Council, suggested 10 per cent as a broad target for coverage by protective designation as 'sites of special scientific interest' which are considered as the minimum needed to conserve the UK's natural heritage of biodiversity and are the cornerstone of nature conservation in the country. Nature Conservancy Council, 1989. *Guidelines for selection of biological SSSI's* Peterborough: NCC. In 1992, at the fourth World Congress on National Parks and Protected Areas (held in Caracas, Venezuela) the World Conservation Union (IUCN) established a goal of protecting 10 per cent of each of the world's major biomes (a broad regional ecological community) **8** SSSIs would not meet the standards required by the IUCN for categorisation as I-III (the standards recommended by the Wuppertal Institute to categorise protected land for the environmental space methodology). Indeed their protection would not meet even the standards of IUCN categories IV-V which are more applicable to the almost entirely human-modified landscapes of the UK. International Union for Conservation of Nature 1994 *Parks for life: action for protected areas in Europe* Gland: IUCN **9** Friends of the Earth 1995 *Losing Interest: A Survey of threats to sites of special scientific interest in England and Wales* London: FOE **10** Rowell, T 1992 *SSSIs: A health check* Report for Wildlife Link. London: Wildlife Link **11** Juniper, T 1994 *Gaining Interest* London: Friends of the Earth **12** However, many SSSIs are small in area and need to be managed, so would still fail to meet IUCN criteria for categories I-III, which means that they would not contribute to a crudely defined target for a protected area **13** To increase the area of SSSIs from 8 to 10 per cent involves an extra 460,000 ha – 10 per cent restoration equals 46,000 ha **14** Girardet, H 1996 *Getting London in shape for 2000* London: London First **15** World Resources Institute, 1996 *World Resources 1996–7* Oxford: Oxford University Press **16** US Agency for International Development 1988 *Urbanization in the Developing Countries. Interim report to Congress* Washington, DC: USAID **17** Jones, P 1995 *The UK Environmental Economy – Do we value it or weigh it?* Working Paper. High Wycombe: Biffa Waste Services **18** Newman, P, and Kenworth, J 1989 *Cities and automobile dependence* Aldershot: Gower Technical; Tarry, S 1992 Accessibility factors at the neighbourhood level. In PTRC, 20th Summer Annual Meeting *Environmental issues: Proceedings of Seminar B* London: PTRC. Some of the energy costs involved in low density development could, in theory, be reduced by higher use of solar energy in low-rise buildings but the possible solar gains are less significant than the gains that can be obtained by good design and effective massing of buildings. See McLaren, D 1993 Compact or dispersed: dilution is no solution *Built Environment* 18 (4) pp 268–84; Liddell, H, Mackie, D and MacFarlane, G 1996 *Energy conservation and planning. A report to the Scottish Office by Gaia Planning* Edinburgh: Scottish Office Central Research Unit **19** McLaren, D 1993 *Op cit.* Freeman, H 1984 *Mental Health and the Environment* Edinburgh, Churchill Livingstone **20** Breheny, M 1993 Counterurbanisation and sustainable urban forms. In Brotchie, J, Batty, M, Hall, P and Newton, P (eds) *Cities in Competition: the emergence of productive and sustainable cities for the 21st century* Melbourne: Longman Cheshire **21** The policies needed to promote compact cities also converge with those needed to regenerate rural areas and villages. Many of the current problems of our rural areas arise from the invasion of urban commuters seeking a quieter and cleaner environment and a traditional village way of life. They do not find it, but push up house prices, damaging local communities. Improving our urban environments and increasing the costs of private transport will both help reverse this insidious trend. McLaren, D 1993 *Op cit.* **22** This is cautious, as around 0.5 million of the new English households are expected to arise because of net migration to England, much of it from the rest of the UK. The overall increase is not the consequence of population growth, but of smaller family sizes, longer lives, higher divorce rates, and a number of other factors which mean that the average household size will fall over the same period from 2.51 (in 1991) to 2.17 (based on predicted population and predicted number of households). **23** Friends of the Earth 1993 *Nothing Ventured, Nothing Gained* London: FOE **24** McLaren, D 1993 Compact or dispersed: dilution is no solution *Built Environment* 18 (4) **25** Statement by Minister for Planning 14 April 1991, cited by Trainer, E 1995 *The Conserver Society: Alternatives for Sustainability* London: Zed Press. Equivalent figures for the UK do not appear to be available **26** Cited in McLaren, D 1993 *Op cit.* **27** Cited by Clover, C 1996 Plea to use waste land for building 4.4 m new homes *Daily Telegraph*, 18 November **28** UK Round Table on Sustainable Development 1997 *Housing and Urban Capacity* London: Department of the Environment **29** Needham, D and Waters, B 1995 Rate of housing conversions collapses despite bigger target *Planning in London*, 15, pp5–6 **30** According to Bob Lawrence, the Head of the Empty Homes Agency, the VAT differential issue is only one of the problems faced in encouraging refurbishment. He commends the Department of the Environment for the advice already given to local authorities to encourage mixed use, but feels sterner guidance is needed. Lawrence, B 1996. *Personal communication with Friends of the Earth* 8 December **31** A typical survey by the market research group Mintel identified three principal reasons for people wanting to move out of cities. The belief that cities are too noisy and dirty, was cited most commonly, with over 50 per cent of the sample giving this as their main reason. The appeal of open spaces in rural areas attracted 45 per cent while just over 20 per cent felt that rural life would be less stressful. Mintel 1992 *Regional Lifestyles* London: Mintel International Group **32** Duke of Westminster 1992 *The problems in rural areas. A report of the recommendations arising from an inquiry chaired by His Grace the Duke of Westminster* Leominster, Orphans Press; House of Lords Select Committee on European Communities 1990 *The Future of Rural Society.* Paper 80. London: HMSO **33** McLaren, D 1993 Counter Urbanisation: How do we achieve a trend breach? *Velocity Conference paper* 6–10 September. Nottingham: Nottinghamshire County Council **34** Rogerson, R 1989 *Quality of life in the UK's intermediate cities* Glasgow: Glasgow Quality of Life Group **35** House of Commons Environment Committee 1996 *Housing need* London: HMSO **36** The House of Commons Environment Committee believe that a realistic target for the vacancy rate is no more than one in 50, or 2 per cent, of the housing stock. *Ibid.* **37** Based on data from the Empty Homes Agency **38** Reading Borough Council 1996 *Environmental strategy for* *housing: sustainability* March. Reading: RBC **39** Royal Institution of Chartered Surveyors, Empty Homes Agency, Incorporated Society of Valuers and Auctioneers 1995 *Empty Property Guide for Professionals and Owners* London: RICS. This excludes vandalism and depreciation, and includes £4000 forgone rent. Properties also deteriorate less quickly when occupied, so requiring less expenditure on maintenance. **40** Holmans, A 1995 *Housing demand and need in England 1991 to 2011* York: Joseph Rowntree Foundation. At present there are 127,000 people accepted as homeless by councils. This includes only those in 'priority need' who have not made themselves 'intentionally homeless'. There are many more who are not included in the statistics including many of the single young people who sleep rough **41** The Living Over the Shop (LOTS) programme evolved because most commercial owners were not willing to grant residential leases at all, since they saw them as devaluing the property and creating potential management problems. LOTS solved one of the major problems by introducing a two-stage leasing arrangement: the first is a commercial lease between the property owner/leaseholder, and an intermediary, such as a housing association, who then gives an assured shorthold tenancy. The intermediary thus protects the interests of both parties, at the same time as freeing the owner from all management responsibilities. But this has not been enough, the LOTS project has not received the resources necessary to publicise itself widely amongst those who own and control commercial property. Living Over the Shop 1995 *Information Pack* York, LOTS **42** McLaren, D and Bosworth, T 1994 *Planning for the Planet* London: Friends of the Earth **43** Conversions from gross figures used by Newman and Kenworthy to net figures applicable in the UK can be found in McLaren, D 1993 Compact or dispersed: dilution is no solution *Built Environment* 18 (4). Net figures are for the residential development, gross figures include non-residential land uses, and account for occupancy rates of residential properties **44** Fulford, C 1996 The compact city and the market: The case of residential development. In Jenks, Burton and Williams (eds) *The Compact City: A Sustainable Urban Form?* London: E&FN Spon **45** Llewellyn Davies 1994 *Providing more homes in urban areas* Bristol: School for Advanced Urban Studies **46** TEST 1991 *Wrong side of the tracks?* London: TEST **47** Falkenbergen, J 1994 New car-free residential areas *Paper to Car free Cities Conference* Amsterdam **48** Llewellyn Davies 1994 *Op cit.* **49** Living Over the Shop 1995 *Information Pack* York: LOTS **50** *Ibid.* **51** *Ibid.* For example, in Stamford, Lincolnshire, in 1900 there were 390 people living in the High Street. By 1991, there were only seven and the upper floors of the street's shops were no longer even classed as residential. Since 1992, LOTS have completed 13 projects (24 homes) through a Peterborough-based Housing Association. **52** Based on 20,400 hectares of derelict urban land in England (Department of the Environment 1996 *Digest of Environmental Statistics no 18*, 1996 London: HMSO). Of a total of 39,600 hectares of derelict land in England, 34,600 is classed as 'stock justifying reclamation'. Assuming, conservatively, that the percentage justifying reclamation in urban areas is the same as in all areas, and that extrapolation can be made to the UK based on population, gives us this figure. **53** 21,660/2 x 170/ 2.17, where 2.17 = average household size. We have not included other vacant land in urban areas – perhaps as much as a further 35,000 hectares – in our estimates, partly because much of this 'vacant' land is valued green space. So for this reason too, our estimates are conservative. See UK Round Table on Sustainable Development 1997 *Housing and Urban Capacity* London: Department of the Environment **54** Average of 1985–1993, grossed up from figures for England given in the Department of the Environment's Land-Use Change Statistics **55** This is a conservative assumption. As the existing stock is larger than the future average household size, the average new dwelling need not be even that large **56** Department of the Environment 1993 *English Housing Condition Survey 1991* London: HMSO **57** Redeveloping 3270 hectares at 170 persons per hectare and 2.17 persons per household implies replacing 256,000 homes each year or 0.9 per cent of the increased stock. Research for the Joseph Rowntree Foundation reports that the average design life of the current housing stock is 60 years. This would imply a replacement rate of 1.7 per cent of properties each year. However, at current replacement rates the average home will have to last 4000 years. So replacement rates will need to rise, even if new homes are provided in more durable, longer-lived buildings to reduce material needs in the longer term. See Collins, P 1996 Shaky Foundations *Search* 25, pp4–7 **58** Ridout, G 1994 Keeping up appearances *Building Homes*, 25 November, pp4–7 **59** As Llewellyn Davies note in their report to the Round Table, 'since the market only offers a limited product to the consumer at present it is impossible to gauge preferences from existing house purchasing patterns' UK Round Table on Sustainable Development 1997 *Housing and Urban Capacity* London: Department of the Environment pp22–23 **60** Wedmore, K and Freeman, H 1984 Social pathology and urban overgrowth. Chapter 11 in

Freeman, H *Mental Health and the Environment* Edinburgh: Churchill Livingstone, p36
**61** Wackernagel, M and Rees, W 1996 *Our Ecological Footprint* Gabriola Island BC, New Society
**62** Between 1990 and 2016, we estimate that 5.2 million additional dwellings would be needed in
the UK. However between 1991 and 1996 0.6–0.7 million additional dwellings have already been
built **63** This assumes that the entire gains from reducing vacancy rates could be achieved by
2010, whilst the other measures would reach their full potential by 2016, with the exception of
continued redevelopment, which could go on delivering additional homes for many more years
**64** Assumes average net residential density of 100 persons/hectare and 70 per cent of provision
on greenfield sites **65** Defined by the Food and Agriculture Organisation of the UN as *access at an
affordable cost to basic food of good quality, in sufficient amounts, at all times and without compromising the satisfaction of other essential needs, based on healthy and culturally adequate food habits, thus contributing to a
dignified life and to the full development of the individual* **66** Dyson, T 1994 Recent Global Trends in
Population and Food *GEC Programme Briefing No. 3* Global Environmental Change Programme:
University of Sussex. **67** Food and Agriculture Organisation 1996 *http://www.fao.org/focus/e/
SpeclPr/SProHm-e.htm* **68** UNICEF 1996 *Progress of Nations. Nutrition* New York: UNICEF
**69** Office of Population Censuses and Surveys 1991 *Health Survey for England, 1991* London:
OPCS; Lean, G and Cooper, Y 1996 Not enough for us. *Independent on Sunday*, 21 July, p19
**70** Lees, A and McVeigh, K 1988 *An Investigation of pesticide pollution in drinking water in England and
Wales* London: Friends of the Earth; Evans, R 1996 *Soil Erosion and Its Impacts in England and Wales*
London: Friends of the Earth; Conway, G and Pretty, J 1991 *Unwelcome Harvest: Agriculture and
Pollution* London: Earthscan **71** Postel, S 1994 Carrying Capacity: The Earth's Bottom Line. In
Mazur, L (ed) 1994 *Beyond the Numbers* Washington: Island Press **72** *The Economist* 1996 Cities:
Fiction and Fact 8 June, pp72–3 **73** US Agency for International Development 1988 *Urbanization
in the Developing Countries. Interim Report to Congress* Washington, DC: USAID **74** Dyson, T 1994
Recent Global Trends in Population and Food *GEC Programme Briefing No. 3* Global
Environmental Change Programme: University of Sussex **75** Jules Pretty of the International
Institute for Environment and Development (IIED) suggests that sustainable practices will match
or exceed current yields in 'green revolution' countries, and double or treble yields elsewhere in
developing countries. Sunita Narain of India's Centre for Science and Environment agrees: 'for a
country like India, food is not the problem ... The most central issue in the future will not be
about how we feed the world, but rather about who will feed the world'. Pretty, J 1995 *Regenerating
Agriculture* London: Earthscan. Narain cited in Milieu Defensie 1996 *North-South Perspectives on
Sustainability: towards a global redistribution of environmental space* Amsterdam: Milieu Defensie
**76** Proponents of modern, intensive, 'hi-tech' agriculture are prone to claiming that without it
humanity would risk shortages or famine. They assert, for example, that widespread adoption of
organic agriculture 'would cause famine' or 'result in massive worldwide starvation'. There is
certainly little if any substantive evidence to support such assertions. Gardiner, RA 1997 Beware
organic famine. Letter to *Sunday Times* 9 March; Rosen, A 1996 Organic farming's costly
drawbacks. Letter to *Independent* 19 September **77** Pretty, J 1995 *Regenerating Agriculture* London:
Earthscan. Economic evidence suggests that farmers can significantly reduce external input use
without losing out on gross margins – the financial return per hectare. This is because following
the adoption of resource-conserving technologies, although yields fall a little, variable costs fall
significantly, and so gross margins can be matched or bettered **78** Ministry of Agriculture,
Fisheries and Food 1996 *Information service* September London: MAFF **79** Pretty, J 1997
(forthcoming) *Sustainable Agriculture for Farmers and Food, Communities and Countryside* London:
Friends of the Earth. A study covering 1.9 million farmers and over 4 million hectares found that
in currently low-yield countries (average yields less than half the world average) cereal yields
under sustainable agriculture more than double, while in medium-yield countries (where average
yields are 50–100 per cent of the world average) they increase by two-thirds: Pretty, J 1996
Sustainability Works *Our Planet* 8(4), pp19–22 **80** Postel, S 1994 Carrying Capacity: The Earth's
Bottom Line. In Mazur, L (ed) 1994 *Beyond the Numbers* Washington, DC: Island Press **81** Pretty, J
1995 *Regenerating Agriculture* London: Earthscan **82** Pretty, J 1997 *Sustainable Agriculture for Farmers
and Food, Communities and Countryside* London: Friends of the Earth **83** National Food Alliance
unpublished scoping study, 1996 **84** Younie, D 1994 Economics and viability of organic farming.
*Paper at Grampian ECOLINK conference* September; Lampkin, N 1995 *Estimating the impact of
widespread conversion to organic farming on land use and physical output in the United Kingdom* Aberystwyth:
Centre for Organic Husbandry and Agroecology, University of Wales **85** Bob Evans, a leading
independent soil scientist, has studied upland erosion for over 20 years. He has found that soil

erosion on our hills and moors is largely the result of overstocking with grazing animals. Evans, R 1996 *Soil Erosion and its Impacts in England and Wales* London: Friends of the Earth **86** Friends of the Earth, 1995 *Losing Interest: A Survey of Threats to Sites of Special Scientific Interest in England and Wales* London: Friends of the Earth; Rowell, T 1992 *SSSIs: A health check* Report for Wildlife Link. London: Wildlife Link **87** For example, the rate of salmonella poisoning has rocketed in recent years. Some have attributed this in part to the growing level of immunity to antibiotics in livestock and livestock infections created by the prophylactic use of antibiotics in intensive systems. Because of crowded conditions, modern intensive farming is only made possible by the systematic use of antibiotics. But continued antibiotic use makes bugs evolve resistance more quickly. There is no simple solution short of ceasing to use such intensive production methods. Cannon, G 1996 *Superbug* London, Virgin Publishing **88** Conway, G and Pretty, J 1991 *Unwelcome Harvest: Agriculture and Pollution* London: Earthscan. In the Netherlands, there is now so much manure produced by the country's 14 million animals in feeding pens, mainly pigs, that they have to ship it all over the country to find agricultural land to spread it on **89** Although intensive systems allow a more carefully managed diet, the net effect seems to be to increase overall methane generation levels. Intensive dairy and feedlot production hold 11–17 per cent of all cattle, but account for 22–29 per cent of methane emissions from cattle. In the UK, recent research revealed that heavily fertilised dairy-farm grasslands emit three times more nitrous oxide, another potent greenhouse gas, than ungrazed grasslands – in total exceeding industrial sources of this gas. Gibbs, M and Leng, R 1992 Animal Agriculture Systems. In *IPCC Agriculture and Forestry Options Subgroup Report*; Natural Environment Research Council 1996 *The TIGER's Tale: Terrestrial Initiative in Global Environmental Research* Swindon: NERC **90** Durning, A and Brough, H 1991 *Taking stock: Animal farming and the environment* Washington: WorldWatch Institute **91** To calculate our targets we begin from our estimate of how much land will be available for food production – of no net increase over the present. We will then compare estimates of the average productivity of that land (based on predicted changes in yields in different countries as a result of the adoption of sustainable agricultural techniques) with figures for average productivity in the UK to determine what level of net import or export of land (as agricultural products) is fair. We will then see how consumption patterns in the UK match up to the land available, and what approaches might increase our efficiency of use of the land available **92** Data for 1993 from the Food and Agriculture Organisation *http://apps.fao.org/cgi-bin/nph-db.pl* We assume that our net imported land is of approximately the same quality as domestic land – crops for export in developing countries typically occupy the best and most productive land **93** Assuming that areas of crop and rangeland do not change, there will be 4.809 billion hectares of agricultural land, of which 1.448 billion is cropland **94** The quality factor is the difference in average yields once the effects of unsustainable production techniques have been taken out of the picture. At present for a range of different crops the ratio between UK yields and world average yields, and the ratio of areas harvested between different crop types between the UK and the rest of the world, are both remarkably consistent, although the crop yield ratio is very different from the ratio for livestock. So we can calculate our crop yield factor on the basis of total production and total area harvested. In the UK, sustainable production techniques can be expected to reduce yields slightly. Crop yields will fall by about 5 per cent. The average yield (total production divided by area harvested) of the crops in question in 1995 was 8.75 tonnes per hectare. Reducing this by 5 per cent gives 8.31 tonnes per hectare. Estimating the world average sustainable yield is slightly more complex. In countries with 'intensive' agriculture (Europe, USA, Japan, Canada and Brazil – classed by criteria of yields and amounts of grain fed to livestock, as key indicators of intensive production) yields can be expected to fall in line with the UK, but elsewhere average yields are expected to rise by 50 per cent. So we take current production totals for these two groups and multiply them by these factors, and then divide by the area harvested. For both UK and world average yields we use the same basis, that is area harvested according to FAO, which excludes areas set aside or in fallow. This gives a figure for average yield of 4.79 tonnes per hectare. So for crops, the quality factor is 8.31:4.79, or 1.73:1. Then we calculate a similar factor for livestock. UK livestock production, under sustainable techniques, is estimated to fall by 10–20 per cent. As a result of eliminating factory and feedlot production (as represented by reducing the average livestock feed per unit to the levels that are found in 'non-intensive' countries), production in 'intensive countries' is estimated to drop by 18 per cent. Figures were calculated for the average amount of grain fed to livestock per tonne of meat produced for each country. It was assumed that 'intensive' countries would need to reduce their feed inputs to those of the average of 'other' countries, and the ratio of the two figures for grain per tonne of meat produced was used to calculate a reduced figure for meat production for each 'intensive' country. This leaves UK production at 0.27 tonnes per hectare of 'rangeland' (again using comparable FAO figures). For world averages we adjust 'intensive' countries' production similarly, down to 50 mt; and the rest of the world's yield is unchanged at 116 mt. On 3362.2 million ha of rangeland, this gives an average yield of 0.0494 tonnes per hectare. The ratio for livestock is therefore 1:5.5. The final step in deriving the quality factor is to combine the two. We do this on the basis of the volume of production (as in later analysis we will look at diet in terms of weight of food). This means that as crops account for 96 per cent of the weight of food produced globally, relative crop yields account for 96 per cent of the final quality factor. This gives a quality factor of 1.88. If we weighted it by nutritional contribution to the diet it would be in the order of 2:1 (assuming meat has twice the nutritional value of the average crop) or 2.3:1 (assuming meat has four times the nutritional value of the average crop) **95** The central figure of a 50 per cent increase is based on work by Pretty: Pretty, J 1997 *Sustainable Agriculture for Farmers and Food, Communities and Countryside* London: Friends of the Earth; Pretty, J 1995 *Regenerating Agriculture* London: Earthscan **96** The figures for 2050 availability assume first, rather than an 'across-the board' reduction of 27 per cent in use of land for each product, that we have notionally eliminated our net import of land. This leaves a net reduction of 10 per cent in land available in the UK (to account for our future net export) **97** There is a 22 per cent surplus in crop production and a 13 per cent surplus in meat and dairy production over current diets. Assuming the same ratio of cropland to grassland in 2050 as in 1995 in the UK, this leads to a surplus of 2.5 million hectares **98** *The Guardian*, 26 February 1997 **99** National Food Alliance and SAFE 1996 *Growing Food in Cities* London: NFA/SAFE **100** International Institute for Environment and Development 1995 *Citizen Action to Lighten Ecological Footprints* London: IIED. This report cites many differing changes in yield in the switch from conventional to organic cotton production – average drop 36 per cent in India and Turkey, 29 per cent drop in California, increase of 7 per cent in Missouri and Tennessee **101** Calculation as in note 97 **102** The North Sea cod spawning stock, for example, is reported to have stabilized at a very low level, approximately one-third of what the FAO describes as the 'lowest desirable biological level.' Food and Agriculture Organisation 1996 *Review of the State of World Fisheries Resources: Marine Fisheries* Rome: FAO **103** Brown, L, Flavin, C and Kane, H, 1996 *Vital Signs 1996* London: Earthscan **104** Food and Agriculture Organisation, 1996a. In-depth study: patterns of marine fishery landings and future landings. *http://www.fao.org/waicent/faoinfo/fishery/publ/sofia/sostudye.pdf*. **105** Food and Agriculture Organisation, 1996b. *Global fishery production in 1994*. Rome: FAO; and *http://www.fao.org/waicent/faoinfo/fishery /fishery.html*. **106** Inefficiency also results from wastage in the fisheries sector. The WorldWatch Institute report 'Vital signs' says: 'In the Gulf of Mexico for example 80 per cent of all fish caught – an estimated 450,000 tonnes annually, is discarded in the process, damaged, or killed. This is creating a growing deficit of juvenile and mature stocks of key commercial species, threatening the long-term health of the Gulf fishery.' Brown, L, Flavin, C and Kane, H, 1996 *Vital Signs 1996* London: Earthscan **107** Food and Agriculture Organisation 1996 Major trends in Global Aquaculture production: 1984–1994 *http://www.fao.org/waicent/ faoinfo/fishery/fishery.html*. **108** International Institute for Environment and Development 1995 *Citizen Action to Lighten Ecological Footprints* London: IIED **109** The feed ratio is 2.2 kg for chicken, 4 for pork and 7 for beef. Brown, L, Flavin, C and Kane, H, 1996 *Vital Signs 1996* London: Earthscan **110** Drawbacks of aquaculture include eutrophication due to large quantities of organic wastes from intensive farming; wide use of chemicals; clearance of fragile wetland ecosystems and mangrove forests, especially for brackish water aquaculture – the high-value end of the market **111** Food and Agriculture Organisation 1993 Marine fisheries and the law of the sea: a decade of change *Fisheries circular no 853 http://www.fao.org/* **112** Budiansky, S 1995 *Nature's Keeper: The new science of nature management* London: Phoenix **113** GLASOD cited in World Resources Institute 1992 *World Resources 1992–93: A Guide to the Global Environment* Oxford: Oxford University Press, pp116–17 **114** World Resources Institute 1992 *World Resources 1992–3* Oxford: Oxford University Press **115** Royal Commission on Environmental Pollution, 1995. *Environmental Problems Associated with Soil* London: HMSO **116** Authoritative figures are not available for the UK. Even a comprehensive study on soil-related problems recently undertaken by the Royal Commission on Environmental Pollution was not able to produce figures for degraded areas. The data that does exist suggests that only a relatively small area of soils in the UK is severely degraded (outside of urban areas), but that much greater areas are under threat from several quarters. Royal Commission on Environmental

Pollution 1995 *Environmental Problems Associated with Soil* London: HMSO; ENDS Report 237 1994 Government 'toned down' warnings over threats to soil, pp29–30 **117** Pretty, J 1997 *Sustainable Agriculture for Farmers and Food, Communities and Countryside* London: Friends of the Earth; Evans, R 1996 *Soil Erosion and Its Impacts in England and Wales* London: Friends of the Earth. Acid deposition is predicted to leave over 40 per cent of UK soils over critical loads by 2005. Lowered organic matter levels are estimated to affect between 15 and 30 per cent of soils. Professor Peter Bullock of the Soil Survey believes that: 'Soil organic matter has fallen to dangerous levels in about 30 per cent of UK soils, with serious implications for soil stability, water retention and nutrient holding capacity'. Evans, R 1990 Soils at risk from accelerated erosion in England and Wales *Soil Use and Management* 6, pp125–31; Tickle, A and Sweet, J 1993. *Critical Loads and UK Air Pollution Policy* London, Friends of the Earth; *ENDS Report* 237, *Op cit.*; Bullock, P 1993 Presentation to Soil Protection Problems and Solutions *4th Silsoe Link Conference* 24 March **118** Department of the Environment and the Welsh Office 1993 *Paying for our past* London: HMSO **119** Department of the Environment 1996 *Digest of Environmental Statistics No 18* London: HMSO **120** Davies, R, Hodgkinson, R and Chapman, R 1995 Nitrogen Loss from a Soil Restored after Surface Mining *Journal of Environmental Quality* 24(6) pp12–15 **121** Davies, R et al. (1995) *Op cit*; Bradshaw, AD and Chadwick, MJ 1980 *The restoration of land: the ecology and reclamation of derelict and degraded land* Studies in Ecology 6. London: Blackwell. And despite arguments to the contrary, opencast mining in the UK has not principally been undertaken on already degraded land. For example, between 1983 and 1992, only about one-quarter of new planning permissions for opencast coal mining was on sites in previous deep-mining areas which were 'derelict' before mining was planned. County Planning Officers Society 1992 *Opencast coalmining: statistics 1991/2* Durham: Durham County Council **122** Pretty, J 1997 *Sustainable Agriculture for Farmers and Food, Communities and Countryside* London: Friends of the Earth **123** Vellve, R 1992 *Saving the Seed: genetic diversity and European agriculture* London: Earthscan. In these circumstances, loss of biodiversity, especially in tropical areas, has a knock-on effect for global agriculture. Some modern crops have required regular infusions of genetic variability from wild strains to sustain their productivity or increase their capacity to resist pests and diseases or adverse environmental conditions. Gretchen Daily of Stanford University attributes about half of annual agricultural productivity gains to this factor. Cited in Radford, T 1997 The buck stops here *The Guardian* 6 March **124** Goldburg, R, Rissler, J, Shand, H and Hassebrook, C 1990 *Biotechnology's Bitter Harvest: Herbicide Tolerant Crops and the Threat to Sustainable Agriculture* Washington, DC: Biotechnology Working Group **125** Lipietz, A 1995 Enclosing Policies and North-South trade. In Bhaskar, V and Glyn A (eds) *The North, The South and the Environment* London, Earthscan; McDougall, CL 1995 *Intellectual Property Rights and the Biodiversity Convention: The Impact of GATT* London: Friends of the Earth. A consultative expert seminar organised by the Food and Agriculture Organization of the United Nations (FAO) recommended that: *there should not be any patenting of life forms such as plants, animals, micro-organisms and genetic materials, as such patenting will be detrimental to farmers' and consumers' rights in developing countries and moreover will render sustainable agriculture extremely difficult if not impossible to achieve.* Cited in Khor, M 1993 FAO experts caution on bioengineered products *South North Development Monitor* 17 September **126** Some tree-crops are even higher yielding (and comparable in protein content), for example 100 tonnes of food per year can be produced from carob or honey locust trees on as little as two hectares. Trainer, T 1995 *The Conserver Society: Alternatives for Sustainability* London: Zed Press **127** Commission of the European Communities 1991 *The agricultural situation in the community 1990* Brussels: CEC **128** 'Recommended diet' figures from Deutsche Gesellschaft fur Ernahrung e. V. Vollwerting Essen und Trinken, nach den 10 Regeln der DGE, in Spangenberg, J (ed) 1995 *Towards a Sustainable Europe* Brussels: FOE Europe **129** The Grocer 1995 *Provision, a Supplement to the Grocer* 8 April, p6, William Reed Publishing; Cottee, P and Webster, J 1997 *Waste not, want not* London: Crisis **130** Around £3 million worth of food will be distributed in 1996 and the amount is growing. Some, but not all, of this waste food would find its way to consumers anyway, through secondary markets and market traders, but Provision helps target food to those in need and helps reduce the overall wastage in the system **131** Simple nitrogen taxes, applied without taking account of their distributional effects, could be damaging in the agriculture sector. Although the most intensive farmers would pay more, the costs for many marginal farms could easily be excessive, as at present the demand for nitrogen is 'inelastic' and a high tax per unit would be needed to achieve a significant cut in use. Any further bankruptcies in the agriculture sector would be environmentally damaging, as they would probably trigger further amalgamation of farms into larger, more intensively managed units **132** However, at present, as the Royal

Commission on Environmental Pollution has noted, the use of sewage sludge as a soil conditioner 'is not necessarily ... sustainable in the sense that the land can continue to be used in the long term for food production', because the contamination in sludge would prevent such continued use. The RCEP recommended that substantial further reductions in inputs of heavy metals to the sewerage system should be sought by controlling trade effluent discharges to sewers more stringently. Royal Commission on Environmental Pollution May 1993 *Seventeenth Report, Incineration of Waste* London: HMSO; Foundation for Water Research 1993 *Report on the examination of sewage sludges for polychlorinated-dibenzo-p-dioxins and polychlorinated dibenzofurans* Marlow: Foundation for Water Research **133** Economist Intelligence Unit 1996 *Retail Business. Market Survey Report. Organic and natural health foods* London: EIU **134** Ministry of Agriculture, Fisheries and Food 1996a *Organic Conversion Information Service* London: MAFF **135** Ministry of Agriculture, Fisheries and Food 1996b *Organic Farming* London: MAFF **136** Fowler, S, University of Wales 1996 cited in *Farming News*, 8 November Organic conversion can boost margins **137** Ministry of Agriculture, Fisheries and Food 1996b *Op cit* **138** Lampkin, N 1996 Impact of EC regulation 2078/92 on the development of organic farming in the European Union *CEPFAR/IFOAM Seminar on Organic Agriculture* Vignola, Italy, 6–8 June **139** Germany, Denmark, Sweden, Finland, Austria and the Netherlands have full-time state-funded advisers specialising in organic farming, or contribute to the costs of private sector advisers, working both in existing advisory structures and organic producer organisations **140** Booth, E 1996 Local food links *Paper at the Vegetable Challenge Conference* May 21 London, Guild of Food Writers. Box schemes also seem to offer benefits to consumers' health. A survey by Emma Delow for the Soil Association found that people subscribing to box schemes increased the diversity and freshness of their dietary intake: Delow, E 1995 *Living Earth Magazine* Winter 1995, No.189, Bristol: Soil Association **141** This phase saw whole villages shifting over to organic production, beginning with localised marketing schemes. A poll conducted by the Austrian Ministry of Land asked farmers what the most important motivations were to start organic farming. The most popular answer was the change in general attitudes (23.8 per cent), followed by changes in nutritional consciousness or sickness (16 per cent). Problems with soil fertility, sickness or fertility problems with farm animals, and problems with chemical inputs also featured significantly. The amount available has risen to 700 million Austrian Schillings in 1995. Organic farmers may also obtain funding from a scheme focused on improving their marketing. Bundesministerium Fur Land – und Fortwirtschaft, Austria, 1996 *Fax to Friends of the Earth* 5 March **142** Schoon, N 1996 Can farming go green: the UK grows slow in world *Independent* 12 April. Now 30 per cent of all fresh produce available is organic and this includes not just vegetables, but cheese, milk, noodles and bread. It has become 'fashionable' to produce and consume organic produce. The premium on organic produce is on average 10–15 per cent more than its intensively produced counterpart, but this is less than the average 20 per cent organic premium in the UK. That supermarkets have the power to influence their suppliers in such a way is not doubted: Sainsbury recently reported that 73 per cent of its suppliers were now committed to a low pesticide regime. Sainsburys 1996 *Sainsburys Environmental Report* September, London: Sainsburys **143** Lampkin, N 1995 *Estimating the impact of widespread conversion to organic farming on land use and physical output in the United Kingdom* University of Wales, Aberystwyth: Centre for Organic Husbandry and Agroecology **144** Agricultural support, according to Nic Lampkin, the UK's leading expert on organic agriculture, needs retargeting. It is not enough, he argues, simply to reward farmers for tangible features like hedges and walls. The benefits of sustainable practices – healthier soil, richer wildlife, less pollution – may be harder to quantify, but they are no less deserving of aid. Lampkin, N 1996 Impact of EC regulation 2078/92 on the development of organic farming in the European Union *CEPFAR/IFOAM Seminar on Organic Agriculture* Vignola, Italy, 6–8 June **145** See, for example, Hunter, J 1995 A Land Reform Agenda for a Scottish Parliament *The Second McEwan Memorial Lecture* September **146** Reforesting Scotland 1993 *Norway and Scotland: A study in land use* Edinburgh: Reforesting Scotland. Recently, a number of rural communities in Scotland have succeeded in buying the estates of which they were previously tenants and the previous Secretary of State for Scotland proposed the transfer of ownership of government land to the tenants living on it **147** Friends of the Earth Scotland 1996 *Towards a Sustainable Scotland* Edinburgh: FOE Scotland **148** Ministry of Agriculture, Fisheries and Food 1996 *British Survey of Fertiliser Practice* London: HMSO **149** OECD 1993 *World Energy Outlook* May, Paris: OECD **150** Data for 1995 from Department of Trade and Industry 1996 *Business Monitor: Overseas Trade Statistics of the United Kingdom* London: DTI **151** Intervention figure for October 1995. Personal Communication with European Union Offices **152** Paxton, A 1994 *The Food Miles Report: The dangers of long distance food transport* London:

SAFE Alliance **153** *Ibid.* **154** Sweden, in contrast, plans to increase the area under 'ecological cultivation' to 10 per cent by 2000, an increase of 2 per cent per year. Jonsson, H 1996 Greening the fields *Our Planet* 8(4) pp16–17

# NOTES TO CHAPTER 7

**1** Figures for 1981–90 from World Resources Institute 1994 *World Resources 1994–95. A guide to the Global Environment* Oxford. Oxford University Press. All continents are affected, for example, each year in the 1980s, Brazil lost over 3.6 million hectares, Indonesia over 1.2 million hectares and Zaire almost 0.75 million hectares. Food and Agriculture Organisation 1993 *Forest Resources Assessment. Tropical Countries* FAO Forestry Paper 112. Rome: FAO **2** Barnett, A 1992 *Deserts of Trees: The Environmental and Social Impacts of Large-Scale Tropical Reforestation in Response to Global Climatic Change* London: Friends of the Earth **3** See, for example, Harris, M and Kent, M 1987 Ecological benefits of the Bradford-Hutt system of commercial forestry *Quarterly Journal of Forestry* 81. Although disturbance, even in forests, is part of the natural order of things, the impact of clear felling is generally beyond that of natural fires or storms **4** Postel, S and Ryan, J 1991 Reforming Forestry. In Worldwatch Institute *State of the World 1991* London: Earthscan **5** Kardell, L, Steen, E and Fabiao, A 1986 Eucalyptus in Portugal, *Ambio* XV(1) **6** Isomaki, R 1991 Paper, Pollution and global warming – Unsustainable forestry in Finland *The Ecologist*, 21(1), Jan/Feb **7** *Ibid.* **8** As with many assumptions made for simplicity, this is no simple matter, and will require targeted technology transfer by various development agencies to address the problems identified in Chapter 1 **9** World Resources Institute, 1994 *World Resources 1994–95. A Guide to the Global Environment* Oxford: Oxford University Press. We use this as the best proxy for primary industrial wood production and use **10** Rice, T and Wood, A 1995 Introduction. In Rice, T (ed) *Out of the Woods* London: Friends of the Earth **11** Based on tropics (0.63 bn ha): 164.8–291.57 million m³/year, and temperate (0.57 bn ha): 1022.230–2044.602 million m³/year (Rice, T and Wood, A 1995 *Op cit.*) **12** One exception is multi-use forestry or agroforestry as part of regenerative and sustainable agriculture, especially in fragile dry-land environments, which could provide increased timber production with less or no cost to alternative land uses **13** Food and Agriculture Organisation 1993 *FAO yearbook 1991, Forest Products* Rome: FAO **14** However, by 2010 it is unlikely that techniques and yields will have improved in this way, so, as we will see later, we suggest a more stringent target for 2010 than the 2050 target and environmental space methodology would imply **15** These figures, although of the same order of magnitude, are different in detail from those in Friends of the Earth's previous publication on this issue (Rice, T (ed) 1995 *Out of the Woods* London: FOE). This is for two principal reasons. First, we have used more detailed and up-to-date figures on UK consumption and recycled content of wood products which reduce double counting. This acts to reduce the target cuts required. Second, and more significantly, we have calculated environmental space based on a different year with a larger global population base which increases the target cuts **16** Monbiot, G 1992 *Mahogany is Murder, Mahogany extraction from Indian reserves in Brazil* London: Friends of the Earth **17** This means that the reduction targets suggested here are more stringent than those suggested by the Wuppertal Institute, who calculated a 'continental Environmental Space' for wood of between 0.56m³ per capita (requiring a reduction of 23 per cent) and 1.0m³ per capita (requiring no reduction) depending on how much of Russia they included in Europe. Treating wood as a continental resource means that the environmental space target depends on the European sustainable supply of wood. But the boundary of 'Europe' can either include or exclude European Russia. Including Russia would more or less double the European Environmental Space **18** International Institute for Environment and Development 1995 *Citizen Action to Lighten Ecological Footprints* London: IIED **19** Rice, T (ed) 1995 *Out of the Woods* London: FOE **20** Assuming an additional 3.3 million new homes by 2010 and 5.76 m³ of wood per house **21** Based on International Institute for Environment and Development 1995 *Op cit.* who estimate that 64,000 km² of forest land throughout the world are taken up 'more or less permanently' and that an additional 670 km² are deforested each year to provide wood products for the UK **22** For example, substantial areas of the Flow Country remain allocated for afforestation which will largely destroy their wildlife interest. Yet the Flow Country is one of the few areas in the UK which has been proposed as a World Heritage Site **23** House of Lords Select Committee on Sustainable Development 1995 *Sustainable*

*Development. Volume 1* London: HMSO **24** Whiteman, A 1991 *The Supply and Demand for Wood in the United Kingdom* Occasional Paper 29 Forestry Commission. Edinburgh: Forestry Commission **25** Department of the Environment and Ministry of Agriculture, Fisheries and Food 1995 *Rural England – A Nation Committed to a Living Countryside* London: HMSO **26** 1.4 (40 per cent increase)*14.6 (estimated sustainable production) **27** Rice, T (Ed) 1995 *Out of the Woods* London: FOE **28** *Ibid.* **29** Green, B 1992 *Countryside Conservation* The Resource Management Series 3. London: George Allen and Unwin **30** Croydon's 400 tonnes is equivalent to 0.0127 tonnes per person; if every local authority in the UK recycled its wood waste 74,117 tonnes of wood could be recycled **31** Rice, T (ed) 1995 *Out of the Woods* London: FOE **32** Knight, P 1996 Forest Futures *Tomorrow Magazine* VI(6), Nov–Dec, pp10–12 **33** Audit Commission 1995 and 1996 *Local Authority Performance Indicators* London: HMSO; London Borough of Sutton 1995 *Environmental News Newsletter*, Issue 1. November; London Borough of Sutton 1996 *Environmental News Newsletter*, Issue 2. May. Sutton is not entirely an isolated example. In Milton Keynes, for example, a recycling participation rate of 70 per cent has been achieved by providing a separated collection service. Between 50 and 60 per cent of the paper collected is successfully recycled **34** Kendal, M 1996 Personal communication with Waste and Recycling Manager at London Borough of Sutton, July **35** Based on a population of 173,300 **36** This figure has been reduced by 5 per cent to acount for existing average UK recycling rates **37** Using an average conversion factor to WRME of 2.8 as the waste stream contains mixed papers. This percentage figure is not the full 25 per cent that Sutton's performance might suggest, mainly because only larger towns and cities, where recycling is currently more economical, have been included here **38** Jones, P 1995 *The UK Environmental Economy – Do we value it or weigh it?* Working Paper. High Wycombe: Biffa Waste Services **39** Jenkins, T and McLaren, D 1994 *Working Future?* London: Friends of the Earth **40** At the time of writing, waste pulp paper prices have increased substantially so collection is more viable. However, recovery and collection costs are still relatively high, and recycling plants are currently not working at full capacity, thus not at full economic efficiency. This is partly due to poor demand for recycled paper products **41** *Materials Recycling Week* 1996 Cleveland Tonnage Debate, 20 September **42** Warren Springs Laboratory LR511 1992 *A Review of the Environmental Impacts of Recycling* LR511. Stevenage, WSL **43** Rice, T (ed) 1995 *Out of the Woods* London: FOE **44** *Ibid.* **45** Construction Industry Research and Information Association 1994 *Environmental Impact of Materials* Draft for discussion. London, CIRIA **46** Between 1.68 to 2.3 million m$^3$ WRME is already recycled content. Increasing to 70 per cent recycled content across the UK would mean that 2.7 million m$^3$ WRME would be recycled content, a net saving of 0.4 to 1.02 million m$^3$ WRME. As primary consumption for panels as a whole is between 4.8 and 5.4 million m3 WRME this would be a saving of 7.8 to 20 per cent in wood consumption for the production of panels **47** Rice, T (ed) 1995 *Out of the Woods* London: FOE **48** *Ibid.* **49** Desai , P (ed) 1996 *Local Paper – waste paper and non-wood fibres for a sustainable paper cycle in the south east* London, Bioregional Development Group **50** Assuming pulp yields of 75 per cent can be achieved this would produce 47,000 tonnes of pulp. If added to waste paper at a ratio of 1:9, 470,000 tonnes of high grade printing and writing paper could have been home produced. This is equivalent to 11 per cent of current printing and writing paper consumption; *Ibid.* **51** Equivalent to 2.5 per cent of UK consumption of board panels; Forestry Industry Council of Great Britain 1995 *The Forestry Industry Year-Book 1995* London: FICGB **52** Assuming a tonne of straw is equivalent to approximately 2.6m$^3$ WRME. Rice, T (ed) 1995 *Out of the Woods* London: FOE **53** Rice, T (ed) 1995 *Op cit.* **54** Desai, P (ed) 1996 *Local Paper – waste paper and non-wood fibres for a sustainable paper cycle in the south east* London:Bioregional Development Group. The percentage of virgin fibre is high as high grade printing and writing paper is being produced. We have assumed that 70 per cent is collectable and 20 per cent lost during repulping and recycling and used a conservative figure of 5.25 tonnes/ha for hemp fibres and assuming that both the hurds and short fibres are used. The area required is approximately 1.45 per cent of the total land area of the UK **55** Rice, T (ed) 1995 *Op cit.* **56** *Ibid.* **57** *Ibid.* **58** *Ibid* reports figures as high as 80–90 per cent **59** *ENDS Report* 261 1996 Hubbub over packaging regulations, pp25–6 **60** Pruder, F 1992 The German packaging decree, Multi-trip system decree and the consequences of the Eco packaging directive, Dept of Waste Economics, Umweltbundesamt, Berlin *Paper given at Milieu Defensie Sustainable packaging conference* **61** Richert, W and Venner, H 1994 *Well packaged: examples of environmentally friendly packaging systems* Amsterdam: Milieu Defensie **62** Total packaging in UK is 34 per cent of total paper consumption or 8.568 million m$^3$ WRME. 25 per cent of this is 2.14 million m$^3$ WRME **63** Bank, H (ed) 1995 *Sustainable Production and Consumption: An agenda for change* Oslo: The Norwegian Forum for Development and Environment **64** Department of the Environment 1995

*Making Waste Work, A strategy for sustainable waste management in England & Wales* London: HMSO
**65** Rifkin, J 1995 The Future of the Document *Forbes ASAP* 156(8), p45, October **66** Rice, T (ed)
1995 *Out of the Woods* London: FOE **67** *Ibid.* **68** Although it is not clear from the original source
whether energy use in collection has been accounted for **69** World Resource Foundation 1996.
*Electrical and electronic waste* Tonbridge: WRF. Paper production accounts for 7 per cent of industry
emissions, or 2.18 mt-$CO_2$. Forty per cent energy saving on 50–80 per cent of the total production equals 0.4-0.7 mt-CO2 **70** Rice, T (ed) 1995 *Out of the Woods* London: FOE **71** Department
of the Environment 1991 *Waste Management Paper 28 – Recycling* London: DOE

# NOTES TO CHAPTER 8

**1** World Resources Institute 1994 *World Resources 1994–95. A Guide to the Global Environment*
Oxford: Oxford University Press **2** World Resources Institute 1996 *World Resources 1996–7*
Oxford: Oxford University Press **3** Price, M 1996 Relations between groundwater and surface
water in times of scarcity: a challenge to conventional views *Water Environment '96. Conference by the
Chartered Institution of Water and Environmental Management* **4** National Rivers Authority 1994 *Water,
Nature's Precious Resource* Bristol: NRA **5** National Rivers Authority 1995a *Saving Water – the NRA's
Approach to Water Conservation and Demand Management* Bristol: NRA. In 1992/93 the available yield
of public water supply sources in Scotland was 3560 Ml/day. This compares to an average daily
demand of 2206 Ml/day. Scottish Office 1993, *The Scottish Environment Statistics, no.4* Edinburgh:
The Scottish Office **6** National Rivers Authority 1994 *Op cit.* **7** National Rivers Authority 1995b
*The Drought of 1995: a report to the Secretary of State for the Environment* Bristol: NRA **8** OFWAT 1994
*Future levels of demand and supply for water* Occasional paper 1. Birmingham: OFWAT **9** National
Rivers Authority 1991 *Water Resource Planning – Strategic Options* R&D Note 35. Bristol: NRA
**10** Hunt, ID 1996 *High and Dry: The impacts of over-abstraction of water on wildlife* London:
Biodiversity Challenge **11** National Rivers Authority 1993 *Low flows and water resources* Bristol: NRA
**12** Cited in Council for the Protection of Rural England 1993 *Water for life: strategies for sustainable
water resource management* London: CPRE **13** National Rivers Authority 1993 *Low flows and water
resources* Bristol: NRA **14** Friends of the Earth Scotland 1996 *Towards a Sustainable Scotland*
Edinburgh: FOE Scotland **15** English Nature, 1996 *Impact of water abstraction on wetland SSSIs*
Peterborough: English Nature **16** Hunt, ID 1996 *High and Dry: The impacts of over-abstraction of
water on wildlife* London: Biodiversity Challenge **17** Phillips, M 1996 Water resources and
Biodiversity. In *Proceedings of IBC Conference: Water Management and Use*, London 8–9 December
**18** Department of the Environment 1996 *Review of the potential effects of climate change in the UK*
London, HMSO **19** Accounting for a 15 per cent increase in the number of households – based
on the forecasts given in Chapter 6 – by 2010, implies demand for public water supply for households increasing to 8449 Ml/day. The total demand would therefore be 25,650 Ml/day. The cut in
abstraction to 20,840 Ml/day therefore implies a cut in volume terms for England and Wales of
4810 Ml/day or 5430 Ml/day for the UK. For public water supplies the existing demand forecasts
(low, medium, high to 2021) suggest increases in supplies of 3, 10 and 21 per cent. The difference
between these scenarios and our proposed 15 per cent cut is respectively 3000, 4300 and 6900
megalitres per day. Assuming that scenarios based on public water supply can be applied to all
water abstracted then the differences are 4400, 6100 and 8800 megalitres per day. We assume here
that the only intrinsic reason for net increases in demand is growth in the number of households
**20** Friends of the Earth 1996 *The environmental threats of the Kielder transfer scheme* London: FOE
**21** House of Commons Environment Committee 1996 *Water Conservation and Supply* London:
HMSO **22** Environment Canada 1995 *The Economic Impacts of Water Conservation. Research Summary*
Burlington, Ontario: Environment Canada **23** *Ibid.* **24** House of Commons Environment
Committee 1996 *Op cit.* **25** Kulakowski, S and Martin, WE. 1991 Water price as policy variable in
managing urban waste water use: Tucson Arizona *Water Resources Research* 27(2) pp157–66
**26** *Environmental News from the Netherlands* 1992 Are the salmon returning to the Rhine? 3 pp7–10
**27** Marvin, SJ 1992 Towards Sustainable Urban Environments: The potential for least-cost
planning approaches *Journal of Environmental Planning and Management* 35(2), pp193–200
**28** OFWAT 1996a *Leakage of water in England and Wales* Birmingham: OFWAT **29** Scottish Office
1994 *Scottish Sustainable Systems Project* Edinburgh: The Scottish Office **30** National Rivers Authority
1995a *Saving Water – the NRA's Approach to Water Conservation and Demand Management* Bristol: NRA

**31** OFWAT 1996b *Report on the Cost of Water Delivered and Sewage Collected* Birmingham: OFWAT **32** NOAH 1996 *Sustainable Denmark, National Report. The Sustainable Europe Campaign* Copenhagen: Friends of the Earth Denmark/NOAH **33** OFWAT 1996a *Op cit.* These figures are for water lost in the Water Companies' pipes only: total leakage is on average around 1/3 higher **34** Department of the Environment 1995 *Water Conservation: Government Action* London: HMSO **35** National Rivers Authority 1995a *Saving Water – the NRA's Approach to Water Conservation and Demand Management* Brsitol: NRA This section largely uses figures for England and Wales which will be extrapolated to the UK at a later stage **36** National Rivers Authority 1995b *The Drought of 1995: a report to the Secretary of State for the Environment* Bristol: NRA **37** National Rivers Authority 1995a *Op cit.* **38** Save The Children 1995 *Water tight: The impact of metering on low income families* London: Save the Children **39** British Medical Association, 1994 *Water: A vital resource* London: BMA **40** Department of the Environment and OFWAT 1992 *The Social impacts of water metering* A report from WS Atkins. London: DoE **41** OFWAT 1993 *The distributional effects of different methods of charging households for water and sewage services* A report from the Institute of Fiscal Studies. OFWAT: Birmingham **42** The Environment Agency can already charge according to quality and amount of the resource used: they already charge more for non-returned water (notably spray irrigation, most of which evaporates), and more for summer water. However, this has little effect as the unit price is very low. In combination with 'ecologically acceptable flow' measures to establish absolute limits to abstraction, they need to introduce ecological pricing too, to account better for the environmental effects of water abstraction. These measures would allow adequate control of abstraction at sensitive sites and in sensitive years **43** Council for the Protection of Rural England 1992 *Using Water Wisely: Response to Department of the Environment Consultation Paper* London: CPRE **44** Vickers, A 1990 Water-Use Efficiency Standards for Plumbing Fixtures: Benefits of National Legislation *Journal AWWA, Management and Operations* USA **45** NRA 1995 *Demand Management Bulletin 13* Hippos – by the million? Worthing: NRA **46** National Rivers Authority 1995a *Saving Water – the NRA's Approach to Water Conservation and Demand Management* Bristol: NRA **47** Assumes, following the NRA (1995a *Op cit.*) that showers would be used at the rate of 0.55/day/household, totally at the expense of baths (used at 0.6 times per day per household) saving 28.75 litres per day **48** Currently using 35 x 0.55 litres a day **49** 6.15 litres per flush x 10.5 flushes per day = 65 litres/property/day **50** National Rivers Authority 1995 *Demand Management Bulletin 12* p5. Worthing: NRA **51** Council for the Protection of Rural England 1992 *Using Water Wisely: Response to Department of the Environment Consultation Paper* London: CPRE; OFWAT 1996c *Water and You* Birmingham: OFWAT **52** This assumes that outside uses of water by households without gardens is negligible, but that in houses with gardens 25 per cent of outside use would continue to be met with tap water – for example, for children's paddling pools **53** Based on efficiency gains in washing machines in all homes. The saving is: 0.75 x 0.9 x 38 x 24.7 x 1.15 = 708 Ml/day (uses/day x fraction of houses with one x saving per machine per use x no of households) **54** This includes: public water supply to non-household uses, cooling water evaporated in the electricity supply and other industries, other water consumed in the electricity supply and other industries, water used for mineral washing, and other (miscellaneous uses). It does not include tidal water used, spray irrigation, other agricultural uses, fish farming, and private water supplies **55** Chess Industries plc *Letter to Water Companies and MPs* March 1996 **56** Chess Industries plc 1996 *Personal Communication with Friends of the Earth* August. 42,857 person weeks (35 hr week), or 952 person years (45 weeks per year) **57** OFWAT 1994 *Future levels of demand and supply for water.* Occasional paper 1. Birmingham: OFWAT **58** Assumes 20 per cent savings on all uses except cooling, mineral washing and 'other' uses **59** Our estimate for savings in England and Wales is more conservative than the NRA's (6760 Ml/day). In particular, we are less optimistic than the NRA on the scope for domestic recycling and universal metering **60** Friends of the Earth Scotland 1996 *Towards a Sustainable Scotland* Edinburgh: FOE Scotland **61** House of Commons Environment Committee 1996 *Water Conservation and Supply* London: HMSO

# NOTES TO CHAPTER 9

**1** Jackson T 1996 *Material concerns: Pollution, profit and quality of life* London: Routledge **2** Greyson, J (ed) 1995 *The Natural Step 1995: a collection of articles* Bristol: The Natural Step **3** Hinterberger, F, Kranendonk, S, Wlefens MJ and Schmidt-Bleek, F 1994 Increasing resource productivity through eco-efficient services *Wuppertal papers No.13* May 1994. Wuppertal: Wuppertal Institute **4** Cited in Robert, K-H, Daly, H, Hawken, P and Holmberg, J 1995 Methodology. In Greyson, J (ed) 1995 *The Natural Step 1995: a collection of articles* Bristol: The Natural Step. Similarly, current levels of dissipative losses for major biological nutrients (with the possible exception of nitrogen) exceed natural flows by a considerable margin, potentially destabilising natural systems. The World Resources Institute report that global emissions of toxic metals from human activity exceed amounts mobilised by natural processes by up to 330 times in the case of lead, and are at least four times greater for zinc, nickel and arsenic. Ayres, R and Simonis, U 1994 *Industrial Metabolism* Tokyo: United Nations University; World Resources Institute, 1994 *World Resources 1994–95. A Guide to the Global Environment* Oxford: Oxford University Press **5** Ripley, E, Redmann, R and Crowder, A 1996 *Environmental effects of mining* Florida: St Lucia Press **6** In the 1980s, gold was extracted using cyanide from ore mined in open pits. The site operator, Summitville Consolidated Mining Company, Inc., had already initiated remediation procedures when it declared bankruptcy in 1992. Yet the EPA needed to use emergency powers and 'Superfund' monies to prevent up to 200 million gallons of spent cyanide processing solutions escaping into the Wightman Fork river. Plumlee, G and Edelmann, P 1995 *The Summitville mine and its downstream effects* Washington: US Geological Survey **7** World Resources Institute, 1994 *Op cit.* **8** Knisch, H 1990 *Auto und abfall* Hamburg: Hamburg Environmental Institute **9** Rees, J 1985 *Natural Resources: Allocation, economics and policy* London: Methuen **10** At Minamata in the 1950s, discharges of mercury from copper refining at the Chisso chemical factory did not disperse as expected, but bio-accumulated through the food chain. At least 300 deaths resulted along with severe foetal abnormalities, increased miscarriage rates and the birth of children who were blind, deaf or heavily spastic. Jackson, T 1996 *Material Concerns: pollution, profit and quality of life* London: Routledge; Rees, J 1985 *Op cit.* **11** Jackson, T 1996 *Op cit.* **12** For example, extracting copper from copper ore requires between 50 and 100 MJ of energy per kilogramme of finished copper. *Ibid.* **13** Young, J 1992 *Aluminium's real tab* Washington DC: Worldwatch Institute. Electricity is the second largest cost component of primary aluminium production **14** In Brazil, the Tucurui dam and power station on the Tocantins river sells over a third of its electricity to the aluminium industry. In 1992 this dam was producing 4000 megawatts of power. Its reservoir flooded 2430 km$^2$ of tropical forest and 14 villages, resulting in the compulsory relocation of about 23,800 people. Three indigenous territories were also flooded by the lake and the Parakana and Caviao da Montanha peoples were forced to abandon their villages. *Ibid.* **15** Jackson, T 1996 *Material Concerns: pollution, profit and quality of life* London: Routledge, p32 **16** Hook, G and Lucier, G 1997 Synergism, Antagonism and Scientific Process *Environmental Health Perspectives* 105(8) **17** Department of the Environment, 1991 *Chlorinated organic pollutants in fish from the North East Irish Sea* London: DoE **18** Warhurst, M 1995 *An environmental assessment of alkylphenol ethoxylates and alkylphenols* Edinburgh: Friends of the Earth Scotland **19** Ayres, R and Simonis, U 1994 *Industrial Metabolism* Tokyo: United Nations University. Ayres has developed the dissipative/non-dissipative classification to divide materials uses into three classes: economically and technologically recyclable; potentially recyclable; and those where recycling is inherently not feasible. He states that: *Most industrial metals and catalysts are in the first category, other structural and packaging materials, as well as most refrigerants and solvents, fall into the second category. This leaves coatings, pigments, pesticides, herbicides, germicides, preservatives, flocculants, anti-freezes, explosives, propellants, fire retardants, reagents, detergents, fertilizers, fuels and lubricants in the third category. In fact ... most chemical products belong in the third category, except those physically embodied in plastics, synthetic rubber or synthetic fibres* **20** Jackson, T 1996 *Material Concerns: pollution, profit and quality of life* London: Routledge **21** This was no isolated incident – there are around 15,000 uncontrolled hazardous waste landfills and 80,000 contaminated lagoons in the US alone. *Ibid.* **22** Department of the Environment, 1995 *Waste Management Paper 26B, Landfill design, construction and operational practice* London: HMSO **23** Economists cannot even agree on the shape of the price curve to be expected in practice because this depends upon the effects of technological advances and substitution effects. Most resource economists reviewing the price indicator in recent years conclude that the oil price shock of the 1970s made it look like real costs were rising for all minerals but that this was a short term impact, and that real prices are still declining in general. Ozdemiroglu, E 1993 *Measuring Natural Resource Scarcity: A study of the price indicator* CSERGE Working Paper GEC 93–14. London: CSERGE **24** Rees, J 1985 *Natural resources: Allocation, economics and policy* London: Methuen **25** Chapman, P and Roberts, F 1983 *Metal Resources and Energy* London: Butterworth. They judge that such a rise is imminent, or has already begun, for copper and mercury, is close for nickel, lead and uranium, and not too far off for zinc, tungsten, molybdenum and several other metals **26** *Ibid.* **27** OECD 1993 *Environmental policies and industrial competitiveness* Paris: OECD **28** Ozdemiroglu, E 1993 *Measuring Natural Resource Scarcity: A study of the price indicator* CSERGE Working Paper GEC 93-14. London: CSERGE **29** Business Council on Sustainable Development, 1993 *Getting Eco-efficient. Report of the BCSD Eco-efficiency workshop* Antwerp, November 1993. Geneva: BCSD **30** This reserves figure of 50 years is almost twice that resulting from the current economics of the mineral market. As a result it implies, more or less, a doubling in efforts to develop reserves, or a halving of global consumption rates. However, we must recognise that reserve lifespans could fall or rise because of changing investment return rates elsewhere in the economy changing the economic criteria on which companies invest in material resources development **31** Weterings, RA and Opschoor, JB 1992 *The ecocapacity as a challenge to technological development* Rijswijk: Advisory Council for Research on Nature and Environment **32** Carley, M and Spapens, P 1997 forthcoming *Fair Shares: Sustainable living and global equity in the 21st Century* London: Earthscan **33** Buitenkamp, M, Venner, H and Wams, T 1993 *Action Plan – Sustainable Netherlands* Amsterdam: Milieu Defensie **34** This is the figure recommended by the Wuppertal Institute on the basis of Schmidt-Bleek's work. In practice, use of different materials should be cut by different amounts according to relative environmental impacts. As better data and information become available, it should be possible to suggest such specific cuts, but at present the data are not good enough to support such an attempt **35** World Resources Institute 1994 *World Resource 1994–95. A Guide to the Global Environment* Oxford: Oxford University Press **36** Partha Sen of the Delhi School of Economics, suggests it is quite substantial for the EU and Japan, but less significant for the US. Sen, P 1995 Environmental policies and North-South trade: a selected survey of the issues. In Bhaskar, V and Glyn, A *The North, the South and the Environment: Ecological Constraints and the Global Economy* London: Earthscan **37** Cembureau, 1996 *Data from Statistical Department* Brussels: Cembureau **38** Department of the Environment, 1991 *Minerals Planning Guidance Note 10. Provision of raw material for the cement industry* London: HMSO **39** Department of the Environment, 1994 *Minerals Planning Guidance Note 6. Guidelines for aggregate provision in England* London: HMSO **40** British Aggregate Construction Materials Industries, 1995 *Statistical Year Book 1995* London: BACMI **41** Department of the Environment, 1994 *Op cit.* **42** Based on estimates in *ENDS Report* 199, 1991. The arguments over aggregates: options for boosting secondary waste sales, pp18–20; and assuming the Government's target of 55 mt of secondary aggregates is achieved **43** The Link Quarry Group, 1996 *The case against the Harris SuperQuarry* Edinburgh: RSPB, FoE Scotland, Association for the Protection of Rural Scotland, The Ramblers Scotland **44** A report by consulting engineers Ove Arup for the Department of the Environment argues that an increase in the secondary aggregate market share from 9.6 per cent to 24.1 per cent could be achieved by a 50 per cent relative shift in prices between primary and secondary. This would raise £60 million, and be equivalent to an extra 20p per tonne of primary aggregate sold – a 4 per cent increase on current prices. Department of the Environment 1991 *Occurrence and utilisation of mineral and construction wastes* London: HMSO **45** Another pilot project, on the Isle of Wight, is using polystyrene waste as a basic material. Nuki, P 1996 It's the talcum powder house *Sunday Times*, 16 June **46** Rose, P (ed) 1993 *Social Trends 23* Central Statistical Office. London: HMSO **47** Our calculations in the land chapter suggest that 180,000 dwellings per year will come from new-build and redevelopment, and a further 100,000 or so from conversions and reducing vacancy rates. Although we would also anticipate a higher rate of refurbishment of dwellings to improve energy efficiency, as housing construction uses only about 15 per cent of all aggregates (British Aggregate Construction Materials Industries, 1995 *Statistical Year Book 1995* London: BACMI) we can assume that the impact of this on overall demand is within 'normal' market fluctuations. While energy efficiency measures and an expansion of renewable energy generation may increase demands for some materials, they will most likely reduce net demands for non-metallic construction materials by reducing the demand in the energy supply industry. Similarly reducing leakage in our water supply infrastructure may increase demand for some materials for renewing and relaying pipes, but water conservation will remove the need for major infrastructure development of reservoirs and transfer schemes **48** Tindale, S and Holtham, G 1996 *Green Tax Reform* London: Institute of Public Policy Reform **49** Department of the Environment, 1994 *Managing demolition and construction wastes* London: HMSO **50** *Ibid.* In Scotland the recycling rate is lower – just 1 per cent. Liddell, H, Stevenson, F and Kay, T 1994 *New from old: the potential for re-use and recycling in housing* Edinburgh: Scott Homes **51** Liddell, H, Stevenson, F and Kay, T 1994 *New from old: the potential for re-use and recycling in housing* Edinburgh: Scott Homes **52** *ENDS Report* 199, 1991 The arguments over aggregates: options for boosting secondary waste sales, pp18–20 **53** Following the Wuppertal approach to materials in general, but expressed at a national level as total imports and exports are equivalent to only just over 1 per cent of UK aggregates production. British Aggregate Construction Materials Industries 1996 *Personal Communication* 2 December **54** Department of the Environment, 1994 *Managing demolition and construction wastes* London: HMSO. The Transport and Road Research Laboratory cite cases where around 50 per cent recycled content was used with no detriment to durability and performance of even heavily-trafficked roads: Smith, M 1987 Recycled Roads Cut the Cost of Materials *New Scientist*, 30 July **55** *ENDS Report* 199, 1991 *Op cit.* **56** World cement production is 1.15 billion tonnes (1990). For a projected 2050 world population of 9.83 billion, a 50 per cent cut implies a per capita sustainable production figure of 1.15 x 1000/9 83 x 2 = 58.5 kg/cap. For a UK population of 59.594 million in 2050, UK consumption in 2050 can be 58 x 59.594 = 3.49 million tonnes. Apparent cement consumption in the UK in 1992 was 215 kg per capita, or around 12.36 million tonnes (production = 11.046 Mt, exports = 0.365 Mt, imports = 1.455 Mt) Cembureau 1996 *Data from Statistical Department* Brussels: Cembureau **57** We assume that UK steel consumed has roughly the same proportion of recycled scrap inputs as UK steel produced. Recycled input (1994) was 36.5 per cent so UK primary steel consumption (1994) was 14.04 x 0.635 = 8 9 million tonnes **58** Friends of the Earth Scotland, 1996 *Towards a Sustainable Scotland* Edinburgh: FOE Scotland; Vaze, P and Balchin, S 1996 *The Pilot United Kingdom Environmental Accounts* London: Office for National Statistics **59** We use primary steel consumption as a surrogate for raw material flows. World steel consumption in 1990 was 123 kg per capita, in finished steel equivalents. In crude steel equivalents this is 123 x 1.23 = 151.29 kg per capita (using UK conversion factor of 1.23). The UK proportion of recycled inputs in 1990 was 36.85 per cent. Assuming the same proportion of recycled inputs as the UK, world primary crude steel equivalents = 151.29 x 0.6315 = 95.5 kg per capita. So for a world population 1990 of 5.283 billion, this is 504.53 million tonnes. Current UK consumption is 8.92 million tonnes (153 kg per capita). Calculated as a 50 per cent reduction the global 2050 target is 252.3 million tonnes. For a 9.8 billion population this is 25.7 kg per capita. For a UK 2050 population of 59.6 million the target is 1.534 million tonnes, ie a reduction of 83 per cent is needed. Iron and Steel Statistical Bureau 1996 *Faxes to Friends of the Earth, March 25, April 16, April 18* London ISSB; ISSB/IIASA 1996 *World Steel Statistics* London: ISSB; UNECE 1995 *The steel market in 1994 and prospects for 1995* Geneva: UNECE **60** The 2010 target is 7.1 million tonnes of primary steel, down from 8.92 million in 1994. Total consumption of steel was 14.04 million tonnes (ie recycled input was 5.12 million, 36.5 per cent) in 1994. Assuming that total steel consumption is the same in 2010, the recycled/secondary input needs to be 14.04–7 1 = 6.94 million tonnes, ie 49 per cent, an increase of 1.82 million tonnes **61** World Bureau of Metal Statistics, 1994 *Metal statistics 1983–1993* Ware: WBMS **62** *Ibid.* **63** The figures used for this study are for apparent consumption (production + import – export) of primary aluminium, ignoring uses of secondary aluminium and scrap, from the WBMS data (*Op cit.*) **64** Based on data from the Aluminium Federation, cited in Friends of the Earth Scotland 1996 *Towards a Sustainable Scotland* Edinburgh: FOE Scotland **65** World production of primary aluminium, 1990 = 19.437 million tonnes. Current UK consumption is 477,300 (8.2 kg per capita) A 50 per cent cut leads to a 2050 target of 9.72 million tonnes. For a 9.8 billion population this is 0.99 kg per capita. For a UK 2050 population of 59.6 million the target is 59,004 tonnes ie a reduction of 88 per cent is needed World Bureau of Metal Statistics 1994 *Op cit.* **66** World Bureau of Metal Statistics, 1994 *Op cit.* **67** Total consumption of aluminium in 1993 was 687,300 tonnes. If we assume that total aluminium consumption has not increased by 2010, then recycled/ secondary/ scrap input therefore has to increase from the current 209,700 (687,300–477,600) to 314,300 (687,300–373,000). This means that recycled input has to increase from 31 per cent to 46 per cent, or by 104,600 tonnes **68** Department of the Environment, 1996 *Digest of Environmental Statistics, No 18* London: HMSO **69** For example, in 1992, the International Joint Commission (IJC) on the Great Lakes recommended that the US and Canada 'develop timetables to phase out the use of chlorine and chlorinated compounds as industrial feedstocks'. In 1993 the American Public Health Association (APHA) unanimously passed a resolution urging American industry to stop using chlorine. International Joint Commission 1992 *6th Biennial Report* Windsor, Canada: IJC. American Public Health Association 1993 *Policy Statement 9304.* Reported in the *American Journal of Public Health* 1994 Recognizing and Addressing the Environmental and Occupational Health Problems Posed by Chlorinated Organic Chemicals 84(3), pp 514–15 **70** Mackenzie, D 1994 Clinton backs call to ban chlorine *New Scientist*, 12 February **71** Greenpeace 1995 *Transition planning for the chlorine phaseout: economic benefits, costs and opportunities* Amsterdam:

Greenpeace International **72** UK consumption of chlorine in 1992 was 555,000 tonnes. UNECE 1995 *The steel market in 1994 and prospects for 1995* Geneva: UNECE. The Wuppertal methodology adopted by FOE calls for a phase out of chlorine by 2050, and 25 per cent progress towards this by 2010 **73** 1990 Production = 940,305 tonnes + import (12,728 tonnes) – export (3815 tonnes) UNECE 1995 *The Chemical Industry in 1993. Production and Trade Statistics, 1991–93* Geneva: UNECE **74** SITC Code 522.24 **75** National Farmers Union/Friends of the Earth, 1993 *Non-food uses of crops and land. Conference proceedings* London: NFU **76** *ENDS Report* 258 1996 Plastics producers struggle to increase recovery rates, p11 77 Jackson, T 1996 *Material Concerns: Pollution, Profit and Quality of Life* London: Routledge **78** *Ibid.* **79** *Ibid.* **80** *Ibid.* **81** *Ibid.* In an Austrian scheme in Graz, 54 opportunities were found in just five companies (including a garage, printing shops and a chainstore group). Waste reductions of up to 82 per cent were achieved. Niederl and Schnitzer, cited in *Ibid.* **82** In the Aire and Calder project over 540 measures were identified in 11 companies, of which just 2 per cent were later discarded as unfeasible. Emissions to rivers and sewers were reduced by over 300,000 cubic metres per year of suspended solids. Annual savings for the 11 companies totalled £12 million per year. Centre for Exploitation of Science and Technology 1995 *Waste minimisation: Aire and Calder Final Report – Executive summary* London: CEST. WS Atkins, March Consulting Group and Aspects International,1994 *Project Catalyst: Report to the project completion event* Warrington: WS Atkins North West **83** *ENDS Report* 225 HMIP builds on Yorkshire waste reduction project, pp5–6 **84** In a lower-profile initiative in Leicestershire involving ten smaller companies, waste going to landfill (the majority of solid waste) was reduced by 46 per cent while emissions to water and air were also cut. This project found that waste cost the companies concerned 4.5 per cent of turnover (including wasted energy and raw materials costs) and that over 20 per cent of that could be saved. Leicestershire County Council 1995 *Leicestershire waste minimisation initiative project report* Leicester: LCC, March **85** Biffa Waste Services, 1994 *Waste: A game of Snakes and Ladders? A benchmarking report on waste and business strategy* High Wycombe: Biffa Waste Services **86** Research by FOE into the use of voluntary schemes and information provision to promote cleaner technologies found that a stronger regulatory framework, including taxation measures is essential. Hooper, P and Jenkins, T 1994 International Cleaner Technology Databases: On-line off-target *Journal of Cleaner Production* 3(1&2), pp33–44; Jenkins, T 1995 *A Superficial Attraction: The voluntary approach and sustainable development* London: Friends of the Earth **87** Her Majesty's Government, 1994 *Sustainable Development: the UK Strategy* London: HMSO **88** Jones, P 1995 *The UK Environmental Economy – Do we value it or weigh it? Working paper* High Wycombe: Biffa Waste Services **89** Cited in Bar-Hillel, M 1996 A step nearer the less nervous breakdown *Evening Standard* 7 August. There is no reason why all washing machines should not last 20 years. Unfortunately very few manage more than half of this time. If all washing machines were built to the same durability standards as Miele or ASKO, the Finnish group, lasting two to three times longer than average – then 73,000 tonnes of steel per year would be saved. (Initially, the same number of washing machines each year would be bought. As long-life products take over the market, unit turnover will decrease. This figure assumes one million units will be sold each year.) Assuming average British recycled steel content, this is equivalent to 46,000 tonnes of primary material. To increase repair rates, manufacturers need to offer longer guarantees: covering labour and costs, and stock spare parts for at least the expected lifetime of the product. Reliability of washing machines is generally getting worse; 24 per cent of machines needed repair in the first 12 months of use, and one in three needed repair during their first six years. Centre for Alternative Technology 1996 *Come Clean: A Guide to Green Washing Machines* Machynlleth, Wales: Centre for Alternative Technology **90** Cooper, T 1994 *Beyond Recycling* London: New Economics Foundation **91** *Ibid.*, p16 **92** Cited in Cooper, T 1994 *Op cit.* p16 **93** For example, for washing machines, 95 per cent of energy use and water pollution, and 87 per cent of solid waste is generated in use. Washing machines account for 13 per cent of domestic electricity consumption and 12 per cent of domestic water usage. Jackson, T 1996 *Material Concerns: Pollution, Profit and Quality of Life* London: Routledge. The most efficient machines use only about half the water and only one-third of the electricity of the average. If all washing machines achieved these best practice standards, 700 megalitres of water a day would be saved, and so would 3500 GWh of electricity – equivalent to around 3 million tonnes of carbon dioxide. At current machine lifetimes, every machine in use now will have been replaced by 2010. By 2010 it is very likely that the best technology will be better than is currently available. Ninety per cent of 24 million households use a washing machine 0.75 times a day. Average steel use from Friends of the Earth Netherlands 1996 *While stocks last* Amsterdam: Milieu Defensie. Current average water use at 80 litres per load is a conservative estimate from OFWAT 1996 *Water and You* Birmingham: OFWAT **94** Cited in Victory, KM 1996 *Case Studies in Corporate Environmentalism Volume 4* Arlington MA: Cutter Information **95** *Ibid.* **96** Collins, P 1996 Shaky Foundations *Search* 25, pp4–7 **97** Jenkins, T and McLaren, D 1994 *Working Future?* London: Friends of the Earth; Jenkins, T 1997 *Less Traffic: More jobs* London: Friends of the Earth **98** Tindale, S and Holtham, G 1996 *Green Tax Reform* London: Institute of Public Policy Reform **99** Royal Commission on Environmental Pollution, 1993 *Seventeenth Report, Incineration of Waste* London: HMSO **100** For example, the UK exported 4000 tonnes of lead waste to non-OECD countries in 1993; the major destinations were the Philippines, Indonesia, India and Brazil. At lead recycling facilities in the USA, workers are required to wear full-body protective gear. However, at one facility in the Philippines, for example, Greenpeace report that they witnessed factory workers pulling batteries apart with their bare hands. Many workers at battery recycling facilities in Asia and Latin America suffer from severe lead poisoning. The factories are discharging acid into waterways and dumping residual wastes outside property gates. Greenpeace 1994 *Lead, Astray: The poisonous lead battery waste trade* Amsterdam: Greenpeace International **101** Tindale, S and Holtham, G 1996 *Op cit.* In the four years since the tax was introduced, the proportion of construction waste recycled has risen from 12 per cent to over 80 per cent **102** Commission of the European Communities, 1992 *The State of the Environment in the European Community* Brussels: CEC **103** *ENDS Report* 199, 1991 The arguments over aggregate: options for boosting secondary waste sales, pp18–20 **104** The Building Research Establishment comments: 'Despite a large body of laboratory research data showing that recycled aggregates can give excellent performance in concrete, practical use in the concrete industry has been restricted by questions of specification, risk, availability and cost' Collins, R 1996 *Increasing the use of recycled aggregates in construction* Garston: Building Research Establishment. All of these obstacles can be overcome. Changes in minerals and waste planning and taxation regimes can change the relative costs in favour of secondary materials use, and reform of Building Regulations set without consideration of non-primary materials can encourage changes in specification practices **105** Friends of the Earth Scotland, 1996 *Towards a Sustainable Scotland* Edinburgh: FOE Scotland **106** Jenkins, T and McLaren, D 1994 *Working Future?* London: FOE. A report for Scottish Enterprise estimated that increased rates of recycling domestic waste could create around 1000–2000 new jobs in Scotland alone, and save around £25 million annually. Read, T 1991 *Recycling domestic waste in Scotland: A report to Scottish Enterprise Energy and Environmental Technologies Group* Edinburgh: Scottish Enterprise **107** Audit Commission, 1995 and 1996 *Local Authority Performance Indicators* London: HMSO **108** *Ibid.* **109** Mintel, 1992 *Recycling – Public Attitudes and Market Reality* London: Mintel International Group **110** Aluminium Can Recycling Association, 1996 Fax to Friends of the Earth 11 July **111** Despite increasing our can recycling rate from 2.5 per cent to 28 per cent in six years, we are still throwing away more cans every year. Overall, the percentage of aluminium scrap used in the UK's consumption of aluminium has decreased: from 41 per cent in 1984 to 39 per cent in 1994. Department of the Environment, 1996 *Digest of Environmental Statistics, no.18* London: HMSO **112** This is the recycling rate currently achieved in Sweden. At present annual increases of aluminium can recycling, the UK will meet this target, and the aluminium industry's targets are a convenient midway point. There are signs that the increased demand for aluminium cans may be slowing – aluminium's share of the can market appears to be falling in 1996 **113** Aluminium Can Recycling Association, 1996 Personal Communication with Friends of the Earth 11 July **114** For example, energy-use per container for glass milk bottles decreases from 6.11 MJ if they are not returned, to 1.42 MJ if they are reused ten times – a decrease of 77 per cent. Boustead, I and Hancock, G 1989 *EEC directive 85/339 UK Data 1986, A report for INCPEN, Vol 1 – Main report and summary* Milton Keynes: Open University **115** In 1988 the EC Court of Justice approved the Danish ban on metal containers for beer and soft drinks, and accepted the restricted number of bottle types distributed in a deposit and return system – this order contributes significantly to the fact that the return percentage of bottles for beer and soft drinks in Denmark is 99.5 per cent. Ministry of the Environment, Denmark 1992 *Action Plan for Waste and Recycling* Copenhagen: Ministry of the Environment **116** Sound Resource Management Group Incorporated, 1992 *Recycling versus Incineration. An energy conservation analysis* A report for Pollution Probe, Toronto, and Work on Waste USA, New York **117** Cited in Rifkin, J 1996 *The End of Work* New York: Tarcher Puttnam, p130. Around 33 per cent of the steel comes from recycled material, and 62 per cent of the aluminium used has been recycled. In total, 554 kg of primary steel and 27 kg of primary aluminium is used to make an average car. Each car burns 300 gallons of fuel a year, emitting three tonnes of $CO_2$. Friends of the Earth 1996 *The Environmental Footprint of the Car* (unpublished working paper) **118** Friends of the Earth, 1996 *Op cit.* **119** Lovins, A and Lovins, L 1994 *Reinventing the Wheels* Colorado: Rocky Mountain Institute **120** Each hyper-car thus requires 39 kg of primary steel and 20 kg of primary aluminium **121** Lovins, A 1995 *Hypercars: Answers to Frequently Asked Questions* Colorado: Rocky Mountain Institute **122** Mass-producing hyper- or similar cars is a major risk for car manufacturers. Car manufacturers have relatively small profit margins, well established supply networks for components and raw materials and well established marketing strategies: these would need to be re-organised or redesigned **123** Cited in Jackson, T 1996 *Material Concerns: Pollution, Profit and Quality of Life* London: Routledge, p64 **124** Schmidt, K 1996 The Zero Option *New Scientist*, 1 June, pp33–7 **125** *Local Transport Today*, 1996 Councils look to Europe for lessons in car-free living, 15 February. This is not directly equivalent to an 80 per cent dematerialisation, as each car will be used more intensively. However, even if this effect reduces the effective car lifespan (before it, or most of its parts need to be replaced) by half it still represents a 60 per cent cut in consumption of the materials that make up a car **126** Jackson, T 1996 *Op cit.* There are other products to which similar logic can be applied. Increased use of launderettes or communal laundries with efficient washing machines could achieve even greater savings in materials than more durable machines alone could deliver, especially where easy access to clothes lines is retained. For this to succeed, launderettes need to be made more pleasant places for people to use. The Centre for Alternative Technology reports plans by the Ark Foundation to set up: *launderettes which provide coffee bars, games and television. All the machines will be environmentally friendly and energy efficient and information will be provided to customers. They will be computerised and able to weigh the laundry and calculate the correct amount of detergent and water required. Waste heat from the tumble driers will be used to heat the washing water and the building while the final rinse water from one wash will be used in the first rinse of the next wash.* In Denmark there are more than 120 clusters of housing designed to include common facilities such as dining rooms, laundries, playrooms, workshops and recreation space. In one Danish co-housing estate 100 people found they needed only two washing machines. At this level of sharing it is very easy to find the money to buy the most efficient and most durable machines. In Sweden many flats have shared laundries, and also shared heating systems, bike storage and recreation space, and separated storage of recyclable waste. Centre for Alternative Technology, 1996 *Come Clean: A Guide to Green Washing Machines* Machynlleth, Wales: Centre for Alternative Technology. Trainer, T 1995 *The Conserver Society* London: Zed Press **127** Mayo, E 1996 *Community Banking: a review of the international policy and practice of social lending* Prepared for Credit and Debt Policy Group, Dublin **128** Manchester LETS, 1996 *Manchester LETS* Manchester: Manchester LETS. Aluminium extending ladders are a very popular hire item in Manchester as are step-ladders and numerous other DIY tools. Overall, there are over 3000 pieces of equipment or tools available to members of LETS in Manchester, probably cutting material consumption by more than ten times **129** Jackson, T 1996 *Material Concerns: Pollution, Profit and Quality of Life* London: Routledge

# NOTES TO PART 2 CONCLUSIONS

**1** Wackernagel, M and Rees, W 1996 *Our Ecological Footprint* Gabriola Island BC: New Society, pxi

# NOTES TO CHAPTER 10

**1** European Commission 1994 Communication on Economic Growth and the Environment. *Supplement to Europe Environment* 444: December 6. Brussels: Europe Information Service **2** *ENDS Report* 207 1992 Industrial Winners and Losers in the Carbon Tax Game, pp14–16; *ENDS Report* 218 1993 Battle lines sharpen on carbon tax as EC climate policy advances, pp35–6; *ENDS Report* 257 1996 A new momentum towards green tax reforms, pp18–21 **3** Worcester, R 1996 Business and the Environment: In the aftermath of Brent Spar and BSE. *Lecture to HRH The Prince of Wales' Business and the Environment Programme* University of Cambridge 16 September **4** Hawken, P 1994 *The Ecology of Commerce* London: Phoenix **5** Handy, C 1994 *The Empty Raincoat* London: Hutchinson. **6** Korten, DC 1996 *When Corporations Rule the World* London: Earthscan

**7** Hampden-Turner, C 1996 The Enterprising Stakeholder *Independent* 5 February **8** Bello, W and Rosenfeld, S 1992 *Dragons in Distress: Asia's miracle economies in crisis* London: Penguin, p12 **9** You, Jong-Il 1995 The Korean model of development and its environmental implications. In Bhaskar, V and Glyn, A *The North, the South and the Environment* London: Earthscan **10** Robinson, S 1996 *Out of the Twilight Zone: managing the threats and opportunities of an environmentally sustainable business* London: The Environment Council **11** Korten, DC 1996 *When Corporations Rule the World* London: Earthscan **12** Rowell, A 1996 *Green Backlash* London: Routledge **13** Alliance of Northern People for Environment and Development, undated. Groundwork Series 6: Green Business Policies *Http://www.mbnet.mb.ca/ linkages/consume/an'bus.html* **14** Institute of Environmental Management 1995 *Members Annual Survey* Edinburgh: IEM **15** Cited in Victory, KM (ed) *Case Studies in Corporate Environmentalism, Vol 1* Arlington MA: Cutter Information, p20 **16** *ENDS Report* 258 1996 Policy machine moves up a gear to meet global warming challenge, pp13–18 **17** Jenkins, T and Hunter, D 1993 *Multinational Corporations and the Environment: An introduction for central and eastern Europeans* Brussels: FOE Europe **18** Dow Chemical Company v. Alfaro 768 S.W.2d 674, 679 (Texas 1990), cert denied 111 S.Ct. 671 (1991) **19** Jenkins, T and Hunter, D 1993 Op cit. In a similar act, Texaco was recently proven to have falsified reports under the Tidal Waters Act in the USA for testing of oil-rigs **20** Hutton, W 1995 *The State We're In* London: Jonathan Cape **21** *International Environment Reporter* 1996 Law makes some environment crimes capital offences punishable by death 3 April **22** Jenkins, T 1995 *A Superficial Attraction. Sustainable Development and the Voluntary Approach* London: FOE **23** Industry Council for Electronic Equipment Recycling 1994 *UK Plan for Recovering Value from End-of-life Electronic and Electrical Equipment* Bath: ICER **24** *ENDS Report* 257 1996 Doubts raised over accuracy of appliance energy labels, p27 **25** Spencer Cooke, A and Elkington, J 1996 Making a Statement. *Tomorrow Magazine* VI(4) pp52–7 **26** Cited in Business Council for Sustainable Development 1994 *Getting Eco-efficient. Report of the BCSD First Antwerp Eco-efficiency workshop* November 1993. Geneva: BCSD **27** Loughran, K 1996 No turning back. *Tomorrow Magazine* VI(1), January–February **28** Interview with Professor Siefert, Head of Research and Development, *BBC Radio 4 Today programme* 30 May 1990 **29** Kernwick, I and Ausubel, JH 1995 National material flows and the environment. *Annual Review of Energy and the Environment* 20; Jones, P 1995 *The UK Environmental Economy – Do we value it or weigh it?* Working Paper. High Wycombe: Biffa Waste Services **30** Business Council for Sustainable Development 1994 *Op cit.* p10 **31** Factor Ten Club 1994 *The Carnoules Declaration* Wuppertal: Factor Ten Club **32** Maizels, A 1992 *Commodities in Crisis* Oxford: Clarendon Press discusses this literature **33** Department of the Environment 1996 *Indicators of Sustainable Development for the United Kingdom* London: HMSO **34** Maizels, A 1992 *Op cit.* **35** Glyn, A 1995 Northern growth and environmental constraints. In Bhaskar, V and Glyn, A (eds) *The North, the South and the Environment* London: Earthscan **36** Business Council for Sustainable Development 1994 *Getting Eco-efficient. Report of the BCSD First Antwerp Eco-efficiency Workshop* November 1993. Geneva: BCSD, p9, emphasis added **37** Hart, S 1997 Beyond Greening. *Harvard Business Review*, Jan–Feb, pp66–76 **38** Business Council for Sustainable Development 1994 Op cit. **39** Jackson, T 1996 *Material Concerns: Pollution, Profit and Quality of Life* London: Routledge **40** Weaver, PM 1993 Synergies of association: Ecorestructuring, scale, and the industrial landscape *Paper for United Nations University, Tokyo, Symposium on Ecorestructuring* 5–7 July **41** Jackson, T 1996 *Op cit.*; Christie, I and Rolfe, H with Legard, R 1995 *Cleaner Production in Industry: Integrating business goals and environmental management* London: Policy Studies Institute **42** *International Environment Reporter* 1996 Ebara announces $235 million project for 'zero emission' city by the turn of the century, 12 June **43** Schmidt, K 1996 The Zero Option. *New Scientist*, 1 June, pp33–7 **44** Cited in *Ibid.* **45** Laurance, B 1997 Multi-armed monsters set to dismember. *Observer* 16 Feb **46** Weaver, PM 1993 Synergies of association: Ecorestructuring, scale, and the industrial landscape *Paper for United Nations University, Tokyo, Symposium on Ecorestructuring* 5–7 July **47** World Business Council for Sustainable Development 1996 *Eco-efficient leadership for improved economic and environmental performance* Geneva: WBCSD **48** Hutton, W 1995 *The State We're In* London: Jonathan Cape **49** Korten, DC 1996 *When Corporations Rule the World* London: Earthscan **50** Hampden-Turner, C 1996 The Enterprising Stakeholder *Independent* 5 February **51** Multinational Monitor 1996 When Corporations Rule the World: an interview with David Korten. *Multinational Monitor* Jan/Feb, pp25–9 **52** Christie, I and Rolfe, H with Legard, R 1995 *Cleaner Production in Industry: Integrating business goals and environmental management* London: Policy Studies Institute. The BCSD has called for financial innovation: new instruments which can channel capital to eco-efficient products and companies. Business Council for Sustainable Development 1994 *Getting Eco-efficient: Report of the BCSD First Antwerp Eco-efficiency Workshop* November 1993. Geneva: BCSD **53** Jackson, T 1996 *Material Concerns: Pollution,*

*Profit and Quality of Life* London: Routledge **54** The UN Environment Programme estimates that 16 US$1bn-plus catastrophes linked to the environment occurred between 1987 and 1993, resulting in worldwide insured losses of over US$50bn. Cited by Boulton, L 1996 Weather Worries *Financial Times* 9 September **55** Cited in Boulton, L 1996 Debate warms up *Financial Times* 28 May **56** *ENDS Report* 249 1995 Pollution insurance 'freebies' come under fire, pp19–21 **57** UNI Storebrand in Norway are already refusing to insure companies that fail to take on environmental responsibilities. So far, those rejected include several shipping companies. They are also promoting environmental management and certification in car-repair workshops, to reduce materials waste in repair work funded from insurance claims. Frankel, C 1996 Putting a premium on the Environment *Tomorrow magazine* VI(3) p18 **58** *ENDS Report* 250 1995 Insurance businesses promise environmental commitment, p6 **59** Wright, M 1996 God, Mammon and the Markets. *Tomorrow Magazine* VI(3), pp10–11 **60** Elkington, J and Spencer-Cooke, A 1996 The Banks Come Clean. *Tomorrow Magazine* VI(3) pp54–60 **61** Cited in *Ibid.* **62** Krouwel, BJ and Steiner, T 1997 Working for a better world for business. *Environmental News from the Netherlands* Feb 1997 pp5–7 **63** Nitsche, C and Hope, C 1996 *The Banking sector and environmental issues* University of Cambridge, Judge Institute of Management Studies: Research Papers in Management Studies No 7 **64** Business in the Environment/Extel Financial 1994 *City Analysts and the Environment: a survey of environmental attitudes in the City of London* London: BiE. On the other hand 69 per cent of analysts reported taking account of likely financial costs of environmental liabilities such as site clean-up **65** Holden Meehan 1994 *An independent guide to ethical and green investment funds* London: Holden Meehan **66** Cited by *Ibid.* **67** Holden Meehan 1994 *Op cit.* **68** They are partly responsible for the growing number of 'investor proxy' resolutions to company AGMs on environmental issues, which increased over 20 times in the US between 1988 and 1990. Hoffman, AJ 1996 Environmental management withers away. *Tomorrow Magazine* VI(2), pp60–2 **69** Business in the Environment/Extel Financial 1994 *City Analysts and the Environment: a survey of environmental attitudes in the City of London* London: BiE **70** Gale, R, Barg, S and Gillies, A 1995 *Green Budget Reform. An international casebook of leading practices* London: Earthscan **71** Christie, I and Rolfe, H with Legard, R 1995 *Cleaner Production in Industry: Integrating business goals and environmental management* London: Policy Studies Institute **72** Handy, C 1994 *The Empty Raincoat* London: Hutchinson **73** Hutton, W 1995 *The State We're In* London: Jonathan Cape **74** He suggests: first, constraining banks' dividend distribution so they build up reserves for long-term lending (as in Germany), and second, encouraging banks to take equity stakes, if they are to have any effective claim on company assets in the event of business failure. In such circumstances, the government would need to offer loan guarantees to support borrowing by smaller enterprises, so that banks did not focus on lower-risk loans to established companies **75** Mayo, E 1996 *Community Banking: a review of the international policy and practice of social lending.* Paper for the Credit and Debt Policy Group, Dublin, Ireland **76** In the USA, on the other hand, the Community Reinvestment Act of 1977 required banks to reveal the distribution of their lending and to meet the credit needs of their entire communities. There are now five Community Development Banks in the USA, which have made loans of US$400m since inception. They provide finance for a range of community needs. For example, the South Shore Bank in Chicago has financed rehabilitation of 30 per cent of the area's housing in a community of 75,000 mainly black people, over 20 years. There are also around 125 ethnic minority or women owned banks in the US. Mayo, E 1996 *Op cit.* **77** *Multinational Monitor* 1996 When Corporations Rule the World: an interview with David Korten Jan/Feb, pp25–9 **78** Mayo, E 1996 *Op cit.* **79** *Ibid.* In the Emilian region of Northern Italy, a network of mainly small firms and self-employed workers is supported by the availability of low-interest credit (even to home-workers) from such sources **80** Millais, C 1996 Greenpeace solutions campaigns – closing the implementation gap *ECOS* 17(2), pp50–58 **81** Institute of Directors 1995 *Business opinion survey: the environment* London: Director Publications **82** UN Centre on Transnational Corporations 1991 *Benchmark Corporate Environmental Survey* New York: UNCTC **83** Cited by Vidal, J 1992 Environment: briefing *The Guardian* 11 December **84** Vaze, P and Balchin, S 1996 *The Pilot UK Environmental Accounts* London: Office for National Statistics. *ENDS Report* 259 1996 Study finds lower environmental costs in chemical, power industries pp3–4 **85** Entec and The Green Alliance 1996 Business and the Environment Trends Survey. *News Release* 22 May **86** *ENDS Report* 236 1994 NRA calls for regulations to curb industrial pollution, p10; *ENDS Report* 248 1995 HMIP reports another rise in pollution incidents, pp8–9 **87** Environmental Industries Commission 1996 *Weak standards, delayed implementation and poor enforcement of environmental legislation* London: EIC **88** Environmental Industries Commission 1995

*Government Policies as the Catalyst for the British Environmental Industry* London: EIC **89** Christie, I and Rolfe, H with Legard, R 1995 *Cleaner Production in Industry: Integrating business goals and environmental management* London: Policy Studies Institute **90** European Commission 1994 Communication on Economic Growth and the Environment *Supplement to Europe Environment* 444: December 6. Brussels: Europe Information Service **91** Foundation for Economic Research (Amsterdam University) and Centre for European Economic Research (Mannheim) 1996 *The impact of parameters provided by environmental policy on the innovative behaviour of companies in selected European countries* Amsterdam: Foundation for Economic Research **92** Christie, I and Rolfe, H with Legard, R 1995 *Op cit.*, p222 **93** US Environmental Protection Agency 1988 *Toxics in the Community* Washington DC: US EPA, pxxxi **94** Jackson, T 1996 *Material Concerns: Pollution, Profit and the Quality of Life* London: Routledge **95** Robert, KH, Daly, H, Hawken, P and Holmberg, J 1995 'Methodology' in Greyson, J (ed) 1995 *The Natural Step 1995: A Collection of Articles* Bristol: The Natural Step **96** Marvin, SJ 1992 Towards Sustainable Urban Environments: The potential for least-cost planning approaches *Journal of Environmental Planning and Management* 35(2), pp193–200 **97** Jackson, T 1992 *Efficiency without tears: no-regrets policy to combat climate change* London: Friends of the Earth **98** Marvin, SJ 1992 *Op cit.* **99** Levett, R 1994 Sustainable Pricing Structures *Town and Country Planning* 63(10) pp270–272 **100** European Commission 1993 *White Paper on Growth, Competitiveness, Employment: The challenges and ways forward into the twenty first century* Brussels: European Commission; Poitier, M 1995 Environmental Policies, Employment and International Competitiveness. In Friends of the Earth 1995 *Working Futures. Proceedings of a Seminar on Growth, Jobs and the Environment* London: Friends of the Earth **101** Tindale, S and Holtham, G 1996 *Green Tax Reform* London: Institute of Public Policy Reform. Not all of the new jobs would be taken by those currently recognised as unemployed **102** Deutsches Institut fur Wirtschaftforschung 1994 *The economic effects of ecological tax reform* Berlin: DIW **103** OECD 1993 *Environmental policies and industrial competitiveness*. Paris: OECD **104** Warren Spring Laboratory 1993 *Report of the current work of the Warren Spring Laboratory* Investigation of Air Pollution Standing Conference **105** Weightman, F 1994 *Renewable Energy and NFFO3* London: Friends of the Earth; Inland Revenue 1996 *Inland Revenue Statistics 1996* London, HMSO **106** Greyson, J (ed) 1995 *Op cit*, p36 **107** OECD 1993 *Op cit*; Barker, T 1993 Is green growth possible *New Economy* 1, pp20–25 **108** Templet, PH 1996 The energy transition in international economic systems: an empirical analysis of change in development *International Journal of Sustainable Development and World Ecology* 3, pp13–30 **109** European Commission 1994 Communication on Economic Growth and the Environment *Supplement to Europe Environment* 444: December 6. Brussels: Europe Information Service **110** Jenkins, T and McLaren, D 1994 *Working Future?* London: Friends of the Earth **111** DRI 1994 *The potential benefits of integration of environmental and economic policies: an incentive based approach to policy integration* Brussels: European Commission **112** Another area where our proposals might have a direct effect on the economy is in the property market. Property value is an important factor in economic stability. Too rapid growth in property values can fuel inflation, while falls in property values, especially if negative equity becomes widespread, can reinforce economic recession and hardship. The measures suggested in Chapter 6 would see an increase in the rate of housing starts (especially in the social housing sector), and given growing household numbers would have little net effect on house prices in comparison with the effects of wider economic confidence **113** Currently PSBR is around 3.5 per cent of GDP, and investment about 1 per cent – the golden rule can be reached by increasing investment as well as cutting borrowing **114** Corry, D and Holtham, G 1995 *Growth with Stability: Progressive macroeconomic policy* London: Institute for Public Policy Research **115** *Ibid.* **116** Tindale, S and Holtham, G 1996 *Green Tax Reform* London: Institute of Public Policy Reform **117** DRI 1994 *The Potential Benefits of integration of environmental and economic policies: an incentive based approach to policy integration* Brussels: European Commission **118** Tindale, S and Holtham, G 1996 *Op cit.* **119** European Commission 1994 Communication on Economic Growth and the Environment *Supplement to Europe Environment* 444: December 6. Brussels: Europe Information Service **120** de Wit, G 1995 Employment effects of ecological tax reform. In Friends of the Earth 1995 *Working Futures. Proceedings of a Seminar on Growth, Jobs and the Environment* London: FOE **121** Majocchi, A 1994 The employment effects of eco-taxes: a review of empirical models and results *Paper presented at the OECD workshop on implementation of Environmental Taxes* Paris, February **122** Jacobs, M 1996 *The Politics of the Real World* London: Earthscan **123** Cooper, Y 1996 A blunt instrument that would fail to cure poverty? No *Independent* 9th September, p6 **124** Hudson, R and Weaver, P 1995 Economic Restructuring and Public Expenditure for sustainable development: An Eco-Keynesian Model. In Friends of the Earth

1995 *Op cit.* **125** Tindale, S and Holtham, G 1996 *Green Tax Reform* London: Institute of Public Policy Reform; DRI 1994 *The potential benefits of integration of environmental and economic policies: an incentive based approach to policy integration* Brussels: European Commission **126** Lowe, MD 1994 *Back on Track: The Global Rail Revival* Washington DC: Worldwatch Institute **127** Hutton, W 1995 Myth that sets the world to right *Guardian* 12 June; Wolf, M 1996 The Global Economy Myth *Financial Times*, 13 Feb **128** Cited in Wolf, M 1996 *Op cit.* **129** Cited in Agarwal, A and Narain, S 1993 Sustainability and the Southern Perspective. *Down to Earth* 15 July, pp32–6 **130** Redclift, M 1996 *Wasted: counting the costs of global consumption* London: Earthscan **131** *ENDS Report* 260. 1996 ISO under fire over environmental standards pp3–4 **132** Agarwal, A and Narain, S 1993 *Op cit.* **133** Bhaskar, V and Glyn A (eds) 1995 *The North, the South and the Environment* London: Earthscan

# NOTES TO CHAPTER 11

**1** UN Development Programme 1996 *Human Development Report 1996* Oxford: Oxford University Press **2** Wilkinson, R 1996 *Unhealthy societies: the afflictions of inequality* London: Routledge **3** In the US, researchers from Harvard and Berkeley found that the states with the most unequal distribution of household income had the highest death rates, and the wider the inequality the lower the overall decline in death rates over recent decades. This was found to hold for heart disease, cancer and homicide, amongst other causes of death. Kaplan, G, Pamuk, E, Lynch, J, Cohen, R and Balfour, J 1996 Inequality in income and mortality in the United States: analysis of mortality and potential pathways. *British Medical Journal* 312, 20 April, pp999–1003; Kennedy, B, Kawachi, I and Prothrow-Stith, D 1996 Income distribution and mortality: cross-sectional ecological study of the Robin Hood index in the United States. *British Medical Journal* 312, 20 April, pp1004–8 **4** Benezeval, M, Judge, K and Whitehead, M 1995 *Tackling inequalities in health. An Agenda for Action* London: Kings Fund, p xviii **5** Jacobs, M 1996 *The Politics of the Real World* London: Earthscan **6** Merva and Fowles, cited by Rifkin, J 1996 *The End of Work* New York: Tarcher Puttnam **7** Wilkinson, R 1996 *Op cit.* **8** Jacobs, M 1996 *Op cit.* **9** Kaplan, G *et al.* 1996 Inequality in income and mortality in the United States: analysis of mortality and potential pathways *British Medical Journal* 312 20 April, pp999–1003 **10** OECD 1996 *Employment Outlook, July 1996* Paris: OECD; Bruno, M 1996 Unpublished World Bank paper cited by Lean, G and Cooper, Y 1996 Not enough for us *Independent on Sunday* 21 July, p19 **11** Cited by Lean, G and Cooper, Y 1996 *Op cit.* **12** Lean, G and Cooper, Y 1996 *Op cit.*; Jacobs, M 1996 *The Politics of the Real World* London: Earthscan **13** Leadbeater, C 1996 How Fat Cats Rock the Boat. *Independent on Sunday* 3 November **14** OECD 1996 *Op cit.* **15** Corry, D and Glyn, A 1994 The macro-economics of equality, stability and growth. In Glyn, A and Milliband, D (eds) *Paying for inequality: the economic cost of social injustice* London: Institute for Public Policy Research **16** These arguments are backed by economic theory based on the work of mathematical economists such as Paul Romer at Berkeley in California, and by the work of urban economists looking at regional trends across the USA which found the highest increases in unemployment where inequality rose most. Bernstein, A 1994 Inequality: how the gap between rich and poor hurts the economy *Business Week* 15 August **17** Deininger, K and Squire, L 1996 Measuring income inequality: a new database *World Bank Economic Review* September **18** Hampden-Turner, C 1996 The Enterprising Stakeholder *The Independent* 5 February **19** UN Development Programme 1996 *Human Development Report 1996* Oxford: Oxford University Press **20** Jacobs, M 1996 *The Politics of the Real World* London: Earthscan **21** Wilkinson, R 1996 *Unhealthy societies: the afflictions of inequality* London: Routledge **22** Wilkinson, MJ 1996 Our At-Risk Society: Exclusion as a threat to health and democracy. *Journal of Contemporary Health* 4, pp62–4 **23** Merva and Fowles, cited by Rifkin, J 1996 *The End of Work* New York: Tarcher Puttnam **24** Jacobs, M 1996 *Op cit.* **25** *Ibid.* **26** *Ibid.* **27** DRI 1994 *The potential benefits of integration of environmental and economic policies: an incentive based approach to policy integration* Brussels: European Commission **28** Hutton, W 1995 *The State We're In* London: Jonathan Cape. The bottom 30 per cent generally lack employment and live on state benefits, the top 40 per cent still have reasonably secure jobs and incomes, and the middle 30 per cent live in insecurity **29** Judd, J 1996 Inner city pupils stunted by gap in growth and development *The Independent* 2 October **30** *The Economist* 1996 Opportunity Knocks. 10 August, pp24–6 **31** UN Development Programme 1996 *Human Development Report 1996* Oxford: Oxford University Press **32** Holterman, S 1996 The impact of public expenditure and fiscal policies on the UK's children and young people. *Children and Society*

10, pp3–13 **33** Handy, C 1994 *The Empty Raincoat* London: Hutchinson; Wilkinson, MJ 1996 Our
At-risk Society: Exclusion as a threat to health and democracy *Journal of Contemporary Health* 4,
pp62–4 **34** *The Independent* 1996 Leading article: Wake up unions: there's a mighty job to do 9
September, p13 **35** Jacobs, M 1996 *The Politics of the Real World* London: Earthscan **36** Rifkin, J
1996 *The End of Work* New York: Tarcher Puttnam **37** *Ibid.* **38** de Wit, G 1995 Employment
effects of ecological tax reform. In Friends of the Earth 1995 *Working Futures. Proceedings of a
seminar on Growth, Jobs and the Environment* London: FOE **39** Schor, J 1995 Can the North stop
consumption growth? Escaping the cycle of work and spend. In Glyn, A and Bhaskar, V (eds)
*The North, the South and the Environment* London: Earthscan **40** Robertson, J 1991 *Future Wealth: A
new economics for the twenty first century* London: Cassell; Robertson, J 1994 *Taxes and Benefits* London:
New Economics Foundation **41** Stroeken, J 1996 A Case for basic income *New Economy* 3(3),
pp187–191 **42** Jacobs, M 1996 *The Politics of the Real World* London: Earthscan **43** Corry, D
Indirect taxation is not as bad as you think. In Tindale, S and Holtham, G 1996 *Green Tax Reform*
London: Institute of Public Policy Research **44** Jenkins, T and McLaren, D 1994 *Working Future?*
London: Friends of the Earth **45** The £16 billion contract to build 230 jet fighters, announced in
1996, will 'safeguard' some 14,000 jobs **46** Cited in Rifkin, J 1996 *The End of Work* New York:
Tarcher Puttnam, p242 **47** Wilkinson, MJ 1996 Our At-risk Society: Exclusion as a threat to
health and democracy *Journal of Contemporary Health* 4, pp62–4 **48** Jacobs, M 1996 *Op cit.*
**49** Independent Commission on Population and Quality of Life 1996 *Caring for the Future* Oxford:
Oxford University Press **50** UN Development Programme 1996 *Human Development Report 1996*
Oxford: Oxford University Press **51** Boardman, B 1995 *Personal Communication to Friends of the
Earth* 31 May **52** Cited by Lean, G and Cooper, Y 1996 Not enough for us *Independent on Sunday*
21 July, p19 **53** Bullard, R (ed) 1993 *Confronting Environmental Racism* Boston MA: South End Press
**54** Agyeman, J 1989 Black People, White Landscape *Town and Country Planning* 58(12), pp336–8
**55** Newell, P 1994 What a way to treat a child *The Independent* 15 January **56** Department of the
Environment 1991 *English Housing Condition Survey* London, HMSO **57** Hunt, S and Boardman, B
1994 Chapter 2: Defining the problem. In Markus, T (ed) *Domestic energy and affordable warmth*
Report 30 London: Watt Committee **58** Freeman, H 1984. Scientific Background, p44. in
Freeman, H (ed) *Mental Health and the Environment* London: Churchill Livingstone **59** *ENDS Report*
230 1994 Energy efficiency bill hits treasury blockage, pp30–31 **60** Appleyard, D and Lintell, M
1972 The environmental quality of city streets: the resident's viewpoint *American Institute of
Planners' Journal* March, pp84–101. They studied three similar streets in San Francisco, differenti-
ated only by the volumes of traffic (2000–16,000 vehicles per day). There were three times as
many social contacts in the street with the least traffic as in the street with the most **61** Berkman,
L and Syme, D 1979. Social Networks, Host Resistance and Mortality: a Nine year Follow-up
Study of Alameda County Residents *American Journal of Epidemiology* 109, pp186–204 **62** Hillman,
M, Whitelegg, J and Adams, J 1991 *One False Move* London: Policy Studies Institute **63** *Ibid.* p81
**64** Cited in Bullock, S 1995 *Prescription for Change* London: Friends of the Earth **65** Bullock, S
1995 *Op cit.* **66** Independent Commission on Population and Quality of Life 1996 *Caring for the
Future* Oxford: Oxford University Press **67** UN Conference on Environment and Development
1992 *Agenda 21: the United Nations Programme of Action from Rio* Geneva: United Nations
Publications, paras 23.1–23.2 **68** Major, J 1991 *Speech to Sunday Times Conference* London, July
**69** Toynbee, P 1997 Beware new housing traps for the poor *The Independent* 10 Feb **70** Wilkinson,
MJ 1996 Our At-risk Society: Exclusion as a threat to health and democracy *Journal of
Contemporary Health* 4, pp62–4 **71** Cited by Wilkinson, MJ 1996 *Op cit.* **72** Barrie Green
Community near Toronto has achieved 25 per cent water savings in its first year, through improving 7000 out of 26,000 households. The savings from this exceeded the provincial funding for all
25 green communities for the last three years. In total the Green Communities Initiative has
created 10,000 person years of work. Overall the return on investment in the province is over 400
per cent. Ministry of the Environment, Canada 1995 Green Communities Initiative, 13 October,
Toronto. In a similar initiative in the USA, an organisation called Habitat for Humanity is building
green-design houses to fulfil social needs. Surveys for the US Department of Housing showed
that low-income families spend 20–30 per cent of their income on utility bills, compared with
10–15 per cent for middle-income house owners. Habitat for Humanity, 1996 *Information Pack*
Americus, Georgia: Habitat for Humanity International. By purposely building affordable,
energy-efficient houses with a range of green-design features, they are lowering costs for potential home-owners, and are opening home-ownership to a lot more people. Habitat for Humanity
1996 *Information Pack.* Americus, Georgia: Habitat for Humanity International **73** Ministry of the
Environment Canada 1995 *Op cit.* **74** Agyeman, J 1996 *Personal Communication* 15 November

# NOTES TO CHAPTER 12

**1** European Commission 1992 *Towards Sustainability* Brussels: CEC p3 **2** UN Conference on Environment and Development 1992 *Agenda 21: the United Nations Programme of Action from Rio* Geneva: United Nations Publications, para 8.3 **3** Instead of addressing each pollutant and its impacts separately, European negotiations on the UN Economic Commission for Europe Convention on Long-range Transboundary Air Pollution are seeking cost-effective strategies to control emissions of sulphur dioxide, nitrogen oxides, ammonia and volatile organic compounds in order to limit damage from acidification, eutrophication and tropospheric ozone simultaneously. And the European Environment Agency is exploring wider application of such principles to the range of pollution problems we face **4** Tindale, S and Holtham, G 1996 *Green Tax Reform* London: Institute of Public Policy Reform; Barker, T and Lewney, R 1991 A green scenario for the UK economy. In Barker, T (ed) *Green futures for the UK – economic growth in 2010* Cambridge: Cambridge Econometrics **5** The House of Lords select committee on sustainable development found that progress on policy integration in the UK was 'uneven', and were especially critical of the role of the Treasury in this respect, which they saw as key to other policy areas. House of Lords Select Committee on Sustainable Development 1995 *Sustainable Development* Volume 1. London: HMSO **6** European Commission 1996 *Progress Report on implementation of the European Community Programme of policy and action in relation to the environment and sustainable development 'Towards Sustainability'* Brussels: EC **7** This was the background to the conflict over Twyford Down, which was the last link in upgrading the whole route between London and Southampton to motorway standard. Progress on a proposed EU Directive on assessment of plans and programmes has been limited. The latest draft seeks to apply environmental assessment to land-use and related plans and programmes for major sectors but does not cover policies, nor extend to the activities of the European Commission itself. *ENDS Report* 248. 1995 Brussels drafts revised rules on SEA, pp37–8 **8** United Nations Development Programme 1996 *Human Development Report 1996* Oxford: Oxford University Press **9** Independent Commission on Population and Quality of Life 1996 *Caring for the Future* Oxford: Oxford University Press **10** Cited by Redefining Progress undated Information pack, San Francisco: Redefining Progress. The largest companies working with the 'Natural Step' in Sweden have formed a 'Challenge' group. In March 1995, their chief executives met with the Prime Minister of Sweden to tell him that the goal of economic growth is illusory – reportedly, he agreed. Greyson, J (ed) 1995 *The Natural Step 1995: a collection of articles* Bristol: The Natural Step **11** The need for a new headline indicator does not make redundant the work of other researchers to develop useful indicators of sustainability. But when such indicators are put into practical use it is very rare for action to be justified without reference to economic costs and the impacts on GDP. For example the UK Department of the Environment's 'Indicators of Sustainable Development' use rates of pollution and resource use per unit of economic output to measure sustainability. This is misleading on two main counts. First, economic growth is a poor measure of welfare. And second, even with increasing efficiency which such measures are designed to illustrate, the absolute use – or abuse – of the environment can go on increasing. Thus environmental limits to such exploitation can be breached. Department of the Environment 1996 *Indicators of Sustainable Development for the United Kingdom* London: HMSO **12** *The Economist* 1996 Booming Busts, 3 August, p29 **13** See Mayo, E, MacGillivray, A and McLaren, D 1997 *More Isn't Always Better* London: Friends of the Earth and the New Economics Foundation for a brief explanation **14** Hicks, JR 1946. *Value and Capital* 2nd edition. Oxford: Oxford University Press **15** Lintott, J 1996 Environmental accounting: useful to whom and for what? *Ecological Economics* 16, pp179–190 **16** Commission of the European Communities 1992 *Towards Sustainability* Brussels: CEC **17** European Environment Agency 1996 Current EU measures insufficient to prevent further increase of $CO_2$ emissions after the year 2000 *Press Release* 6 September Copenhagen: EEA **18** Rowell, A 1996 Armies of the Right *Guardian* 20 September **19** *ENDS Report* 236 1994 Growing tension over global warming review, pp3–4; Rowell, A 1996 *Green Backlash* London: Routledge **20** Hawken, P 1994 *The Ecology of Commerce* London: Phoenix **21** Gladwin, TN, Krause, TS and Kennelly, JJ 1995 Beyond Eco-efficiency: towards socially sustainable business. *Sustainable Development* 3, pp35–43 **22** Cited by Weir, S and Dunleavy, P 1996 The nation in a state *The Independent* 23 September, p14 **23** Weir, S and Dunleavy, P 1996 *Op cit.* **24** Jacobs, M 1996 *The Politics of the Real World* London: Earthscan **25** Holtham, G, Hillman, J, Spencer, S and Tindale, S 1996 Why Government is Good for You *IPPR In Progress* Summer **26** According to figures collected by Demos, cited by Oxford, E 1995

Clowns to the left of us, jokers to the right *The Independent* 25 January **27** Weir, S and Dunleavy, P 1996 The nation in a state *The Independent* 23 September **28** Sands, R 1996 Creating a sustainable global community through citizenship. *Journal of Contemporary Health* 4, Summer, pp65–69 **29** *ENDS Report* 255.1996 IGC set to alter framework for EC environment policy, pp40–42 **30** *Ibid.* **31** *ENDS Report* 258. 1996 Push for access to justice in new ECE treaty, pp42–3 **32** Rowell, A 1996 Armies of the Right *Guardian* 20 September **33** *ENDS Report* 255 1996 *Op cit.* **34** Association of County Councils, Association of District Councils and Association of Metropolitan Authorities 1996 *Environmental manifesto for local government: a consultation document* London: Association of Metropolitan Authorities **35** As Roger Levett, sustainability expert at CAG management consultants, says, with reference to Garrett Hardin's classic work on public environmental goods such as the atmosphere and the oceans, 'only commons without planning authorities are tragic'. Levett, R 1996 *Personal communication* November **36** Blair, T 1996 *Speech to the Royal Society* London, 27 February **37** Professor James Mirrlees of Cambridge University recently won the Nobel prize for economics for his work on the theory of asymmetric information. Essentially this shows that where one of the two parties to a market transaction systematically has worse information than the other, an effective market cannot be formed. Even if we attempt to bring environmental and social goods into the market it is unlikely that this will maximise social welfare without continued intervention **38** Holtham, G et al. 1996 Why Government is Good for You *IPPR In Progress* Summer **39** Cross-country comparisons don't support the notion that tax-cuts boost growth through increasing incentives. *The Economist* 1996 The supply-siders ride again: do tax cuts help to promote economic growth? 24 August, p74 **40** The House of Lords Select Committee on Sustainable Development urged the Government to consider hypothecation in the form of 'earmarked' levies more seriously. They see potential for such measures at a local level too. House of Lords Select Committee on Sustainable Development 1995 *Sustainable Development* Vol 1. London: HMSO **41** *ENDS Report* 257. 1996 A new momentum towards green tax reforms, pp18–21 **42** United Nations Development Programme 1996 *Human Development Report 1996* Oxford: Oxford University Press **43** Rifkind, M 1996 *Partners in Development. Speech to the UN General Assembly* New York, 24 September **44** Friends of the Earth 1992 *Whose Hand on the Chainsaw? UK Government Policy and the Tropical Rainforests* London: Friends of the Earth **45** Coyle, D 1996 IMF will sell gold reserves to reduce debt in Third World *The Independent*, 23 September, p18 **46** Korten, D 1996 *When Corporations Rule the World* London: Earthscan **47** Weaver, PM 1993 Synergies of association: Ecorestructuring, scale, and the industrial landscape. *Paper for United Nations University, Tokyo, Symposium on Ecorestructuring* 5–7 July **48** Cited in Redclift, M 1996 *Wasted: counting the costs of global consumption* London: Earthscan **49** Independent Commission on Population and Quality of Life 1996 *Caring for the Future* Oxford: Oxford University Press **50** Nobel Laureate economist James Tobin proposed this tax not simply as a means of raising money – important as that might be, but to help dampen currency speculation, and thus protect fragile developing economies from the destabilising effects of such speculation and provide more confidence in the longer term stability of exchange rates **51** Cited by Weaver, PM 1993 *Op cit* **52** United Nations Centre on Transnational Corporations 1991 *Benchmark Corporate Environmental Survey* New York: UNCTC

# NOTES TO CONCLUSION AND AFTERWORD

**1** Millais, C 1996 Greenpeace solutions campaigns – closing the implementation gap *ECOS* 17(2) pp50–58 **2** Independent Commission on Population and Quality of Life 1996 *Caring for the Future* Oxford: Oxford University Press **3** See Friends of the Earth 1994 *Nothing Ventured, Nothing Gained* London: FOE **4** Marquand, D 1988 *The Unprincipled Society* London: Fontana **5** Schoon, N 1996 Whatever happened to the green market? *The Independent* 10 September **6** Carey, G 1996 The Archbishop of Canterbury talks to Andrew Marr about his campaign for a debate on the UK's moral decline *The Independent* 24 June

# Index

Figures in **bold** refer to boxes, illustrations or tables.

374 *Index*

Open University 277
Opschoor, J.B. 82, 211–12, **212**
Oregon, timber production **163**
organic farming 141, **142**, 150, 157, 159, 160, 224
  Austria **142**, 153, 154–5, **155**, 156, 160
  Europe **154**
  food distribution schemes 155–6
  Germany **142**
  Italy **155**
  Netherlands 264
  UK 153, 154–6, **155**, 160
Organisation for Economic Cooperation and Development (OECD) **18**, 33, 91
  agricultural energy consumption 157
  carbon dioxide emissions 38, 89
  on environmental innovation 254
  inequity 284
  study of energy-saving proposals 122
  study on inequity 283, 287
Orwell, George, *The Road to Wigan Pier* 23
overgrazing 72, 141, **150**
overproduction, in Northern countries 33
Oxfam
  book banks 173
  report on losses to developing countries 33
  report on SAPs 30–1, 32
  report on trade liberalisation 24
Oxford Solar House 100–1
Oxfordshire 107
ozone layer 72, 85
  Antarctic 21
  depletion **11**, 15, 24, 40, 51, 62, 73, 207

Pacific Gas and Electric, California 95–6, 255
Pacific Northwest Pollution Prevention Research Centre 252
packaging
  consumption of aluminium 220
  consumption of wood 178–9
  minimisation 178
  recycling and reuse 233, 254
Pakistan, growth of cities 138
paper 72, 161
  bleaching 222
  demand in developing countries 161
  environmental space **248**
  recycling 172–4, **174**, **175**, 209, 230
  reduction of consumption 177–9
  Scandinavian forests 10
  TCF bleaching methods **223**
  UK consumption 169–70
  UK imports 71
  use of chlorine in industry 222
  use of fibre 160, 176–7
  use in offices 179
Paris, INSEAD 208
Pearce, David **50–1**
peatlands 164, 170

Pergau Dam 35
pesticides 207
  companies 253
  health risks **142**
  pollution **16**, 137, 152, **184**
  threat to insects **142**
  use of chlorine 73, 222
Pesticides Safety Directorate **142**
petrol 272, 276, 291
Philippines 14–15, 34, 38, **158**
Philips electrical company 227
Phillips, Matt 189
phosphates, as chemical feedstock 222–4
phosphorus, emissions 224
photocopiers
  leasing 236
  redesign and repair 236
photovoltaics 91, **92**, 96, 100, 119
  Japanese investment 101
  projects 101
  UK energy generation estimates **103**
phytoplankton 15, 20
Pilkington Tiles, Clifton Junction (Manchester) **200**
Pintasilgo, Maria de Lourdes 290
Plaid Cymru, promotion of Road Traffic Reduction Act 118
planets, needed to sustain global consumption **7**
planning and development
  damage to land 124
  housing 124, 129, 131–2, 136
  regulations 299
plant species, destruction of 10–11
plastics 234
  recycling 209, 224, 230, **232**
  use of chlorine in industry 222
  waste 259
platinum, South Africa 10
PNEM (Dutch electricity company) 102
polar bears, contamination by toxins 10
Policy Studies Institute 268
political concerns
  companies 249, 315
  conflict over resources 42, 183
  international perspectives 309–12
  North–South divide 29
  sustainability 245, 298–312, 316
  *see also* democracy
pollution
  absorption by natural environment 73, 207
  chemicals **11**, **16**, 20, **31**, 73, **184**, 207, 209
  from fuels 84–5, 88, 207
  from humans 13, 15
  from intensive agriculture 137, 143
  from mining wastes **31**, 205, **206**
  from oil industry 86
  from pesticides **16**, 137, 152, **184**
  from traffic 253

*Index*